BEGINNING
iOS 4 APPLICATION DEVELOPMENT

Continues

BEGINNING

iOS 4 Application Development

Wei-Meng Lee

Wiley Publishing, Inc.

Beginning iOS 4 Application Development

Published by
Wiley Publishing, Inc.
10475 Crosspoint Boulevard
Indianapolis, IN 46256
www.wiley.com

Copyright © 2010 by Wiley Publishing, Inc., Indianapolis, Indiana

Published simultaneously in Canada

ISBN: 978-0-470-91802-9

ISBN: 978-0-470-94983-2 (ebk)
ISBN: 978-1-118-00480-7 (ebk)
ISBN: 978-1-118-00481-4 (ebk)

Manufactured in the United States of America

10 9 8 7 6 5 4 3 2 1

For general information on our other products and services please contact our Customer Care Department within the United States at (877) 762-2974, outside the United States at (317) 572-3993 or fax (317) 572-4002.

Wiley also publishes its books in a variety of electronic formats. Some content that appears in print may not be available in electronic books.

Library of Congress Control Number: 2010932418

To my family:

Thanks for the understanding and support while I worked on getting this book ready! I love you all!

CREDITS

ACQUISITIONS EDITOR
Scott Meyers

SENIOR PROJECT EDITOR
Ami Frank Sullivan

TECHNICAL EDITOR
Trenton Shumay

PRODUCTION EDITOR
Rebecca Anderson

COPY EDITOR
Luann Rouff

EDITORIAL DIRECTOR
Robyn B. Siesky

EDITORIAL MANAGER
Mary Beth Wakefield

ASSOCIATE DIRECTOR OF MARKETING
David Mayhew

PRODUCTION MANAGER
Tim Tate

**VICE PRESIDENT AND
EXECUTIVE GROUP PUBLISHER**
Richard Swadley

VICE PRESIDENT AND EXECUTIVE PUBLISHER
Barry Pruett

ASSOCIATE PUBLISHER
Jim Minatel

PROJECT COORDINATOR, COVER
Lynsey Stanford

COMPOSITOR
James D. Kramer,
Happenstance Type-O-Rama

PROOFREADER
Nancy Carrasco

INDEXER
Johnna VanHoose Dinse

COVER DESIGNER
Michael E. Trent

COVER IMAGE
© istockphoto.com/-M-I-S-H-A-

ABOUT THE AUTHOR

WEI-MENG LEE is a technologist and founder of Developer Learning Solutions (www.learn2develop.net), a technology company specializing in hands-on training for the latest Microsoft and Mac OS X technologies. He is also an established author with Wrox and O'Reilly.

Wei-Meng first started the iPhone programming course in Singapore, and it has since received much positive feedback. His hands-on approach to iPhone/iPad programming makes understanding the subject much easier than reading books, tutorials, and documentation from Apple.

Contact Wei-Meng at weimenglee@learn2develop.net.

ABOUT THE TECHNICAL EDITOR

TRENT SHUMAY is the founder and Chief Architect at Finger Food Studios Inc. in the Vancouver, BC area. After graduating from the UBC Computer Science program, Trent spent thirteen years in the gaming and interactive entertainment space, where handheld gaming devices ignited his passion for mobile development. Today, Finger Food Studios focuses on developing media-rich, interactive mobile and Web applications. You can reach Trent directly at trent@fingerfoodstudios.com.

ACKNOWLEDGMENTS

AFTER MUCH SPECULATION and rumor, Apple has finally released the iPhone 4 amid fanfare and excitement. With the new iPhone 4 comes a new OS — iOS 4, which incorporates many enhancements, most notably the ability to support background applications. I was very fortunate to be able to work with the new OS while it was in its beta phase and even more excited to learn that I would be working on an iPhone 4 book! Writing a book is always exciting, but along with it come long hours of hard work, straining to get things done accurately and correctly. For this, I would like to take this opportunity to thank a number of people who made this book possible.

First, I want to thank my acquisitions editor Scott Meyers, who had faith in me when he signed me up for this book. Thanks for standing by me and always being there to help. I hope I have not disappointed you. Thank you, Scott!

Next, a huge thanks to Ami Sullivan, my editor, who is always a pleasure to work with. After working together on three books, we have built up a rapport and totally understand how each other works. With every new book that I work on with Ami, I learn new things. Thanks for the guidance, Ami!

I should not forget the heroes behind the scene: copy editor Luann Rouff and technical editor Trenton Shumay. They have been eagle-eye editing the book, making sure that every sentence makes sense — both grammatically as well as technically. Thanks, Luann and Trent!

Last, but not least, I want to thank my parents, and my wife, Sze Wa, for all the support they have given me. They have selflessly adjusted their schedules to accommodate my busy schedule when I was working on this book. My wife, as always, has stayed up with me on numerous nights as I was furiously working to meet the deadlines, and for this I would like to say to her and my parents: "I love you all!" Finally, to our lovely dog, Ookii, thanks for staying by our side. Now that the book is done, we can look forward to an earlier night.

CONTENTS

PART II: DISPLAYING AND PERSISTING DATA

INTRODUCTION

WITHIN A SHORT TIME SPAN OF SIX MONTHS, Apple revised the iPhone OS twice. The first time was in January 2010, when Apple announced a magical and revolutionary product: the iPad. Because the iPad is a tablet computer that is based on the iPhone OS, this meant that there were instantly more than 250,000 applications that could run on the iPad. Then, in April Apple announced (and subsequently shipped in June) the next major release of the iPhone OS — 4.0. Apple also took this opportunity to rename this new release of the OS, calling it *iOS*. This signifies Apple's grand plan to run the iPhone OS on a wide variety of devices, not just on phones. Included with the new release of the OS is a new SDK, the iPhone SDK 4, which enables developers to take advantage of the various features provided by the operating system — key of which is the capability to run background applications.

When I first started learning about iPhone and iPad development, I went through the same journey that most developers go through: Write a Hello World application, play around with Interface Builder, try to understand what the code is doing, and repeat that process. I was also overwhelmed by the concept of a View Controller, and wondered why it was needed if I simply wanted to display a view. My background in developing for Windows Mobile and Android did not help much, and I had to start working with this concept from scratch.

This book was written to help jumpstart beginning iPhone and iPad developers. It covers the various topics in such a manner that you will progressively learn without being overwhelmed by the details. I adopt the philosophy that the best way to learn is by doing, hence the numerous hands-on "Try It Out" sections in each chapter, which first show you how to build something and then explain "How It Works."

Although iPhone and iPad programming is a huge topic, my aim for this book is to get you started with the fundamentals, help you understand the underlying architecture of the SDK, and appreciate why things are done certain ways. It is beyond the scope of this book to cover everything under the sun related to iPhone and iPad programming, but I am confident that after reading this book (and doing the exercises), you will be well equipped to tackle your next iPhone or iPad programming challenge.

WHO THIS BOOK IS FOR

This book is for the beginning iPhone and iPad developer who wants to start developing applications using the Apple iPhone SDK. To truly benefit from this book, you should have some background in programming and at least be familiar with object-oriented programming concepts. If you are totally new to the Objective-C language, you might want to jump straight to Appendix D, which provides an overview of the language. Alternatively, you can use Appendix D as a quick reference while you tackle the various chapters, checking out the syntax as you try the exercises. Depending on your learning style, one of those approaches should work best for you.

While most of the chapters are geared toward developing for the iPhone, the concepts apply to iPad development as well. In cases where specific features are available only on the iPad, they will be pointed out.

NOTE *All the examples discussed in this book were written and tested using the iPhone SDK 4.0. Even though Apple continues to call it the iPhone SDK, it can be used to develop iPhone, iPod touch, and iPad applications. At the time of writing (July 2010), Apple continues to use the term "iPhone Simulator" to refer to the simulator that enables you to simulate both an iPhone and iPad. While every effort has been made to ensure that the screen shots are as current as possible, the actual screen that you see may differ when the iPhone SDK is revised.*

WHAT THIS BOOK COVERS

This book covers the fundamentals of iPhone and iPad programming using the iPhone SDK. It is divided into 21 chapters and five appendices.

Chapter 1: Getting Started with iOS 4 Programming covers the various tools found in the iPhone SDK and explains their uses in iPhone and iPad development.

Chapter 2: Write Your First Hello World! Application gets you started with Xcode and Interface Builder to build a Hello World application. The focus is on giving you some hands-on practice getting a project up and running quickly. More details on the various project components are covered in subsequent chapters.

Chapter 3: Views, Outlets, and Actions covers the fundamental concepts of iPhone and iPad programming: outlets and actions. You learn how outlets and actions allow your code to interact with the visual elements in Interface Builder and why they are an integral part of every iPhone and iPad application. You will also learn about the various UI widgets known as *views* that make up the user interface of your application.

Chapter 4: View Controllers discusses the various View Controllers available in the iPhone SDK. You will learn how to develop different types of applications — View-based, Window-based, Split View–based, as well as Tab Bar applications.

Chapter 5: Multi-Platform Support for the iPhone and iPad shows how you can port your iPhone applications to the iPad platform. You will also learn how to create universal applications that will run on both the iPhone and the iPad.

Chapter 6: Keyboard Inputs shows you how to deal with the virtual keyboard in your iPhone or iPad. You learn how to hide the keyboard on demand and how to ensure that your views are not blocked by the keyboard when it is displayed.

Chapter 7: Screen Rotations demonstrates how you can reorient your application's UI when the device is rotated. You learn about the various events that are fired when the device is rotated, and how to force your application to be displayed in a certain orientation.

Chapter 8: Using the Table View explores one of the most powerful views in the iPhone SDK — the Table view. The Table view is commonly used to display rows of data. In this chapter, you also learn how to implement search capabilities in your Table view.

Chapter 9: Application Preferences discusses the use of application settings to persist application preferences. Using application settings, you can access preferences related to your application through the Settings application available on the iPhone and iPad.

Chapter 10: File Handling shows how you can persist your application data by saving the data to files in your application's sandbox directory. You also learn how to access the various folders available in your application sandbox.

Chapter 11: Database Storage Using SQLite3 covers the use of the embedded SQLite3 database library to store your data.

Chapter 12: Simple Animations and Video Playback provides an overview of the various techniques you can use to implement basic animations on the iPhone and iPad. You also learn about the various affine transformations supported by the iPhone SDK. In addition, you learn how to playback video on the iPhone and iPad.

Chapter 13: Accessing Built-In Applications describes the various ways you can access the iPhone and iPad's built-in applications, such as the Photo Library, Contacts, and others. You also learn how you can invoke built-in applications such as Mail and Safari from within your applications.

Chapter 14: Recognizing Gestures provides an overview of the various gesture recognizers available in the iPhone SDK to help your device interpret user's input gestures.

Chapter 15: Accessing the Accelerometer shows how you can access the accelerometer that is included with every iPhone and iPad. You will also learn how to detect shakes to your device.

Chapter 16: Web Services teaches you how to consume Web services from within your iPhone and iPad application. You will learn the various ways to communicate with Web services — SOAP, HTTP GET, and HTTP POST. You will also learn how to parse the XML result returned by the Web service.

Chapter 17: Bluetooth Programming explores the use of the Game Kit framework for Bluetooth programming. You will learn how to enable two devices to communicate using a Bluetooth connection, and how to implement voice chatting over a Bluetooth connection.

Chapter 18: Bonjour Programming shows how you can publish services on the network using the Bonjour protocol.

Chapter 19: Apple Push Notification Services explains how you can implement applications that use push notifications. The APNs allows your applications to continuously receive status updates from a service provider even though the application may not be running.

Chapter 20: Displaying Maps demonstrates how to build a location-based services application using the Map Kit framework. You will also learn how to obtain geographical location data and use it to display a map.

Chapter 21: Background Applications shows how to build applications that can continue to run in the background when the user switches to another application. You will also learn how to use the new local notifications feature to schedule notifications that will fire at specific time intervals.

Appendix A: Testing on an Actual Device outlines the steps you need to take to test your application on a real device.

Appendix B: Getting Around in Xcode provides a quick run-through of the many features in Xcode.

Appendix C: Getting Around in Interface Builder provides an overview of the many features of Interface Builder.

Appendix D: Crash Course in Objective-C offers a brief tutorial in Objective-C. Readers who are new to this language should read this chapter before getting started.

Appendix E: Answers to Exercises contains the solutions to the end-of-chapter exercises found in every chapter except Chapter 1. Please note, Appendix E is located online at Wrox.com.

HOW THIS BOOK IS STRUCTURED

This book breaks down the task of learning iPhone and iPad programming into several smaller chunks, enabling you to digest each foundational topic before delving into a more advanced topic. In addition, some chapters cover topics already discussed in a previous chapter. That's because there is usually more than one way of doing things in Xcode and Interface Builder, so this approach enables you to learn the different techniques available for developing iPhone and iPad applications.

If you are a total beginner to iPhone programming, start with Chapters 1 and 2. After you are comfortable with the basics, head to the appendices to read more about the tools and language you are using. Once you are ready, you can continue with Chapter 3 and gradually move into more advanced topics.

A useful feature of this book is that all the code samples in each chapter are independent of those discussed in previous chapters. That gives you the flexibility to dive right into the topics that interest you and start working on the Try It Out projects.

WHAT YOU NEED TO USE THIS BOOK

Most of the examples in this book run on the iPhone Simulator (which is included with the iPhone SDK). For exercises that access the hardware (such as the accelerometer), you need a real iPhone or iPad. In general, to get the most out of this book, having a real iPhone or iPad device is not necessary (although it is definitely required for testing if you plan to deploy your application on the App Store).

CONVENTIONS

To help you get the most from the text and keep track of what's happening, we've used a number of conventions throughout the book.

TRY IT OUT   These Are Exercises or Examples for You to Follow

The Try It Out sections, which appear once or more per chapter, provide hands-on exercises to work through as you follow the text in the book.

1. They usually consist of a set of numbered steps.

2. Follow the steps with your copy of the project files.

How It Works

After each Try It Out section, these sections explain the code you've typed in detail.

As for other conventions in the text:

- ➤ New terms and important words are *highlighted* in italics when first introduced.
- ➤ Keyboard combinations are treated like this: Control-R.
- ➤ Filenames, URLs, and code within the text are treated like so: `persistence.properties`.
- ➤ Code is presented in two different ways:

  ```
  We use a monofont type with no highlighting for most code examples.
  ```

  We use bold to emphasize code that is of particular importance in the present context.

 WARNING *Boxes like this one hold important, not-to-be forgotten information that is directly relevant to the surrounding text.*

 NOTE *Notes, tips, hints, tricks, and asides to the current discussion look like this.*

 COMMON MISTAKES *This feature, Common Mistakes, helps you avoid the obstacles that many new practitioners find themselves negotiating.*

SOURCE CODE AND ANSWERS APPENDIX

As you work through the examples in this book, you may choose either to type in all the code manually or to use the source code files that accompany the book. All the source code used in this book is available for download at www.wrox.com. When at the site, simply locate the book's title (use the Search box or one of the title lists) and click the Download Code link on the book's detail page to obtain all the source code for the book. Code that is included on the website is highlighted by the following icon and/or CodeNote, as shown following the icon:

Available for download on Wrox.com

Listings include the filename in the title. If it is just a code snippet, you'll find the filename in a CodeNote such as this:

Code zip filename available for download at wrox.com

After you download the code, just decompress it with your favorite compression tool. Alternatively, go to the main Wrox code download page at www.wrox.com/dynamic/books/download.aspx to see the code available for this book and all other Wrox books.

Please note, Appendix E, Answers to Exercises, is available as a PDF for download.

 NOTE *Because many books have similar titles, you may find it easiest to search by ISBN; this book's ISBN is 978-0-470-91802-9.*

ERRATA

We make every effort to ensure that there are no errors in the text or the code. However, no one is perfect and mistakes do occur. If you find an error in one of our books, such as a spelling mistake or a faulty piece of code, we would be very grateful for your feedback. By sending in errata, you may save another reader hours of frustration and at the same time help us provide even higher-quality information.

To find the errata page for this book, go to www.wrox.com and locate the title using the Search box or one of the title lists. Then, on the book details page, click the Book Errata link. On this page, you can view all errata that has been submitted for this book and posted by Wrox editors. A complete book list, including links to each book's errata, is also available at www.wrox.com/misc-pages/booklist.shtml.

If you don't spot "your" error on the Book Errata page, go to `www.wrox.com/contact/techsupport .shtml` and complete the form there to send us the error you have found. We'll check the information and, if appropriate, post a message to the book's errata page and fix the problem in subsequent editions of the book.

P2P.WROX.COM

For author and peer discussion, join the P2P forums at `p2p.wrox.com`. The forums are a Web-based system for you to post messages relating to Wrox books and related technologies and interact with other readers and technology users. The forums offer a subscription feature to e-mail you topics of interest of your choosing when new posts are made to the forums. Wrox authors, editors, other industry experts, and your fellow readers are present on these forums.

At `http://p2p.wrox.com`, you will find a number of different forums that will help you not only as you read this book, but also as you develop your own applications. To join the forums, just follow these steps:

1. Go to `p2p.wrox.com` and click the Register link.

2. Read the terms of use and click Agree.

3. Complete the required information to join as well as any optional information you want to provide and click Submit.

4. You will receive an e-mail with information describing how to verify your account and complete the joining process.

After you join, you can post new messages and respond to messages that other users post. You can read messages at any time on the Web. If you want to have new messages from a particular forum e-mailed to you, click the Subscribe to This Forum icon by the forum name in the forum listing.

For more information about how to use the Wrox P2P, be sure to read the P2P FAQs for answers to questions about how the forum software works as well as for many common questions specific to P2P and Wrox books. To read the FAQs, click the FAQ link on any P2P page.

PART I
Getting Started

1

Getting Started with iOS 4 Programming

WHAT YOU WILL LEARN IN THIS CHAPTER

➤ How to obtain the iPhone SDK

➤ Components included in the iPhone SDK

➤ Features of the development tools — Xcode, Interface Builder, iPhone Simulator

➤ Capabilities of the iPhone Simulator

➤ Architecture of the iPhone OS

➤ Characteristics of the iPhone

Welcome to the world of iPhone programming! That you are now holding this book shows that you are fascinated with the idea of developing your own iPhone (and iPad) applications and want to join the ranks of the tens of thousands of developers whose applications are already deployed in the App Store.

As the Chinese adage says, "To accomplish your mission, first sharpen your tools." Successful programming requires that you first know your tools well. Indeed, this couldn't be more true for iPhone programming — you need to know quite a few tools before you can even get started. Hence, this chapter describes the various relevant tools and information you need to jump on the iPhone development bandwagon.

Without further ado, it's time to get down to work.

OBTAINING THE IPHONE SDK

To develop for the iPhone, you first need to sign up as a registered iPhone developer at `http://developer` `.apple.com/iphone/program/start/register/`. Registration is free and provides you with access to the iPhone SDK (software development kit) and other resources that are useful for getting started.

> **NOTE** At the time of writing, iOS (the iPhone OS) 4 is supported only on the iPhone and the iPod touch. The iPad still runs on the older iPhone OS 3.2 version. However, the iPhone SDK 4.0 supports both iPhone and iPad development.
>
> Because the iPad also uses the iPhone OS, throughout this book you will often see the term "iPhone" used.

After signing up, you can download the iPhone SDK (version 4; see Figure 1-1).

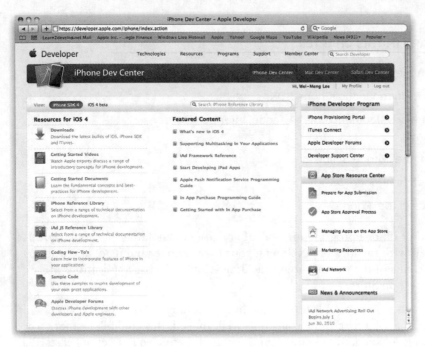

FIGURE 1-1

Before you install the iPhone SDK, make sure you satisfy the following system requirements:

➤   Only Intel Macs are supported, so if you have another processor type (such as the older G4 or G5 Macs), you're out of luck.

➤   Your system is updated with the latest Mac OS X release.

An actual iPhone/iPad is highly recommended, although not strictly necessary. To test your application, you can use the included iPhone Simulator (which enables you to simulate an iPhone or an iPad). However, to test certain hardware features like GPS, the accelerometer, and such, you need to use a real device.

When the SDK is downloaded, proceed with installing it (see Figure 1-2). Accept a few licensing agreements and then select the destination folder in which to install the SDK.

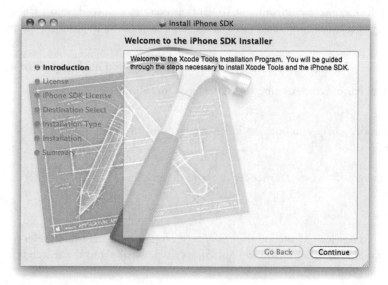

FIGURE 1-2

If you select the default settings during the installation phase, the various tools will be installed in the /Developer/Applications folder (see Figure 1-3).

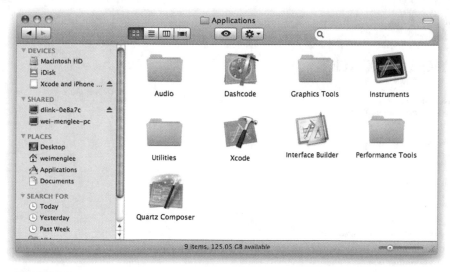

FIGURE 1-3

COMPONENTS OF THE IPHONE SDK

The iPhone SDK includes a suite of development tools to help you create applications for your iPhone, iPod touch, and iPad. It includes the following:

➤ **Xcode** — Integrated development environment (IDE) that enables you to manage, edit, and debug your projects

➤ **Dashcode** — Integrated development environment (IDE) that enables you to develop web-based iPhone and iPad applications and Dashboard Widgets. Dashcode is beyond the scope of this book.

➤ **iPhone Simulator** — Provides a software simulator to simulate an iPhone or an iPad on your Mac.

➤ **Interface Builder** — Visual editor for designing user interfaces for your iPhone and iPad applications

➤ **Instruments** — Analysis tool to help you both optimize your application and monitor for memory leaks in real time

The following sections discuss each tool (except Dashcode) in more detail.

Xcode

To launch Xcode, double-click the Xcode icon located in the `/Developer/Applications` folder (refer to Figure 1-3). Alternatively, go the quicker route and use Spotlight: Simply type **Xcode** into the search box and Xcode should be in the Top Hit position.

Figure 1-4 shows the Xcode Welcome screen.

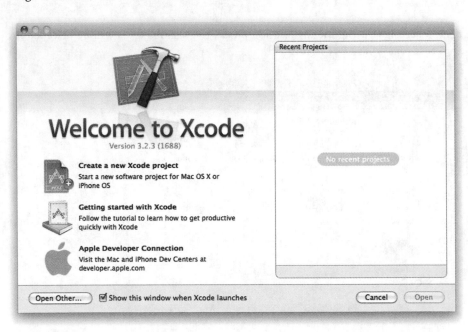

FIGURE 1-4

Using Xcode, you can develop different types of iPhone, iPad, and Mac OS X applications using the various project templates shown in Figure 1-5.

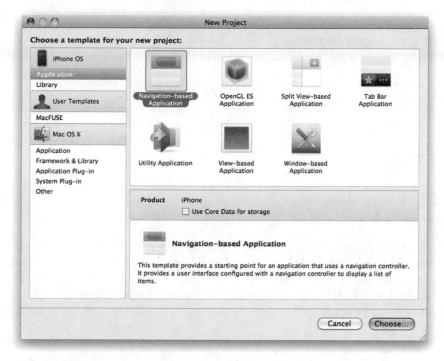

FIGURE 1-5

Each template gives you the option to select the platform you are targeting — iPhone or iPad.

 NOTE *Note that not every application template is available for iPhone and iPad. For example, Navigation-based application templates do not support the iPad, and Split-View application templates do not support the iPhone.*

The IDE in Xcode provides many tools and features that make your development life much easier. One such feature is Code Sense (see Figure 1-6), which displays a popup list showing the available classes and members, such as methods, properties, and so on.

 NOTE *For a more comprehensive description of some of the most commonly used features in Xcode, refer to Appendix B.*

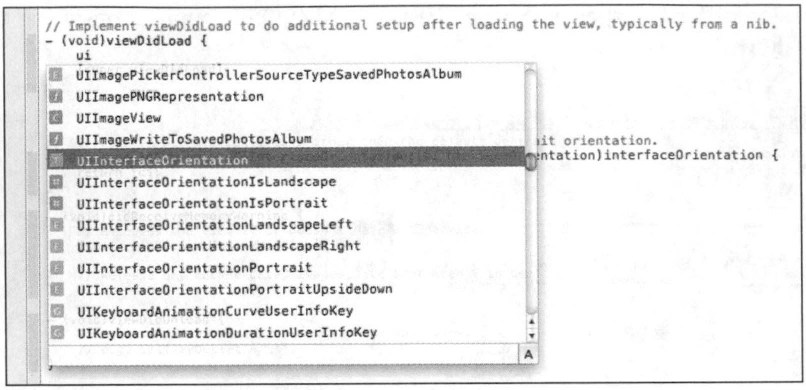

```
// Implement viewDidLoad to do additional setup after loading the view, typically from a nib.
- (void)viewDidLoad {
    ui
    UIImagePickerControllerSourceTypeSavedPhotosAlbum
    UIImagePNGRepresentation
    UIImageView
    UIImageWriteToSavedPhotosAlbum
    UIInterfaceOrientation                              it orientation.
                                                        ntation)interfaceOrientation {
    UIInterfaceOrientationIsLandscape
    UIInterfaceOrientationIsPortrait
    UIInterfaceOrientationLandscapeLeft
    UIInterfaceOrientationLandscapeRight
    UIInterfaceOrientationPortrait
    UIInterfaceOrientationPortraitUpsideDown
    UIKeyboardAnimationCurveUserInfoKey
    UIKeyboardAnimationDurationUserInfoKey
                                                        A
```

FIGURE 1-6

iPhone Simulator

The iPhone Simulator, shown in Figure 1-7, is a very useful tool that you can use to test your application without using your actual iPhone/iPod touch/iPad. The iPhone Simulator is located in the `/Developer/Platforms/iPhoneSimulator.platform/Developer/Applications` folder. Most of the time, you don't need to launch the iPhone Simulator directly — running (or debugging) your application in Xcode automatically brings up the iPhone Simulator. Xcode installs the application on the iPhone Simulator automatically.

> **THE IPHONE SIMULATOR IS NOT AN EMULATOR**
>
> To understand the difference between a simulator and an emulator, keep in mind that a simulator tries to mimic the behavior of a real device. In the case of the iPhone Simulator, it simulates the real behavior of an actual iPhone/iPad device. However, the Simulator itself uses the various libraries installed on the Mac (such as QuickTime) to perform its rendering so that the effect looks the same as an actual iPhone. In addition, applications tested on the Simulator are compiled into x86 code, which is the byte-code understood by the Simulator. A real iPhone device, on the other hand, uses ARM-based code.
>
> In contrast, an emulator emulates the working of a real device. Applications tested on an emulator are compiled into the actual byte-code used by the real device. The emulator executes the application by translating the byte-code into a form that can be executed by the host computer running the emulator.
>
> A good way to understand the subtle difference between simulation and emulation is this: Imagine you are trying to convince a child that playing with knives is dangerous. To *simulate* this, you pretend to cut yourself with a knife and groan in pain. To *emulate* this, you actually cut yourself.

FIGURE 1-7

The iPhone Simulator can simulate different versions of the iPhone OS (see Figure 1-8). To support older versions of the SDK, you need to install the previous versions of the SDKs). This capability is useful if you need to support older versions of the platform, as well as test and debug errors reported in the application on specific versions of the OS.

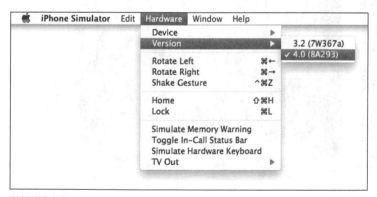

FIGURE 1-8

In addition, the iPhone Simulator can simulate different devices — iPad, iPhone (3G and 3GS), and iPhone 4 (see Figure 1-9).

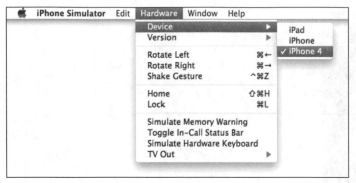

FIGURE 1-9

Figure 1-10 shows the iPhone Simulator simulating the older iPhone 3G/3GS, while Figure 1-11 shows it simulating the iPad.

FIGURE 1-10   **FIGURE 1-11**

Features of the iPhone Simulator

The iPhone Simulator simulates various features of a real iPhone, iPod touch, or iPad device. Features you can test on the iPhone Simulator include the following:

➤   Screen rotation — left, top, and right

➤ Support for gestures:

   ➤ Tap

   ➤ Touch and Hold

   ➤ Double-tap

   ➤ Swipe

   ➤ Flick

   ➤ Drag

   ➤ Pinch

➤ Low-memory warning simulations

However, the iPhone Simulator, being a software simulator for the real device, does have its limitations. The following features are not available on the iPhone Simulator:

➤ Making phone calls

➤ Accessing the accelerometer

➤ Sending and receiving SMS messages

➤ Installing applications from the App Store

➤ Camera

➤ Microphone

➤ Several features of OpenGL ES

 NOTE *In the previous version of the SDK (3.1.3), the iPhone Simulator supports location data by always returning a fixed coordinate, such as Latitude 37.3317 North and Longitude 122.0307 West. In the newer release of the SDK (3.2 and later), the iPhone Simulator uses the location data of the Mac it is currently running on to return the current location.*

Note also that the speed of the iPhone Simulator is more tightly coupled to the performance of your Mac than the actual device. Therefore, it is important that you test your application on a real device, rather than rely exclusively on the iPhone Simulator for testing.

Despite the iPhone Simulator's limitations, it is definitely a useful tool for testing your applications. That said, testing your application on a real device is imperative before you deploy it on the App Store.

Uninstalling Applications from the iPhone Simulator

The user domain of the iPhone OS file system for the iPhone Simulator is stored in the `~/Library/ Application Support/iPhone Simulator/` folder.

NOTE *The* `~/Library/Application Support/iPhone Simulator/` *folder is also known as the* `<iPhoneUserDomain>`.

All third-party applications are stored in the `<iPhoneUserDomain>/<version_no>/Applications/` folder. When an application is deployed onto the iPhone Simulator, an icon is created on the Home screen (shown on the left in Figure 1-9) and a file and a folder are created within the `Applications` folder (shown on the right in Figure 1-12).

FIGURE 1-12

To uninstall (delete) an application, execute the following steps:

1. Click and hold the icon of the application on the Home screen until all the icons start wriggling. Observe that all the icons now have an X button displayed on their top-left corner.

2. Click the X button (see Figure 1-13) next to the icon of the application you want to uninstall.

3. An alert window appears asking if you are sure you want to delete the icon. Click Delete to confirm the deletion.

FIGURE 1-13

 WARNING *When an application is uninstalled, the corresponding file and folder in the Applications folder are deleted automatically.*

The easiest way to reset the iPhone Simulator to its original state is to select iPhone Simulator ⇨ Reset Content and Settings.

Interface Builder

Interface Builder is a visual tool that enables you to design the user interfaces for your iPhone/iPad applications. Using Interface Builder, you drag and drop views onto windows and then connect the various views with outlets and actions so that they can programmatically interact with your code.

 NOTE *Outlets and actions are discussed in more detail in Chapter 3, and Appendix C discusses Interface Builder in more detail.*

Figure 1-14 shows the various windows in Interface Builder.

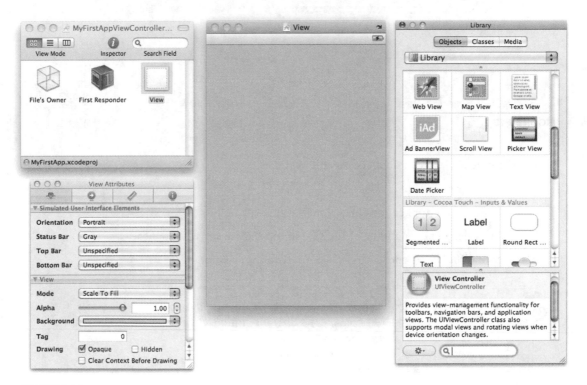

FIGURE 1-14

Instruments

The Instruments application (see Figure 1-15) enables you to dynamically trace and profile the performance of your Mac OS X, iPhone, and iPad applications.

FIGURE 1-15

Using Instruments, you can do all of the following:

➤ Stress test your applications

➤ Monitor your applications for memory leaks

➤ Gain a deep understanding of the executing behavior of your applications

➤ Track difficult-to-reproduce problems in your applications

> **NOTE** *Covering the Instruments application is beyond the scope of this book. For more information, refer to Apple's documentation at:* `http://developer` `.apple.com/mac/library/documentation/DeveloperTools/Conceptual/` `InstrumentsUserGuide/Introduction/Introduction.html`

ARCHITECTURE OF THE IPHONE OS

Although this book doesn't explore the innards of the iPhone OS, understanding some of its important characteristics is useful. Figure 1-16 shows the different abstraction layers that make up the Mac OS X and the iPhone OS (which is used by the iPhone, iPod touch, and iPad).

NOTE *The iPhone OS is architecturally very similar to the Mac OS X except that the topmost layer is Cocoa Touch for iPhone instead of the Cocoa Framework.*

The bottom layer is the Core OS, which is the foundation of the operating system. It is in charge of memory management, the file system, networking, and other OS tasks, and it interacts directly with the hardware. The Core OS layer consists of components such as the following:

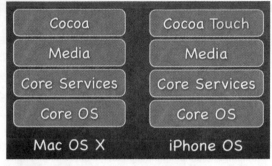

FIGURE 1-16

➤ OS X Kernel

➤ Mach 3.0

➤ BSD

➤ Sockets

➤ Security

➤ Power Management

➤ Keychain

➤ Certificates

➤ File System

➤ Bonjour

The Core Services layer provides an abstraction over the services provided in the Core OS layer. It provides fundamental access to iPhone OS services and consists of the following components:

➤ Collections

➤ Address Book

➤ Networking

➤ File Access

➤ SQLite

➤ Core Location

➤ Net Services

➤ Threading

➤ Preferences

➤ URL Utilities

The Media layer provides multimedia services that you can use in your iPhone and iPad applications. It consists of the following components:

➤ Core Audio

➤ OpenGL

➤ Audio Mixing

➤ Audio Recording

➤ Video Playback

➤ JPG, PNG, TIFF

➤ PDF

➤ Quartz

➤ Core Animation

➤ OpenGL ES

The Cocoa Touch layer provides an abstraction layer to expose the various libraries for programming the iPhone and iPad, such as the following:

➤ Multi-Touch events

➤ Multi-Touch controls

➤ Accelerometer

➤ View Hierarchy

➤ Localization

➤ Alerts

➤ Web Views

➤ People Picker

➤ Image Picker

➤ Controllers

In iPhone programming, all the functionalities in each layer are exposed through various frameworks which you will use in your project. Subsequent chapters in this book will show you how to use these frameworks in your projects.

 NOTE *A framework is a software library that provides specific functionalities. Refer to Apple's documentation at* `http://developer.apple.com/iphone/library/documentation/Miscellaneous/Conceptual/iPhoneOSTechOverview/iPhoneOSFrameworks/iPhoneOSFrameworks.html` *for a list of frameworks included in the SDK.*

SOME USEFUL INFORMATION BEFORE YOU GET STARTED

You now have a good idea of the tools involved in iPhone and iPad application development. Before you go ahead and take the plunge, the following sections discuss some useful information that can make your journey more pleasant.

Versions of the iPhone OS

At the time of writing, the iOS (iPhone OS) is in its fourth revision — that is, version 4.0. Its major versions are as follows:

- **1.0** — Initial release of iPhone
- **1.1** — Additional features and bug fixes for 1.0
- **2.0** — Released with iPhone 3G; comes with App Store.
- **2.1** — Additional features and bug fixes for 2.0
- **2.2** — Additional features and bug fixes for 2.1
- **3.0** — Third major release of the iPhone OS
- **3.1** — Additional features and bug fixes for 3.0
- **3.2** — This version release is for the iPad only; see the sidebar for what is new in iPhone OS 3.2.
- **4.0** — Fourth major release of the iPhone OS. Renamed as iOS. This version is designed for the new iPhone 4 and it also supports older devices, such as the iPod touch and iPhones.

For a detailed description of the features in each release, check out `http://en.wikipedia.org/wiki/IPhone_OS_version_history`.

WHAT'S NEW IN IPHONE OS 3.2 AND IOS 4

In January 2010, Apple announced a new device based on the existing iPhone OS — the iPad. The iPad is a tablet computer that resembles an iPod touch, except that it has a much bigger screen. The iPad comes in six different editions, three with Wi-Fi and another three with Wi-Fi and 3G networks. The iPad was released in three storage configurations: 16GB, 32GB, and 64GB.

Some of the important new features of the iPhone OS 3.2 SDK include the following:

- Support for existing iPhone applications by running them either in their original screen size or in pixel-doubled mode
- New UI features such as popovers, split views, and custom input views
- Support for external displays
- Support for gestures detection using gesture recognizers for iPad applications

continues

WHAT'S NEW IN IPHONE OS 3.2 AND IOS 4 *(continued)*

➤ Improved text support to provide applications with more sophisticated text-handling capabilities

➤ New file and document support to facilitate building document-centric applications

In June 2010, Apple officially released the latest version of the iPhone OS — version 4.0 (with an updated 4.0.1 in July). It also renamed it iOS, signifying Apple's intention to use the OS not just for phones, but for other devices such as the iPad. iOS 4 comes with more than 100 new features, but here are some notable features supported by the iPhone SDK 4.0:

➤ Support for multitasking; third-party applications can now run in the background

➤ Improved support for sending SMS and e-mail from within your applications

➤ Support of the new gesture recognizers for iPhone applications

Testing on Real Devices

One of the most common complaints about developing applications for the iPhone and iPad is how difficult Apple makes it to test a new application on an actual device. Nonetheless, for security reasons, Apple requires all applications to be signed with a valid certificate; and for testing purposes, a developer certificate is required.

To test your applications on a device, you must sign up for the iPhone Developer Program and request that a developer certificate be installed onto your device. Appendix E outlines the steps in detail.

Screen Resolutions

The iPhone 4 is a beautiful device with a high-resolution screen. At 3.5 inches (diagonally), the iPhone screen supports multi-touch operation and allows a pixel resolution of 960 × 640 at 326 ppi (see Figure 1-17). When designing your application, note that because of the status bar, the actual resolution is generally limited to 920 × 640 pixels. Of course, you can turn off the status bar programmatically to gain access to the full 960 × 640 resolution.

Also, be mindful that users may rotate the device to display your application in landscape mode. You need to make provisions to your user interface so that the applications can still work properly in landscape mode.

 NOTE *Chapter 7 discusses how to handle screen rotations.*

FIGURE 1-17

The older iPhones (iPhone 3G/3GS) and the iPod touch have lower resolutions compared to the iPhone 4. They have a resolution of 480 × 320 pixels, which is exactly a quarter of the resolution of the iPhone 4.

When programming for the iPhones, it is important to note the difference between *points* and *pixels*. For example, the following statement specifies a frame that starts from the *point* (20,10) with a width of 280 points and a height of 50 points:

```
CGRect frame = CGRectMake(20, 10, 280, 50);
```

On the older iPhones, a point corresponds to a pixel. Thus, the preceding statement translates directly to the pixel (20,10), with a width of 280 pixels and a height of 50 pixels. However, if the statement is executed within the iPhone 4, a point translates to *two* pixels. Thus, the preceding statement translates into the pixel (40,20), with a width of 560 pixels and a height of 100 pixels. The translation is performed automatically by the OS, which is very useful because it allows older applications to run and scale correctly without modifications on the iPhone 4.

The iPad has a pixel resolution of 1024 × 768 at 132 ppi.

Table 1-1 summarizes the screen resolutions for the various platforms.

TABLE 1-1: Platform Resolutions

PLATFORM	RESOLUTION (PIXELS)	VISIBLE REAL ESTATE WITHOUT THE STATUS BAR (PIXELS) — LANDSCAPE MODE	VISIBLE REAL ESTATE WITHOUT THE STATUS BAR (PIXELS) — PORTRAIT MODE
iPhone 4	960 × 640	960 × 600	920 × 640
iPhone 3G/3GS, iPod touch	480 × 320	480 × 300	460 × 320
iPad	1024 × 768	1024 × 748	1004 × 768

SUMMARY

This chapter offered a quick tour of the available tools used for iPhone and iPad application development. You had a look at the iPhone Simulator, which you will use to test your applications without using a real device. The Simulator is a very powerful tool that you will be using very often in your iPhone development journey.

You also learned some of the characteristics of the iPhone and iPad, such as screen resolutions and the difference between iPhone OS 3.2 and 4.0. In the next chapter, you will develop your first iPhone application, and soon be on your way to iPhone nirvana!

▶ **WHAT YOU LEARNED IN THIS CHAPTER**

TOPIC	KEY CONCEPTS
Obtaining the iPhone SDK	Register as an iPhone developer at `http://developer.apple.com` first and download the free SDK.
iPhone Simulator	Most of the testing can be done on the iPhone Simulator. However, it is strongly recommended that you have a real device for actual testing.
Limitations of the iPhone Simulator	Access to hardware is generally not supported by the Simulator. For example, the camera, accelerometer, voice recording, and so on are not supported.
Frameworks in the iPhone SDK	The iPhone SDK provides several frameworks that perform specific functionalities on the iPhone. You program your iPhone applications using all these frameworks.

Write Your First Hello World! Application

WHAT YOU WILL LEARN IN THIS CHAPTER

- ➤ How to create a new iPhone project
- ➤ Building your first iPhone application using Xcode
- ➤ Designing the user interface (UI) of your iPhone application with Interface Builder
- ➤ How to add an icon to your iPhone application

Now that you have installed the SDK, you are ready to start developing for the iPhone! Programming books customarily start by demonstrating how to develop a "Hello World!" application. This approach enables you to use the various tools quickly without getting bogged down with the details. It also provides you with instant gratification: You see for yourself that things really work, which can be a morale booster that inspires you to learn more.

GETTING STARTED WITH XCODE

Power up Xcode and you should see the Welcome screen, shown in Figure 2-1.

 NOTE *The easiest way to start Xcode is to type* **Xcode** *in Spotlight and then press the Enter key to launch it.*

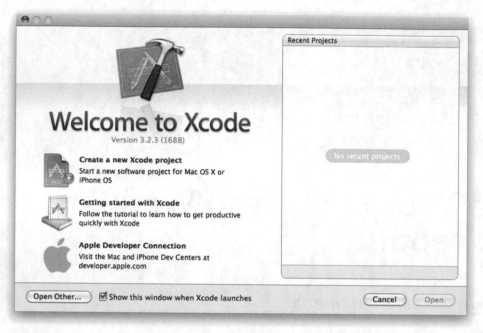

FIGURE 2-1

To create a new iPhone project, choose File ➪ New Project. Figure 2-2 shows the different types of projects you can create using Xcode. The left panel shows the two primary categories — iPhone OS and Mac OS X. The iPhone uses the iPhone OS (which has since been renamed as iOS), so click the Application item listed under iPhone OS to view the different templates available for developing your iPhone application.

Although there are quite a few types of iPhone applications you can create, for this chapter select the View-based Application template; and for the product, select iPhone (to target the iPad, select the iPad as the product). Click the Choose... button.

> **NOTE** Subsequent chapters show you how to develop some of the other types of iPhone applications, such as Tab Bar applications and Split View-based applications.

Name the project HelloWorld and click Save. Xcode proceeds to create the project for the template you have selected. Figure 2-3 shows the various files and folders automatically created for your project.

The left panel of Xcode shows the groups in the project. You can expand each group or folder to reveal the files contained in it. The right panel of Xcode shows the files contained within the group or folder you have selected from the left panel. To edit a particular file, select it from the list, and the editor at the bottom of the right panel opens the file for editing. If you want a separate window for editing, simply double-click the file to edit it in a new window.

FIGURE 2-2

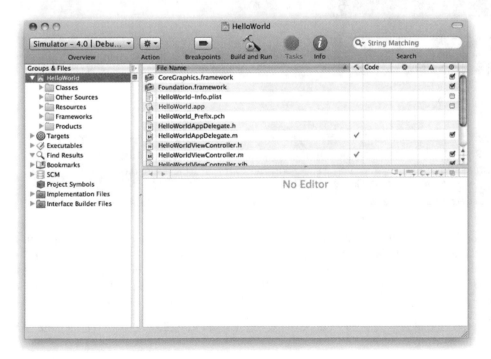

FIGURE 2-3

Using Interface Builder

At this point, the project has no UI. To prove this, simply press Command-R (or select Run ➪ Run), and your application is deployed to the included iPhone 4 Simulator. Figure 2-4 shows the blank screen displayed on the iPhone Simulator. It's good to see this now, because as you go through the chapter you will see changes occur based on your actions.

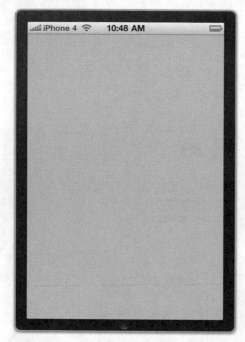

iPhone 4   10:48 AM

FIGURE 2-4

NOTE *If you are not seeing the Simulator as shown in Figure 2-4, that's because it is still simulating the older iPhone. To change to the iPhone 4 Simulator, select Hardware ➪ Device ➪ iPhone 4.*

Obviously, a blank screen is not very useful. Therefore, it's time to try adding some views to your application's UI. In the list of files in your project, you'll notice two files with the `.xib` extension — `MainWindow.xib` and `HelloWorldViewController.xib`. Files with `.xib` extensions are basically XML files containing the UI definitions of an application. You can edit `.xib` files by either modifying their XML content or, more easily (and more sanely), editing them using Interface Builder.

Interface Builder, included as part of the iPhone SDK, enables you to build the UI of iPhone (and Mac) applications by using drag and drop.

Double-click the `HelloWorldViewController.xib` file to launch Interface Builder. Figure 2-5 shows Interface Builder displaying the content of `HelloWorldViewController.xib`, which contains three items: File's Owner, First Responder, and View. As you can see, the Library window shows the various views that you can add to the UI of your iPhone application. The View window shows the graphical layout of your UI. You will see the use of the other windows shortly.

 NOTE *Refer to Appendix C for a crash course on Interface Builder if you are not familiar with it.*

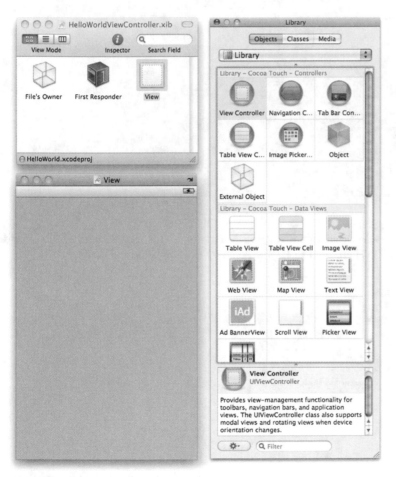

FIGURE 2-5

Scroll down to the Label view in the Library window and drag and drop a Label view onto the View window (see Figure 2-6).

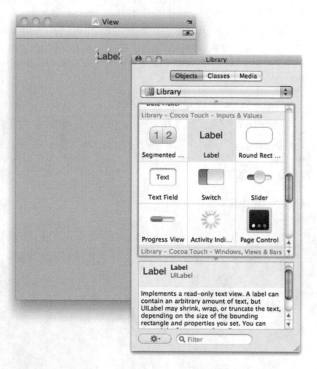

FIGURE 2-6

After the Label view is added, select it and choose Tools ⇨ Attributes Inspector. Enter **Hello World!** in the Text field (see Figure 2-7). Then, next to Layout, click the center Alignment type.

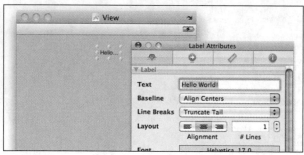

FIGURE 2-7

With the Label view still selected, press Command-T to invoke the Fonts window (see Figure 2-8). Set the font size to 36.

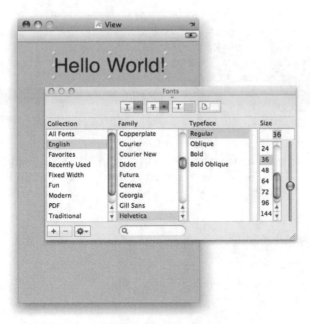

FIGURE 2-8

Next, from the Library window, drag and drop a Text Field view to the View window, followed by a Round Rect Button view. Modify the attribute of the Round Rect Button view by entering **Click Me!** in the Title field (see Figure 2-9).

FIGURE 2-9

NOTE *Rather than specify the* Text *or* Title *property of a view to make the text display in the view (for example, the Label and the Round Rect Button views), you can simply double-click the view itself and type the text directly. After you've done this, you can rearrange the views and resize them to suit your needs. Interface Builder provides you with alignment guidelines to help you arrange your controls in a visually pleasing layout.*

Save the `HelloWorldViewController.xib` file by pressing Command-S. Then, return to Xcode and run the application again by pressing Command-R. The iPhone 4 Simulator now displays the modified UI (see Figure 2-10).

FIGURE 2-10

 NOTE *Always remember to save all your changes in Interface Builder before you run the application in Xcode.*

Click the Text Field view and watch the keyboard automatically appear (see Figure 2-11).

Click the Home button on the iPhone 4 Simulator, and you will see that your application has been installed on the Simulator. To go back to the application, simply click the HelloWorld icon (see Figure 2-12).

FIGURE 2-11

FIGURE 2-12

 NOTE *By default, starting with iOS 4, all applications built using the iPhone 4.0 SDK support multi-tasking. Hence, when you press the Home button on your iPhone, your application is not terminated; it is sent to the background and suspended. Tapping an application icon resumes the application. Chapter 21 contains more details about background execution of your iPhone applications.*

Writing Some Code

By now you should be comfortable enough with Xcode and Interface Builder to write some code. This section will give you a taste of programming the iPhone.

In the `HelloWorldViewController.h` file, add a declaration for the `btnClicked:` action:

```
#import <UIKit/UIKit.h>

@interface HelloWorldViewController : UIViewController {

}

-(IBAction) btnClicked:(id) sender;

@end
```

The bold statement creates an action (commonly known as an *event handler*) named `btnClicked:`. With the action declared, save the file and return to Interface Builder.

Earlier in this chapter, you saw a window labeled `HelloWorldViewController.xib`. Within this window are three components: File's Owner, First Responder, and View. Control-click the Round Rect Button view in the View window and drag it to the File's Owner item in the `HelloWorldViewController.xib` window (see Figure 2-13). A small popup containing the `btnClicked:` action appears. Select the `btnClicked:` action. Basically, what you are doing here is linking the Round Rect Button view with the action (`btnClicked:`) so that when the user clicks the button, the action is invoked.

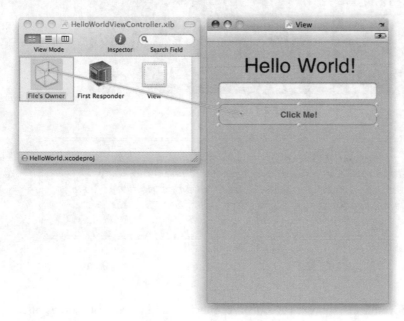

FIGURE 2-13

In the `HelloWorldViewController.m` file, add the code that provides the implementation for the `btnClicked:` action:

```
#import "HelloWorldViewController.h"

@implementation HelloWorldViewController

-(IBAction) btnClicked:(id) sender {
    //--display an alert view--
    UIAlertView *alert =
        [[UIAlertView alloc] initWithTitle:@"Hello World!"
                                   message:@"iPhone, here I come!"
                                  delegate:self
                         cancelButtonTitle:@"OK"
                         otherButtonTitles:nil];
    [alert show];
    [alert release];
}
```

The preceding code displays an alert containing the sentence "iPhone, here I come!"

That's it! Go back to Xcode and run the application again. This time, when you click the Button view, an Alert view displays (see Figure 2-14).

FIGURE 2-14

CUSTOMIZING YOUR APPLICATION ICON

As you saw earlier, the application installed on your iPhone Simulator uses a default white image as an icon. It is possible, however, to customize this icon. When designing icons for your iPhone and iPad applications, bear the following in mind:

➤ Design your icon to be 57 × 57 pixels (for iPhone), 114 × 114 pixels (for iPhone high-resolution), or 72 × 72 pixels (for iPad). Larger size is acceptable because the iOS automatically sizes it for you. For distribution through the App Store, you also need to prepare a 512 × 512 pixel image.

➤ Use square corners for your icon image because iPhone automatically rounds them. It also adds a glossy surface (you can turn off this feature, though).

 NOTE *Apple has published a technical Q&A on the various icon files that you can use in your iPhone application. This document is located at* `http://developer.apple.com/iphone/library/qa/qa2010/qa1686.html`*.*

HOW TO TURN OFF THE GLOSSY SURFACE ON YOUR ICON

To turn off the glossy effect applied on your icon, you need to add the `UIPrerenderedIcon` key to the `HelloWorld-Info.plist` file in your Xcode project and then set it to YES. For more details on the various keys that you can set in your `HelloWorld-Info.plist` file, refer to Apple's documentation at: `http://developer.apple.com/iphone/library/documentation/General/Reference/InfoPlistKeyReference/Articles/iPhoneOSKeys.html`

The following Try It Out demonstrates how to add an icon to your application so that the iPhone will use it instead of the default white image.

TRY IT OUT Adding an Icon to the Application

1. To add an icon to your application, drag and drop an image onto the Resources folder of your project (see Figure 2-15). You will be asked if you want to make a copy of the image you are dropping. Check this option so that a copy of the image will be stored in your project folder.

2. Select the `HelloWorld-Info.plist` item (also located under the Resources folder; the `HelloWorld-Info.plist` file is commonly referred to as the `info.plist` file). Select the Icon file item and set its value to the name of the icon, `app-icon.png` (see Figure 2-16). This specifies the name of the image to be used as the application icon.

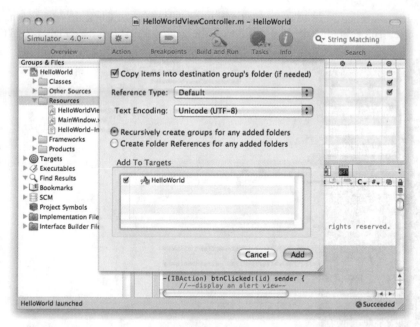

FIGURE 2-15

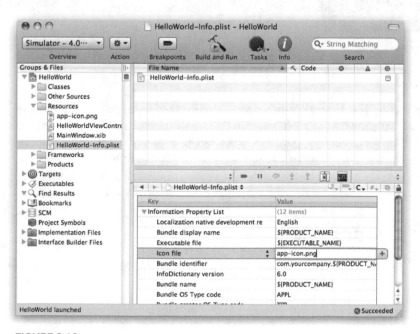

FIGURE 2-16

3. Press Command-R to run the application and test it on the iPhone 4 Simulator. Click the Home but-ton to return to the main screen of the iPhone. You should see the newly added icon (see Figure 2-17).

FIGURE 2-17

How It Works

Setting an icon for your application is very straight-forward — simply specify the icon filename in the Icon file item and it will appear in your iPhone when you run the application again. For more informa-tion about all the icons used in a typical iPhone application, check out Apple's documentation at: http://developer.apple.com/iphone/library/documentation/userexperience/conceptual/mobilehig/IconsImages/IconsImages.html.

DISPLAYING A SPLASH SCREEN

Most iPhone applications display a splash screen whenever they are loaded. The splash screen serves as both a good way to display the logo of the company/application and a distraction to keep the user entertained while the application is busily loading itself into memory.

Displaying a splash screen is very easy using Xcode. You just need to include an image named `Default.png` in your application bundle (e.g., the `Resources` folder). This image needs to have a

e high resolution). When your application is
ge and hide it when the first View window of

ing a photo-editing application, or easily cap-
e. All you need to do is view and capture the
one. The following Try It Out describes how

pplication

le and select Window ⇨ Organizer.

e attached to your Mac. Click the Use for
ab.

os in the Photo Library) and then click the
e right in Organizer (see Figure 2-18).

anizer window. Select the image that you
n.

o use for the default image (see Figure 2-19).

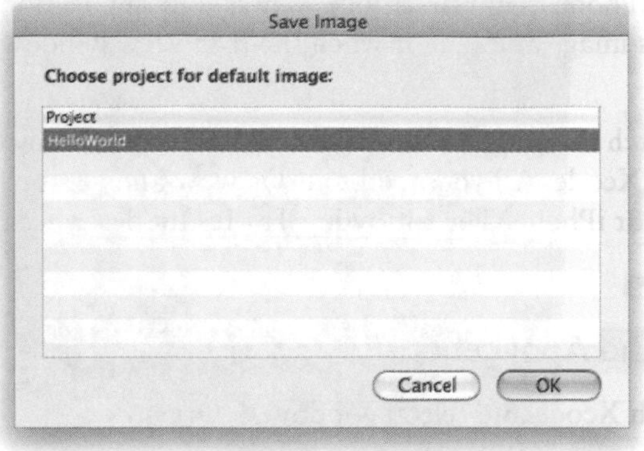

FIGURE 2-19

6. The name will be copied to the Resources folder of the HelloWorld Xcode project (see Figure 2-20).

FIGURE 2-20

7. Press Command-R to test the application on the iPhone 4 Simulator. The splash screen will appear momentarily, followed by the HelloWorldViewController View window in your project.

8. If you want the splash screen to appear for a few seconds before it goes away, insert the following bold code into the `HelloWorldAppDelegate.m` file:

```
- (BOOL)application:(UIApplication *)application
  didFinishLaunchingWithOptions:(NSDictionary *)launchOptions {

    //--insert a delay of 5 seconds before the splash screen disappears--
    [NSThread sleepForTimeInterval:5.0];

    // Override point for customization after application launch.

    // Add the view controller's view to the window and display.
    [window addSubview:viewController.view];
    [window makeKeyAndVisible];

    return YES;
}
```

9. Press Command-R to test the application on the iPhone 4 Simulator again. This time, you will see the splash screen for about five seconds before it goes away.

How It Works

When you include an image named `Default.png` in your project, it will be displayed when your application is being loaded. This is a good chance to display your company's logo, or some information to keep the user occupied when your application is being loaded. Keep in mind the dimension of the image; it will not be displayed during loading if you have an image of the wrong size.

SUMMARY

This chapter provided a brief introduction to developing your first iPhone application. Although you likely still have many questions, the aim of this chapter was to get you started. The next few chapters dive deeper into the details of iPhone programming, and the secret of how all those components that seem so mysterious now work together is gradually revealed.

EXERCISES

1. You want to add an icon to an iPhone project in Xcode. What is the size of the image that you should provide?

2. What is the easiest way to add a splash screen to an iPhone application?

3. When adding an image to the Resources folder in your Xcode project, why do you need to check the "Copy items into destination group's folder (If needed)" option?

Answers to the Exercises can be found in Appendix E, on Wrox.com.

▶ **WHAT YOU LEARNED IN THIS CHAPTER**

TOPIC	KEY CONCEPTS
Xcode	Create your iPhone Application project and write code that manipulates your application.
Interface Builder	Build your iPhone UI using the various views located in the Library.
Adding an application icon	Add an image to the project and then specify the image name in the Icon file property of the `info.plist` file.
Adding a splash screen	Add an image named `Default.png` to the `Resources` folder of your project.
Creating icons for your iPhone applications	Icon size is 57 × 57 pixels and 114 × 114 pixels (high resolution). For App Store hosting, size is 512 × 512 pixels.

3

Views, Outlets, and Actions

WHAT YOU WILL LEARN IN THIS CHAPTER

- ➤ How to declare and define outlets
- ➤ How to declare and define actions
- ➤ How to connect outlets and actions to the views in your View window
- ➤ How to use the UIAlertView to display an alert view to the user
- ➤ How to use the UIActionSheet to display some options to the user
- ➤ How to use the UIPageControl to control paging
- ➤ How to use the UIImageView to display images
- ➤ How to use the UIWebView to display Web content in your application
- ➤ How to add views dynamically to your application during runtime

In the previous chapter, you built a simple Hello World! iPhone application without understanding much of the underlying details of how things work together. In fact, one of the greatest hurdles in learning iPhone programming is the large number of details you need to learn before you can get an application up and running. This book aims to make the iPhone programming experience both fun and bearable. Hence, this chapter starts with the basics of creating the user interface (UI) of an iPhone application and how your code connects with the various graphical widgets.

OUTLETS AND ACTIONS

One of the first things you need to understand in iPhone programming is outlets and actions. If you are familiar with traditional programming languages such as Java or C#, this is a concept that requires some time to get used to — the concepts are similar, just that it is a different way of doing things. At the end of this section, you will have a solid understanding of what outlets and actions are and how to create them, and be on your way to creating great iPhone applications.

TRY IT OUT Creating Outlets and Actions

1. Using Xcode, create a View-based Application (iPhone) project and name it **OutletsAndActions**.

2. Edit the `OutletsAndActionsViewController.xib` file by double-clicking it to open it in Interface Builder. When Interface Builder is loaded, double-click the View item in the `OutletsAndActionsViewController.xib` window to visually display the View window (see Figure 3-1). Populate the three views onto the View window — Label, Text Field, and Round Rect Button. Set the Label view with the text "Enter your name" by double-clicking on it. Also, set the Round Rect Button with the "OK" string.

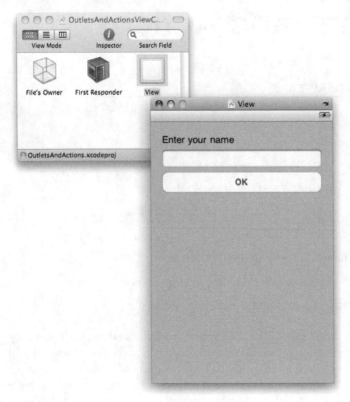

FIGURE 3-1

3. In Xcode, modify the `OutletsAndActionsViewController.h` file with the following statements shown in bold:

```
#import <UIKit/UIKit.h>

@interface OutletsAndActionsViewController : UIViewController {
    //---declaring the outlet---
    IBOutlet UITextField *txtName;
```

```
    }

    //---expose the outlet as a property---
    @property (nonatomic, retain) UITextField *txtName;

    //---declaring the action---
    -(IBAction) btnClicked:(id) sender;

    @end
```

4. In the `OutletsAndActionsViewController.m` file, define the following statements in bold:

```
    #import "OutletsAndActionsViewController.h"

    @implementation OutletsAndActionsViewController

    //---synthesize the property---
    @synthesize txtName;

    //---displays an alert view when the button is clicked---
    -(IBAction) btnClicked:(id) sender {
        NSString *str = [[NSString alloc]
                           initWithFormat:@"Hello, %@", txtName.text];
        UIAlertView *alert = [[UIAlertView alloc]
                                 initWithTitle:@"Hello!"
                                       message:str
                                      delegate:self
                              cancelButtonTitle:@"Done"
                              otherButtonTitles:nil];
        [alert show];
        [str release];
        [alert release];
    }

    - (void)dealloc {
        //---release the outlet---
        [txtName release];
        [super dealloc];
    }
```

5. In the `OutletsAndActionsViewController.xib` window, control-click and drag the File's Owner item to the Text Field view (see Figure 3-2). A popup will appear; select the outlet named `txtName`.

6. Control-click and drag the OK Button view to the File's Owner item (see Figure 3-3). Select the action named `btnClicked:`.

7. Right-click the OK Button view to display its events (see Figure 3-4). Notice that the Button view has several events, but one particular event — Touch Up Inside — is now connected to the action you specified (`btnClicked:`). Because the Touch Up Inside event is so commonly used, it is automatically connected to the action when you control-click and drag it to the File's Owner item. To connect other events to the action, simply click the circle displayed next to each event and then drag it to the File's Owner item.

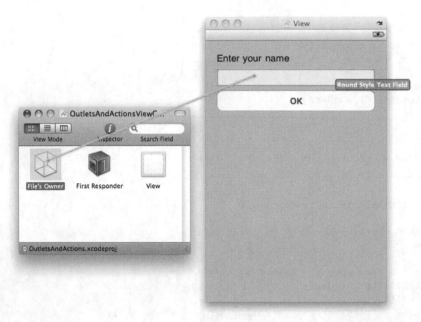

FIGURE 3-2

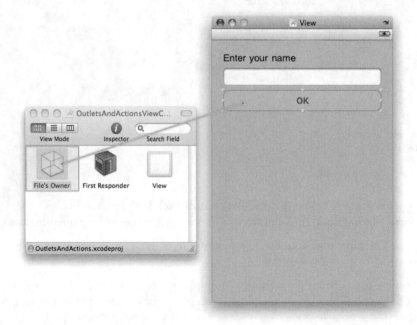

FIGURE 3-3

8. That's it! Press Command-R to test the application on the iPhone 4 Simulator. Enter a name in the Text Field and click the OK button. An alert view displays a welcome message (see Figure 3-5).

FIGURE 3-4   **FIGURE 3-5**

How It Works

In iPhone, you use actions and outlets to connect your code to the various views in your UI. Think of actions as methods in the traditional object-oriented programming world and outlets as object references. Actions are represented using the IBAction keyword while outlets use the IBOutlet keyword:

```
#import <UIKit/UIKit.h>

@interface OutletsAndActionsViewController : UIViewController {
    //---declaring the outlet---
    IBOutlet UITextField *txtName;
}

//---expose the outlet as a property---
@property (nonatomic, retain) UITextField *txtName;

//---declaring the action---
-(IBAction) btnClicked:(id) sender;

@end
```

The IBOutlet identifier is used to prefix variables so that Interface Builder can synchronize the display and connection of outlets with Xcode. The @property keyword indicates to the compiler that you want the txtName outlet to be exposed as a property. The nonatomic keyword indicates that there is no need to ensure that the property is used in a thread-safe manner because it is not used in multiple threads. The default behavior is atomic, and specifying nonatomic actually improves the performance of your application.

> **NOTE** The IBOutlet tag can also be added to the @property identifier. This syntax is common in the Apple documentation:
>
>   @property (nonatomic, retain) IBOutlet UITextField *txtName;

> **NOTE** For the use of the nonatomic and retain identifiers, refer to Appendix D, where you can find an introduction to Objective-C, the language used for iPhone programming. Also, the @synthesize keyword, discussed shortly, is explained in more detail there as well.

The IBAction identifier is used to synchronize action methods. An *action* is a method that can handle events raised by views (for example, when a button is clicked) in the View window. An outlet, on the other hand, allows your code to programmatically reference a view on the View window.

Once your actions and outlets are added to the header (.h) file of the View Controller, you then need to connect them to your views in Interface Builder.

When you control-click and drag the File's Owner item to the Text Field view and select txtName, you essentially connect the outlet you have created (txtName) with the Text Field view on the View window. In general, to connect outlets you control-click and drag the File's Owner item to the view on the View window.

CONNECTING OUTLETS AND ACTIONS TO VIEWS

A quick tip: To connect outlets to the views, you drag the File's Owner item onto the required view in the View window.

To connect an action, you control-click and drag a view to the File's Owner item. Hence, for the OK Button view, you control-click and drag the OK Button view to the File's Owner item and then select the action named btnClicked:.Another quick tip: To connect actions, you drag from the view in the View window onto the File's Owner item.

In the implementation file (.m), you use the @synthesize keyword to indicate to the compiler to create the getter and setter for the specified property:

 COMMON MISTAKES *Forgetting to add the* @synthesize *keyword is one of the most common mistakes that developers make. Remember to add this statement or else you will encounter a runtime error when the application is executed. Appendix D covers getter/setter in more details.*

```
#import "OutletsAndActionsViewController.h"

@implementation OutletsAndActionsViewController

//---synthesize the property---
@synthesize txtName;

//---displays an alert view when the button is clicked---
-(IBAction) btnClicked:(id) sender {
    NSString *str = [[NSString alloc]
                        initWithFormat:@"Hello, %@", txtName.text];
    UIAlertView *alert = [[UIAlertView alloc]
                             initWithTitle:@"Hello!"
                                   message:str
                                  delegate:self
                         cancelButtonTitle:@"Done"
                         otherButtonTitles:nil];
    [alert show];
    [str release];
    [alert release];
}

- (void)dealloc {
    //---release the outlet---
    [txtName release];
    [super dealloc];
}
```

The btnClicked: action simply displays an alert view with a message containing the user's name. Note that it has a parameter sender of type id. The sender parameter allows you to programmatically find out who actually invokes this action. This is useful when you have multiple views connecting to one single action. For such cases, you often need to know which is the view that invokes this method and the sender parameter will contain a reference to the calling view.

USING VIEWS

So far, you have seen quite a number of views in action — Round Rect Button, Text Field, and Label. All these views are quite straightforward, but they give you a good opportunity to understand how to apply the concepts behind outlets and actions.

To use more views, you can locate them from the Library window in Interface Builder (see Figure 3-6).

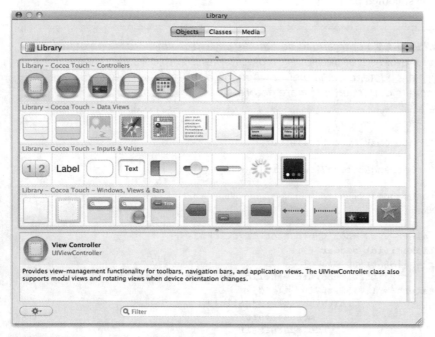

FIGURE 3-6

The Library is divided into sections:

➤ Controllers — Contains views that control other views, such as the View Controller, Tab Bar Controller, Navigation Controller, and so on.

➤ Data Views — Contains views that display data, such as the Image View, Table View, Data Picker, Picker View, and so on.

➤ Inputs and Values — Contains views that accept input from users as well as display values, such as the Label, Round Rect Button, Text Field, and so on.

➤ Windows, Views & Bars — Contains views that display other, miscellaneous views, such as View, Search Bar, Toolbar, and so on.

In the following sections, you learn how to use some of the views available in the Library. Although it is beyond the scope of this book to show the use of every view, you have the opportunity to see a number of views in action throughout the book. In this chapter, you learn some of the fundamental concepts of dealing with views so that you can use other views without problems.

Using the Alert View

One of the views not listed in the Library is the `UIAlertView`. The `UIAlertView` displays an alert view to the user and is usually created during runtime. Hence, you have to create it using code.

NOTE *You actually saw the* `UIAlertView` *in the previous section. In this section, you will understand how it actually works.*

The `UIAlertView` is useful for cases in which you have to display a message to the user. In addition, it can serve as a quick debugging tool when you want to observe the value of a variable during runtime.

The following Try It Out explores the `UIAlertView` in more detail. Download the code as indicated.

TRY IT OUT Using the Alert View

codefile UsingViews.zip available for download at Wrox.com

1. Using Xcode, create a new View-based Application (iPhone) project and name it **UsingViews**.

2. In the `UsingViewsViewController.m` file, add the following bold code to the `viewDidLoad` method:

```
- (void)viewDidLoad {
    UIAlertView *alert = [[UIAlertView alloc]
                            initWithTitle:@"Hello"
                                message:@"This is an alert view"
                                delegate:self
                          cancelButtonTitle:@"OK"
                          otherButtonTitles:nil];
    [alert show];
    [alert release];
    [super viewDidLoad];
}
```

3. Press Command-R to test the application on the iPhone 4 Simulator. When the application is loaded, you see the alert view shown in Figure 3-7.

4. In Xcode, modify the `otherButtonTitles` parameter by setting it with the value shown in bold:

```
- (void)viewDidLoad {
    UIAlertView *alert = [[UIAlertView alloc]
                            initWithTitle:@"Hello"
                                message:@"This is an alert view"
                                delegate:self
                          cancelButtonTitle:@"OK"
                          otherButtonTitles:@"Option 1", @"Option 2", nil];
    [alert show];
    [alert release];
    [super viewDidLoad];
}
```

5. In the `UsingViewsViewController.h` file, add the following line that appears in bold:

```
#import <UIKit/UIKit.h>

@interface UsingViewsViewController : UIViewController
    <UIAlertViewDelegate> {
}

@end
```

FIGURE 3-7

6. In the `UsingViewsViewController.m` file, add the following method:

```
- (void)alertView:(UIAlertView *)alertView
clickedButtonAtIndex:(NSInteger)buttonIndex {
    NSLog(@"%d", buttonIndex);
}
```

7. Press Command-R to test the application in the iPhone 4 Simulator. Notice that there are now two buttons in addition to the OK button (see Figure 3-8).

8. Click any one of the buttons — Option 1, Option 2, or OK.

9. In Xcode, press Command-Shift-R to view the Debugger Console window. Observe the values printed. You can rerun the application a number of times, clicking the different buttons to observe the values printed. The values printed for each button clicked are as follows:

➤ OK button — 0

➤ Option 1 — 1

➤ Option 2 — 2

FIGURE 3-8

How It Works

To use UIAlertView, you first instantiate it and initialize it with the various arguments:

```
UIAlertView *alert = [[UIAlertView alloc]
                        initWithTitle:@"Hello"
                              message:@"This is an alert view"
                             delegate:self
                    cancelButtonTitle:@"OK"
                    otherButtonTitles:nil];
```

The first parameter is the title of the alert view, which you set to "Hello". The second is the message, which you set to "This is an alert view". The third is the delegate, which you need to set to an object that will handle the events fired by the UIAlertView object. In this case, you set it to self, which means that the event handler will be implemented in the current class, that is, the View Controller. The cancelButtonTitle parameter displays a button to dismiss your alert view. Last, the otherButtonTitles parameter allows you to display additional buttons if needed. If no additional buttons are needed, simply set this to nil.

To show the alert view modally, use the show method:

```
[alert show];
```

 COMMON MISTAKES *It is important to note that showing the alert view modally using the* show *method does not cause the program to stall execution at this statement. The subsequent statements after this line continue to execute even though the user may not have dismissed the alert.*

For simple use of the alert view, you don't really need to handle the events fired by it. Tapping the OK button (as set in the cancelButtonTitle parameter) simply dismisses the alert view.

If you want more than one button, you need to set the otherButtonTitles parameter, like this:

```
UIAlertView *alert = [[UIAlertView alloc]
                        initWithTitle:@"Hello"
                              message:@"This is an alert view"
                             delegate:self
                    cancelButtonTitle:@"OK"
                    otherButtonTitles:@"Option 1", @"Option 2", nil];
```

Note that you need to end the otherButtonTitles parameter with a nil or a runtime error will occur.

Now that you have three buttons, you need to be able to know which button the user pressed — in particular, whether Option 1 or Option 2 was pressed. To do so, you need to handle the event raised by the UIAlertView class. You do so by ensuring that your View Controller implements the UIAlertViewDelegate protocol:

```
@interface UsingViewsViewController : UIViewController
    <UIAlertViewDelegate> {
}
```

The `UIAlertViewDelegate` protocol contains several methods associated with the alert view. To know which button the user tapped, you need to implement the `alertView:clickedButtonAtIndex:` method:

```
- (void)alertView:(UIAlertView *)alertView
clickedButtonAtIndex:(NSInteger)buttonIndex {
    NSLog(@"%d", buttonIndex);
}
```

The index of the button clicked will be passed in via the `clickedButtonAtIndex:` parameter.

 NOTE *Refer to Appendix D for a discussion of the concept of protocols in Objective-C.*

Using the Action Sheet

Although the Alert view can display multiple buttons, its primary use is still as a tool to alert users when something happens. If you need to display a message with multiple choices for the user to select, you should use an Action Sheet rather than the Alert view. An *action sheet* displays a collection of buttons among which the user can select one.

To use an action sheet, use the code snippet below:

```
UIActionSheet *action = [[UIActionSheet alloc]
                     initWithTitle:@"Title of Action Sheet"
                          delegate:self
                 cancelButtonTitle:@"OK"
            destructiveButtonTitle:@"Delete Message"
                 otherButtonTitles:@"Option 1", @"Option 2",
                                    nil];
[action showInView:self.view];
[action release];
```

To handle the event fired by the action sheet when one of the buttons is tapped, implement the `UIActionSheetDelegate` protocol in your View Controller, like this:

```
#import <UIKit/UIKit.h>

@interface UsingViewsViewController : UIViewController
    <UIActionSheetDelegate>{
}
```

When a button is tapped, the `actionSheet:clickedButtonAtIndex:` event will be fired:

```
- (void)actionSheet:(UIActionSheet *)actionSheet
clickedButtonAtIndex:(NSInteger)buttonIndex{
    NSLog(@"%d", buttonIndex);
}
```

Figure 3-9 shows the action sheet when it is displayed on the iPhone 4 Simulator. Observe that the action sheet pops up from the bottom of the View window.

One important aspect of the action sheet is that when it is used on the iPad, you should not display an action sheet in the viewDidLoad method — doing so causes an exception to be raised during runtime. Instead, you can display it in say, an IBAction method.

Figure 3-10 shows the action sheet when displayed on the iPad. Interestingly, on the iPad the OK button (set by the cancelButtonTitle: parameter) is not displayed.

FIGURE 3-9   **FIGURE 3-10**

The value (buttonIndex) of each button is as follows:

➤ Delete Message — 0

➤ Option 1 — 1

➤ Option 2 — 2

➤ OK — 3

On the iPad, when the user taps on an area outside of the action sheet, the action sheet is dismissed and the value of buttonIndex becomes 3. Interestingly, if you specified nil for the cancelButtonTitle: part, the value of buttonIndex would be –1 when the action sheet is dismissed.

Page Control and Image View

Near the bottom of iPhone's Home screen is a series of dots (see Figure 3-11). A lighted dot represents the currently selected page. As you swipe the page to the next page, the next dot lights, and the first one dims. In the figure, the dots indicate that the first page is the active page. In the iPhone SDK, the series of dots is represented by the `UIPageControl` class.

FIGURE 3-11

In the following Try it Out, you learn to use the page control view within your own application to switch between images displayed in the ImageView.

TRY IT OUT Using the Page Control and the Image View

1. Using the `UsingViews` project created in the previous section, add five images to the Resources folder by dragging and dropping them from the Finder. Figure 3-12 shows the five images added to the project.

2. Double-click the `UsingViewsViewController.xib file` to edit it using Interface Builder.

3. Drag and drop two ImageViews onto the View window (see Figure 3-13). At this point, overlap them (but not entirely) as shown in the figure.

4. With the first ImageView selected, open the Attributes Inspector window and set the `Tag` property to 0. Select the second ImageView and set the `Tag` property to 1 (see Figure 3-14).

5. Drag and drop the Page Control view onto the View window and set its number of pages to 5 (see Figure 3-15).

FIGURE 3-12

Ensure that you increase the width of the Page Control view so that all the dots are now visible.

6. Set the Background color of the View window to black so that the dots inside the Page Control are clearly visible (see Figure 3-16).

7. In Xcode, declare three outlets and two `UIImageView` objects in the `UsingViewsViewController.h` file:

```
#import <UIKit/UIKit.h>

@interface UsingViewsViewController : UIViewController {
    IBOutlet UIPageControl *pageControl;
    IBOutlet UIImageView *imageView1;
    IBOutlet UIImageView *imageView2;
    UIImageView *tempImageView, *bgImageView;
}

@property (nonatomic, retain) UIPageControl *pageControl;
@property (nonatomic, retain) UIImageView *imageView1;
@property (nonatomic, retain) UIImageView *imageView2;

@end
```

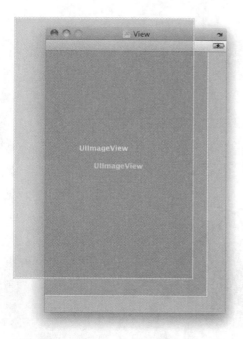

FIGURE 3-13

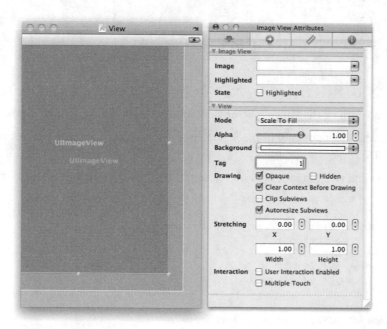

FIGURE 3-14

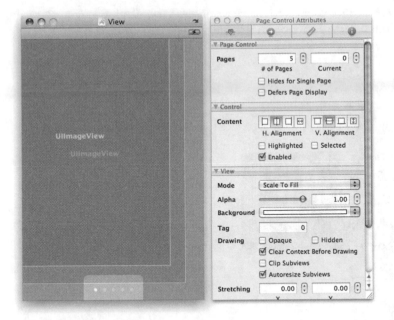

FIGURE 3-15

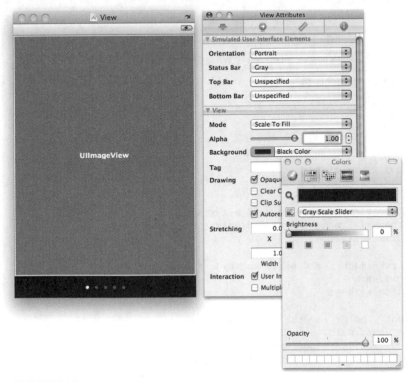

FIGURE 3-16

8. In Interface Builder, connect the three outlets to the views on the View window. Figure 3-17 shows the connections made for the `imageView1`, `imageView2`, and `pageControl` outlets.

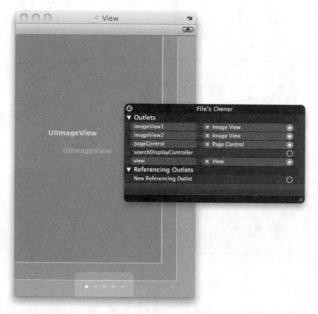

FIGURE 3-17

9. You can now rearrange the ImageViews on the View window so that they overlap each other.

10. In Xcode, add the following statements that appear in bold to the `UsingViewsViewController.m` file:

```objc
#import "UsingViewsViewController.h"

@implementation UsingViewsViewController

@synthesize pageControl;
@synthesize imageView1, imageView2;

- (void)viewDidLoad {
    //---initialize the first imageview to display an image---
    [imageView1 setImage:[UIImage imageNamed:@"iMac_old.jpeg"]];
    tempImageView = imageView2;

    //---make the first imageview visible and hide the second---
    [imageView1 setHidden:NO];
    [imageView2 setHidden:YES];

    //---add the event handler for the page control---
    [pageControl addTarget:self
                    action:@selector(pageTurning:)
          forControlEvents:UIControlEventValueChanged];

    [super viewDidLoad];
```

```objc
}

//---when the page control's value is changed---
- (void) pageTurning: (UIPageControl *) pageController {
    //---get the page number you can turning to---
    NSInteger nextPage = [pageController currentPage];
    switch (nextPage) {
        case 0:
            [tempImageView setImage:
                [UIImage imageNamed:@"iMac_old.jpeg"]];
            break;
        case 1:
            [tempImageView setImage:
                [UIImage imageNamed:@"iMac.jpeg"]];
            break;
        case 2:
            [tempImageView setImage:
                [UIImage imageNamed:@"Mac8100.jpeg"]];
            break;
        case 3:
            [tempImageView setImage:
                [UIImage imageNamed:@"MacPlus.jpeg"]];
            break;
        case 4:
            [tempImageView setImage:
                [UIImage imageNamed:@"MacSE.jpeg"]];
            break;
        default:
            break;
    }

    //---switch the two imageview views---
    if (tempImageView.tag == 0) { //---imageView1---
        tempImageView = imageView2;
        bgImageView = imageView1;
    }
    else {                          //---imageView2---
        tempImageView = imageView1;
        bgImageView = imageView2;
    }

    //---animate the two views flipping---
    [UIView beginAnimations:@"flipping view" context:nil];
    [UIView setAnimationDuration:0.5];
    [UIView setAnimationCurve:UIViewAnimationCurveEaseInOut];
    [UIView setAnimationTransition:UIViewAnimationTransitionFlipFromLeft
                        forView:tempImageView
                            cache:YES];

    [tempImageView setHidden:YES];

    [UIView commitAnimations];

    [UIView beginAnimations:@"flipping view" context:nil];
```

```
    [UIView setAnimationDuration:0.5];
    [UIView setAnimationCurve:UIViewAnimationCurveEaseInOut];
    [UIView setAnimationTransition:UIViewAnimationTransitionFlipFromRight
                        forView:bgImageView
                          cache:YES];

    [bgImageView setHidden:NO];

    [UIView commitAnimations];
}

- (void)dealloc {
    [pageControl release];
    [imageView1 release];
    [imageView2 release];
    [super dealloc];
}
```

11. Press Command-R to test the application on the iPhone 4 Simulator. When you tap the Page
Control located at the bottom of the screen, the image view flips to display the next one.

How It Works

When the View is first loaded, you get one of the ImageViews to display an image and then hide the other:

```
    //---initialize the first imageview to display an image---
    [imageView1 setImage:[UIImage imageNamed:@"iMac_old.jpeg"]];
    tempImageView = imageView2;

    //---make the first imageview visible and hide the second---
    [imageView1 setHidden:NO];
    [imageView2 setHidden:YES];
```

You then wire the Page Control so that when the user taps it, an event is fired and triggers a method.
In this case, the pageTurning: method is called:

```
    //---add the event handler for the page control---
    [pageControl addTarget:self
                    action:@selector(pageTurning:)
            forControlEvents:UIControlEventValueChanged];
```

In the pageTurning: method, you determine which image you should load based on the value of the
Page Control:

```
    //---when the page control's value is changed---
    - (void) pageTurning: (UIPageControl *) pageController {

        //---get the page number you can turning to---
        NSInteger nextPage = [pageController currentPage];
        switch (nextPage) {
            case 0:
                [tempImageView setImage:
                 [UIImage imageNamed:@"iMac_old.jpeg"]];
                break;
            case 1:
```

```
                [tempImageView setImage:
                 [UIImage imageNamed:@"iMac.jpeg"]];
                break;
            case 2:
                [tempImageView setImage:
                 [UIImage imageNamed:@"Mac8100.jpeg"]];
                break;
            case 3:
                [tempImageView setImage:
                 [UIImage imageNamed:@"MacPlus.jpeg"]];
                break;
            case 4:
                [tempImageView setImage:
                 [UIImage imageNamed:@"MacSE.jpeg"]];
                break;
            default:
                break;
        }
        //...
    }
```

You then switch the two ImageViews and animate them by using the various methods in the UIView class:

```
    //---switch the two imageview views---
    if (tempImageView.tag == 0) { //---imageView1---
        tempImageView = imageView2;
        bgImageView = imageView1;
    }
    else {                          //---imageView2---
        tempImageView = imageView1;
        bgImageView = imageView2;
    }

    //---animate the two views flipping---
    [UIView beginAnimations:@"flipping view" context:nil];
    [UIView setAnimationDuration:0.5];
    [UIView setAnimationCurve:UIViewAnimationCurveEaseInOut];
    [UIView setAnimationTransition:UIViewAnimationTransitionFlipFromLeft
                          forView:tempImageView
                            cache:YES];

    [tempImageView setHidden:YES];

    [UIView commitAnimations];

    [UIView beginAnimations:@"flipping view" context:nil];
    [UIView setAnimationDuration:0.5];
    [UIView setAnimationCurve:UIViewAnimationCurveEaseInOut];
    [UIView setAnimationTransition:UIViewAnimationTransitionFlipFromRight
                          forView:bgImageView
                            cache:YES];

    [bgImageView setHidden:NO];

    [UIView commitAnimations];
```

Specifically, you apply the flipping transitions to the ImageViews:

```
[UIView setAnimationTransition:UIViewAnimationTransitionFlipFromLeft
                forView:tempImageView
                cache:YES];
```

Using the Web View

To load Web pages from within your application, you can embed a Web browser in your application through the use of the `UIWebView`. Using the Web view, you can send a request to load Web content, which is very useful if you want to convert an existing Web application into a native application (such as those written using Dashcode). All you need to do is to embed all the HTML pages into your Resources folder in your Xcode project and load the HTML pages into the Web view during runtime.

 NOTE *Depending on how complex your Web applications are, you may have to do some additional work to port your Web application to a native application if it involves server-side technologies such as CGI, PHP, or others.*

The following Try It Out shows how to use the Web view to load a Web page.

TRY IT OUT Loading a Web Page Using the Web View

codefile UsingViews2.zip available for download at Wrox.com

1. Using Xcode, create a new View-based Application project and name it `UsingViews2`.

2. Double-click the `UsingViews2ViewController.xib` file to edit it using Interface Builder.

3. In the View window, add a Web View from the Library (see Figure 3-18). In the Attributes Inspector window for the Web view, check the `Scales Page to Fit` property.

4. In the `UsingViews2ViewController.h` file, declare an outlet for the Web view:

```
#import <UIKit/UIKit.h>

@interface UsingViews2ViewController : UIViewController {
    IBOutlet UIWebView *webView;
}

@property (nonatomic, retain) UIWebView *webView;

@end
```

5. In Interface Builder, connect the `webView` outlet to the Web view.

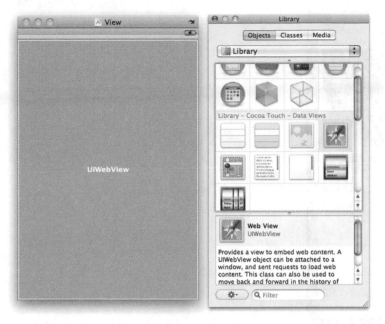

FIGURE 3-18

6. In the `UsingViews2ViewController.m` file, add the following statements that appear in bold:

```
#import "UsingViews2ViewController.h"

@implementation UsingViews2ViewController

@synthesize webView;

- (void)viewDidLoad {
    NSURL *url = [NSURL URLWithString:@"http://www.apple.com"];
    NSURLRequest *req = [NSURLRequest requestWithURL:url];
    [webView loadRequest:req];
    [super viewDidLoad];
}

- (void)dealloc {
    [webView release];
    [super dealloc];
}
```

7. Press Command-R to test the application on the iPhone 4 Simulator. You should see the application loading the page from Apple.com (see Figure 3-19).

FIGURE 3-19

How It Works

To load the Web view with a URL, you first instantiate an NSURL object with a URL via the URLWithString method:

```
NSURL *url = [NSURL URLWithString:@"http://www.apple.com"];
```

You then create an NSURLRequest object by passing the NSURL object to its requestWithURL: method:

```
NSURLRequest *req = [NSURLRequest requestWithURL:url];
```

Finally, you load the Web view with the NSURLRequest object via the loadRequest: method:

```
[webView loadRequest:req];
```

ADDING VIEWS DYNAMICALLY USING CODE

Up to this point, all the UIs of your application have been created visually using Interface Builder. Although Interface Builder makes it relatively easy to build a UI using drag-and-drop, sometimes you are better off using code to create it. One such instance is when you need a dynamic UI, such as for games.

NOTE *Interface Builder may be easy to use, but it can be confusing to some people. Because you often have more than one way of doing things in Interface Builder, it may create unnecessary complications. I know of developers who swear by creating their UIs using code.*

In the following Try It Out, you learn how to create views dynamically from code, which will help you understand how views are constructed and manipulated.

TRY IT OUT   Creating Views from Code

codefile DynamicViews.zip available for download at Wrox.com

1. Using Xcode, create a View-based Application project and name it DynamicViews.

2. In the DynamicViewsViewController.m file, add the following statements that appear in bold:

```
#import "DynamicViewsViewController.h"

@implementation DynamicViewsViewController

- (void)loadView {
    //---create a UIView object---
    UIView *view =
    [[UIView alloc] initWithFrame:[UIScreen mainScreen].applicationFrame];

    //---set the background color to light gray---
    view.backgroundColor = [UIColor lightGrayColor];

    //---create a Label view---
    CGRect frame = CGRectMake(10, 15, 300, 20);
    UILabel *label = [[UILabel alloc] initWithFrame:frame];
    label.textAlignment = UITextAlignmentCenter;
    label.backgroundColor = [UIColor clearColor];
    label.font = [UIFont fontWithName:@"Verdana" size:20];
    label.text = @"This is a label";
    label.tag = 1000;

    //---create a Button view---
    frame = CGRectMake(10, 70, 300, 50);
    UIButton *button = [UIButton buttonWithType:UIButtonTypeRoundedRect];
    button.frame = frame;

    [button setTitle:@"Click Me, Please!" forState:UIControlStateNormal];
    button.backgroundColor = [UIColor clearColor];
    button.tag = 2000;
    [button addTarget:self
                action:@selector(buttonClicked:)
     forControlEvents:UIControlEventTouchUpInside];

    [view addSubview:label];
```

```
    [view addSubview:button];

    self.view = view;
    [label release];
}

-(IBAction) buttonClicked: (id) sender{
    UIAlertView *alert = [[UIAlertView alloc]
                              initWithTitle:@"Action invoked!"
                                    message:@"Button clicked!"
                                   delegate:self
                          cancelButtonTitle:@"OK"
                          otherButtonTitles:nil];
    [alert show];
    [alert release];
}
```

3. Press Command-R to test the application in the iPhone 4 Simulator. Figure 3-20 shows that the Label and Round Rect Button views are displayed on the View window. Click the button to see an alert view displaying a message.

How It Works

You implement the `loadView` method defined in your View Controller to programmatically create your views. You implement this method only if you are generating your UI during runtime. This method is automatically called when the `view` property of your View Controller is called but its current value is `nil`.

 NOTE *Chapter 4 discusses some of the commonly used methods in a View Controller.*

The first view you create is the `UIView` object, which allows you to use it as a container for more views:

```
//---create a UIView object---
UIView *view =
[[UIView alloc] initWithFrame:[UIScreen mainScreen].applicationFrame];
 //---set the background color to light gray---
view.backgroundColor = [UIColor lightGrayColor];
```

Next, you create a Label view and set it to display a string:

```
//---create a Label view---
CGRect frame = CGRectMake(10, 15, 300, 20);
UILabel *label = [[UILabel alloc] initWithFrame:frame];
label.textAlignment = UITextAlignmentCenter;
label.backgroundColor = [UIColor clearColor];
label.font = [UIFont fontWithName:@"Verdana" size:20];
label.text = @"This is a label";
label.tag = 1000;
```

FIGURE 3-20

Notice that you have also set the `tag` property, which is very useful for allowing you to search for particular views during runtime.

You also create a Button view by calling the `buttonWithType:` method with the `UIButtonTypeRoundedRect` constant. This method returns a `UIRoundedRectButton` object (which is a subclass of `UIButton`).

```
//---create a Button view---
frame = CGRectMake(10, 70, 300, 50);
UIButton *button = [UIButton buttonWithType:UIButtonTypeRoundedRect];
button.frame = frame;

[button setTitle:@"Click Me, Please!" forState:UIControlStateNormal];
button.backgroundColor = [UIColor clearColor];
button.tag = 2000;
```

You then wire an event handler for its `Touch Up Inside` event so that when the button is tapped, the `buttonClicked:` method is called:

```
[button addTarget:self
          action:@selector(buttonClicked:)
 forControlEvents:UIControlEventTouchUpInside];
```

Finally, you add the `label` and `button` views to the `view` you created earlier:

```
[view addSubview:label];
[view addSubview:button];
```

Finally, you assign the `view` object to the `view` property of the current View Controller:

```
self.view = view;
```

 NOTE *One important point to note here is that within the* `loadView` *method, you should not get the value of the* `view` *property (setting it is all right), like this:*

```
[self.view addSubview:label];   //---this is not OK---
self.view = view;               //---this is OK---
```

Trying to get the value of the `view` property in this method will result in a circular reference and cause memory overflow.

UNDERSTANDING VIEW HIERARCHY

As views are created and added, they are added to a tree data structure. Views are displayed in the order that they are added. To verify this, modify the location of the `UIButton` object you created earlier by changing its location to `CGRectMake(10, 30, 300, 50)`, as in the following:

```
frame = CGRectMake(10, 30, 300, 50);

UIButton *button = [UIButton buttonWithType:UIButtonTypeRoundedRect];
button.frame = frame;

[button setTitle:@"Click Me, Please!" forState:UIControlStateNormal];
button.backgroundColor = [UIColor clearColor];
button.tag = 2000;
[button addTarget:self
           action:@selector(buttonClicked:)
  forControlEvents:UIControlEventTouchUpInside];
```

When you now run the application again, you will notice that the button overlaps the label control (see Figure 3-21) because the button was added last:

```
[view addSubview:label];
[view addSubview:button];
```

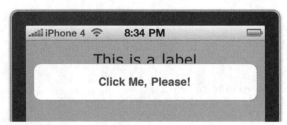

FIGURE 3-21

To switch the order in which the views are displayed after they have been added, use the
exchangeSubviewAtIndex:withSubviewAtIndex: method, like this:

```
[view addSubview:label];
[view addSubview:button];
[view exchangeSubviewAtIndex:1 withSubviewAtIndex:0];
self.view = view;
[label release];
```

The preceding statement in bold swaps the order of the Label and Button views. When the application is run again, the Label view will now appear on top of the Button view (See Figure 3-22).

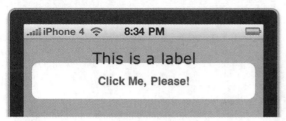

FIGURE 3-22

To learn the order of the various views already added, you can use the following code segment to print the value of the tag property for each view:

```
[view addSubview:label];
[view addSubview:button];
[view exchangeSubviewAtIndex:1 withSubviewAtIndex:0];
for (int i=0; i<[view.subviews count]; ++i) {
    UIView *v = [view.subviews objectAtIndex:i];
    NSLog(@"%d", v.tag);
}
```

The following method recursively prints out all the views contained in a UIView object:

```
-(void) printViews:(UIView *) view {
    if ([view.subviews count] > 0){
        for (int i=0; i<[view.subviews count]; ++i) {
            UIView *v = [view.subviews objectAtIndex:i];
            NSLog(@"View index: %d Tag: %d",i, v.tag);
            [self printViews:v];
        }
    } else
        return;
}
```

To remove a view from the current view hierarchy, use the removeFromSuperview method of the view you want to remove. For example, the following statement removes the label view:

```
[label removeFromSuperview];
```

SUMMARY

This chapter explored the roles played by outlets and actions in an iPhone application. Outlets and actions are the cornerstone of iPhone development, so understanding their use is extremely important. Throughout this book, you will come across them frequently. You have also seen the use of some of the commonly used views in the Library.

In the next chapter, you learn about the various types of View Controllers supported by the iPhone SDK, and how you can use them to build different types of iPhone and iPad applications.

EXERCISES

1. Declare and define an outlet for a `UITextField` view using code.

2. Declare and define an action using code.

3. When do you use an Alert view and when do you use an action sheet?

4. Create a `UIButton` from code and wire its `Touch Up Inside` event to an event handler.

Answers to the Exercises can be found in Appendix E, on Wrox.com.

▶ WHAT YOU LEARNED IN THIS CHAPTER

TOPIC	KEY CONCEPTS
Action	An action is a method that can handle events raised by views (for example, when a button is clicked, etc.) in the View window.
Outlet	An outlet allows your code to programmatically reference a view on the View window.
Adding outlet using code	Use the `IBOutlet` keyword: `IBOutlet UITextField *txtName;`
Adding action using code	Use the `IBAction` keyword: `-(IBAction) btnClicked:(id) sender;`
Connecting actions	To link actions, you commonly drag from the view in the View window onto the File's Owner item.
Connection outlets	To link outlets, you commonly drag from the File's Owner item onto the required view in the View window.

Using the `UIAlertView`	```
	UIAlertView *alert =
	    [[UIAlertView alloc]
	        initWithTitle:@"Hello!"
	            message:@"Hello, world!"
	            delegate:self
	        cancelButtonTitle:@"Done"
	        otherButtonTitles:nil];
	
	[alert show];
	[alert release];
	``

Handling events fired by `UIAlertView`	Ensure that your View Controller conforms to the `UIAlertViewDelegate` protocol.

Using the `UIActionSheet`	```
	UIActionSheet *action =
	    [[UIActionSheet alloc]
	        initWithTitle:@"Title of Action Sheet"
	            delegate:self
	        cancelButtonTitle:@"OK"
	    destructiveButtonTitle:@"Delete Message"
	        otherButtonTitles:@"Option 1", @"Option 2",
	                            nil];
	
	[action showInView:self.view];
	[action release];
	``

Handling events fired by `UIActionSheet`	Ensure that your View Controller conforms to the `UIActionSheetDelegate` protocol.

TOPIC	KEY CONCEPTS
Wiring up the events for the `UIPageControl`	```[pageControl addTarget:self action:@selector(pageTurning:) forControlEvents:UIControlEventValueChanged];```
Using the `UIImageView`	```[imageView1 setImage: [UIImage imageNamed:@"iMac_old.jpeg"]];```
Using the `UIWebView`	```NSURL *url = [NSURL URLWithString:@"http://www.apple.com"]; NSURLRequest *req = [NSURLRequest requestWithURL:url]; [webView loadRequest:req];```

View Controllers

WHAT YOU WILL LEARN IN THIS CHAPTER

➤ Understanding the structure of a View-based Application project

➤ How to create a Window-based Application project and manually add a View Controller and a View window to it

➤ Creating views dynamically during runtime

➤ Wiring up events of views with event handlers via code

➤ How to switch to another view during runtime

➤ How to animate the switching of views

➤ How to create a Split View-based application

➤ How to create a Tab Bar application

So far you've dealt only with single-view applications — that is, applications with a single View Controller. The previous chapters all use the View-based Application template available in the iPhone SDK because it is the simplest way to get started with iPhone programming. When you create a View-based Application project, there is one View Controller (named `<project_name>ViewController` by the iPhone SDK) by default.

In real-life applications, you often need more than one View Controller, with each controlling a different view displaying different information. This chapter explains the various types of projects you can create for your iPhone and iPad and how each utilizes a different type of View Controller. You will also learn how to create multiple views in your application and then programmatically switch among them during runtime. In addition, you learn how to animate the switching of views using the built-in animation methods available in the iPhone SDK.

THE VIEW-BASED APPLICATION TEMPLATE

When you create a View-based Application project using Xcode, you automatically have a single view in your application. Until now, you have been using it without understanding much about how it works under the hood. In the following Try It Out, you dive into the details and unravel all the magic that makes your application work.

TRY IT OUT Creating a View-based Application Project

codefile viewBasedApp.zip available for download at Wrox.com

1. Using Xcode, create a View-based Application (iPhone) project and name it `viewBasedApp`.

2. Press Command-R to test the application on the iPhone 4 Simulator. The application displays an empty screen, as shown in Figure 4-1.

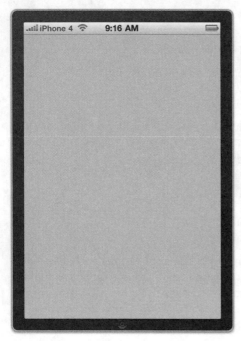

FIGURE 4-1

How It Works

What you have just created is a View-based Application project. By default, the View-based Application template includes a single view, controlled by a View Controller class.

First, take a look at the files and folders created for your project in Xcode. In particular, note the `Classes` and `Resources` folders listed under the project name (see Figure 4-2).

FIGURE 4-2

As you can see, many files are created for you by default when you create a new project. The iPhone SDK tries to make your life simpler by creating some of the items that you will use most often when you develop an iPhone application. Table 4-1 describes the various files created in the project by default.

 NOTE *The types and number of files created vary according to the type of project you have selected. The View-based Application template is a good starting point for understanding the various files involved.*

TABLE 4-1: Project Files Created by Default

FILE	DESCRIPTION
viewBasedApp.app	The application bundle (executable), which contains the executable as well as the data that is bundled with the application

continues

TABLE 4-1 *(continued)*

FILE	DESCRIPTION
viewBasedApp_Prefix.pch	Contains the prefix header for all files in the project. The prefix header is included by default in the other files in the project.
viewBasedAppAppDelegate.h	Header file for the application delegate
viewBasedAppAppDelegate.m	Implementation file for the application delegate
viewBasedAppViewController.h	Header file for a View Controller
viewBasedAppViewController.m	Implementation file for a View Controller
viewBasedAppViewController.xib	XIB file containing the UI of a view
CoreGraphics.framework	C-based APIs for low-level 2D rendering
Foundation.framework	APIs for foundational system services such as data types, XML, URL, and so on
UIKit.framework	Provides fundamental objects for constructing and managing your application's UI.
viewBasedApp-Info.plist	A dictionary file that contains information about your project, such as icon, application name, and more; information is stored in key/value pairs.
main.m	The main file that bootstraps your iPhone/iPad application
MainWindow.xib	XIB file for the main window of the application

The main.m file contains code that bootstraps your application, and you rarely need to modify it:

```
#import <UIKit/UIKit.h>

int main(int argc, char *argv[]) {

    NSAutoreleasePool * pool = [[NSAutoreleasePool alloc] init];
    int retVal = UIApplicationMain(argc, argv, nil, nil);
    [pool release];
    return retVal;
}
```

Most of the hard work is done by the UIApplicationMain() function, which examines the viewBasedApp-Info.plist file to obtain more information about the project. In particular, it looks at the main NIB file you will use for your project. Figure 4-3 shows the content of the viewBasedApp-Info.plist file. Notice that the Main nib file base name key is pointing to MainWindow, which is the name of the NIB file to load when the application is started.

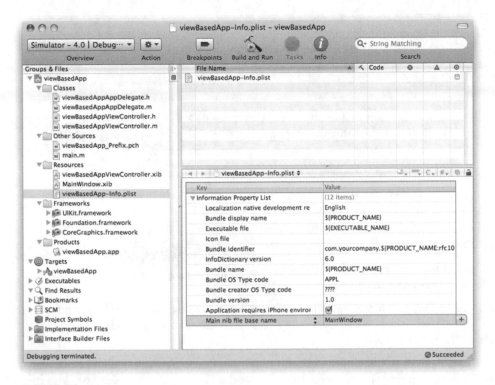

FIGURE 4-3

THE XIB AND NIB EXTENSIONS

iPhone application development always includes files with the `.xib` extension (sometimes also known as NIB files), so it is useful to know what these extensions stand for. The current Mac OS X was built upon an operating system called NeXTSTEP, from a company known as NeXT (founded by Apple's cofounder, Steve Jobs, in 1985). The N in NIB stands for NeXTSTEP. As for .xib, the X presumably stands for XML because its content is saved as an XML file. The *IB* stands for Interface Builder, the design tool that enables you to visually construct the UI for your application.

Editing XIB Files

Double-click the `MainWindow.xib` file to edit it using Interface Builder. As mentioned, the XIB file represents the UI of your application, and it is used almost exclusively by Interface Builder.

NOTE *An XIB file is actually an XML file. You can view and edit an XIB file using applications such as TextEdit, but it is usually preferable, to maintain your sanity, to use Interface Builder to visually modify your application's UI.*

When the `MinWindow.xib` file is opened by Interface Builder, you see a window with the same title as the filename (see Figure 4-4).

This window contains five items:

FIGURE 4-4

➤ **File's Owner** — Represents the object that is set to the owner of the user interface (that is, the class responsible for managing the content of the XIB file).

➤ **First Responder** — Represents the object with which the user is currently interacting.

➤ **viewBasedApp App Delegate** — Points to the `viewBasedAppAppDelegate` class. You can see this when you select the `viewBasedApp App Delegate` item and view its Identity Inspector window (see Figure 4-5).

➤ **View Based App View Controller** — Points to a View Controller that you will be using to display your UI. In this case, it points to the `viewBasedAppViewController` class. You can see this when you select the `View Based App View Controller` item and view its Identity Inspector window (see Figure 4-6).

➤ **Window** — The screen that you see when the application is launched.

FIGURE 4-5

FIGURE 4-6

Application Delegate

The viewBasedAppAppDelegate.m file contains code that is typically executed after the application has finished loading, or just before it is terminated. For this example, its content is as follows:

 NOTE *When creating your project using Xcode, the filename of your application delegate will always be appended with the string* AppDelegate. *For example, if the project name is* viewBasedApp, *then the application delegate will be called* viewBasedAppAppDelegate.

```objc
#import "viewBasedAppAppDelegate.h"
#import "viewBasedAppViewController.h"

@implementation viewBasedAppAppDelegate

@synthesize window;
@synthesize viewController;

#pragma mark -
#pragma mark Application lifecycle

- (BOOL)application:(UIApplication *)application
didFinishLaunchingWithOptions:(NSDictionary *)launchOptions {

    // Override point for customization after application launch.

    // Add the view controller's view to the window and display.
    [window addSubview:viewController.view];
    [window makeKeyAndVisible];

    return YES;
}

- (void)applicationWillResignActive:(UIApplication *)application {
    /*
    Sent when the application is about to move from active to inactive state. This
    can occur for certain types of temporary interruptions (such as an incoming
    phone call or SMS message) or when the user quits the application and it
    begins the transition to the background state.
    Use this method to pause ongoing tasks, disable timers, and throttle  down
    OpenGL ES frame rates. Games should use this method to pause the game.
    */
}

- (void)applicationDidEnterBackground:(UIApplication *)application {
    /*
    Use this method to release shared resources, save user data, invalidate
    timers, and store enough application state information to restore your
    application to its current state in case it is terminated later.
    If your application supports background execution, called instead of
    applicationWillTerminate: when the user quits.
```

```objc
        */
    }

    - (void)applicationWillEnterForeground:(UIApplication *)application {
        /*
        Called as part of  transition from the background to the inactive state:
        here you can undo many of the changes made on entering the background.
        */
    }

    - (void)applicationDidBecomeActive:(UIApplication *)application {
        /*
        Restart any tasks that were paused (or not yet started) while the application
        was inactive. If the application was previously in the background, optionally
        refresh the user interface.
        */
    }

    - (void)applicationWillTerminate:(UIApplication *)application {
        /*
        Called when the application is about to terminate.
        See also applicationDidEnterBackground:.
        */
    }

    #pragma mark -
    #pragma mark Memory management

    - (void)applicationDidReceiveMemoryWarning:(UIApplication *)application {
        /*
        Free up as much memory as possible by purging cached data objects that can be
        recreated (or reloaded from disk) later.
        */
    }

    - (void)dealloc {
        [viewController release];
        [window release];
        [super dealloc];
    }

    @end
```

When the application has finished launching, it sends its delegate the
`application:DidFinishLaunchingWithOptions:` message. In the preceding case, it uses a View
Controller to obtain its view and then adds it to the current window so that it can be displayed.

The `viewBasedAppDelegate.h` file contains the declaration of the members of the
`viewBasedAppAppDelegate` class:

```objc
    #import <UIKit/UIKit.h>

    @class viewBasedAppViewController;

    @interface viewBasedAppAppDelegate : NSObject <UIApplicationDelegate> {
```

```
        UIWindow *window;
        viewBasedAppViewController *viewController;
}

@property (nonatomic, retain) IBOutlet UIWindow *window;
@property (nonatomic, retain) IBOutlet viewBasedAppViewController
    *viewController;

@end
```

Of particular interest is this line:

```
@interface viewBasedAppAppDelegate : NSObject <UIApplicationDelegate> {
```

The `<UIApplicationDelegate>` statement specifies that the delegate class should implement the `UIApplicationDelegate` protocol. Put simply, it means that the delegate class will handle events (or messages) defined in the `UIApplicationDelegate` protocol. Examples of events in the `UIApplicationDelegate` protocol include the following:

➤ `Application:DidFinishLaunchingWithOptions:` (You saw this implemented in the `viewBasedAppAppDelegate.m` file.)

➤ `applicationWillTerminate:`

➤ `applicationDidDidReceiveMemoryWarning:`

➤ Other methods that inform you if the application is receding into the background or coming back into the foreground. You will learn more about these methods in Chapter 21.

The application delegate class is also a good place to put your global objects and functions, as they are accessible from all the other classes in your project.

 NOTE *Protocols are discussed in more detail in Appendix D.*

Controlling Your UI Using View Controllers

In iPhone programming, you typically use a View Controller to manage a view, as well as to perform navigation and memory management. In the project template for a View-based Application, Xcode automatically uses a View Controller to help you manage your *view*. Think of a view as a screen (or window) you see on your iPhone.

Earlier in this chapter, you saw that the `MainWindow.xib` window contains the `View Based App View Controller` item. When you double-click that, it shows a window of the same name (see Figure 4-7).

As you can see, the view says that it is loaded from `viewBasedAppViewController`, which refers to the name of the `viewBasedAppViewController.xib` file that's also in your project.

Double-click the `viewBasedAppViewController.xib` file to edit it in Interface Builder. As with the `MainWindow.xib` file, a few objects are contained inside the `viewBasedAppViewController.xib` window. In this case, it contains File's Owner, First Responder, and View.

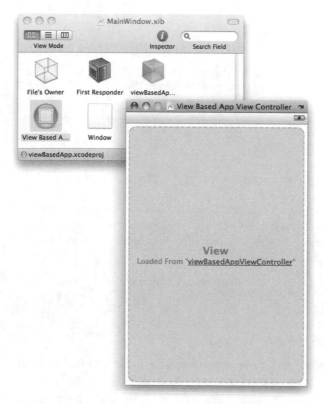

FIGURE 4-7

 NOTE *When creating your project using Xcode, the filename of your View Controller will always be appended with the string* `ViewController`. *For example, if the project name is* `viewBasedApp`, *then the application delegate will be called* `viewBasedAppViewController`. *When the View Controller is displayed in Interface Builder, Interface Builder examines the name and displays the View Controller with spaces inserted wherever capitalization changes, e.g.,* `viewBasedAppViewController` *becomes* `View Based App View Controller`.

You can right-click (or Control-click) the File's Owner item to view its properties (see Figure 4-8). Note that the `view` outlet is connected to the `View` item.

The `View` item represents the screen that appears on your application. Double-click View to display it (see Figure 4-9).

When you select the File's Owner item and view its Identity Inspector window, you should see that the class is pointing to the `viewBasedAppViewController`

FIGURE 4-8

class (see Figure 4-10). This means that the View window is being controlled by the
`viewBasedAppViewController` class.

FIGURE 4-9   **FIGURE 4-10**

The `viewBasedAppViewController` class is represented by two files — `viewBasedAppViewController.h`
and `viewBasedAppViewController.m`. The `viewBasedAppViewController` class is where you write the
code to interact with the views of your application.

The content of the `viewBasedAppViewController.h` file looks like this:

```
#import <UIKit/UIKit.h>

@interface viewBasedAppViewController : UIViewController {

}

@end
```

Note that the `viewBasedAppViewController` class inherits from the `UIViewController` base class,
which provides most of the functionality available on a View window.

The content of the `viewBasedAppViewController.m` file looks like this:

```
#import "viewBasedAppViewController.h"

@implementation viewBasedAppViewController

/*
// The designated initializer. Override to perform setup that is required
```

```
    before the view is loaded.
- (id)initWithNibName:(NSString *)nibNameOrNil bundle:(NSBundle *)nibBundleOrNil {
    if ((self = [super initWithNibName:nibNameOrNil bundle:nibBundleOrNil])) {
        // Custom initialization
    }
    return self;
}
*/

/*
// Implement loadView to create a view hierarchy programmatically, without
 using a nib.
- (void)loadView {
}
*/


/*
// Implement viewDidLoad to do additional setup after loading the view,
typically from a nib.
- (void)viewDidLoad {
    [super viewDidLoad];
}
*/


/*
// Override to allow orientations other than the default portrait orientation.
- (BOOL)shouldAutorotateToInterfaceOrientation:(UIInterfaceOrientation)
interfaceOrientation {
    // Return YES for supported orientations
    return (interfaceOrientation == UIInterfaceOrientationPortrait);
}
*/

- (void)didReceiveMemoryWarning {
    // Releases the view if it doesn't have a superview.
    [super didReceiveMemoryWarning];

    // Release any cached data, images, etc that aren't in use.
}

- (void)viewDidUnload {
    // Release any retained subviews of the main view.
    // e.g. self.myOutlet = nil;
}

- (void)dealloc {
    [super dealloc];
}

@end
```

THE WINDOW-BASED APPLICATION TEMPLATE

In this section, you discover another type of application template you can create using the iPhone SDK: the *Window-based Application* template. Unlike the View-based Application template, the Window-based Application template does not include a View Controller by default. Instead, it provides only the skeleton of an iPhone application, leaving the rest to the developer — you need to add your own views and their respective View Controllers. Therefore, a Window-based Application project presents a good opportunity for you to understand how View Controllers work and appreciate all the work needed to connect the View Controllers and XIB files. When you understand how View Controllers work, you will be on your way to creating more sophisticated applications.

To put first things first, execute the following Try it Out to create a Window-based Application project and then progressively add a View Controller to it.

TRY IT OUT Creating a Window-based Application Project

codefile windowBasedApp.zip available for download on Wrox.com

1. Using Xcode, create a Window-based Application (iPhone) project and name it `windowBasedApp`. Observe the files created for this project type (see Figure 4-11). Apart from the usual supporting files, note that there is only one XIB file (`MainWindow.xib`) and two delegate files (`windowBasedAppAppDelegate.h` and `windowBasedAppAppDelegate.m`).

2. Press Command-R to test the application. An empty screen is displayed on the iPhone Simulator. This is because the Window-based application template provides only the skeleton structure for a simple iPhone application — just a window and the application delegate.

FIGURE 4-11

3. In Xcode, double-click `MainWindow.xib` to edit it in Interface Builder. Note that there are four items in the `MainWindow.xib` window (see Figure 4-12):

> File's Owner

> First Responder

> Window

> Window Based App App Delegate

4. From the Library window, drag and drop a `View Controller` item onto the `MainWindow.xib` window (see Figure 4-13). You will connect this `View Controller` item to a view that you will add to the project in the next step.

FIGURE 4-12

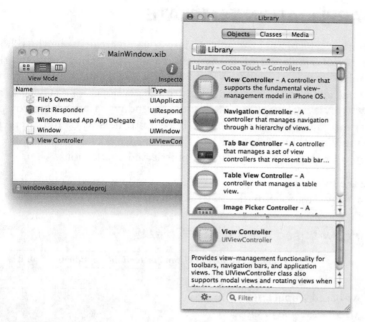

FIGURE 4-13

5. In Xcode, right-click the Classes group and add a new file (see Figure 4-14). In the New File window, click the Cocoa Touch Class item and select the `UIViewController` subclass template (see Figure 4-15). Ensure that the "With XIB for user interface" check box is checked. Click Next and name the item **HelloWorldViewController.m**. Xcode should now look like Figure 4-16. The two files (.h and .m) will serve as the `View Controller` class for the `View Controller` item you added previously in Interface Builder. The .xib file serves as the UI for the View Controller.

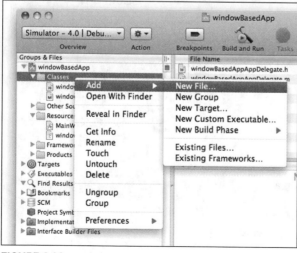

FIGURE 4-14

FIGURE 4-15

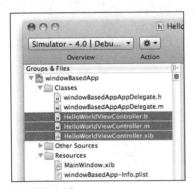

FIGURE 4-16

 NOTE *To keep your project neat, it is recommended that you drag the* `.xib` *file into the* `Resources` *folder.*

6. Double-click the `HelloWorldViewController.xib` file to edit it in Interface Builder.

7. Add a Round Rect Button to the View window and label the button as shown in Figure 4-17.

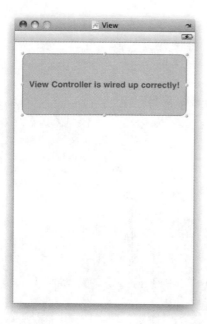

FIGURE 4-17

8. In Interface Builder, select the `View Controller` item in the `MainWindow.xib` window and view its Identity Inspector window. In the Class drop-down list, select `HelloWorldViewController` (see Figure 4-18). The name of the View Controller will now change to `Hello World View Controller`.

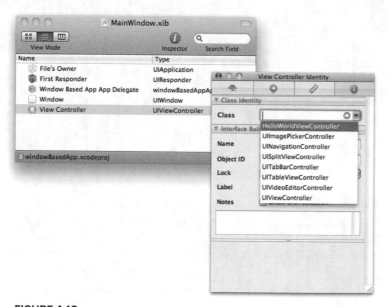

FIGURE 4-18

9. View the Attributes Inspector window for the `Hello World View Controller`; and for the NIB Name drop-down list, select `HelloWorldViewController` (see Figure 4-19).

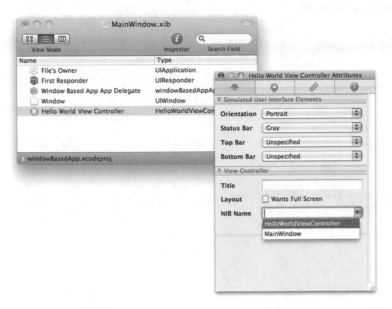

FIGURE 4-19

10. Back in Xcode, insert the bold lines in the following code into the `windowBasedAppAppDelegate.h` file:

```objc
#import <UIKit/UIKit.h>

//---add a forward reference to the
// HelloWorldViewController class---
@class HelloWorldViewController;

@interface windowBasedAppAppDelegate : NSObject
    <UIApplicationDelegate> {
    UIWindow *window;

    //---create an instance of the view controller---
    HelloWorldViewController *viewController;
}

@property (nonatomic, retain) IBOutlet UIWindow *window;

//---expose the view controller as a property---
@property (nonatomic, retain) IBOutlet
    HelloWorldViewController *viewController;

@end
```

11. In the `windowBasedAppAppDelegate.m` file, insert the following code that appears in bold:

```
#import "windowBasedAppAppDelegate.h"
#import "HelloWorldViewController.h"

@implementation windowBasedAppAppDelegate

@synthesize window;

//---synthesize the property---
@synthesize viewController;

- (BOOL)application:(UIApplication *)application
didFinishLaunchingWithOptions:(NSDictionary *)launchOptions {

    // Override point for customization after application launch.

    //---add the new view to the current window---
    [window addSubview:viewController.view];

    [window makeKeyAndVisible];

    return YES;
}

- (void)dealloc {
    [viewController release];
    [window release];
    [super dealloc];
}
```

12. In the `MainWindow.xib` window, Control-click and drag the `Window Based App App Delegate` item to the `Hello World View Controller` item (see Figure 4-20). Select `viewController`. This will associate the window with the View Controller.

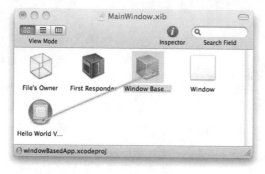

FIGURE 4-20

13. That's it! Press Command-R to test the application on the iPhone Simulator. The button should appear on the main screen of the application as shown in Figure 4-21.

How It Works

When you create an iPhone project using the Window-based Application template, Xcode provides you with only the bare minimum number of items in your project — a MainWindow.xib file and the application delegate. You need to add your own View Controller(s) and view(s).

In the preceding exercise, you first added a View Controller item to the MainWindow.xib window. You then added an instance of the UIViewController class (which you named HelloWorldViewController) so that it could be connected to the View Controller you just added. This controller class contains the code that you will write to handle the interactions between the view and the user.

When the application has finished launching, you add the view represented by the HelloWorldViewController object to the window so that it is visible, using the addSubview: method of the UIWindow instance:

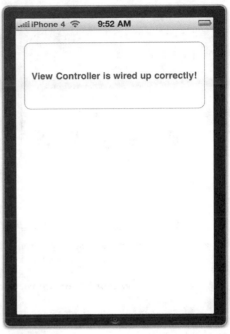

FIGURE 4-21

```
//---add the new view to the current window---
[window addSubview:viewController.view];
```

Adding a View Controller and Views Programmatically

Another commonly used technique is to programmatically create the views during runtime without using Interface Builder. This provides a lot of flexibility, especially when you are writing games for which the application's UI is constantly changing.

In the following Try It Out, you learn how to create a View window using an instance of the UIViewController class and then programmatically add views to it.

TRY IT OUT   Adding a View Controller and Views Programmatically

1. Using the windowBasedApp project, right-click the Classes group in Xcode and add a new file. Select the UIViewController subclass item and name it MySecondViewController. Ensure that the "With XIB for user interface" checkbox is unchecked. Xcode should now look like Figure 4-22.

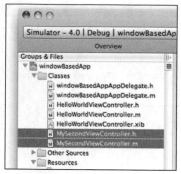

FIGURE 4-22

2. In the `windowBasedAppAppDelegate.m` file, add the following bold code:

```
#import "windowBasedAppAppDelegate.h"
#import "HelloWorldViewController.h"

#import "MySecondViewController.h"

@implementation windowBasedAppAppDelegate

@synthesize window;

//---synthesize the property---
@synthesize viewController;

//---a second view controller object---
MySecondViewController *mySecondViewController;

- (BOOL)application:(UIApplication *)application
didFinishLaunchingWithOptions:(NSDictionary *)launchOptions {

    // Override point for customization after application launch.

    //---instantiate the second view controller---
    mySecondViewController = [[MySecondViewController alloc]
                                initWithNibName:nil
                                        bundle:nil];

    //---add the view from the second view controller---
    [window addSubview:mySecondViewController.view];

    //---comment this out so that it doesn't load the viewController---
    //---add the new view to the current window---
    //[window addSubview:viewController.view];

    [window makeKeyAndVisible];

    return YES;
```

```
    }

    - (void)dealloc {
        [mySecondViewController release];
        [viewController release];
        [window release];
        [super dealloc];
    }
```

3. In the `MySecondViewController.h` file, insert the following bold lines of code:

```
    #import <UIKit/UIKit.h>

    @interface MySecondViewController : UIViewController {
        //---create two outlets - label and button---
        UILabel *label;
        UIButton *button;
    }

    //---expose the outlets as properties---
    @property (nonatomic, retain) UILabel *label;
    @property (nonatomic, retain) UIButton *button;

    @end
```

4. In the `MySecondViewController.m` file, add the `viewDidLoad()` method and modify the `dealloc` method:

```
    #import "MySecondViewController.h"

    @implementation MySecondViewController

    @synthesize label, button;

    - (void)viewDidLoad {
        //---create a CGRect for the positioning---
        CGRect frame = CGRectMake(20, 10, 280, 50);

        //---create a Label view---
        label = [[UILabel alloc] initWithFrame:frame];
        label.textAlignment = UITextAlignmentCenter;
        label.font = [UIFont fontWithName:@"Verdana" size:20];
        label.text = @"This is a label";

        //---create a Button view---
        frame = CGRectMake(20, 60, 280, 50);
        button = [UIButton buttonWithType:UIButtonTypeRoundedRect];
        button.frame = frame;
        [button setTitle:@"OK" forState:UIControlStateNormal];
        button.backgroundColor = [UIColor clearColor];

        //---add the views to the View window---
        [self.view addSubview:label];
```

```
    [self.view addSubview:button];
    [super viewDidLoad];
}

- (void)dealloc {
    [label release];
    [button release];
    [super dealloc];
}
```

5.   Press Command-R to test the application on the iPhone 4 Simulator. The Label and Button views appear on the main screen of the application (see Figure 4-23).

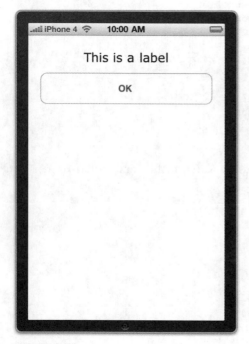

FIGURE 4-23

How It Works

In contrast to the previous example, in which you added a View Controller item, an instance of the UIViewController class, and a XIB file to your project, this example simply creates an instance of the UIViewController class and adds the views programmatically to the main View window.

In the application delegate, after the application has finished launching, you create an instance of the UIViewController class that you have created:

```
    //---instantiate the second view controller---
    mySecondViewController = [[MySecondViewController alloc]
```

```
                              initWithNibName:nil
                                   bundle:nil];
```

You do not need a XIB file because the various views that you will be using are added programmatically. Hence, the `initWithNibName:` parameter can be set to `nil`.

To load the View window represented by the instance of the `UIViewController` class, you use the `addSubview:` method of the `UIWindow` instance:

```
//---add the view from the second view controller---
[window addSubview:mySecondViewController.view];
```

To programmatically create your views during runtime, you need to override the `viewDidLoad()` method of the `UIViewController` class. Here, you create instances of the Label and Button views programmatically, specifying their positions as well as their text captions. Finally, you add them to the main View window:

```
- (void)viewDidLoad {
    //---create a CGRect for the positioning---
    CGRect frame = CGRectMake(20, 10, 280, 50);

    //---create a Label view---
    label = [[UILabel alloc] initWithFrame:frame];
    label.textAlignment = UITextAlignmentCenter;
    label.font = [UIFont fontWithName:@"Verdana" size:20];
    label.text = @"This is a label";

    //---create a Button view---
    frame = CGRectMake(20, 60, 280, 50);
    button = [UIButton buttonWithType:UIButtonTypeRoundedRect];
    button.frame = frame;
    [button setTitle:@"OK" forState:UIControlStateNormal];
    button.backgroundColor = [UIColor clearColor];

    //---add the views to the View window---
    [self.view addSubview:label];
    [self.view addSubview:button];
    [super viewDidLoad];
}
```

Creating and Connecting Actions

In the previous example, you saw how you can add a Label and Button view to the main View window. However, you need to handle the events raised by the Button view so that when the user presses it, the application can respond appropriately. Chapter 3 covered outlets and actions and how you connect your code to them using Interface Builder; but in the following Try it Out, the views are created using code, so you cannot use Interface Builder to connect the actions and outlets — you have to do it with code too.

TRY IT OUT Linking Actions to Views

1. Continuing with the `windowBasedApp` project, declare the following `buttonClicked:` action (shown in bold) in the `MySecondViewController.h` file:

```
#import <UIKit/UIKit.h>

@interface MySecondViewController : UIViewController {
    //---create two outlets - label and button---
    UILabel *label;
    UIButton *button;
}

//---expose the outlets as properties---
@property (nonatomic, retain) UILabel *label;
@property (nonatomic, retain) UIButton *button;

//---declaring the IBAction---
-(IBAction) buttonClicked: (id) sender;

@end
```

2. In the `MySecondViewController.m` file, provide the implementation for the `buttonClicked:` action:

```
#import "MySecondViewController.h"

@implementation MySecondViewController

@synthesize label, button;

-(IBAction) buttonClicked: (id) sender{
    UIAlertView *alert =
        [[UIAlertView alloc] initWithTitle:@"Action invoked!"
                                   message:@"Button clicked!"
                                  delegate:self
                         cancelButtonTitle:@"OK"
                         otherButtonTitles:nil];
    [alert show];
    [alert release];
}
```

3. To connect the relevant event (`Touch Up Inside`) of the Button view with the `buttonClicked:` action, add the following bold code to the `viewDidLoad()` method:

```
- (void)viewDidLoad {
    //---create a CGRect for the positioning---
    CGRect frame = CGRectMake(20, 10, 280, 50);

    //---create a Label view---
    label = [[UILabel alloc] initWithFrame:frame];
    label.textAlignment = UITextAlignmentCenter;
    label.font = [UIFont fontWithName:@"Verdana" size:20];
    label.text = @"This is a label";

    //---create a Button view---
    frame = CGRectMake(20, 60, 280, 50);
```

```
button = [UIButton buttonWithType:UIButtonTypeRoundedRect];
button.frame = frame;
[button setTitle:@"OK" forState:UIControlStateNormal];
button.backgroundColor = [UIColor clearColor];

//---add the action handler and set current class as target---
[button addTarget:self
          action:@selector(buttonClicked:)
 forControlEvents:UIControlEventTouchUpInside];

//---add the views to the View window---
[self.view addSubview:label];
[self.view addSubview:button];
[super viewDidLoad];
}
```

4. That's it! Press Command-R to test the application on the iPhone 4 Simulator. Clicking the OK button displays an Alert view (see Figure 4-24).

FIGURE 4-24

How It Works

To connect an action to a view, you use the addTarget:action:forControlEvents: method of a view. In this case, the view is the Round Rect Button:

```
//---add the action handler and set current class as target---
[button addTarget:self
          action:@selector(buttonClicked:)
 forControlEvents:UIControlEventTouchUpInside];
```

The action: parameter specifies the name of the method (buttonClicked:) that will handle the event, while the forControlEvents: method specifies the type of event that you want to handle. In this example, the event is Touch Up Inside.

CONTROL EVENTS

You can use the following list of events for control objects:

UIControlEventTouchDown

UIControlEventTouchDownRepeat

UIControlEventTouchDragInside

UIControlEventTouchDragOutside

UIControlEventTouchDragEnter

UIControlEventTouchDragExit

UIControlEventTouchUpInside

UIControlEventTouchUpOutside

UIControlEventTouchCancel

UIControlEventValueChanged

UIControlEventEditingDidBegin

UIControlEventEditingChanged

UIControlEventEditingDidEnd

UIControlEventEditingDidEndOnExit

UIControlEventAllTouchEvents

UIControlEventAllEditingEvents

UIControlEventApplicationReserved

UIControlEventSystemReserved

UIControlEventAllEvents

The use of each event is detailed at http://developer.apple.com/iphone/library/documentation/UIKit/Reference/UIControl_Class/Reference/Reference.html#//apple_ref/doc/constant_group/Control_Events.

Switching to Another View

In real life, your application often has a number of views, each representing different pieces of information. Depending on the selections made by the user, the application switches to different views to perform different tasks.

This section describes how your application can switch to another view based on the user's selection.

TRY IT OUT Switching Views

1. Using the same project created in the previous section, add the following bold code to the `MySecondViewController.m` file:

```objc
#import "MySecondViewController.h"
#import "HelloWorldViewController.h"

@implementation MySecondViewController

@synthesize label, button;

//---create an instance of the view controller---
HelloWorldViewController *viewController;

-(IBAction) buttonClicked: (id) sender {
    //---add the view of the view controller to the current View---
    viewController =
        [[HelloWorldViewController alloc]
            initWithNibName:@"HelloWorldViewController"
                    bundle:nil];

    [self.view addSubview:viewController.view];

    /*
    UIAlertView *alert =
        [[UIAlertView alloc] initWithTitle:@"Action invoked!"
                                   message:@"Button clicked!"
                                  delegate:self
                         cancelButtonTitle:@"OK"
                         otherButtonTitles:nil];

    [alert show];
    [alert release];
    */
}

- (void)dealloc {
    [viewController release];
    [label release];
    [button release];
    [super dealloc];
}
```

2. Declare a `btnClicked:` action in the `HelloWorldViewController.h` file (and remember to save the file after editing it):

```
#import <UIKit/UIKit.h>

@interface HelloWorldViewController : UIViewController {

}

-(IBAction) btnClicked:(id) sender;

@end
```

3. In the `HelloWorldViewController.m` file, define the `btnClicked:` action as follows:

```
#import "HelloWorldViewController.h"

@implementation HelloWorldViewController

-(IBAction) btnClicked:(id) sender{
    //---remove the current view; essentially hiding the view---
    [self.view removeFromSuperview];
}
```

4. Double-click the `HelloWorldViewController.xib` file to edit it in Interface Builder. Control-click and drag the Round Rect Button in the View window to the File's Owner item in the `HelloWorldViewController.xib` window and select `btnClicked:`.

5. In Xcode, press Command-R to test the application. Now when you click the OK button in the main View, you are brought to the Hello World View. To close the View, click the button.

How It Works

For this example, you simply add the view of the View Controller (that you are switching to) to the current View window using the `addSubview:` method:

```
    //---add the view of the view controller to the current View---
    viewController =
        [[HelloWorldViewController alloc]
            initWithNibName:@"HelloWorldViewController"
                    bundle:nil];

    [self.view addSubview:viewController.view];
```

To dismiss a view, you use the `removeFromSuperview:` method:

```
    //---remove the current view; essentially hiding the view---
    [self.view removeFromSuperview];
```

Animating the Switching of Views

The switching of Views that you have just seen in the previous section happens instantaneously — the two Views change immediately without any visual cues. One of the key selling points of the iPhone is its animation capabilities. Therefore, for the switching of views, you can make the display a little more interesting by performing some simple animations, such as flipping one View window to reveal another. The following Try It Out shows you how.

TRY IT OUT | Animating View Transitions

1. Using the same project, add the following bold code to the `MySecondViewController.m` file:

```
-(IBAction) buttonClicked: (id) sender{
    //---add the view of the view controller to the current View---
    viewController =
        [[HelloWorldViewController alloc]
            initWithNibName:@"HelloWorldViewController"
                    bundle:nil];

    [UIView beginAnimations:@"flipping view" context:nil];
    [UIView setAnimationDuration:1];
    [UIView setAnimationCurve:UIViewAnimationCurveEaseInOut];
    [UIView setAnimationTransition:UIViewAnimationTransitionFlipFromLeft
                        forView:self.view
                          cache:YES];
    [self.view addSubview:viewController.view];
    [UIView commitAnimations];

    /*
    UIAlertView *alert =
        [[UIAlertView alloc] initWithTitle:@"Action invoked!"
                                   message:@"Button clicked!"
                                  delegate:self
                         cancelButtonTitle:@"OK"
                         otherButtonTitles:nil];

    [alert show];
    [alert release];
    */
}
```

2. In the `HelloWorldViewController.m file`, add the following code that appears in bold:

```
#import "HelloWorldViewController.h"

@implementation HelloWorldViewController

-(IBAction) btnClicked:(id) sender{
    [UIView beginAnimations:@"flipping view" context:nil];
    [UIView setAnimationDuration:1];
    [UIView setAnimationCurve:UIViewAnimationCurveEaseIn];
    [UIView setAnimationTransition:UIViewAnimationTransitionFlipFromRight
```

```
                            forView:self.view.superview
                                cache:YES];
        //---remove the current view; essentially hiding the view---
        [self.view removeFromSuperview];
        [UIView commitAnimations];
    }
```

3. Press Command-R to test the application on the iPhone 4 Simulator. Click the OK buttons on both Views and notice the direction in which the two Views flip to one another.

How It Works

First, examine the animation that is applied to the MySecondViewController. You perform the animation by first calling the beginAnimations: method of the UIView class to start the animation block:

```
    [UIView beginAnimations:@"flipping view" context:nil];
```

The setAnimationDuration: method specifies the duration of the animation, in seconds. Here, you set it to one second:

```
    [UIView setAnimationDuration:1];
```

The setAnimationCurve: method sets the curve of the animating property changes within an animation:

```
    [UIView setAnimationCurve:UIViewAnimationCurveEaseInOut];
```

You can use the following constants for the curve of the animation:

➤ UIViewAnimationCurveEaseInOut — Causes the animation to begin slowly, accelerate through the middle of its duration, and then slow again before completing.

➤ UIViewAnimationCurveEaseIn — Causes the animation to begin slowly and then speed up as it progresses.

➤ UIViewAnimationCurveEaseOut — Causes the animation to begin quickly and then slow as it completes.

➤ UIViewAnimationCurveLinear — Causes an animation to occur evenly over its duration.

The setAnimationTransition: method specifies a transition type to be applied to a view during the animation's duration:

```
    [UIView setAnimationTransition:UIViewAnimationTransitionFlipFromLeft
                           forView:self.view
                             cache:YES];
```

The cache: parameter specifies whether the iPhone should cache the image of the view and use it during the transition. Caching the image speeds up the animation process. The following constants can be used for the animation transition:

➤ UIViewAnimationTransitionNone — No transition.

➤ UIViewAnimationTransitionFlipFromLeft — Flips a view around a vertical axis from left to right.

➤ UIViewAnimationTransitionFlipFromRight — Flips a view around a vertical axis from right to left.

➤   `UIViewAnimationTransitionCurlUp` — Curls a view up from the bottom.

➤   `UIViewAnimationTransitionCurlDown` — Curls a view down from the top.

To end the animation, call the `commitAnimations:` method:

```
[UIView commitAnimations];
```

The animation performed on the `HelloWorldViewController` is similar to that of the `MySecondViewController`, except that the view to animate must be set to `self.view.superview`:

```
[UIView setAnimationTransition:UIViewAnimationTransitionFlipFromRight
                       forView:self.view.superview
                         cache:YES];
```

THE SPLIT VIEW-BASED APPLICATION TEMPLATE

Beginning with the iPhone SDK 3.2, there is a new application template that is exclusive to the iPad: Split View–based application. It enables you to create a split-view interface for your iPad application, which is essentially a master-detail interface. The left side of the screen displays a list of selectable items, while the right-side displays details about the item selected.

To see how the Split View–based application works, take a look at the following Try It Out.

TRY IT OUT   Creating a Split View–based Application

codefile splitViewBasedApp.zip available for download at Wrox.com

1. Using Xcode, create a new Split View–based Application project and name it `splitViewBasedApp`.

2. Observe the files created in the `Classes` and `Resources` folders (see Figure 4-25). Notice that there are two View Controller classes (`RootViewController` and `DetailViewController`), as well as two XIB files.

3. Press Command-R in Xcode to test the application on the iPhone 3.2 Simulator (for iPad). Figure 4-26 shows the application when it is displayed in landscape mode. When you rotate the Simulator to portrait mode, the application looks like Figure 4-27.

FIGURE 4-25

How It Works

The magic of a Split View–based application lies in its transformation when the device is rotated. In landscape mode, the application displays a list of rows on the left. When it is turned to portrait mode, the list of rows is hidden in a Popover view. Here's how this is done.

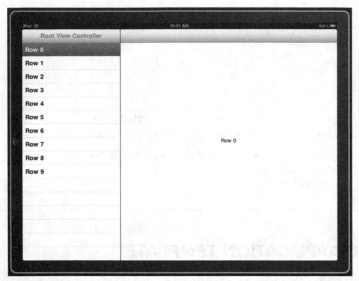

FIGURE 4-26

FIGURE 4-27

First, observe the content of the splitViewBasedAppAppDelegate.h file:

```
#import <UIKit/UIKit.h>

@class RootViewController;
```

```objc
@class DetailViewController;

@interface splitViewBasedAppDelegate : NSObject <UIApplicationDelegate> {

    UIWindow *window;

    UISplitViewController *splitViewController;

    RootViewController *rootViewController;
    DetailViewController *detailViewController;
}

@property (nonatomic, retain) IBOutlet UIWindow *window;

@property (nonatomic, retain) IBOutlet UISplitViewController
    *splitViewController;
@property (nonatomic, retain) IBOutlet RootViewController
    *rootViewController;
@property (nonatomic, retain) IBOutlet DetailViewController
    *detailViewController;

@end
```

Notice that it contains a View Controller object of type UISplitViewController (splitViewController), as well two View Controllers (rootViewController and detailViewController). The UISplitViewController is a container View Controller that contains two View Controllers, allowing you to implement a master-detail interface.

Next, look at the content of the splitViewBasedAppAppDelegate.m file:

```objc
#import "splitViewBasedAppDelegate.h"

#import "RootViewController.h"
#import "DetailViewController.h"

@implementation splitViewBasedAppDelegate

@synthesize window, splitViewController, rootViewController, detailViewController;

#pragma mark -
#pragma mark Application lifecycle

- (BOOL)application:(UIApplication *)application
didFinishLaunchingWithOptions:(NSDictionary *)launchOptions {

    // Override point for customization after app launch.

    // Add the split view controller's view to the window and display.
    [window addSubview:splitViewController.view];
    [window makeKeyAndVisible];

    return YES;
}

- (void)applicationWillResignActive:(UIApplication *)application {
    /*
     Sent when the application is about to move from active to inactive state. This
```

```
        can occur for certain types of temporary interruptions (such as an incoming phone
        call or SMS message) or when the user quits the application and it begins the
        transition to the background state.
        Use this method to pause ongoing tasks, disable timers, and throttle down OpenGL
        ES frame rates. Games should use this method to pause the game.
        */
    }

    - (void)applicationDidBecomeActive:(UIApplication *)application {
        /*
        Restart any tasks that were paused (or not yet started) while the
        application was inactive.
        */
    }

    - (void)applicationWillTerminate:(UIApplication *)application {
        /*
        Called when the application is about to terminate.
        */
    }

    #pragma mark -
    #pragma mark Memory management

    - (void)applicationDidReceiveMemoryWarning:(UIApplication *)application {
        /*
        Free up as much memory as possible by purging cached data objects that
        can be recreated (or reloaded from disk) later.
        */
    }

    - (void)dealloc {
        [splitViewController release];
        [window release];
        [super dealloc];
    }

    @end
```

When the application is loaded, the view contained in the splitViewController object is added to the window.

Now, double-click the MainWindow.xib file to edit it in Interface Builder. You'll see that the MainWindow .xib contains an item named Split View Controller (recall that for a View-based Application project, you had a View Controller item instead).

Switch the MainWindow.xib file to display in list view mode and observe the items located within the Split View Controller item (see Figure 4-28):

➤ Navigation Controller

➤ Detail View Controller

The Navigation Controller controls the left side of a Split-view application. Figure 4-29 shows that it consists of a Navigation Bar as well as a Root View Controller.

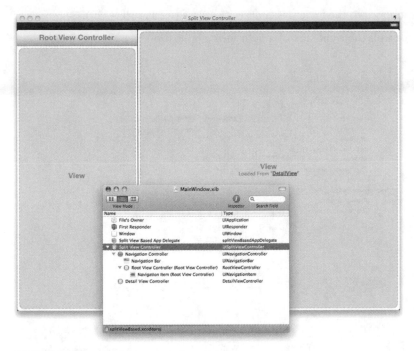

FIGURE 4-28

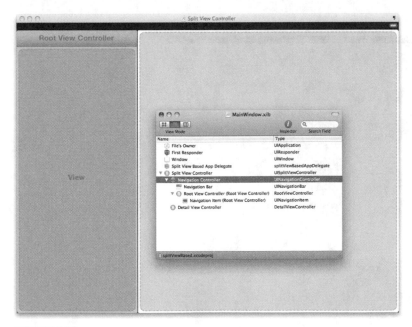

FIGURE 4-29

The Root View Controller is mapped to the `RootViewController` class (see Figure 4-30).

The Detail View Controller controls the right side of a Split-view application (see Figure 4-31).

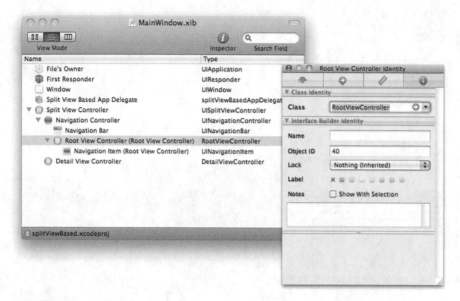

FIGURE 4-30

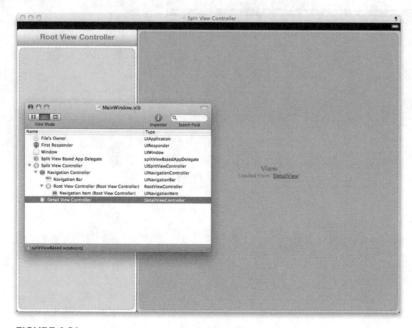

FIGURE 4-31

The Detail View Controller is mapped to the `DetailViewController` class (see Figure 4-32).

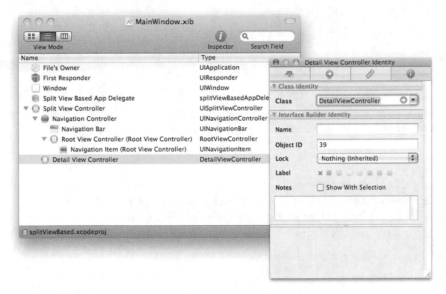

FIGURE 4-32

The application delegate is connected to the various View Controllers, as you can see when you right-click the Split View Based App Delegate item (see Figure 4-33).

FIGURE 4-33

Let's examine the two View Controllers contained within the Split View Controller: `RootViewController` and `DetailViewController`.

Observe the content of the RootViewController.h file:

```
#import <UIKit/UIKit.h>

@class DetailViewController;

@interface RootViewController : UITableViewController {
    DetailViewController *detailViewController;
}

@property (nonatomic, retain) IBOutlet DetailViewController
    *detailViewController;

@end
```

Note that the RootViewController class inherits from the UITableViewController class, not the UIViewController class shown earlier. The UITableViewController class is a subclass of the UIViewController class, providing the capability to display a table containing rows of data. (Chapter 8 discusses the Table view in more detail.)

The content of the RootViewController.m file looks like this:

```
#import "RootViewController.h"
#import "DetailViewController.h"

@implementation RootViewController

@synthesize detailViewController;

#pragma mark -
#pragma mark View lifecycle

- (void)viewDidLoad {
    [super viewDidLoad];
    self.clearsSelectionOnViewWillAppear = NO;
    self.contentSizeForViewInPopover = CGSizeMake(320.0, 600.0);
}

/*
    Other commented out code is omitted from this code listing
*/

// Ensure that the view controller supports rotation and that the split
   view can therefore show in both portrait and landscape.
- (BOOL)shouldAutorotateToInterfaceOrientation:(UIInterfaceOrientation)
interfaceOrientation {
    return YES;
}

- (NSInteger)numberOfSectionsInTableView:(UITableView *)aTableView {
    // Return the number of sections.
    return 1;
}

- (NSInteger)tableView:(UITableView *)aTableView
```

```objc
numberOfRowsInSection:(NSInteger)section {
    // Return the number of rows in the section.
    return 10;
}

- (UITableViewCell *)tableView:(UITableView *)tableView
cellForRowAtIndexPath:(NSIndexPath *)indexPath {

    static NSString *CellIdentifier = @"CellIdentifier";

    // Dequeue or create a cell of the appropriate type.
    UITableViewCell *cell = [tableView
        dequeueReusableCellWithIdentifier:CellIdentifier];
    if (cell == nil) {
        cell = [[[UITableViewCell alloc]
            initWithStyle:UITableViewCellStyleDefault
          reuseIdentifier:CellIdentifier] autorelease];
        cell.accessoryType = UITableViewCellAccessoryNone;
    }

    // Configure the cell.
    cell.textLabel.text =
        [NSString stringWithFormat:@"Row %d", indexPath.row];
    return cell;
}

- (void)tableView:(UITableView *)aTableView
didSelectRowAtIndexPath:(NSIndexPath *)indexPath {

    /*
     When a row is selected, set the detail view controller's detail item
    to the item associated with the selected row.
     */
    detailViewController.detailItem =
        [NSString stringWithFormat:@"Row %d", indexPath.row];
}

- (void)didReceiveMemoryWarning {
    // Releases the view if it doesn't have a superview.
    [super didReceiveMemoryWarning];

    // Relinquish ownership any cached data, images, etc. that aren't in use.
}

- (void)viewDidUnload {
    // Relinquish ownership of anything that can be recreated in
  viewDidLoad or on demand.
    // For example: self.myOutlet = nil;
}

- (void)dealloc {
    [detailViewController release];
    [super dealloc];
}

@end
```

While the `RootViewController.m` file contains many methods related to the Table view, here is a quick summary of some of the most important methods:

➤ `contentSizeForViewInPopoverView` — The size of the PopoverView to display

➤ `numberOfSectionsInTableView:` — The number of sections to be displayed in the Table view

➤ `tableView:numberOfRowsInSection:` — The number of rows to be displayed in the Table view

➤ `tableView:cellForRowAtIndexPath:` — The data to populate for each row

➤ `tableView:didSelectRowAtIndexPath:` — The row selected by the user

Now take a look at the `DetailsViewController.h` file:

```
#import <UIKit/UIKit.h>

@interface DetailViewController : UIViewController
    <UIPopoverControllerDelegate, UISplitViewControllerDelegate> {

    UIPopoverController *popoverController;
    UIToolbar *toolbar;

    id detailItem;
    UILabel *detailDescriptionLabel;
}

@property (nonatomic, retain) IBOutlet UIToolbar *toolbar;

@property (nonatomic, retain) id detailItem;
@property (nonatomic, retain) IBOutlet UILabel *detailDescriptionLabel;

@end
```

Notice that the `DetailsViewController` class implements the following protocols:

➤ `UIPopoverControllerDelegate` — It needs to implement this protocol because when the iPad is held in portrait orientation, the Popover view will display the content of the Table view `UISplitViewControllerDelegate` — It needs to implement this protocol because when the iPad changes orientation, it needs to hide/display the Popover view.

Examine the content of the `DetailsViewController.m` file:

```
#import "DetailViewController.h"
#import "RootViewController.h"

@interface DetailViewController ()
@property (nonatomic, retain) UIPopoverController *popoverController;
- (void)configureView;
@end

@implementation DetailViewController

@synthesize toolbar, popoverController, detailItem, detailDescriptionLabel;

/*
```

```
   When setting the detail item, update the view and dismiss the popover
    controller if it's showing.
   */
- (void)setDetailItem:(id)newDetailItem {
     if (detailItem != newDetailItem) {
          [detailItem release];
          detailItem = [newDetailItem retain];

          // Update the view.
          [self configureView];
     }

     if (popoverController != nil) {
          [popoverController dismissPopoverAnimated:YES];
     }
}


- (void)configureView {
     // Update the user interface for the detail item.
     detailDescriptionLabel.text = [detailItem description];
}


- (void)splitViewController:(UISplitViewController*)svc
      willHideViewController:(UIViewController *)aViewController
           withBarButtonItem:(UIBarButtonItem*)barButtonItem
        forPopoverController:(UIPopoverController*)pc {

     barButtonItem.title = @"Root List";
     NSMutableArray *items = [[toolbar items] mutableCopy];
     [items insertObject:barButtonItem atIndex:0];
     [toolbar setItems:items animated:YES];
     [items release];
     self.popoverController = pc;
}

// Called when the view is shown again in the split view, invalidating the
    button and popover controller.
- (void)splitViewController:(UISplitViewController*)svc
    willShowViewController:(UIViewController *)aViewController
invalidatingBarButtonItem:(UIBarButtonItem *)barButtonItem {

     NSMutableArray *items = [[toolbar items] mutableCopy];
     [items removeObjectAtIndex:0];
     [toolbar setItems:items animated:YES];
     [items release];
     self.popoverController = nil;
}

// Ensure that the view controller supports rotation and that the split
    view can therefore show in both portrait and landscape.
- (BOOL)shouldAutorotateToInterfaceOrientation:(UIInterfaceOrientation)
interfaceOrientation {
     return YES;
```

```
}

/*
    Other commented out code is omitted from this code listing
*/

- (void)viewDidUnload {
    // Release any retained subviews of the main view.
    // e.g. self.myOutlet = nil;
    self.popoverController = nil;
}

- (void)dealloc {
    [popoverController release];
    [toolbar release];

    [detailItem release];
    [detailDescriptionLabel release];
    [super dealloc];
}

@end
```

You need to handle two important events in this View Controller (both events are defined in the
UISplitViewControllerDelegate protocol):

➤ splitViewController:willHideViewController:withBarButtonItem:forPopover-
   Controller: — Fired when the iPad switches to portrait mode (where the PopoverView will
   be shown and the Table View will be hidden).

➤ splitViewController:willShowViewController:invalidatingBarButtonItem: — Fired when the
   iPad switches to landscape mode (where the PopoverView will be hidden and the Table View will
   be shown).

Displaying Some Items in the Split View-Based Application

Now that you have seen a Split View-based application in action, it is time to make some changes to
it and see how it is useful for the iPad. The following Try It Out displays a list of movies, and when
a movie is selected a picture is displayed on the detail view.

TRY IT OUT Displaying Some Items

1. Using the splitViewBasedApp project, double-click the DetailView.xib file to edit it in Interface
Builder.

2. Add an ImageView to the View window and set its Mode to Aspect Fit in the Attributes Inspector
window (see Figure 4-34).

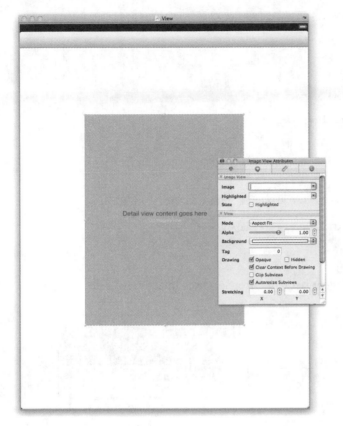

FIGURE 4-34

3. In the Size Inspector window, set the Autosizing attribute as follows (see Figure 4-35):

➤ X: 152

➤ Y: 163

➤ W: 463

➤ H: 644

4. In Xcode, add the images listed in Figure 4-36 to the `Resources` folder (you can download the images along with this project from Wrox.com; see the section in the book's Introduction titled "Source Code" for details).

5. In the `DetailViewController.h` file, insert the following bold statements:

```
#import <UIKit/UIKit.h>

@interface DetailViewController : UIViewController
```

```
      <UIPopoverControllerDelegate, UISplitViewControllerDelegate> {

      UIPopoverController *popoverController;
      UIToolbar *toolbar;

      id detailItem;
      UILabel *detailDescriptionLabel;

      IBOutlet UIImageView *imageView;
}

@property (nonatomic, retain) IBOutlet UIToolbar *toolbar;

@property (nonatomic, retain) id detailItem;
@property (nonatomic, retain) IBOutlet UILabel *detailDescriptionLabel;

@property (nonatomic, retain) UIImageView *imageView;

@end
```

6. Control-click and drag the File's Owner item and drop it on the ImageView. Select `imageView`.

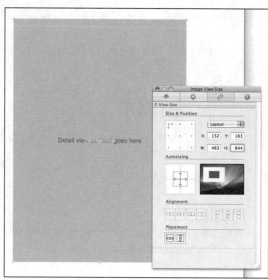

FIGURE 4-35

FIGURE 4-36

7. Add the following bold statements to the `RootViewController.m` file:

```objc
#import "RootViewController.h"
#import "DetailViewController.h"

@implementation RootViewController

@synthesize detailViewController;

NSMutableArray *listOfMovies;

- (void)viewDidLoad {
    //---initialize the array---
    listOfMovies = [[NSMutableArray alloc] init];
    [listOfMovies addObject:@"Training Day"];
    [listOfMovies addObject:@"Remember the Titans"];
    [listOfMovies addObject:@"John Q."];
    [listOfMovies addObject:@"The Bone Collector"];
    [listOfMovies addObject:@"Ricochet"];
    [listOfMovies addObject:@"The Siege"];
    [listOfMovies addObject:@"Malcolm X"];
    [listOfMovies addObject:@"Antwone Fisher"];
    [listOfMovies addObject:@"Courage Under Fire"];
    [listOfMovies addObject:@"He Got Game"];
    [listOfMovies addObject:@"The Pelican Brief"];
    [listOfMovies addObject:@"Glory"];
    [listOfMovies addObject:@"The Preacher's Wife"];

    //---set the title---
    self.navigationItem.title = @"Movies";

    [super viewDidLoad];
    self.clearsSelectionOnViewWillAppear = NO;
    self.contentSizeForViewInPopover = CGSizeMake(320.0, 600.0);
}

- (NSInteger)tableView:(UITableView *)aTableView
numberOfRowsInSection:(NSInteger)section {
    // Return the number of rows in the section.
    //return 10;
    return [listOfMovies count];
}

- (UITableViewCell *)tableView:(UITableView *)tableView
        cellForRowAtIndexPath:(NSIndexPath *)indexPath {

    static NSString *CellIdentifier = @"CellIdentifier";

    // Dequeue or create a cell of the appropriate type.
    UITableViewCell *cell = [tableView
        dequeueReusableCellWithIdentifier:CellIdentifier];

    if (cell == nil) {
```

```
        cell =
            [[[UITableViewCell alloc]
                initWithStyle:UITableViewCellStyleDefault
              reuseIdentifier:CellIdentifier] autorelease];
        cell.accessoryType = UITableViewCellAccessoryNone;
    }

    // Configure the cell.
    //cell.textLabel.text = [NSString stringWithFormat:@"Row %d", indexPath.row];
    cell.textLabel.text = [listOfMovies objectAtIndex:indexPath.row];

    return cell;
}

- (void)tableView:(UITableView *)aTableView
didSelectRowAtIndexPath:(NSIndexPath *)indexPath {

    /*
    When a row is selected, set the detail view controller's detail item
  to the item associated with the selected row.
    */
    //detailViewController.detailItem =
    //    [NSString stringWithFormat:@"Row %d", indexPath.row];
    detailViewController.detailItem =
        [NSString stringWithFormat:@"%@",
            [listOfMovies objectAtIndex:indexPath.row]];
}

- (void)dealloc {
    [listOfMovies release];
    [detailViewController release];
    [super dealloc];
}
```

8. Add the following bold statements to the DetailViewController.m file:

```
#import "DetailViewController.h"
#import "RootViewController.h"

@interface DetailViewController ()
@property (nonatomic, retain) UIPopoverController *popoverController;
- (void)configureView;
@end

@implementation DetailViewController

@synthesize toolbar, popoverController, detailItem, detailDescriptionLabel;

@synthesize imageView;

/*
```

```
      When setting the detail item, update the view and dismiss the popover
      controller if it's showing.
   */
- (void)setDetailItem:(id)newDetailItem {
    if (detailItem != newDetailItem) {
        [detailItem release];
        detailItem = [newDetailItem retain];

        // Update the view.
        NSString *imageName = [NSString stringWithFormat:@"%@.jpg",
            [detailItem description]];
        imageView.image = [UIImage imageNamed:imageName];

        [self configureView];
    }

    if (popoverController != nil) {
        [popoverController dismissPopoverAnimated:YES];
    }
}
```

9. Press Command-R to test the application on the iPhone Simulator. As shown in Figure 4-37, when the Simulator is in landscape mode, the application shows a list of movies on the left. Selecting a movie displays the movie image. You can also switch to portrait mode and select the movies from the PopoverView (see Figure 4-38).

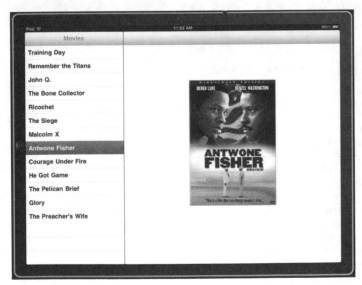

FIGURE 4-37

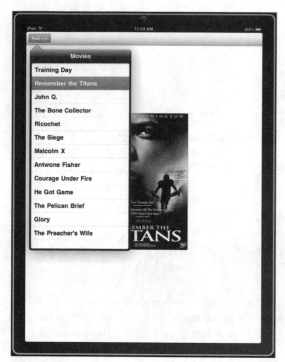

FIGURE 4-38

How It Works

First, you initialize a mutable array with a list of movie names:

```objc
- (void)viewDidLoad {
    //---initialize the array---
    listOfMovies = [[NSMutableArray alloc] init];
    [listOfMovies addObject:@"Training Day"];
    [listOfMovies addObject:@"Remember the Titans"];
    [listOfMovies addObject:@"John Q."];
    [listOfMovies addObject:@"The Bone Collector"];
    [listOfMovies addObject:@"Ricochet"];
    [listOfMovies addObject:@"The Siege"];
    [listOfMovies addObject:@"Malcolm X"];
    [listOfMovies addObject:@"Antwone Fisher"];
    [listOfMovies addObject:@"Courage Under Fire"];
    [listOfMovies addObject:@"He Got Game"];
    [listOfMovies addObject:@"The Pelican Brief"];
    [listOfMovies addObject:@"Glory"];
    [listOfMovies addObject:@"The Preacher's Wife"];

    //---set the title---
    self.navigationItem.title = @"Movies";

    [super viewDidLoad];
```

```
            self.clearsSelectionOnViewWillAppear = NO;
            self.contentSizeForViewInPopover = CGSizeMake(320.0, 600.0);
    }
```

The value returned by the `tableView:numberOfRowsInSection:` method sets the number of rows to be displayed, which in this case is the size of the mutable array:

```
    - (NSInteger)tableView:(UITableView *)aTableView
    numberOfRowsInSection:(NSInteger)section {
        // Return the number of rows in the section.
        //return 10;
        return [listOfMovies count];
    }
```

The `tableView:cellForRowAtIndexPath:` method is fired for each item in the mutable array, thereby populating the Table view:

```
    - (UITableViewCell *)tableView:(UITableView *)tableView
            cellForRowAtIndexPath:(NSIndexPath *)indexPath {

        static NSString *CellIdentifier = @"CellIdentifier";

        // Dequeue or create a cell of the appropriate type.
        UITableViewCell *cell = [tableView
            dequeueReusableCellWithIdentifier:CellIdentifier];

        if (cell == nil) {
            cell =
                [[[UITableViewCell alloc]
                    initWithStyle:UITableViewCellStyleDefault
                  reuseIdentifier:CellIdentifier] autorelease];
            cell.accessoryType = UITableViewCellAccessoryNone;
        }

        // Configure the cell.
        //cell.textLabel.text =
        //    [NSString stringWithFormat:@"Row %d", indexPath.row];
        cell.textLabel.text = [listOfMovies objectAtIndex:indexPath.row];

        return cell;
    }
```

When an item is selected in the Table view, you pass the movie selected to the `DetailViewController` object via its `detailItem` property:

```
    - (void)tableView:(UITableView *)aTableView
    didSelectRowAtIndexPath:(NSIndexPath *)indexPath {

        /*
         When a row is selected, set the detail view controller's detail item
        to the item associated with the selected row.
         */

        //detailViewController.detailItem =
```

```
//      [NSString stringWithFormat:@"Row %d", indexPath.row];
    detailViewController.detailItem =
        [NSString stringWithFormat:@"%@",
            [listOfMovies objectAtIndex:indexPath.row]];
}
```

In the `DetailViewController.m` file, you modified the `setDetailItem:` method (which is really a setter for the `detailItem` property) so that an image can be displayed. For the image name, you simply appended a `.jpg` to the movie name:

```
- (void)setDetailItem:(id)newDetailItem {
    if (detailItem != newDetailItem) {
        [detailItem release];
        detailItem = [newDetailItem retain];

        // Update the view.
        NSString *imageName = [NSString stringWithFormat:@"%@.jpg",
            [detailItem description]];
        imageView.image = [UIImage imageNamed:imageName];

        [self configureView];
    }

    if (popoverController != nil) {
        [popoverController dismissPopoverAnimated:YES];
    }
}
```

THE TAB BAR APPLICATION TEMPLATE

You have seen the use of three types of application template provided by the iPhone SDK: View-based application, Window-based application, and Split View–based application. A fourth type of application template exists for the iPhone: The Tab Bar application template. The following Try it Out uses the Tab Bar Application template to create a project and shows what a Tab Bar application looks like. Download the necessary project files as indicated.

TRY IT OUT   Creating a Tab Bar Application

codefile TabBarApplication.zip available for download at Wrox.com

1. Using Xcode, create a new Tab Bar Application project and name it `tabBarApp`.

2. Examine the content of the project (see Figure 4-39). In addition to the usual application delegate files, it also contains one View Controller (`FirstViewController`) and three XIB files: `MainWindow.xib`, `FirstView.xib`, and `SecondView.xib`.

FIGURE 4-39

3. Examine the content of the `tabBarAppAppDelegate.h` file, which is as follows:

```objc
#import <UIKit/UIKit.h>

@interface tabBarAppAppDelegate : NSObject
    <UIApplicationDelegate, UITabBarControllerDelegate> {

    UIWindow *window;
    UITabBarController *tabBarController;
}

@property (nonatomic, retain) IBOutlet UIWindow *window;
@property (nonatomic, retain) IBOutlet UITabBarController
    *tabBarController;

@end
```

Instead of the usual `UIViewController` class, you are now using the `UITabBarController`
class, which inherits from the `UIViewController` class. A `TabBarController` is a specialized
`UIViewController` class that contains a collection of View Controllers.

4. When the application has finished loading, the current view of the `UITabBarController` instance is
loaded, an occurrence that is evident in the `tabBarAppAppDelegate.m` file:

```objc
#import "tabBarAppAppDelegate.h"

@implementation tabBarAppAppDelegate

@synthesize window;
@synthesize tabBarController;

- (BOOL)application:(UIApplication *)application
```

```
didFinishLaunchingWithOptions:(NSDictionary *)launchOptions {

    // Override point for customization after application launch.

    // Add the tab bar controller's view to the window and display.
    [window addSubview:tabBarController.view];
    [window makeKeyAndVisible];

    return YES;
}
```

5. Double-click the `MainWindow.xib` file to edit it in Interface Builder. Observe the two Tab Bar Item views contained within the Tab Bar view shown at the bottom of the View window.

6. Click the first Tab Bar Item labeled First (see Figure 4-40). In the Identity Inspector window, observe that this is a View Controller and that the implementing class is FirstViewController. If you view its Attributes Inspector window, you will see that it is linked to the `FirstView.xib` file (see Figure 4-41).

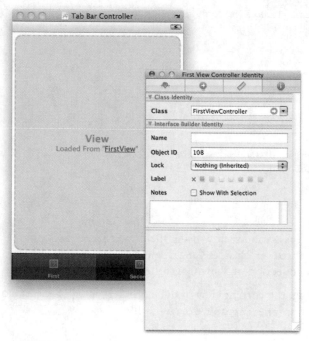

FIGURE 4-40

7. Click the second Tab Bar Item and view its Attributes Inspector window. Like the first Tab Bar Item, it is pointing to an XIB file, in this case it is pointing to the `SecondView.xib` file. However, if you examine the Identity Inspector window of the second Tab Bar Item, you will realize that it is not pointing to any specific View Controller class.

FIGURE 4-41

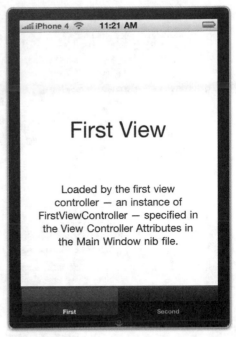

FIGURE 4-42

8. In Xcode, press Command-R to run the application on the iPhone 4 Simulator (see Figure 4-42). You can now touch the Tab Bar Items at the bottom of the screen to switch between the two views.

How It Works

Basically, the magic of a Tab Bar application is in the use of the `UITabBarController` class. Double-click the `MainWindow.xib` file; you'll see that it has a Tab Bar Controller item (see Figure 4-43).

The Tab Bar Controller contains a collection of View Controllers. In this case, it has two View Controllers. The first View Controller inside the `UITabBarController` instance is always displayed when it is added to the current view:

```
- (BOOL)application:(UIApplication *)application
didFinishLaunchingWithOptions:(NSDictionary *)launchOptions {

    // Override point for customization after application launch.

    // Add the tab bar controller's view to the window and display.
    [window addSubview:tabBarController.view];
    [window makeKeyAndVisible];

    return YES;
}
```

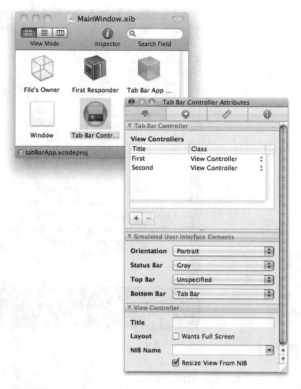

FIGURE 4-43

When the user touches the Tab Bar Items, each corresponding View Controller is loaded to display its view.

 NOTE *A Tab Bar Item actually is comprised of a View Controller and a Tab Bar Item object.*

By default, the Tab Bar Application template includes only two Tab Bar Items, so in this section you'll learn how to add more Tab Bar Items to the existing Tab Bar.

TRY IT OUT   Adding Tab Bar Items

1. Using the TabBarApplication project, in Interface Builder, drag and drop a Tab Bar Item from the Library onto the Tab Bar view (see Figure 4-44).

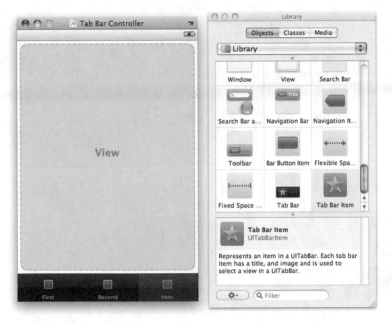

FIGURE 4-44

2. Select the newly added Tab Bar Item and view its Attributes Inspector window. Set the Badge property to 5 and the Identifier property to **Search** (see Figure 4-45). Observe the change in appearance of the Tab Bar Item. Be sure to click the center of the Tab Bar Item so that it can be selected; if you click the outside, the View Controller is selected.

 NOTE *The Badge property is a nifty way you can set some numbers or other text on the Tab Bar Item so that it can serve as a quick visual reminder to users about something.*

3. In Xcode, right-click the Classes folder in Xcode and choose Add ⇨ New File. Click the Cocoa Touch Classes category and select the UIViewController subclass. Name the file SearchViewController.m and check the "With XIB for user interface" option.

4. Double-click the newly created SearchViewController.xib file to open it in Interface Builder. Add a Label view to it (see Figure 4-46).

 NOTE *You won't be doing much in this SearchViewController.xib file. You're just adding a Label view so that you can confirm that this view loads successfully when the user taps the Tab Bar Item.*

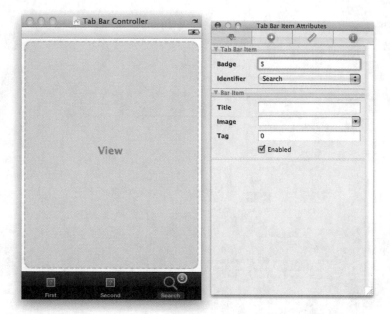

FIGURE 4-45

FIGURE 4-46

5. Back in `MainWindow.xib`, select the Tab Bar Item and view its Attributes Inspector window (see Figure 4-47). Set its NIB name to `SearchViewController`.

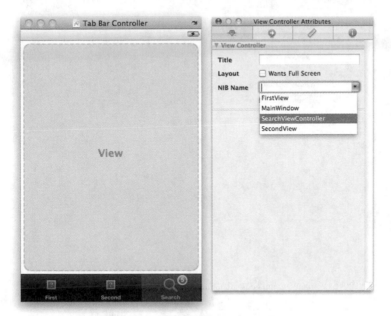

FIGURE 4-47

6. In the Identity Inspector window for the Search Tab Bar Item, set the Class name to `SearchViewController` (see Figure 4-48). This step is important; without it, you will get a runtime error later when you create outlets and actions on the View Controller class.

7. Save the project in Interface Builder.

8. That's it! Press Command-R to test the application on the iPhone Simulator. You can now touch the third Tab Bar Item (Search) to view the label (see Figure 4-49).

How It Works

In this example, you added a Tab Bar Item view to the Tab Bar view and connected it to a XIB file and its corresponding View Controller class.

Adding new Tab Bar Item views is straightforward: Simply drag the Tab Bar Item from the Library and drop it into the Tab Bar view. Alternatively, you can add it through the Attributes Inspector window for the Tab Bar Controller item in the `MainWindow.xib` window (see Figure 4-50). Click the + (plus) button to add new View Controllers, and the Tab Bar view automatically inserts a new Tab Bar Item view for you.

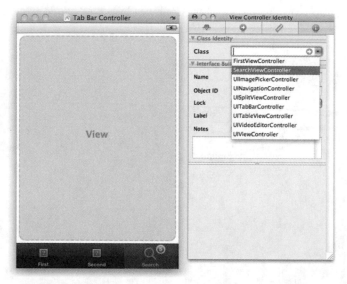

FIGURE 4-48

FIGURE 4-49

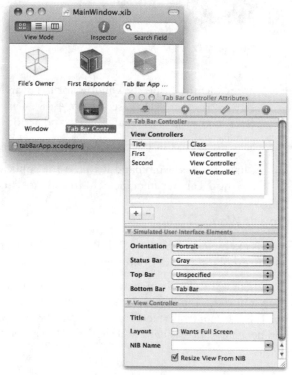

FIGURE 4-50

SUMMARY

This chapter provided a detailed look at the various application templates provided by the iPhone SDK: View-based Application, Window-based Application, Split View–based Application, and Tab Bar Application. Each one uses a different type of View Controller. It is important to have a good understanding of how the various pieces of an iPhone project are put together — knowing that will enable you to build applications with sophisticated user interfaces.

EXERCISES

1. Write the code snippet that enables you to create a View Controller programmatically.

2. Write the code snippet that creates a view dynamically during runtime.

3. Write the code snippet that wires an event of a view to an event handler.

4. In the `windowBasedApp` project created earlier in this chapter, create an action to display an Alert view when the button in the `HelloWorldViewController` class is pressed.

Answers to the Exercises can be found in Appendix E, on Wrox.com.

▶ WHAT YOU LEARNED IN THIS CHAPTER

TOPIC	KEY CONCEPTS
Types of iPhone/iPad Applications	View-based application, Window-based application, Split View-based application, and Tab Bar Application

Creating a Label view by code	```label = [[UILabel alloc] initWithFrame:frame];```
	```label.textAlignment = UITextAlignmentCenter;```
	```label.font = [UIFont fontWithName:@"Verdana" size:20];```
	```label.text = @"This is a label";```

Creating a Button view by code	```frame = CGRectMake(20, 60, 280, 50);```
	```button = [UIButton buttonWithType:UIButtonTypeRoundedRect];```
	```button.frame = frame;```
	```[button setTitle:@"OK" forState:UIControlStateNormal];```
	```button.backgroundColor = [UIColor clearColor];```

Wiring up an event to an event handler	```[button addTarget:self```
	``` action:@selector(buttonClicked:)```
	``` forControlEvents:UIControlEventTouchUpInside];```

Switching to another view	```//---instantiate the second view controller---```
	```mySecondViewController = [[MySecondViewController alloc]```
	``` initWithNibName:nil```
	``` bundle:nil];```
	```//---add the view from the second view controller---```
	```[window addSubview:mySecondViewController.view];```

Animating the view transition	```[UIView beginAnimations:@"flipping view" context:nil];```
	```[UIView setAnimationDuration:1];```
	```[UIView setAnimationCurve:UIViewAnimationCurveEaseInOut];```
	```[UIView setAnimationTransition: UIViewAnimationTransitionFlipFromLeft```
	``` forView:self.view cache:YES];```
	
	```[self.view addSubview:viewController.view];```
	
	```[UIView commitAnimations];```

5

Multi-Platform Support for the iPhone and iPad

WHAT YOU WILL LEARN IN THIS CHAPTER

➤ Modifying a project's Targeted Device Family setting to support both the iPhone and the iPad

➤ How to programmatically detect the device being run

➤ How to create a Universal application

➤ Creating separate targets for different devices

Besides the iPhone and iPod touch, another device using the iOS is the iPad. Out-of-the-box, the iPad will run your existing iPhone applications using the same screen size that is available on the iPhone and iPod touch — 320 × 480 pixels. Therefore, your applications will utilize only a portion of the screen. However, applications running in this default mode do not do justice to the much bigger screen real estate afforded by the iPad. Clearly, this is merely an interim size that can be used until developers port their application's UI to the much bigger iPad screen. In order to support the different devices, you need to modify your applications so that they can take advantage of the capabilities of each device type.

Though the iPad is also running the iPhone OS, you should be aware of some subtle differences when porting your applications over to the new device. This chapter examines three techniques you can use to port your existing iPhone apps to support both the iPhone and iPad.

 NOTE *At the time of writing, the iPad runs an older version of the iPhone OS, 3.2; whereas the iPhone 4 and iPod touch run the newer 4.0. Apple has announced that the iPad will be running iOS 4.0 later in the fall of 2010. iPhone 3 and iPhone 3GS users can also upgrade their devices to run iOS 4.*

TECHNIQUE 1 — MODIFYING THE DEVICE TARGET SETTING

The easiest way to ensure that your iPhone application runs as an iPad application (that is, full screen) is to modify the Targeted Device Family setting in your Xcode project. The following Try It Out shows you how to achieve this.

TRY IT OUT Modifying the Device Target Setting

codefile MyiPhoneApp.zip available for download at Wrox.com

1. Using Xcode, create a new View-based Application (iPhone) project (see Figure 5-1) and name it **MyiPhoneApp**.

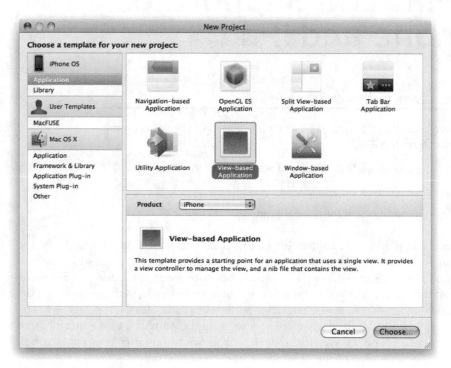

FIGURE 5-1

2. Double-click the `MyiPhoneAppViewController.xib` file to edit it in Interface Builder.

3. Populate the View window with the following views (see Figure 5-2):

➤ Label (set it to display "Please enter your name")

> ➤ Text field

> ➤ Round Rect button (set it to display "OK")

4. Back in Xcode, press Command-R to test the application on the iPhone 4.0 Simulator. You should see the screen shown in Figure 5-3.

FIGURE 5-2

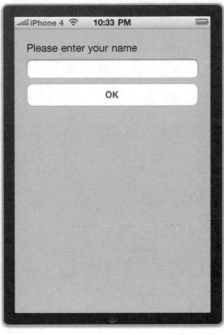

FIGURE 5-3

5. Expand the Targets item in the project and double-click the MyiPhoneApp item (see Figure 5-4).

6. Click the Build tab and scroll down the list. Under the Architectures section, select Base SDK ➪ iPhone Device 3.2 (see Figure 5-5).

7. In Xcode, change the simulator to Simulator 3.2 and press Command-R again. This time, the application will be shown running in the iPhone Simulator (simulating the iPad), running as an iPhone application (see Figure 5-6). This is the default behavior of iPhone applications running on the iPad.

 NOTE *If the iPhone Simulator continues to simulate the iPhone, restart it. After this, it will simulate the iPad.*

FIGURE 5-4

FIGURE 5-5

FIGURE 5-6

8. In Xcode, double-click the MyiPhoneApp item listed under Targets again. Click the Build tab and scroll down the list. Under the Deployment section, select Targeted Device Family ➪ iPhone/iPad (see Figure 5-7).

9. Press Command-R to test the application on the iPhone 3.2 Simulator again. This time, your application will run natively as an iPad application (see Figure 5-8).

How It Works

In this example, you first created an iPhone application that you then tested on the iPhone 4 and iPhone 3.2 (iPad) Simulator. By default, all iPhone applications will run in their original screen size — 320 x 480. If you want your iPhone application to run full screen on the iPad, you have to modify the Targeted Device Family setting in your project.

FIGURE 5-7

The Targeted Device Family setting provides three different values: iPhone, iPad, or iPhone/iPad. Setting it to iPhone/iPad ensures that your application can automatically detect the device on which it is running, and runs your application full screen.

Notice that the UI of the application is exactly the same as that on the iPhone. It is your responsibility to re-layout your UI when the application is running on the iPad. One way would be to programmatically reposition your views when your application detects that it is running on an iPad. The next section describes how to detect the device on which an application is currently running.

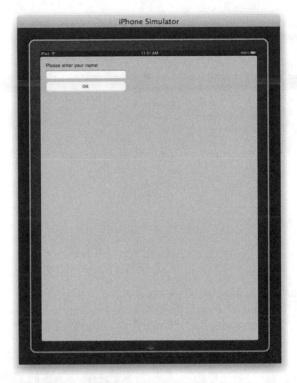

FIGURE 5-8

Detecting the Platform Programmatically

In order to re-layout your UI according to the device on which it is running, it is important to be able to programmatically detect if your application is running on an iPhone/iPod touch or an iPad. The following Try It Out shows you how.

TRY IT OUT Detecting the Device

1. Using the project created in the previous section, add the following statements shown in bold to the MyiPhoneAppViewController.m file:

```
- (void)viewDidLoad {

    #if (__IPHONE_OS_VERSION_MAX_ALLOWED >= 30200)

    NSString *str;
    if (UI_USER_INTERFACE_IDIOM() == UIUserInterfaceIdiomPad) {
        str = [NSString stringWithString:@"Running as an iPad application"];
```

```
    } else {
        str = [NSString stringWithString:
                    @"Running as an iPhone/iPod touch application"];
    }

    UIAlertView *alert = [[UIAlertView alloc] initWithTitle:@"Platform"
                                            message:str
                                            delegate:nil
                                    cancelButtonTitle:@"OK"
                                    otherButtonTitles:nil];

    [alert show];
    [alert release];

#endif

    [super viewDidLoad];
}
```

2. Press Command-R to test the application on the iPhone 3.2 Simulator. You will see the message displayed in Figure 5-9.

3. In Xcode, select iPhone for the Targeted Device Family setting (see the previous section for the steps to modify this setting) and choose the Simulator 3.2 item. Press Command-R; you will notice that the application now runs on the iPhone 3.2 Simulator as an iPhone application. Figure 5-10 shows the alert that it will display.

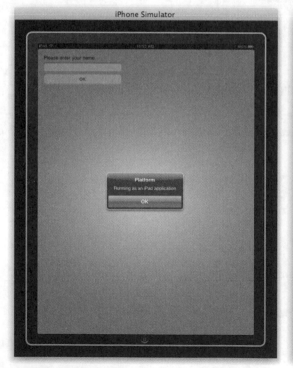

FIGURE 5-9

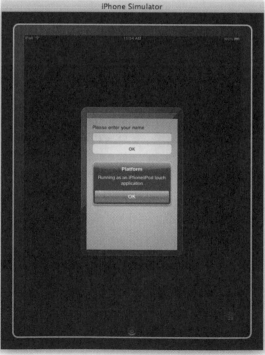

FIGURE 5-10

How It Works

The preceding code includes a conditional compilation directive to indicate that if the application is compiled against the minimum iPhone OS version of 3.2, it will then include a block of code to programmatically detect the type of application it is currently running as:

```
#if (__IPHONE_OS_VERSION_MAX_ALLOWED >= 30200)

//---code within this block will be compiled if application is compiled
// for iPhone OS 3.2 and above---

#endif
```

To detect if the application is running on an iPad, you check the result of the `UI_USER_INTERFACE_IDIOM()` function. This function returns the interface idiom supported by the current device. If it is an iPad, the result of this function will be `UIUserInterfaceIdiomPad`:

```
NSString *str;
if (UI_USER_INTERFACE_IDIOM() == UIUserInterfaceIdiomPad) {
    str = [NSString stringWithString:@"Running as an iPad application"];
} else {
    str = [NSString stringWithString:
                @"Running as an iPhone/iPod touch application"];
}
```

If the application is running as an iPhone application on the iPad, the `UI_USER_INTERFACE_IDIOM()` function will return `UIUserInterfaceIdiomPhone`.

TECHNIQUE 2 — CREATING UNIVERSAL APPLICATIONS

The previous technique shows how you can modify the Targeted Device Family setting to create a single application that runs on both the iPhone and iPad, called a *Universal* application. The challenge is adapting the UI of the application for each platform — you have to programmatically detect the type of device the application is running on and then modify the layout of the UI dynamically.

Apple recommends that you create a Universal application, one that targets both the iPhone and the iPad, with separate XIB files representing the UI for each platform. The following Try It Out shows you how you can create a Universal application.

TRY IT OUT   Creating a Universal Application

codefile Universal.zip available for download at Wrox.com

1. Using Xcode, create a View-based Application (iPhone) project and name it **Universal**.

2. Double-click on the `UniversalViewController.xib` file to edit it in Interface Builder.

3. Add a Label view to the View window and label it as shown in Figure 5-11.

4. Press Command-R to test the application on the iPhone 4 Simulator. You will see the application running on the iPhone 4 Simulator (see Figure 5-12).

FIGURE 5-11   FIGURE 5-12

5. Back in Xcode, select Targets ⇨ Universal. Then select Project ⇨ Upgrade Current Target for iPad (see Figure 5-13).

6. In the dialog box that appears, check the One Universal application option and click OK (see Figure 5-14).

You will now see a folder named `Resources-iPad` containing a XIB file named `MainWindow-iPad.xib` (see Figure 5-15).

7. Examine the `Universal-Info.plist` file located within the `Resources` folder. You will see a key named "Main nib file base name (iPad)," with its value set to `MainWindow-iPad` (see Figure 5-16).

8. Right-click on the `Resources-iPad` folder and select Add ⇨ New File (see Figure 5-17).

9. Select Cocoa Touch Class and then select the UIViewController subclass template (see Figure 5-18). Make sure that the Targeted for iPad and With XIB for user interface options are checked. Click Next.

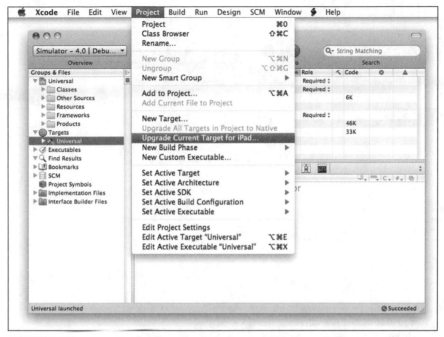

FIGURE 5-13

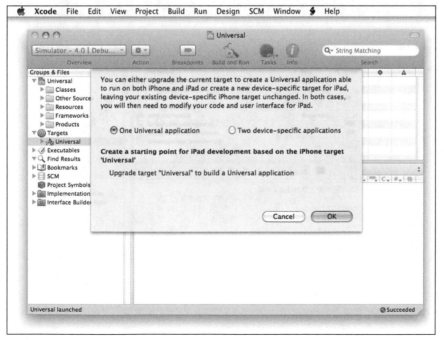

FIGURE 5-14

FIGURE 5-15

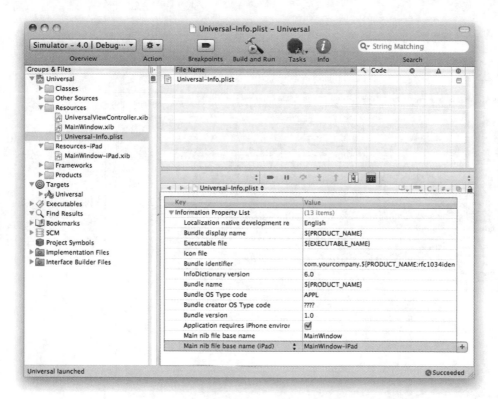

FIGURE 5-16

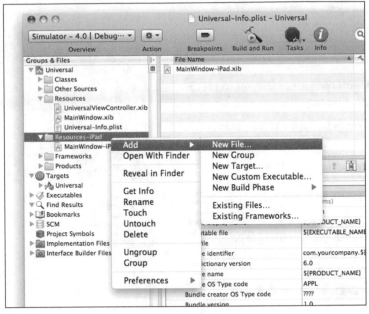

FIGURE 5-17

FIGURE 5-18

10. Name the class **iPadUniversalViewController.m**. The `Resources-iPad` folder should now look like Figure 5-19.

11. Double-click on the `iPadUniversalViewController.xib` file to edit it in Interface Builder.

12. Populate the View window with the Label view and set it to display the string as shown in Figure 5-20.

13. Double-click the `MainWindow-iPad.xib` file to edit it in Interface Builder.

14. Select the Universal View Controller item and view its Identity Inspector window. Set its Class to `iPadUniversalViewController` (see Figure 5-21).

15. With the same View Controller selected, view its Attributes Inspector window and set its NIB Name attribute to `iPadUniversalViewController` (see Figure 5-22).

FIGURE 5-19

I am an iPad Application!

FIGURE 5-20

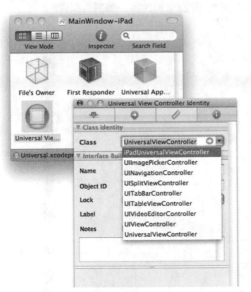

FIGURE 5-21   **FIGURE 5-22**

16. In Xcode, select Universal – iPad Simulator 3.2 (see Figure 5-23) and press Command-R to test the application on the iPhone 3.2 Simulator. You will see the application as shown in Figure 5-24.

17. If you now select the Universal – iPhone Simulator 4 option and press Command-R to test the application on the iPhone 4 Simulator, you should see the application as shown in Figure 5-25.

How It Works

This has been a pretty long Try It Out, but the concepts covered in it are actually very straightforward.

First, you asked Xcode to upgrade the device target for this project to the iPad. Essentially, Xcode modified the Targeted Device Family setting (located under the Deployment section of your target in Xcode) to iPhone/iPad.

FIGURE 5-23

Xcode will automatically create a copy of the `MainWindow.xib` file and name it `MainWindow-iPad.xib`. When the application is loaded in an iPhone or iPod touch, the `MainWindow.xib` file will be loaded. When the application is loaded in an iPad, the `MainWindow-iPad.xib` file will be loaded.

FIGURE 5-24

FIGURE 5-25

By default, both `MainWindow.xib` and `MainWindow-iPad.xib` will automatically load `UniversalViewController.xib` when the application is started. In this example, you have added another View window, which is comprised of the following three files:

➤   `iPadUniversalViewController.xib`

➤   `iPadUniversalViewController.h`

➤   `iPadUniversalViewController.m`

This new View window will be loaded by the `MainWindow-iPad.xib` file. Essentially, you design your iPhone UI in the `UniversalViewController.xib` file, and the iPad UI in the `iPadUniversalViewController.xib` file.

Note that strictly speaking, the additional View Controller class (the `iPadUniversalViewController.h` and the `iPadUniversalViewController.m`) is not needed. The new XIB file (`iPadUniversalViewController.xib`) can be connected to the existing View Controllers class (`UniversalViewController`), which is currently connected to `UniverslViewController.xib`. Essentially, the two XIB files can be connected to the same View Controller class.

The important thing to keep in mind about a Universal application is that you need to create separate XIB files for the different platforms — one for iPhone and one for the iPad. Once you do that, the application itself will automatically detect whether it is running on the iPhone or the iPad and then load the appropriate XIB file. It is your responsibility to create separate XIB files for the user interface in the iPhone and iPad.

The result of using this approach is that you have only one executable for your application.

So far, this chapter has covered two of the three techniques available for porting your existing apps to the iPad (modifying the Targeted Device Family setting and creating universal apps). Next, you will learn about maintaining separate targets with different code bases.

TECHNIQUE 3 — MAINTAINING TWO CODE BASES

The third technique for developing your application for multiple devices is to maintain separate targets for your application. Using this approach, you will have two executables eventually — one for the iPhone/iPod touch, and one for the iPad. The following steps explain how to accomplish this.

TRY IT OUT Maintaining Separate Targets with Different Code Bases

codefile MyAppiPhone.zip available for download at Wrox.com

1. Using Xcode, create a View-based Application (iPhone) project and name it **MyAppiPhone**.

2. Select Targets ⇨ MyAppiPhone, and then select Project ⇨ Upgrade Current Target for iPad.

3. In the dialog box that appears, select the Two device-specific applications option and click OK (see Figure 5-26).

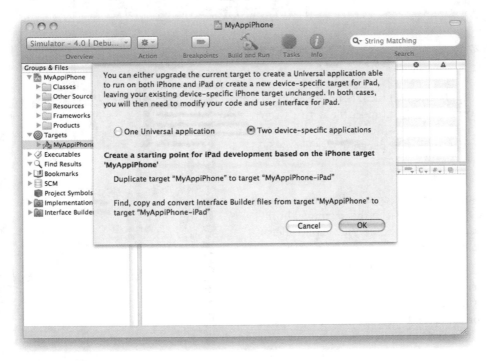

FIGURE 5-26

4. Observe the items created by Xcode (see Figure 5-27). Two sets of resources and targets are created for you — one for the iPhone and one for the iPad. You need to maintain two separate sets of files for each platform.

5. To test the application on the iPhone 4 Simulator, select MyAppiPhone (under the Active Target; see Figure 5-28) and press Command-R. Your application will run as an iPhone application (see Figure 5-29).

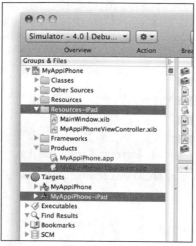

FIGURE 5-27

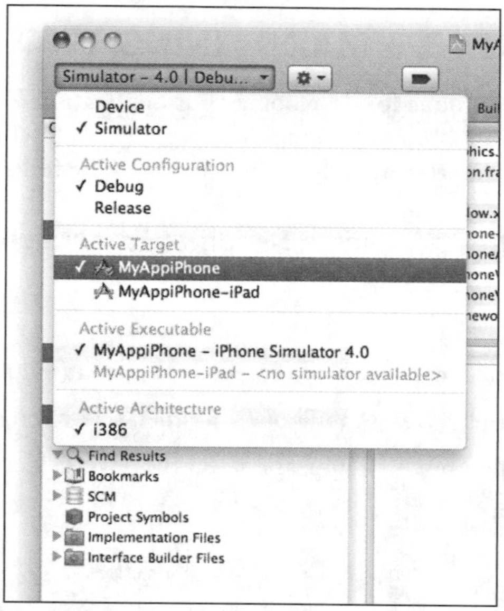

FIGURE 5-28

6. To test the application on the iPhone 3.2 Simulator, select MyAppiPhone-iPad (under the Active Target; see Figure 5-30) and press Command-R. Your application will run as an iPad application (see Figure 5-31).

How It Works

Like the Universal application approach, you need to maintain two sets of resources. In this example, both XIB files are connected to the same View Controller (MyAppiPhoneViewController). You can connect each XIB file to its own View Controller if you like.

The main difference between this technique and the universal approach is that this technique results in two separate targets — one for the iPhone and one for the iPad. Because of this, there will be two separate executables for your application (listed under the Products folder in your Xcode project). When you are ready to deploy your application to the AppStore, you need to submit these two executables separately.

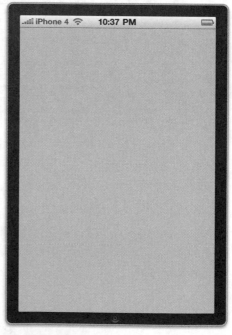

FIGURE 5-29

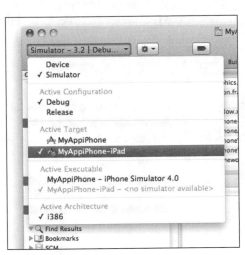

FIGURE 5-30

FIGURE 5-31

MAKING YOUR CHOICE

Now that you have seen the three techniques for porting your iPhone application to support the iPad, which technique should you adopt?

If your application does not have many UI changes when running on either the iPhone or iPad, using the first technique (modifying the device target setting) is the easiest way to support two platforms with a single code base and a single UI. All you need to do is to ensure that when the application runs on the iPad, the UI is rearranged correctly — this can be done programmatically in your View Controller.

Most developers should benefit from creating Universal applications. When you have an application that supports two different platforms, creating a Universal application allows you to have one code base and several XIB files designed specifically for the iPhone and iPad. This technique and the first save you the trouble of uploading two different editions of your application to AppStore. You need to upload just one version of your application and it will automatically support both platforms.

The last technique, maintaining two different code bases, is useful if your application behaves differently when it is running on different platforms. When your application does not support certain features while running on the iPhone, you might have quite a different code base for each platform. In this case, maintaining different code bases might be a better idea and save you the trouble of bundling all the unnecessary files into a single application.

SUMMARY

In this chapter, you have seen how to port an existing iPhone application to support both the iPhone and the iPad. In general, the Universal application approach is the recommended one, as it allows you to maintain just one code base that can target multiple platforms.

EXERCISES

1. What is the difference between creating a Universal application versus creating separate targets?

2. What function enables you to determine the device platform on which your application is currently running?

3. What are the different values available for the Targeted Device Family setting in your Xcode project?

Answers to exercises can be found in Appendix E, on Wrox.com.

▶ **WHAT YOU LEARNED IN THIS CHAPTER**

TOPIC	KEY CONCEPTS
Supporting an application natively on the iPhone and iPad	Modify the Target Device Setting of the project in Xcode and set it to iPhone/iPad.
Detecting the device programmatically	Use the `UI_USER_INTERFACE_IDIOM()` function.
Creating a Universal application	Select the target in the Xcode project and then select Project ⇨ Upgrade Current Target for iPad. Choose the One Universal application option.
Creating separate targets	Select the target in the Xcode project and then select Project ⇨ Upgrade Current Target for iPad. Choose the Two device-specific applications option.

Keyboard Inputs

WHAT YOU WILL LEARN IN THIS CHAPTER

➤ How to customize the keyboard for different types of inputs

➤ How to hide the keyboard when you are done typing

➤ How to detect when a keyboard is visible or not

➤ How to use ScrollView to contain other views

➤ How to shift views to make way for the keyboard

One of the controversial aspects of the iPhone is the multi-touch keyboard that enables users to input data into their iPhone. Critics of the iPhone have criticized its lack of a physical keyboard for data entry, whereas ardent supporters of virtual keyboards swear by its ease of use.

What makes the iPhone keyboard so powerful is its intelligence in tracking what you type, followed by suggestions for the word you are typing, and automatically correcting the spelling and inserting punctuation for you. What's more, the keyboard knows when to appear at the right time — it appears when you tap a Text Field view, and it goes away automatically when you tap a non-input view. You can also input data in different languages.

For iPhone application programmers, the key concern is how to integrate the keyboard into the application. How do you make the keyboard go away naturally when it is no longer needed? And how do you ensure that the view the user is currently interacting with is not blocked by the keyboard? In this chapter, you learn various ways to deal with the keyboard programmatically.

USING THE KEYBOARD

In iPhone programming, the views most commonly associated with the keyboard are the Text Field view and the TextView view. When a Text Field view is tapped (or clicked, if you are using the Simulator), the keyboard is automatically displayed. The data that the user taps on the keyboard is then inserted into the Text Field view. The following Try It Out demonstrates this.

TRY IT OUT **Using a TextField for Inputs**

codefile KeyboardInputs.zip available for download at Wrox.com

1. Using Xcode, create a new View-based Application (iPhone) project and name it `KeyboardInputs`.

2. Double-click the `KeyboardInputsViewController.xib` file to edit it using Interface Builder.

3. Populate the View window with the Label and Text Field views (see Figure 6-1). Set the Label view to display the text "Alphanumeric Input."

FIGURE 6-1

4. Save the `KeyboardInputsViewController.xib` file and press Command-R in Xcode to run the application on the iPhone 4 Simulator. When the application is loaded, the keyboard is initially hidden, and when the user clicks the Text Field view, the keyboard automatically appears (see Figure 6-2).

How It Works

The beauty of the iPhone user interface is that when the system detects that the current active view is a Text Field view, the keyboard automatically appears; you don't need to do anything to bring up the keyboard. Using the keyboard, you can enter alphanumeric data as well as numbers and special characters (such as symbols). The keyboard in the iPhone also supports characters of languages other than English, such as Chinese and Hebrew.

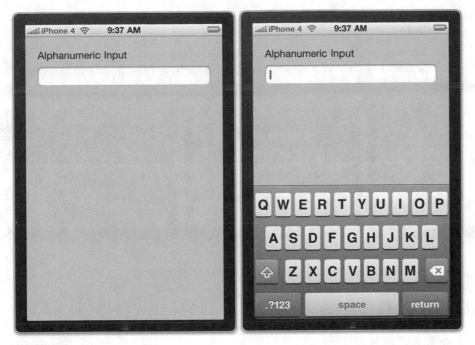

FIGURE 6-2

CUSTOMIZING THE TYPE OF INPUTS

To learn more about the input behaviors, go to Interface Builder, select the Text Field view, and view its Attributes Inspector window (choose Tools ➪ Attributes Inspector). Figure 6-3 shows that window. In particular, pay attention to the section at the bottom labeled Text Input Traits.

The Text Input Traits section contains several items you can configure to determine how the keyboard handles the text entered:

➤ **Capitalize** — Enables you to capitalize the words, sentences, or all characters of the data entered via the keyboard.

➤ **Correction** — Enables you to indicate whether you want the keyboard to provide suggestions for words that are not spelled

FIGURE 6-3

correctly. You can also choose the Default option, which defaults to the user's global text correction settings.

➤ **Keyboard** — Enables you to choose the different types of keyboard for entering different types of data. Figure 6-4 shows (from left to right) the keyboard configured with the following Keyboard types: Email Address, Phone Pad, and Number Pad.

FIGURE 6-4

➤ **Appearance** — Enables you to choose how the keyboard should appear.

➤ **Return Key** — Enables you to show different types of Return key in your keyboard (see Figure 6-5). Figure 6-6 shows the keyboard set with the Google key serving as the Return key (the Return key appears as "Search").

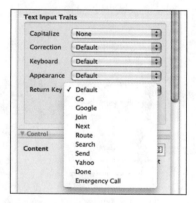

FIGURE 6-5

FIGURE 6-6

➤ **Auto-Enable Return Key check box** — Indicates that if no input is entered for a field, the Return key will be disabled (grayed out). It is enabled again if at least one character is entered.

➤ **Secure check box** — Indicates whether the input will be masked (see Figure 6-7). This is usually used for password input.

FIGURE 6-7

Making the Keyboard Go Away

You know that the keyboard in the iPhone automatically appears when a Text Field view is selected. What about making it go away when you are done typing? You have two ways to dismiss the keyboard.

> **NOTE** *On the iPad, there is a third way of making the keyboard go away without any programming effort on your part — simply tapping the bottom right key on the keyboard dismisses the keyboard.*

First, you can dismiss the keyboard by tapping the Return key on the keyboard. This method requires you to handle the `Did End on Exit` event of the Text Field view that caused the keyboard to appear. This method is demonstrated in the following Try It Out.

Second, you can dismiss the keyboard when the user taps outside a Text Field view. This method, which requires some additional coding, makes your application much more user-friendly. The subsequent Try It Out illustrates this method.

TRY IT OUT Dismissing the Keyboard (Technique 1)

1. Using the `KeyboardInputs` project, edit the `KeyboardInputsViewController.h` file by adding the following bold statements:

```
#import <UIKit/UIKit.h>

@interface KeyboardInputsViewController : UIViewController {

}

-(IBAction) doneEditing:(id) sender;

@end
```

2. Double-click the `KeyboardInputsViewController.xib` file to edit it in Interface Builder. Right-click the Text Field view in the View window and then click the circle next to the `Did End on Exit` event and drag it to the File's Owner item (see Figure 6-8). The `doneEditing:` action you have just created should appear. Select it.

3. Save the `KeyboardInputsViewController.xib` file.

4. In the `KeyboardInputsViewController.m` file, provide the implementation for the `doneEditing:` action:

```
#import "KeyboardInputsViewController.h"

@implementation KeyboardInputsViewController

-(IBAction) doneEditing:(id) sender {
    [sender resignFirstResponder];
}
```

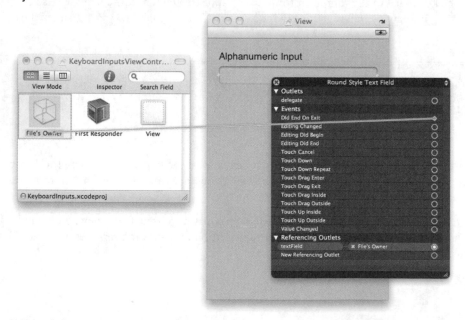

FIGURE 6-8

5. Save the project and press Command-R to run the application on the iPhone 4 Simulator.

6. When the application appears on the iPhone 4 Simulator, tap the Text Field view. The keyboard should appear. Using the keyboard, type some text into the view and click the Return key when you are done. The keyboard now goes away.

How It Works

What you have just done is connect the `Did End on Exit` event of the Text Field view with the `doneEditing:` action you have created. When you are editing the content of a Text Field view using the keyboard, clicking the Return key on the keyboard fires the `Did End on Edit` event of the Text Field view. In this case, it invokes the `doneEditing:` action, which contains the following statement:

```
[sender resignFirstResponder];
```

The `sender` in this case refers to the Text Field view, and `resignFirstResponder` asks the Text Field view to resign its First-Responder status. Essentially, it means that you do not want to interact with the Text Field view anymore and that the keyboard is no longer needed. Hence, the keyboard should hide itself.

 NOTE *The First Responder in a view always refers to the current view with which the user is interacting. In this example, when you click the Text Field view, it becomes the First Responder and activates the keyboard automatically.*

An alternative way to hide the keyboard is when the user taps an area outside of the Text Field view. This method is more natural and does not require the user to manually tap the Return key on the keyboard to hide the keyboard. The following Try It Out shows how this method can be implemented.

TRY IT OUT Dismissing the Keyboard (Technique 2)

1. Using the `KeyboardInputs` project, double-click the `KeyboardInputsViewController.xib` file to edit it using Interface Builder.

2. Add a Round Rect Button view to the View window (see Figure 6-9).

3. With the Round Rect Button view selected, choose Layout ⇨ Send to Back. This makes the button appear behind the other controls.

4. Resize the Round Rect Button view so that it now covers the entire screen (see Figure 6-10).

5. In the Attributes Inspector window, set the Type of the Round Rect Button view to Custom (see Figure 6-11).

FIGURE 6-9

FIGURE 6-10

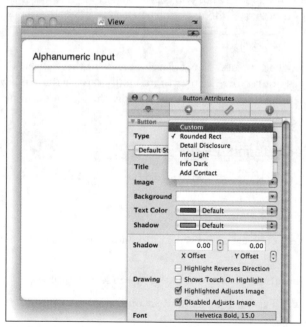

FIGURE 6-11

6. In Xcode, edit the `KeyboardInputsViewController.h` file by adding the following bold statements:

```
#import <UIKit/UIKit.h>

@interface KeyboardInputsViewController : UIViewController {
    IBOutlet UITextField *textField;
}

@property (nonatomic, retain) UITextField *textField;

-(IBAction) doneEditing:(id) sender;
-(IBAction) bgTouched:(id) sender;

@end
```

7. In Interface Builder, Control-click and drag the File's Owner item onto the Text Field view. The `textField` outlet should appear. Select it.

8. Control-click and drag the Round Rect Button view onto the File's Owner item in the `KeyboardInputsViewController.xib` window (see Figure 6-12). Select the `bgTouched:` action.

 NOTE The `Touch Up Inside` *event of the Round Rect Button view is wired to the* `bgTouched:` *action.*

9. Save the XIB file in Interface Builder.

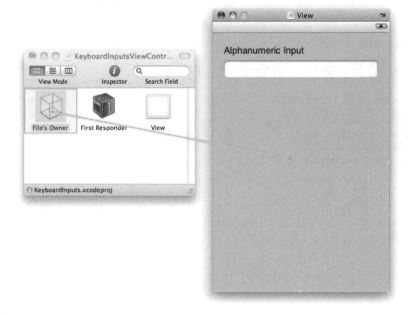

FIGURE 6-12

10. In the `KeyboardInputsViewController.m` file, add the following statements highlighted in bold:

```
#import "KeyboardInputsViewController.h"

@implementation KeyboardInputsViewController

@synthesize textField;

-(IBAction) bgTouched:(id) sender {
    [textField resignFirstResponder];
}

-(IBAction) doneEditing:(id) sender {
    [sender resignFirstResponder];
}
```

11. That's it. Press Command-R in Xcode to deploy the application onto the iPhone 4 Simulator. Then, try the following:

➤ Click the Text Field view to bring up the keyboard.

➤ When you are done, click the Return key on the keyboard to dismiss it. Alternatively, click any of the empty spaces outside the Text Field view to dismiss the keyboard.

How It Works

In this example, you added a Round Rect Button view to cover up all the empty spaces in the View window of your application. Essentially, the button acts as a net to trap all touches outside of the Text Field view on the View window, so when the user clicks (or taps, on a real device) the screen outside the keyboard and the Text Field view, the Round Rect Button fires the `Touch Up Inside` event, which is handled by the `bgTouched:` action. In the `bgTouched:` action, you explicitly asked `textField` to resign its First-Responder status, which causes the keyboard to disappear.

The technique used in this example applies even if you have multiple TextField views on your view. Suppose you have three Text Field views, with outlets named `textField`, `textField2`, and `textField3`. In that case, the `bgTouched:` action looks like this:

```
-(IBAction) bgTouched:(id) sender {
    [textField resignFirstResponder];
    [textField2 resignFirstResponder];
    [textField3 resignFirstResponder];
}
```

When the `bgTouched:` action is invoked, all three `TextField` views are asked to relinquish their First-Responder status. Calling the `resignFirstResponder` method on a view that is currently not the First Responder is harmless; hence, the preceding statements are safe and will not cause a runtime exception.

UNDERSTANDING THE RESPONDER CHAIN

The prior Try It Out is a good example of the responder chain in action. In the iPhone, events are passed through a series of event handlers known as the *responder chain*. As you touch the screen of your iPhone, the iPhone generates events that are passed up the responder chain. Each object in the responder chain checks whether it can handle the event. In the preceding example, when the user taps on the Label view, the Label view checks whether it can handle the event. Because the `Label` event does not handle the `Touch` event, it is passed up the responder chain. The large background button that you have added is now next in line to examine the event. Because it handles the `Touch Up Inside` event, the event is consumed by the button.

In summary, objects higher up in the responder chain examine the event first and handle it if it is applicable. Any object can then stop the propagation of the event up the responder chain, or pass the event up the responder chain if it only partially handles the event.

Automatically Displaying the Keyboard When the View Is Loaded

Sometimes you might want to straightaway set a Text Field view as the active view and display the keyboard without waiting for the user to do so. In such cases, you can use the `becomeFirstResponder` method of the view. The following code shows that the Text Field view will be the First Responder as soon as the View window is loaded:

```
- (void)viewDidLoad {
    [textField becomeFirstResponder];
    [super viewDidLoad];
}
```

DETECTING THE PRESENCE OF THE KEYBOARD

Up to this point, you have seen the various ways to hide the keyboard after you are done using it. However, there is one problem to note: When the keyboard appears, it takes up a significant portion of the screen. If your Text Field view is located at the bottom of the screen, it would be covered by the keyboard. As a programmer, it is your duty to ensure that the view is relocated to a visible portion of the screen. Surprisingly, this is not taken care of by the SDK; you have to do the hard work yourself.

NOTE *The keyboard in the iPhone (3G and 3GS) takes up 216 pixels (432 pixels for iPhone 4) in height when in portrait mode, and 162 pixels (324 pixels for iPhone 4) when in landscape mode. For the iPad, the keyboard takes up 264 pixels in height when in portrait mode, and 352 pixels when in landscape mode.*

First, though, it is important that you understand a few key concepts related to the keyboard:

➤ You need to be able to programmatically know when a keyboard is visible or hidden. To do so, your application needs to register `UIKeyboardDidShowNotification` and `UIKeyboardDidHideNotification`.

➤ You also need to know when and which Text Field view is currently being edited so that you can relocate it to a visible portion of the screen. You can determine this information through the — `textFieldDidBeginEditing:` event available in the `UITextFieldDelegate` protocol.

Confused? Worry not; the following sections make it all clear.

Using the Scroll View

The key to relocating the view that is currently being hidden by the keyboard is to use a Scroll View to contain all the views on the View window. When a view (such as the Text Field) is hidden by the keyboard when the user taps on it, you can scroll all the views contained in the Scroll View upwards so that the view currently responding to the tap is visible. Before you learn how to do that, however, you need to first understand how the Scroll View works. The following Try It Out shows you that.

TRY IT OUT   Understanding the Scroll View

codefile Scroller.zip available for download at Wrox.com

1. Using Xcode, create a new View-based Application (iPhone) project and name it `Scroller`.

2. Double-click on the `ScrollerViewController.xib` file located in the Resources folder to edit it in Interface Builder.

3. Populate the View window with a Scroll View (see Figure 6-13).

4. Add two Round Rect Button views to the Scroll View (see Figure 6-14).

5. To add more views to the Scroll View so that the user can view more than what the View window typically displays at a time, perform the following steps:

➤ Click the Scroll View to select it. If you cannot select it, click on the title bar of the View window first and then click the Scroll View again.

➤ Shift the Scroll View upwards (see the left of Figure 6-15).

➤ Expand the height of the Scroll View by clicking and dragging the center-dot of the Scroll View downwards. The Scroll View should now look like Figure 6-15 (on the right).

6. Add a Text Field view onto the bottom of the Scroll View (see Figure 6-16).

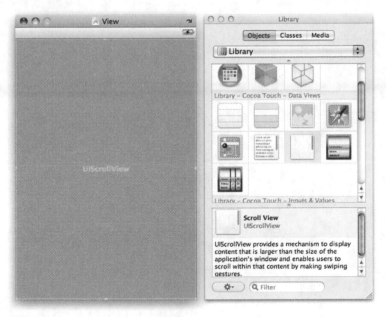

FIGURE 6-13

FIGURE 6-14

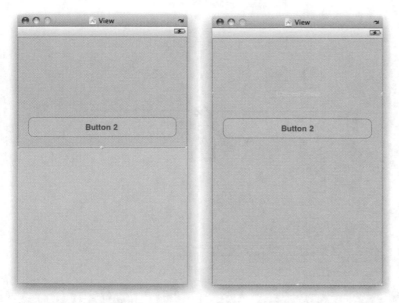

FIGURE 6-15

FIGURE 6-16

7. Select the Scroll View and view its Size Inspector window (see Figure 6-17). Observe that its size is 320 × 713 points. You will need to use this value in your code, which you will do next.

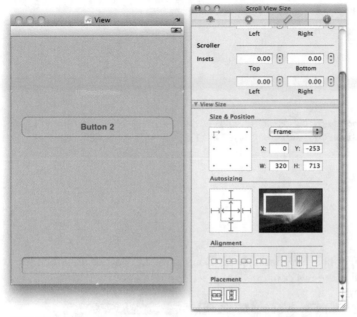

FIGURE 6-17

 NOTE *The unit of dimension used in Interface Builder is* points. *For the iPhone 3G/3GS, a point corresponds to a pixel. For the iPhone 4, a point is equal to two pixels. Specifying the size in points allows your application to work correctly on both the older and newer iPhones. The conversion between points and pixels is done automatically by the iOS.*

8. Back in Xcode, add the following code in bold to the `ScrollViewController.h` file:

```
#import <UIKit/UIKit.h>

@interface ScrollerViewController : UIViewController {
    IBOutlet UIScrollView *scrollView;
}

@property (nonatomic, retain) UIScrollView *scrollView;

@end
```

9. In Interface Builder, Control-click and drag the File's Owner item over the Scroll View. Select `scrollView`.

10. Insert the following bold code in the `ScrollerViewController.m` file:

```
#import "ScrollerViewController.h"

@implementation ScrollerViewController

@synthesize scrollView;

- (void)viewDidLoad {
    scrollView.frame = CGRectMake(0, 0, 320, 460);
    [scrollView setContentSize:CGSizeMake(320, 713)];
    [super viewDidLoad];
}

- (void)dealloc {
    [scrollView release];
    [super dealloc];
}
```

11. To test the application on the iPhone 4 Simulator, press Command-R. You can now flick the Scroll View up and down to reveal all the views contained in it (see Figure 6-18)!

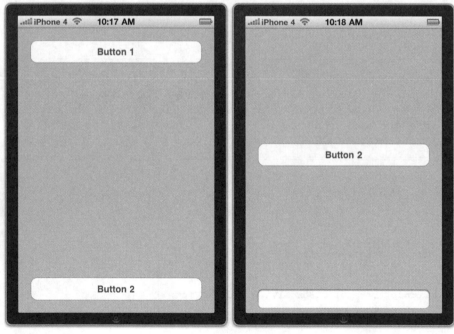

FIGURE 6-18

12. Tap on the Text Field view located at the bottom. The keyboard will automatically appear. However, observe that the Text Field view is now covered by the keyboard (see Figure 6-19). It is your duty to ensure that the current view is not hidden by the keyboard; the next section shows you how.

FIGURE 6-19

How It Works

This example is pretty straightforward. You use the Scroll View as a container for other views. If you have more views than what you can display on screen, you can expand the Scroll View and put all your views in it. The important point to remember is that you need to set the content size and the frame size of the Scroll View. The frame size determines the visible area of the Scroll View. The content size sets the overall size of the Scroll View. As long as the content size is larger than the frame size, the Scroll View will be scrollable.

Scrolling Views When the Keyboard Appears

Now that you understand how the Scroll View works, it is time to see how you can scroll all the views contained within it when the keyboard appears.

TRY IT OUT   Shifting Views

1.   Using the same project created in the previous section, add a few more Label and Text Field views to the bottom of the Scroll View (see Figure 6-20) in Interface Builder.

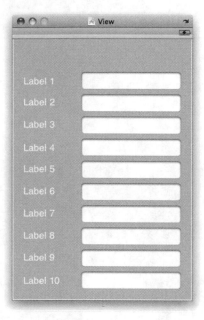

FIGURE 6-20

2.   In the `ScrollerViewController.h` file, add the following code in bold:

```
#import <UIKit/UIKit.h>

@interface ScrollerViewController : UIViewController {
    IBOutlet UIScrollView *scrollView;

    UITextField *currentTextField;
    BOOL keyboardIsShown;
}

@property (nonatomic, retain) UIScrollView *scrollView;

@end
```

3.   In Interface Builder, right-click each Text Field view and connect the `delegate` outlet to the File's Owner item.

> **NOTE** Step 3 is important because it enables the various events (`textFieldDid-BeginEditing:`, `textFieldDidEndEditing:` and `textFieldShouldReturn:`) to be handled by your View Controller.

4. Change the content size of the Scroll View to match its new size:

```
- (void)viewDidLoad {
    scrollView.frame = CGRectMake(0, 0, 320, 460);
    [scrollView setContentSize:CGSizeMake(320, 1040)];
    [super viewDidLoad];
}
```

 NOTE *You can confirm the new content size of the Scroll View by looking at its Size Inspector window.*

5. Add the following methods to the `ScrollerViewController.m` file:

```
//---before the View window appears---
-(void) viewWillAppear:(BOOL)animated {
    //---registers the notifications for keyboard---
    [[NSNotificationCenter defaultCenter]
        addObserver:self
            selector:@selector(keyboardDidShow:)
                name:UIKeyboardDidShowNotification
              object:self.view.window];

    [[NSNotificationCenter defaultCenter]
        addObserver:self
            selector:@selector(keyboardDidHide:)
                name:UIKeyboardDidHideNotification
              object:nil];
}

//---when a TextField view begins editing---
-(void) textFieldDidBeginEditing:(UITextField *)textFieldView {
    currentTextField = textFieldView;
}

//---when the user taps on the return key on the keyboard---
-(BOOL) textFieldShouldReturn:(UITextField *) textFieldView {
    [textFieldView resignFirstResponder];
    return NO;
}

//---when a TextField view is done editing---
-(void) textFieldDidEndEditing:(UITextField *) textFieldView {
    currentTextField = nil;
}

//---when the keyboard appears---
-(void) keyboardDidShow:(NSNotification *) notification {
    if (keyboardIsShown) return;

    NSDictionary* info = [notification userInfo];

    //---obtain the size of the keyboard---
```

```objectivec
    NSValue *aValue =
        [info objectForKey:UIKeyboardFrameEndUserInfoKey];
    CGRect keyboardRect =
        [self.view convertRect:[aValue CGRectValue] fromView:nil];

    NSLog(@"%f", keyboardRect.size.height);

    //---resize the scroll view (with keyboard)---
    CGRect viewFrame = [scrollView frame];
    viewFrame.size.height -= keyboardRect.size.height;
    scrollView.frame = viewFrame;

    //---scroll to the current text field---
    CGRect textFieldRect = [currentTextField frame];
    [scrollView scrollRectToVisible:textFieldRect animated:YES];

    keyboardIsShown = YES;
}


//---when the keyboard disappears---
-(void) keyboardDidHide:(NSNotification *) notification {
    NSDictionary* info = [notification userInfo];

    //---obtain the size of the keyboard---
    NSValue* aValue =
        [info objectForKey:UIKeyboardFrameEndUserInfoKey];
    CGRect keyboardRect =
        [self.view convertRect:[aValue CGRectValue] fromView:nil];

    //---resize the scroll view back to the original size
    // (without keyboard)---
    CGRect viewFrame = [scrollView frame];
    viewFrame.size.height += keyboardRect.size.height;
    scrollView.frame = viewFrame;

    keyboardIsShown = NO;
}


 //---before the View window disappear---
-(void) viewWillDisappear:(BOOL)animated {
    //---removes the notifications for keyboard---
    [[NSNotificationCenter defaultCenter]
        removeObserver:self
                name:UIKeyboardWillShowNotification
              object:nil];

    [[NSNotificationCenter defaultCenter]
        removeObserver:self
                name:UIKeyboardWillHideNotification
              object:nil];
}
```

6. Press Command-R to test the application on the iPhone 4 Simulator. Tap on the various Text Field views and observe the different views scrolling into position (see Figure 6-21).

FIGURE 6-21

How It Works

The first thing you did was connect the `delegate` outlet of each Text Field to the File's Owner item. This step is important, as it ensures that when any of the Text Field views are tapped, the following three events will be handled:

➤ `textFieldDidBeginEditing:`

➤ `textFieldDidEndEditing:`

➤ `textFieldShouldReturn:`

Because there are more views in the Scroll View than what it can display, you need to change its content size:

```
- (void)viewDidLoad {
    scrollView.frame = CGRectMake(0, 0, 320, 460);
    [scrollView setContentSize:CGSizeMake(320, 1040)];
    [super viewDidLoad];
}
```

Next, before the View window appears, you register two notifications: `UIKeyboardDidShowNotification` and `UIKeyboardDidHideNotification`. These two notifications enable you to know when the keyboard has either appeared or disappeared. You register the notifications via the `viewWillAppear:` event:

```
//---before the View window appears---
-(void) viewWillAppear:(BOOL)animated {
    //---registers the notifications for keyboard---
    [[NSNotificationCenter defaultCenter]
        addObserver:self
            selector:@selector(keyboardDidShow:)
                name:UIKeyboardDidShowNotification
              object:self.view.window];

    [[NSNotificationCenter defaultCenter]
        addObserver:self
            selector:@selector(keyboardDidHide:)
                name:UIKeyboardDidHideNotification
              object:nil];
}
```

When any of the Text Field views is tapped, the `textFieldDidBeginEditing:` event will fire:

```
//---when a TextField view begins editing---
-(void) textFieldDidBeginEditing:(UITextField *)textFieldView {
    currentTextField = textFieldView;
}
```

Here, you save a copy of the Text Field currently being tapped. When the user taps the Return key on the keyboard, the `textFieldShouldReturn:` event will be fired:

```
//---when the user taps on the return key on the keyboard---
-(BOOL) textFieldShouldReturn:(UITextField *) textFieldView {
    [textFieldView resignFirstResponder];
    return NO;
}
```

Next, you hide the keyboard by calling the `resignFirstResponder` method of the Text Field view, which then triggers another event, `textFieldDidEndEditing:`. Here, you set the `currentTextField` to `nil`:

```
//---when a TextField view is done editing---
-(void) textFieldDidEndEditing:(UITextField *) textFieldView {
    currentTextField = nil;
}
```

When the keyboard appears, it will call the `keyboardDidShow:` method (which is set via the notification):

```
//---when the keyboard appears---
-(void) keyboardDidShow:(NSNotification *) notification {
    if (keyboardIsShown) return;

    NSDictionary* info = [notification userInfo];

    //---obtain the size of the keyboard---
    NSValue *aValue =
        [info objectForKey:UIKeyboardFrameEndUserInfoKey];
```

```
    CGRect keyboardRect =
        [self.view convertRect:[aValue CGRectValue] fromView:nil];

    NSLog(@"%f", keyboardRect.size.height);

    //---resize the scroll view (with keyboard)---
    CGRect viewFrame = [scrollView frame];
    viewFrame.size.height -= keyboardRect.size.height;
    scrollView.frame = viewFrame;

    //---scroll to the current text field---
    CGRect textFieldRect = [currentTextField frame];
    [scrollView scrollRectToVisible:textFieldRect animated:YES];

    keyboardIsShown = YES;
}
```

This obtains the size of the keyboard, in particular its height. This is important, as the keyboard has different heights depending on whether it is in landscape mode or portrait mode. You then resize the view frame of the Scroll View and scroll the Text Field until it is visible.

What happens when the keyboard is visible and the user taps on another Text Field? In this case, the keyboardDidShow: method will be called again, but since the keyboardIsShown is set to YES, the method will immediately exit. If the Text Field view that is tapped is partially hidden, it will automatically be scrolled to a visible region on the View window.

When the keyboard disappears, the keyboardDidHide: method will be called:

```
    //---when the keyboard disappears---
    -(void) keyboardDidHide:(NSNotification *) notification {
        NSDictionary* info = [notification userInfo];

        //---obtain the size of the keyboard---
        NSValue* aValue =
            [info objectForKey:UIKeyboardFrameEndUserInfoKey];
        CGRect keyboardRect =
            [self.view convertRect:[aValue CGRectValue] fromView:nil];

        //---resize the scroll view back to the original size
        // (without keyboard)---
        CGRect viewFrame = [scrollView frame];
        viewFrame.size.height += keyboardRect.size.height;
        scrollView.frame = viewFrame;

        keyboardIsShown = NO;
    }
```

This restores the size of the view frame of the Scroll View to the one without the keyboard.

Finally, before the View window disappears, you remove the notifications that you set earlier:

```
    //---before the View window disappear---
    -(void) viewWillDisappear:(BOOL)animated {
        //---removes the notifications for keyboard---
        [[NSNotificationCenter defaultCenter]
```

```
            removeObserver:self
                    name:UIKeyboardWillShowNotification
                  object:nil];

    [[NSNotificationCenter defaultCenter]
         removeObserver:self
                    name:UIKeyboardWillHideNotification
                  object:nil];
    }
```

SUMMARY

In this chapter, you learned the various techniques to deal with the keyboard in your iPhone application. In particular, this chapter showed you how to hide the keyboard when you are done entering data, how to detect the presence or absence of the keyboard, and how to ensure that views are not blocked by the keyboard.

EXERCISES

1. How do you hide the keyboard for a UITextField object?

2. How do you detect whether the keyboard is visible or not?

3. How do you get the size of the keyboard?

4. How do you display more views than what the View window can display at any one time?

Answers to the Exercises can be found in Appendix E, on Wrox.com.

▶ **WHAT YOU LEARNED IN THIS CHAPTER**

TOPIC	KEY CONCEPTS
Making the keyboard go away	Use the `resignFirstResponder` method on a `UITextField` object to resign its First-Responder status.
Displaying the different types of keyboard displayed	Modify the keyboard type by changing the Text Input Traits of a `UITextField` object in the Attributes Inspector window.
Handling the return key of the keyboard	Either handle the `Did End on Exit` event of a `UITextField` object or implement the `textFieldShouldReturn:` method in your View Controller (remember to ensure that your View Controller class is the delegate for the `UITextField` object).
Making a Scroll View scrollable	Set its frame size and content size. As long as the content size is larger than the frame size, the Scroll View is scrollable.
Detecting when the keyboard appears or hides	Register for the two notifications — `UIKeyboardDidShowNotification` and `UIKeyboardDidHideNotification`.
Detecting which `UITextField` object has started editing	Implement the `textFieldDidBeginEditing:` method in your View Controller.
Detecting which `UITextField` object has ended editing	Implement the `textFieldDidEndEditing:` method in your View Controller.

7

Screen Rotations

WHAT YOU WILL LEARN IN THIS CHAPTER

➤ How to support the four different types of screen orientations

➤ The various events that are fired when a device rotates

➤ How to reposition the views on a View when the orientation of a device changes

➤ How to change the screen rotation dynamically during runtime

➤ How to set the orientation of your application before it is loaded

The Hello World! application in Chapter 2 showed you how your iPhone application supports viewing in either the portrait or landscape mode. This chapter dives deeper into the topic of screen orientation. In particular, it demonstrates how to manage the orientation of your application when the device is rotated. You will also learn how to reposition your views when the device is rotated so that your application can take advantage of the change in screen dimensions.

RESPONDING TO DEVICE ROTATIONS

One of the features that modern mobile devices support is the capability to detect the current orientation — portrait or landscape — of the device. An application can take advantage of this to readjust the device's screen to maximize use of the new orientation. A good example is Safari on the iPhone. When you rotate the device to landscape orientation, Safari automatically rotates its view so that you have a wider screen to view the content of the page (see Figure 7-1).

In the iPhone SDK, there are several events that you can handle to ensure that your application is aware of changes in orientation. Check them out in the following Try it Out.

FIGURE 7-1

TRY IT OUT | **Supporting Different Screen Orientations**

codefile ScreenRotations.zip available for download at Wrox.com

1. Using Xcode, create a new View-based Application (iPhone) project and name it ScreenRotations.

2. Press Command-R to test the application on the iPhone 4 Simulator.

3. Change the iPhone 4 Simulator orientation by pressing either the Command-→ (rotate it to the right) or Command-← (rotate it to the left) key combination. Notice that the screen orientation of your application changes with the change in device orientation (see Figure 7-2 and Figure 7-3).

How It Works

By default, the iPhone Application project you created using Xcode supports a single orientation — portrait mode. If you want to support screen orientations other than the default portrait mode, you can do so by overriding the

FIGURE 7-2

`shouldAutorotateToInterfaceOrientation:` method in a View Controller. This event is commented out by default in the `ScreenRotationsViewController.m` file:

```
// Override to allow orientations other than the default portrait orientation.
- (BOOL)shouldAutorotateToInterfaceOrientation:
(UIInterfaceOrientation)interfaceOrientation {
    // Return YES for supported orientations
    return (interfaceOrientation == UIInterfaceOrientationPortrait);
}
```

FIGURE 7-3

 NOTE On the iPad, the default behavior of an application supports all orientations — portrait as well as landscape. While you can specify the orientation supported by your application, based on the UI guidelines provided by Apple, iPad applications should support all screen orientations.

 NOTE On the iPhone and iPad, screen rotation is automatically handled by the OS. When the OS detects a change in screen orientation, it fires the `shouldAutorotateToInterfaceOrientation:` event; it is up to the developer to decide how the application should display in the target orientation.

The `shouldAutorotateToInterfaceOrientation:` method is called when the View is loaded and whenever orientation of the device changes. This method passes in a single parameter — the orientation to which the device has been changed. The returning value of this method determines whether the current orientation is supported. By default, your iPhone application supports only the portrait orientation; hence, it simply returns a YES only when the interfaceOrientation argument is equal to portrait mode (UIInterfaceOrientationPortrait):

```
return (interfaceOrientation == UIInterfaceOrientationPortrait);
```

This means that your application will display upright only in portrait mode. To support all orientations, simply return a YES to allow your application to display upright for all orientations:

```
// Override to allow orientations other than the default portrait
// orientation.
- (BOOL)shouldAutorotateToInterfaceOrientation:
(UIInterfaceOrientation)interfaceOrientation {
    // Return YES for supported orientations
    //return (interfaceOrientation ==
    //        UIInterfaceOrientationPortrait);
    return YES;
}
```

> **NOTE** To easily differentiate between UIInterfaceOrientationLandscapeLeft and UIInterfaceOrientationLandscapeRight, *just remember that* UIInterface OrientationLandscapeLeft *refers to the Home button positioned on the left, and* UIInterfaceOrientationLandscapeRight *refers to the Home button positioned on the right.*

Different Types of Screen Orientations

You have a total of four constants to use for specifying screen orientations:

➤ UIInterfaceOrientationPortrait — Displays the screen in portrait mode.

➤ UIInterfaceOrientationPortraitUpsideDown — Displays the screen in portrait mode but with the Home button at the top of the screen.

➤ UIInterfaceOrientationLandscapeLeft — Displays the screen in landscape mode with the Home button on the left.

➤ UIInterfaceOrientationLandscapeRight — Displays the screen in landscape mode with the Home button on the right.

If your application supports multiple screen orientations, override the shouldAutorotateTo-InterfaceOrientation: method and then use the || (logical OR) operator to specify all the orientations it supports, like this:

```
- (BOOL)shouldAutorotateToInterfaceOrientation:
(UIInterfaceOrientation)interfaceOrientation {
    // Return YES for supported orientations
```

```
     return (interfaceOrientation == UIInterfaceOrientationPortrait ||
            interfaceOrientation == UIInterfaceOrientationLandscapeLeft);
}
```

The preceding code snippet enables your application to support both the portrait and landscape left modes.

Handling Rotations

The View Controller exposes several events that you can handle during the rotation of the screen. The capability to handle events fired during rotation is important because it enables you to reposition the views on the View, or you can stop media playback while the screen is rotating. You can handle the following events:

➤   willAnimateFirstHalfOfRotationToInterfaceOrientation:

➤   willAnimateSecondHalfOfRotationFromInterfaceOrientation:

➤   willRotateToInterfaceOrientation:

➤   willAnimateRotationToInterfaceOrientation:

The next several sections take a more detailed look at each of these events.

willAnimateFirstHalfOfRotationToInterfaceOrientation:

The willAnimateFirstHalfOfRotationToInterfaceOrientation: event is fired just before the rotation of the View window starts. The method looks like this:

```
- (void)willAnimateFirstHalfOfRotationToInterfaceOrientation:
(UIInterfaceOrientation) toInterfaceOrientation
    duration:(NSTimeInterval) duration {

}
```

The toInterfaceOrientation parameter indicates the orientation to which the View window is changing, and the duration parameter indicates the duration of the first half of the rotation, in seconds.

In this event, you can insert your code to carry out tasks that you want to perform before the rotation starts, such as pausing media playback, pausing animations, and so on.

willAnimateSecondHalfOfRotationFromInterfaceOrientation:

The willAnimateSecondHalfOfRotationFromInterfaceOrientation: event is fired when the rotation is halfway through. The method looks like this:

```
- (void)willAnimateSecondHalfOfRotationFromInterfaceOrientation:
(UIInterfaceOrientation) fromInterfaceOrientation
    duration:(NSTimeInterval) duration {

}
```

The `fromInterfaceOrientation` parameter indicates the orientation from which it is changing, whereas the `duration` parameter indicates the duration of the second half of the rotation, in seconds.

In this event, you typically perform tasks such as repositioning the views on the View window, resuming media playback, and so on.

willRotateToInterfaceOrientation:

The previous two events are fired consecutively —
first `willAnimateFirstHalfOfRotationTo-InterfaceOrientation:`, followed by `willAnimateSecondHalfOfRotationFromInterface-Orientation`. If you don't need two separate events for handling rotation, you can use the simpler `willRotateToInterfaceOrientation:` event.

The `willRotateToInterfaceOrientation:` event is fired before the orientation starts. In contrast to the previous two events, this is a one-step process. Note that if you handle this event, the `willAnimateFirstHalfOfRotationToInterfaceOrientation:` and `willAnimateSecondHalfOfRotationFromInterfaceOrientation:` events will still be fired.

The method looks like this:

```
- (void)willRotateToInterfaceOrientation:
(UIInterfaceOrientation) toInterfaceOrientation
    duration:(NSTimeInterval) duration {

}
```

The `toInterfaceOrientation` parameter indicates the orientation to which it is changing, and the `duration` parameter indicates the duration of the rotation, in seconds.

willAnimateRotationToInterfaceOrientation:

The `willAnimateRotationToInterfaceOrientation:` event is fired before the animation of the rotation starts.

> **NOTE** If you handle both the `willRotateToInterfaceOrientation:` and `willAnimateRotationToInterfaceOrientation:` events, the former will fire first, followed by the latter.

The method looks like this:

```
- (void)willAnimateSecondHalfOfRotationFromInterfaceOrientation:
(UIInterfaceOrientation) fromInterfaceOrientation
    duration:(NSTimeInterval) duration {

}
```

The `interfaceOrientation` parameter specifies the target orientation to which it is rotating.

NOTE *If you handle this event, the* `willAnimateFirstHalfOfRotationTo-`
`InterfaceOrientation:` *and*
`willAnimateSecondHalfOfRotationFrom-InterfaceOrientation:`
events will not fire anymore.

In the following Try It Out, you will reposition the views on your user interface (UI) when the device changes orientation.

TRY IT OUT Repositioning Views during Orientation Change

1. Using the project created earlier, double-click the `ScreenRotationsViewController.xib` file and add a Round Rect Button view to the View (see Figure 7-4).

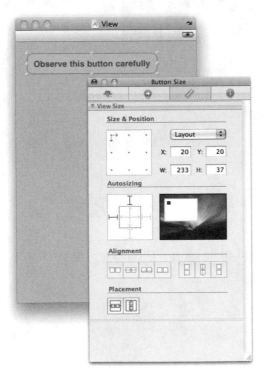

FIGURE 7-4

2. Observe its size and positioning by viewing the Size Inspector window. Here, its position is (20,20) and its size is 233 by 37 points.

3. Rotate the orientation of the View window by clicking the arrow icon on the upper-right corner of the window.

4. Reposition the Round Rect Button view by relocating it to the bottom-right corner of the View window (see Figure 7-5). Also observe and take note of its position.

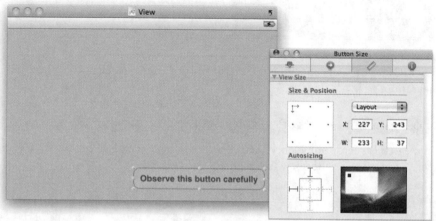

FIGURE 7-5

5. In the `ScreenRotationsViewController.h` file, add the following code shown in bold:

```
#import <UIKit/UIKit.h>

@interface ScreenRotationsViewController : UIViewController {
    IBOutlet UIButton *btn;
}

@property (nonatomic, retain) UIButton *btn;

@end
```

6. In Interface Builder, connect the outlet you have created by control-clicking the File's Owner item and dragging over to the Round Rect Button view. Select `btn`.

7. Save the project in Interface Builder.

8. In the `ScreenRotationsViewController.m` file, add the following bold code:

```
#import "ScreenRotationsViewController.h"

@implementation ScreenRotationsViewController

@synthesize btn;

-(void) positionViews {
    UIInterfaceOrientation destOrientation = self.interfaceOrientation;
    if (destOrientation == UIInterfaceOrientationPortrait ||
        destOrientation == UIInterfaceOrientationPortraitUpsideDown) {
        //---if rotating to portrait mode---
        btn.frame = CGRectMake(20, 20, 233, 37);
    } else {
```

```
            //---if rotating to landscape mode---
            btn.frame = CGRectMake(227, 243, 233, 37);
        }
    }

    - (void)willAnimateSecondHalfOfRotationFromInterfaceOrientation:
    (UIInterfaceOrientation) fromInterfaceOrientation
        duration:(NSTimeInterval) duration {
        [self positionViews];
    }

    - (void)viewDidLoad {
        [self positionViews];
        [super viewDidLoad];
    }

    - (void)dealloc {
        [btn release];
        [super dealloc];
    }
```

9. Save the project and press Command-R in Xcode to deploy the application onto the iPhone 4 Simulator.

10. Observe that when the iPhone 4 Simulator is in portrait mode, the Round Rect Button view is displayed in the top-left corner; but when you change the orientation to landscape mode, it is repositioned to the bottom-right corner (see Figure 7-6).

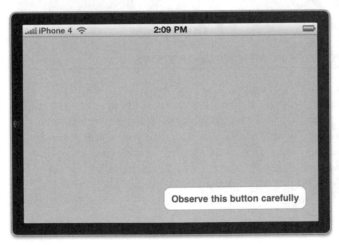

FIGURE 7-6

How It Works

This project illustrates how you can reposition the views on your application when the device changes orientation. You first create an outlet and connect it to the Round Rect Button view on the View window.

When the device is being rotated, you handle the `willAnimateSecondHalfOfRotationFrom-InterfaceOrientation:` event so that you can reposition the Round Rect Button. When this event is fired, you can obtain the destination orientation using the `interfaceOrientation` property of the current View window (`self`), like this:

```
UIInterfaceOrientation destOrientation = self.interfaceOrientation;
```

Using this information, you position the Button view according to the destination orientation by altering its `frame` property via the `positionViews` method, which you have defined:

```
-(void) positionViews {
    UIInterfaceOrientation destOrientation = self.interfaceOrientation;
    if (destOrientation == UIInterfaceOrientationPortrait ||
        destOrientation == UIInterfaceOrientationPortraitUpsideDown) {
        //---if rotating to portrait mode---
        btn.frame = CGRectMake(20, 20, 233, 37);
    } else {
        //---if rotating to landscape mode---
        btn.frame = CGRectMake(227, 243, 233, 37);
    }
}
```

You should also call the `positionViews` method in the `viewDidLoad` method so that the Round Rect Button can be displayed correctly when the View window is loaded:

```
- (void)viewDidLoad {
    [self positionViews];
    [super viewDidLoad];
}
```

PROPERTIES FOR DEALING WITH POSITIONING OF VIEWS

In the previous example, you used the `frame` property to change the position of a view during runtime. The `frame` property defines the rectangle occupied by the view, with respect to its superview (the view that contains it). Using the `frame` property enables you to set the positioning and size of a view. Besides using the `frame` property, you can also use the `center` property, which sets the center of the view, also with respect to its superview. You usually use the `center` property when you are performing some animation and just want to change the position of a view.

PROGRAMMATICALLY ROTATING THE SCREEN

You've seen how your application can handle the changes in device orientation when the user rotates the device. Sometimes (such as when you are developing a game), however, you want to force the application to display in certain rotations independently of the device's orientation.

There are two scenarios to consider:

➤ Rotating the screen orientation during runtime when your application is running

➤ Displaying the screen in a particular orientation when the View window is loaded

Rotating During Runtime

During runtime, you can programmatically rotate the screen by using the `setOrientation:` method on an instance of the `UIDevice` class. Suppose you want users to change the screen orientation: They press the Round Rect Button view. Using the project created earlier, you can code it as follows:

```
-(IBAction) btnClicked: (id) sender{
    [[UIDevice currentDevice]
        setOrientation:UIInterfaceOrientationLandscapeLeft];
}
```

The `setOrientation:` method takes a single parameter specifying the orientation to which you want to change.

> **NOTE** After you have programmatically switched the orientation of your application, your application's rotation can still be changed when the device is physically rotated. The orientation that it can be changed to is dependent on what you set in the `shouldAutorotateToInterfaceOrientation:` method.

Displaying the View Window in a Specific Orientation When Loading

When a View window is loaded, by default it is always displayed in portrait mode. If your application requires that you display the View window in a particular orientation when it is loaded, you can do so by adding a new key (`Initial interface orientation`) to the `info.plist` file located in the `Resources` folder of your Xcode project. Setting it to one of the four values shown in Figure 7-7 will force your application to start in the specified orientation.

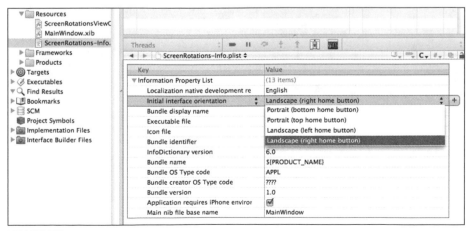

FIGURE 7-7

NOTE *The orientation to which you are changing must first be specified in the* `shouldAutorotateToInterfaceOrientation:` *event.*

SUMMARY

This chapter explained how changes in screen orientations are handled by the various events in the View Controller class. Proper handling of screen orientations will make your application more use-able and improve the user experience.

EXERCISES

1. Suppose you want your application to support only the landscape right and landscape left orientation. How should you modify your code?

2. What is the difference between the `frame` and `center` property of a view?

Answers to the Exercises can be found in Appendix E, on Wrox.com.

▶ **WHAT YOU LEARNED IN THIS CHAPTER**

TOPIC	KEY CONCEPTS

How to handle device rotations	Implement the `shouldAutorotateToInterfaceOrientation:` method
	`willAnimateSecondHalfOfRotationFromInterfaceOrientation:`
	`willRotateToInterfaceOrientation:`
	`willAnimateRotationToInterfaceOrientation:`

Four orientations supported	`UIInterfaceOrientationPortrait`
	`UIInterfaceOrientationLandscapeLeft`
	`UIInterfaceOrientationLandscapeRight`
	`UIInterfaceOrientationPortraitUpsideDown`

Events fired when device is rotated	`willAnimateFirstHalfOfRotationToInterfaceOrientation:`
Properties for changing the position of a view	Use the `frame` property for changing the positioning and size of a view Use the `center` property for changing the positioning of a view
Displaying the View window in a specific orientation when loading	Add a new key (`Initial interface orientation`) to the `info.plist` file in your Xcode project and set it to the desired orientation

PART II
Displaying and Persisting Data

Using the Table View

WHAT YOU WILL LEARN IN THIS CHAPTER

➤ Manually adding a Table view to a view, and wire the data source and delegate to your View Controller

➤ Handling the various events in the Table view to populate it with items

➤ Handling the various events in the Table view so that users can select the items it contains

➤ Displaying text and images in the rows of the Table view

➤ Displaying the items from a property list in a Table view

➤ Grouping the items in a Table view into sections

➤ Adding indexing to the Table view

➤ Adding search capabilities to the Table view

➤ Adding disclosures and checkmarks to rows in the Table view

➤ Navigating to another View window

One of the most commonly used views in iPhone applications is the Table view. The Table view is used to display lists of items from which users can select, or they can tap it to display more information about a particular item. Figure 8-1 shows a Table view in action in the Settings application.

The Table view is such an important topic that it deserves a chapter of its own. Hence, in this chapter, you examine the Table view in details, and learn about the various building blocks that make it such a versatile view.

FIGURE 8-1

A SIMPLE TABLE VIEW

The best way to understand how to use a Table view in your application is to create a new View-based Application project and then manually add a Table view to the View window and wire it to a View Controller. That way, you understand the various building blocks of the Table view.

Without further ado, use the following Try It Out to create a new project and see how to put a Table view together!

TRY IT OUT   Using a Table View

Codefile [TableViewExample.zip] available for download at Wrox.com

1. Create a new View-based Application (iPhone) project and name it TableViewExample.

2. Double-click the TableViewExampleViewController.xib file to edit it in Interface Builder.

3. Drag the Table View Object from the Library and drop it onto the View window (see Figure 8-2).

4. Right-click the Table view and connect the dataSource outlet to the File's Owner item (see Figure 8-3). Do the same for the delegate outlet.

FIGURE 8-2

FIGURE 8-3

5. In the `TableViewExampleViewController.h` file, add the following statement that appears in bold:

```
#import <UIKit/UIKit.h>

@interface TableViewExampleViewController : UIViewController
    <UITableViewDataSource> {

}

@end
```

6. In the `TableViewExampleViewController.m` file, add the following statements that appear in bold:

```
#import "TableViewExampleViewController.h"

@implementation TableViewExampleViewController

NSMutableArray *listOfMovies;

//---insert individual row into the table view---
- (UITableViewCell *)tableView:(UITableView *)tableView
        cellForRowAtIndexPath:(NSIndexPath *)indexPath {

    static NSString *CellIdentifier = @"Cell";

    //---try to get a reusable cell---
    UITableViewCell *cell =
        [tableView dequeueReusableCellWithIdentifier:CellIdentifier];

    //---create new cell if no reusable cell is available---
    if (cell == nil) {
        cell = [[[UITableViewCell alloc] initWithStyle:UITableViewCellStyleDefault
                                    reuseIdentifier:CellIdentifier]
                                    autorelease];
    }

    //---set the text to display for the cell---
    NSString *cellValue = [listOfMovies objectAtIndex:indexPath.row];
    cell.textLabel.text = cellValue;

    return cell;
}

//---set the number of rows in the table view---
- (NSInteger)tableView:(UITableView *)tableView
 numberOfRowsInSection:(NSInteger)section {
    return [listOfMovies count];
}

- (void)viewDidLoad {
    //---initialize the array---
    listOfMovies = [[NSMutableArray alloc] init];

    //---add items---
```

```
    [listOfMovies addObject:@"Training Day"];
    [listOfMovies addObject:@"Remember the Titans"];
    [listOfMovies addObject:@"John Q."];
    [listOfMovies addObject:@"The Bone Collector"];
    [listOfMovies addObject:@"Ricochet"];
    [listOfMovies addObject:@"The Siege"];
    [listOfMovies addObject:@"Malcolm X"];
    [listOfMovies addObject:@"Antwone Fisher"];
    [listOfMovies addObject:@"Courage Under Fire"];
    [listOfMovies addObject:@"He Got Game"];
    [listOfMovies addObject:@"The Pelican Brief"];
    [listOfMovies addObject:@"Glory"];
    [listOfMovies addObject:@"The Preacher's Wife"];

    [super viewDidLoad];
}

- (void)dealloc {
    [listOfMovies release];
    [super dealloc];
}
```

7. Press Command-R to test the application on the iPhone 4 Simulator. Figure 8-4 shows the Table view displaying a list of movies.

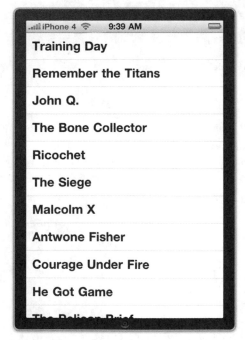

FIGURE 8-4

How It Works

You start the application by creating an NSMutableArray object called listOfMovies containing a list of movie names. The items stored in this array will be displayed by the Table view.

> **NOTE** *The use of an array to contain the items to be displayed by the Table view is purely for demonstration. Of course, in a real-world scenario, your data might be stored in a database or accessed from a Web service.*

```
- (void)viewDidLoad {
    //---initialize the array---
    listOfMovies = [[NSMutableArray alloc] init];

    //---add items---
    [listOfMovies addObject:@"Training Day"];
    [listOfMovies addObject:@"Remember the Titans"];
    [listOfMovies addObject:@"John Q."];
    [listOfMovies addObject:@"The Bone Collector"];
    [listOfMovies addObject:@"Ricochet"];
    [listOfMovies addObject:@"The Siege"];
    [listOfMovies addObject:@"Malcolm X"];
    [listOfMovies addObject:@"Antwone Fisher"];
    [listOfMovies addObject:@"Courage Under Fire"];
    [listOfMovies addObject:@"He Got Game"];
    [listOfMovies addObject:@"The Pelican Brief"];
    [listOfMovies addObject:@"Glory"];
    [listOfMovies addObject:@"The Preacher's Wife"];

    [super viewDidLoad];
}
```

To populate the Table view with items, you need to handle several events contained in the UITableViewDataSource protocol. Hence, you need to ensure that your View Controller conforms to this protocol:

```
@interface TableViewExampleViewController : UIViewController
    <UITableViewDataSource> {

}

@end
```

> **NOTE** *Strictly speaking, if you have connected the dataSource outlet to the File's Owner item, you don't need to add the preceding statement. However, doing both doesn't hurt anything. There is one advantage to adding the <UITableViewDataSource> protocol, though — the compiler will warn you if you forget to implement any mandatory methods in your code, helping to prevent errors.*

The UITableViewDataSource protocol contains several events that you can implement to supply data to the Table view. Two events that you have handled in this example are as follows:

➤ tableView:numberOfRowsInSection:

➤ tableView:cellForRowAtIndexPath:

The tableView:numberOfRowsInSection: event indicates how many rows you want the Table view to display. In this case, you set it to the number of items in the listOfMovies array.

```
//---set the number of rows in the table view---
- (NSInteger)tableView:(UITableView *)tableView
 numberOfRowsInSection:(NSInteger)section {
    return [listOfMovies count];
}
```

The tableView:cellForRowAtIndexPath: event inserts a cell in a particular location of the Table view. This event is fired once for each row of the Table view that is visible.

One of the parameters contained in the tableView:didSelectRowAtIndexPath: event is of the type NSIndexPath. The NSIndexPath class represents the path of a specific item in a nested array collection. To know which row is currently being populated, you simply call the row property of the NSIndexPath object (indexPath) and then use the row number to reference against the listOfMovies array. The value is then used to set the text value of the row in the Table view:

```
//---insert individual row into the table view---
- (UITableViewCell *)tableView:(UITableView *)tableView
         cellForRowAtIndexPath:(NSIndexPath *)indexPath {
    static NSString *CellIdentifier = @"Cell";

    //---try to get a reusable cell---
    UITableViewCell *cell =
        [tableView dequeueReusableCellWithIdentifier:
            CellIdentifier];

    //---create new cell if no reusable cell is available---
    if (cell == nil) {
        cell = [[[UITableViewCell alloc]
                initWithStyle:UITableViewCellStyleDefault
              reuseIdentifier:CellIdentifier]
              autorelease];
    }

    //---set the text to display for the cell---
    NSString *cellValue =
        [listOfMovies objectAtIndex:indexPath.row];
    cell.textLabel.text = cellValue;

    return cell;
}
```

Specifically, you use the dequeueReusableCellWithIdentifier: method of the UITableView class to obtain an instance of the UITableViewCell class. The dequeueReusableCellWithIdentifier: method returns a reusable Table view cell object. This is important because if you have a large table (say, with

10,000 rows) and you create a single UITableViewCell object for each row, you would generate a great performance and memory hit. Also, because a Table view displays only a fixed number of rows at any one time, reusing the cells that have been scrolled out of view makes sense. This is exactly what the dequeueReusableCellWithIdentifier: method does. Therefore, for example, if 10 rows are visible in the Table view, only 10 UITableViewCell objects are ever created — they are always reused when the user scrolls through the Table view.

As the user flicks the Table view to review more rows (that are hidden), the tableView:cellForRowAtIndexPath: event is continually fired, enabling you to populate the newly visible rows with data.

 NOTE *The* tableView:cellForRowAtIndexPath: *event is not fired continuously from start to finish. For example, if the Table view has 100 rows to be displayed, the event is fired continuously for the first, say, 10 rows that are visible. When the user scrolls down the Table view, the* tableView:cellForRowAtIndexPath: *event is fired for the next couple of visible rows.*

Adding a Header and Footer

You can display a header and footer for the Table view by simply implementing the following two methods in your View Controller:

```
- (NSString *)tableView:(UITableView *)tableView
titleForHeaderInSection:(NSInteger)section{
    //---display "Movie List" as the header---
    return @"Movie List";
}

- (NSString *)tableView:(UITableView *)tableView
titleForFooterInSection:(NSInteger)section {
    //---display "by Denzel Washington" as the footer---
    return @"by Denzel Washington";
}
```

If you insert the preceding statements in the TableViewExampleViewController.m file and rerun the application, you see the header and footer of the Table view, as shown in Figure 8-5.

Adding an Image

In addition to text, you can display an image next to the text of a cell in a Table view. Suppose you have an image named apple.jpeg in the Resources folder of your project (see Figure 8-6).

NOTE You can simply drag and drop an image to the Resources *folder of Xcode. When prompted, ensure that you save a copy of the image in your project.*

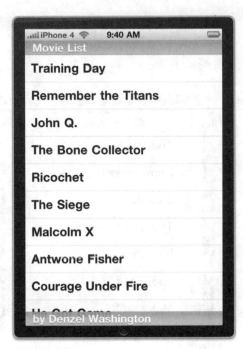

FIGURE 8-5

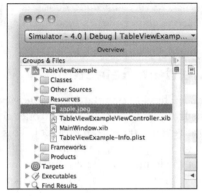

FIGURE 8-6

To display an image next to the text of a cell, insert the following statements that appear in bold into the `tableView:cellForRowAtIndexPath:` method:

```
//---insert individual row into the table view---
- (UITableViewCell *)tableView:(UITableView *)tableView
        cellForRowAtIndexPath:(NSIndexPath *)indexPath {
    static NSString *CellIdentifier = @"Cell";

    //---try to get a reusable cell---
    UITableViewCell *cell =
        [tableView dequeueReusableCellWithIdentifier:CellIdentifier];

    //---create new cell if no reusable cell is available---
    if (cell == nil) {
        cell = [[[UITableViewCell alloc] initWithStyle:UITableViewCellStyleDefault
                                    reuseIdentifier:CellIdentifier]
                                    autorelease];
```

```
        }

        //---set the text to display for the cell---
        NSString *cellValue = [listOfMovies objectAtIndex:indexPath.row];
        cell.textLabel.text = cellValue;

        //---display an image---
        UIImage *image = [UIImage imageNamed:@"apple.jpeg"];
        cell.imageView.image = image;

        return cell;
    }
```

Press Command-R to test the application. You'll see that the image is displayed next to each row (see Figure 8-7).

Notice that the UITableViewCell object already has the imageView property. All you need to do is create an instance of the UIImage class and then load the image from the Resources folder of your project.

Displaying the Item Selected

So far, you have seen how to populate the Table view with items by ensuring that your View Controller conforms to the UITableViewDataSource protocol. This protocol takes care of populating the Table view, but if you want to select the items in a Table view, you need to conform to another protocol — UITableViewDelegate.

The UITableViewDelegate protocol contains events that enable you to manage selections, edit and delete rows, and display a header and footer for each section of a Table view.

To use the UITableViewDelegate protocol, modify the TableViewExampleViewController.h file by adding the statement in bold as follows:

FIGURE 8-7

```
#import <UIKit/UIKit.h>

@interface TableViewExampleViewController : UIViewController
    <UITableViewDataSource,
    UITableViewDelegate> {

}

@end
```

Again, if you have connected the `delegate` outlet to the File's Owner item previously (see Figure 8-8), you don't need to add the preceding statement (`UITableViewDelegate`). However, doing both doesn't hurt.

FIGURE 8-8

The following Try It Out shows how you can enable users to make selections in a Table view.

TRY IT OUT   Making a Selection in a Table View

1.   Using the same project created earlier, add the following method to the `TableViewExampleViewController.m` file:

```
- (void)tableView:(UITableView *)tableView
didSelectRowAtIndexPath:(NSIndexPath *)indexPath {
    NSString *movieSelected = [listOfMovies objectAtIndex:indexPath.row];
    NSString *msg = [NSString stringWithFormat:@"You have selected %@",
                          movieSelected];
    UIAlertView *alert = [[UIAlertView alloc] initWithTitle:@"Movie selected"
                                            message:msg
                                            delegate:self
                                    cancelButtonTitle:@"OK"
                                    otherButtonTitles:nil];

    [alert show];
    [alert release];
}
```

2. Press Command-R to test the application on the iPhone 4 Simulator.

3. Select a row by tapping it. When a row is selected, an Alert view displays the row you have selected (see Figure 8-9).

FIGURE 8-9

How It Works

One of the events declared in the UITableViewDelegate protocol is tableView:didSelectRowAtIndexPath:, which is fired when the user selects a row in the Table view.

As usual, to determine which row has been selected, you simply call the row property of the NSIndexPath object (indexPath) and then use the row number to reference against the listOfMovies array:

```
NSString *movieSelected = [listOfMovies objectAtIndex:indexPath.row];
```

After the selected movie is retrieved, you simply display it using the UIAlertView class:

```
NSString *msg = [NSString stringWithFormat:@"You have selected %@",
                    movieSelected];
UIAlertView *alert = [[UIAlertView alloc] initWithTitle:@"Movie selected"
                                        message:msg
                                        delegate:self
                                  cancelButtonTitle:@"OK"
                                  otherButtonTitles:nil];

[alert show];
[alert release];
```

NOTE The *row* property of the NSIndexPath class is one of the additions made by the UIKit framework to enable the identification of rows and sections in a Table view, so be aware that the original class definition of the NSIndexPath class does not contain the *row* property.

Indenting

Another event in the UITableViewDelegate protocol is tableView:indentationLevelForRowAtIndexPath:. When you handle this event, it is fired for every row that is visible on the screen. To set an indentation for a particular row, simply return an integer indicating the level of indentation:

```
- (NSInteger)tableView:(UITableView *)tableView
indentationLevelForRowAtIndexPath:(NSIndexPath *)indexPath {
    return [indexPath row] % 2;
}
```

In the preceding example, the indentation alternates between 0 and 1, depending on the current row number. Figure 8-10 shows how the Table view looks if you insert the preceding code in the TableViewExampleViewController.m file.

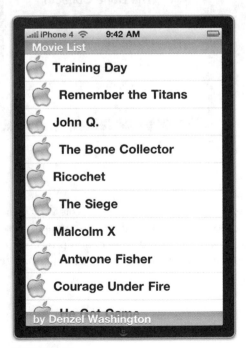

FIGURE 8-10

Modifying the Height of Each Row

Another method defined in the `UITableViewDelegate` protocol is `tableView:heightForRowAtIndexPath:`. This method enables you to modify the height of each row. The following method shows that each row now takes up 70 points (see Figure 8-11):

```
- (CGFloat)tableView:(UITableView *)tableView
heightForRowAtIndexPath:(NSIndexPath *)indexPath {
    return 70;
}
```

USING THE TABLE VIEW IN A NAVIGATION-BASED APPLICATION

In the previous sections, you created a View-based Application project and then manually added a Table view to the View window and connected the data source and delegate to the File's Owner item. You then handled all the relevant events defined in the two protocols, `UITableViewDelegate` and `UITableViewDataSource`, so that you can populate the Table view with items as well as make them selectable.

In real life, the Table view is often used with a Navigation-based Application project because it is very common for users to select an item from a Table view and then navigate to another screen showing the details of the item selected. For this reason, the Navigation-based Application template in the iPhone SDK by default uses the `TableView` class instead of the `View` class. This section demonstrates how to use a Table view from within a Navigation-based Application project.

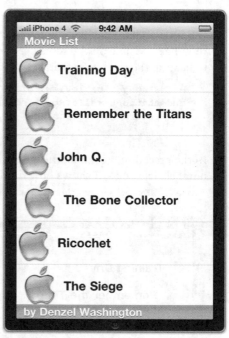

FIGURE 8-11

DISPLAYING SECTIONS

In addition to displaying a series of rows in a Table view, you can group items in a Table view into sections so that you can group related items with a header for each section. In the following Try It Out, you learn how to use the Table view from within a Navigation-based Application project and group the items into sections. At the same time, you learn how to display items stored in a property list, as opposed to an array.

| TRY IT OUT | Displaying Sections in a Table View |

Codefile [TableView.zip] available for download at Wrox.com

1. Create a new Navigation-based Application project and name it `TableView`.

2. Double-click the `RootViewController.xib` file to edit it in Interface Builder.

3. Notice that in the `RootViewController.xib` window you now have a `TableView` item instead of the usual `View` item (see Figure 8-12).

4. Double-click the `TableView` item and observe that you have a Table view within it (see Figure 8-13).

FIGURE 8-12

FIGURE 8-13

5. Examine the `RootViewController.h` file and notice that the `RootViewController` class now extends the `UITableViewController` base class:

```
#import <UIKit/UIKit.h>

@interface RootViewController : UITableViewController {
}

@end
```

6. Also examine the `RootViewController.m` file and observe that it includes a number of event stubs that you can implement.

7. Right-click the `Resources` folder and choose Add ➪ New File.

8. Select the Resource category (under Mac OS X) on the left of the New File dialog and select the Property List template on the right (see Figure 8-14).

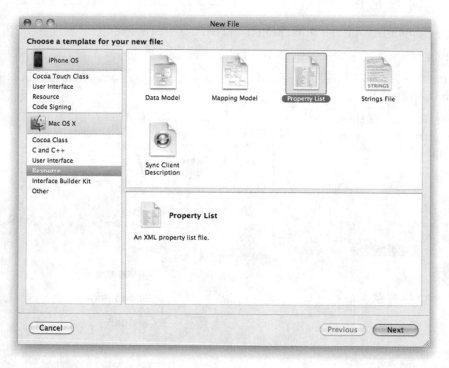

FIGURE 8-14

9. Name the property list `Movies.plist`. The property list is now saved in the `Resources` folder of your project. Select it and create the list of items as shown in Figure 8-15.

10. In the `RootViewController.h` file, add the following statements that appear in bold:

```objc
#import <UIKit/UIKit.h>

@interface RootViewController : UITableViewController {
    NSDictionary *movieTitles;
    NSArray *years;
}

@property (nonatomic, retain) NSDictionary *movieTitles;
@property (nonatomic, retain) NSArray *years;

@end
```

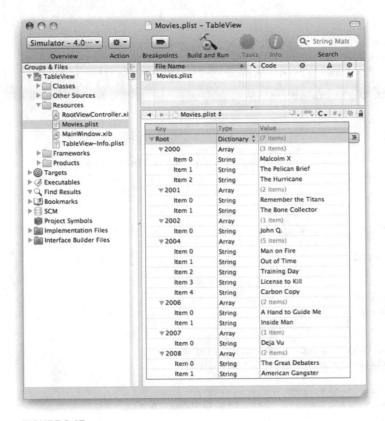

FIGURE 8-15

11. In the `RootViewController.m` file, add the following statements that appear in bold:

```
#import "RootViewController.h"

@implementation RootViewController

@synthesize movieTitles;
@synthesize years;

- (void)viewDidLoad {
    //---path to the property list file---
    NSString *path = [[NSBundle mainBundle] pathForResource:@"Movies"
                                                     ofType:@"plist"];

    //---load the list into the dictionary---
    NSDictionary *dic = [[NSDictionary alloc] initWithContentsOfFile:path];

    //---save the dictionary object to the property---
    self.movieTitles = dic;
```

```objc
    [dic release];

    //---get all the keys in the dictionary object and sort them---
    NSArray *array = [[self.movieTitles allKeys]
                        sortedArrayUsingSelector:@selector(compare:)];

    //---save the keys in the years property---
    self.years = array;

    [super viewDidLoad];

    // Uncomment the following line to display an Edit button in the navigation
        bar for this view controller.
    // self.navigationItem.rightBarButtonItem = self.editButtonItem;
}

- (NSInteger)numberOfSectionsInTableView:(UITableView *)tableView {
    //return 1;
    return [self.years count];
}

- (NSInteger)tableView:(UITableView *)tableView
 numberOfRowsInSection:(NSInteger)section {
    //return 0;

    //---check the current year based on the section index---
    NSString *year = [self.years objectAtIndex:section];

    //---returns the movies in that year as an array---
    NSArray *movieSection = [self.movieTitles objectForKey:year];

    //---return the number of movies for that year as the number of rows in that
    // section ---
    return [movieSection count];
}

- (UITableViewCell *)tableView:(UITableView *)tableView
         cellForRowAtIndexPath:(NSIndexPath *)indexPath {
    static NSString *CellIdentifier = @"Cell";

    UITableViewCell *cell =
        [tableView dequeueReusableCellWithIdentifier:CellIdentifier];

    if (cell == nil) {
        cell = [[[UITableViewCell alloc] initWithStyle:UITableViewCellStyleDefault
                                    reuseIdentifier:CellIdentifier]
                                    autorelease];
    }

    // Configure the cell.
    //---get the year---
    NSString *year = [self.years objectAtIndex:[indexPath section]];

    //---get the list of movies for that year---
```

```
    NSArray *movieSection = [self.movieTitles objectForKey:year];

    //---get the particular movie based on that row---
    cell.textLabel.text = [movieSection objectAtIndex:[indexPath row]];

    return cell;
}

- (NSString *)tableView:(UITableView *)tableView
titleForHeaderInSection:(NSInteger)section {
    //---get the year as the section header---
    NSString *year = [self.years objectAtIndex:section];
    return year;
}

- (void)dealloc {
    [movieTitles release];
    [years release];
    [super dealloc];
}
```

12. Press Command-R to test the application on the iPhone 4 Simulator. You can now see the movies grouped into sections organized by year (see Figure 8-16).

FIGURE 8-16

13. You can also change the style of the Table view by clicking the `TableView` item in Interface Builder and then changing the `Style` property in the Attributes Inspector window to `Grouped` (see Figure 8-17).

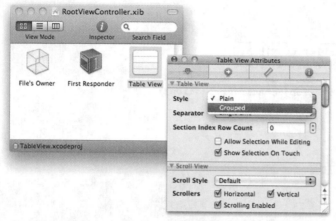

FIGURE 8-17

14. If you rerun the application, the appearance of the Table view is now different (see Figure 8-18).

FIGURE 8-18

How It Works

This exercise covered quite a number of concepts, and you may need some time to absorb them all. First, you created a property list in your project. You populated the property list with several key/value pairs. Essentially, you can visualize the key/value pairs stored in the property list as shown in Figure 8-19.

Key	Value
2000	"Malcolm x", "The Pelican Brief", "The Hurricane"
2001	"Remember the Titans", "The Bone Collector"
2002	"John Q."
2004	"Man on Fire", "Out of Time", "Training Day", "License to Kill", "Carbon Copy"
2006	"A Hand to Guide Me", "Inside Man"
2007	"Deja Vu"
2008	"The Great Debaters", "American Gangster"

FIGURE 8-19

Each key represents a year, and the value for each key represents the movies released in that particular year. You use the values stored in the property list and display them in the Table view.

Within the `RootViewController` class, you create two properties: `movieTitles` (an `NSDictionary` object) and `years` (an `NSArray` object).

When the view is loaded, you first locate the property list and load the list into the `NSDictionary` object, followed by retrieving all the years into the `NSArray` object:

```
- (void)viewDidLoad {
    //---path to the property list file---
    NSString *path = [[NSBundle mainBundle] pathForResource:@"Movies"
                                                     ofType:@"plist"];
    //---load the list into the dictionary---
    NSDictionary *dic = [[NSDictionary alloc] initWithContentsOfFile:path];

    //---save the dictionary object to the property---
    self.movieTitles = dic;
    [dic release];

    //---get all the keys in the dictionary object and sort them---
    NSArray *array = [[self.movieTitles allKeys]
                      sortedArrayUsingSelector:@selector(compare:)];

    //---save the keys in the years property---
    self.years = array;

    [super viewDidLoad];

    // Uncomment the following line to display an Edit button in the navigation
```

```
            bar for this view controller.
        // self.navigationItem.rightBarButtonItem = self.editButtonItem;
    }
```

Because the Table view now displays the list of movies in sections, with each section representing a year, you need to tell the Table view how many sections there are. You do so by implementing the `numberOfSectionsInTableView:` method:

```
- (NSInteger)numberOfSectionsInTableView:(UITableView *)tableView {
    //return 1;
    return [self.years count];
}
```

After the Table view knows how many sections to display, it must also know how many rows to display in each section. You provide that information by implementing the `tableView:numberOfRowsInSection:` method:

```
- (NSInteger)tableView:(UITableView *)tableView
  numberOfRowsInSection:(NSInteger)section {
    //return 0;
    //---check the current year based on the section index---
    NSString *year = [self.years objectAtIndex:section];

    //---returns the movies in that year as an array---
    NSArray *movieSection = [self.movieTitles objectForKey:year];

    //---return the number of movies for that year as the number of rows in that
    // section ---
    return [movieSection count];
}
```

To display the movies for each section, you implement the `tableView:cellForRowAtIndexPath:` method and extract the relevant movie titles from the `NSDictionary` object:

```
- (UITableViewCell *)tableView:(UITableView *)tableView
        cellForRowAtIndexPath:(NSIndexPath *)indexPath {
    static NSString *CellIdentifier = @"Cell";

    UITableViewCell *cell =
        [tableView dequeueReusableCellWithIdentifier:CellIdentifier];

    if (cell == nil) {
        cell = [[[UITableViewCell alloc] initWithStyle:UITableViewCellStyleDefault
                                       reuseIdentifier:CellIdentifier]
                                       autorelease];
    }

    // Configure the cell.
    //---get the year---
    NSString *year = [self.years objectAtIndex:[indexPath section]];

    //---get the list of movies for that year---
```

```
        NSArray *movieSection = [self.movieTitles objectForKey:year];

        //---get the particular movie based on that row---
        cell.textLabel.text = [movieSection objectAtIndex:[indexPath row]];

        return cell;
}
```

Finally, you implement the `tableView:titleForHeaderInSection:` method to retrieve the year as the header for each section:

```
- (NSString *)tableView:(UITableView *)tableView
titleForHeaderInSection:(NSInteger)section {
    //---get the year as the section header---
    NSString *year = [self.years objectAtIndex:section];
    return year;
}
```

Adding Indexing

The list of movies is pretty short, so scrolling through the list is not too much of a hassle. However, imagine a list containing 10,000 titles spanning 100 years. In this case, scrolling from the top of the list to the bottom can take a long time. A useful feature of the Table view is the capability to display an index on the right side of the view. An example is the A–Z index list available in your Contacts list. To add an index list to your Table view, you just need to implement the `sectionIndexTitlesForTableView:` method and return the array containing the section headers, which is the `years` array in this case:

```
- (NSArray *)sectionIndexTitlesForTableView:(UITableView *)tableView {
    return years;
}
```

 NOTE If the Table view's style is set to `Grouped`, the index will overlap with the layout of the Table view.

Figure 8-20 shows the index displayed on the right side of the Table view.

Adding Search Capability

A common function associated with the Table view is the capability to search the items contained within it. For example, the Contacts application has the search bar at the top for easy searching of contacts.

FIGURE 8-20

In the following Try It Out, you will learn how to add search functionality to the Table view.

TRY IT OUT Adding a Search Bar to the Table View

1. Using the same project created in the previous section, in Interface Builder drag a Search Bar from the Library and drop it onto the Table view (see Figure 8-21).

2. Right-click the Search Bar and connect the `delegate` to the File's Owner item (see Figure 8-22).

3. In the `RootViewController.h` file, add the following statements that appear in bold:

```
#import <UIKit/UIKit.h>

@interface RootViewController : UITableViewController
    <UISearchBarDelegate> {
    NSDictionary *movieTitles;
    NSArray *years;

    IBOutlet UISearchBar *searchBar;
}

@property (nonatomic, retain) NSDictionary *movieTitles;
@property (nonatomic, retain) NSArray *years;

@property (nonatomic, retain) UISearchBar *searchBar;

@end
```

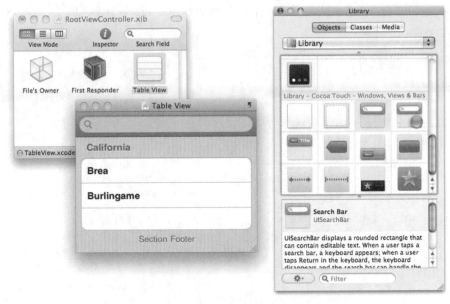

FIGURE 8-21

FIGURE 8-22

4. In Interface Builder, Control-click and drag the File's Owner item to the Search Bar and select
`searchBar`.

5. In the `RootViewController.m` file, add the following statements that appear in bold:

```
#import "RootViewController.h"

@implementation RootViewController

@synthesize movieTitles;
@synthesize years;

@synthesize searchBar;

- (void)viewDidLoad {
    //---path to the property list file---
    NSString *path = [[NSBundle mainBundle] pathForResource:@"Movies"
                                                     ofType:@"plist"];
    //---load the list into the dictionary---
    NSDictionary *dic = [[NSDictionary alloc] initWithContentsOfFile:path];

    //---save the dictionary object to the property---
    self.movieTitles = dic;
    [dic release];

    //---get all the keys in the dictionary object and sort them---
    NSArray *array =
        [[self.movieTitles allKeys]
            sortedArrayUsingSelector:@selector(compare:)];

    //---save the keys in the years property---
    self.years = array;

    //---Search---
    self.tableView.tableHeaderView = searchBar;
    self.searchBar.autocorrectionType = UITextAutocorrectionTypeYes;

    [super viewDidLoad];

    // Uncomment the following line to display an Edit button in the navigation
       bar for this view controller.
    // self.navigationItem.rightBarButtonItem = self.editButtonItem;
}

- (void)dealloc {
    [searchBar release];
    [movieTitles release];
    [years release];
    [super dealloc];
}
```

6. Press Command-R to test the application on the iPhone 4 Simulator. Figure 8-23 shows the Search Bar displayed at the top of the Table view.

FIGURE 8-23

7. Back in Xcode again, edit the RootViewController.h file by adding the following statements that appear in bold:

```objc
#import <UIKit/UIKit.h>

@interface RootViewController : UITableViewController {
    NSDictionary *movieTitles;
    NSArray *years;

    IBOutlet UISearchBar *searchBar;

    BOOL isSearchOn;
    BOOL canSelectRow;
    NSMutableArray *listOfMovies;
    NSMutableArray *searchResult;
}

@property (nonatomic, retain) NSDictionary *movieTitles;
@property (nonatomic, retain) NSArray *years;

@property (nonatomic, retain) UISearchBar *searchBar;

- (void) doneSearching:(id)sender;
- (void) searchMoviesTableView;

@end
```

8. In the `RootViewController.m` file, add the following methods:

```objc
//---fired when the user taps on the searchbar---
- (void)searchBarTextDidBeginEditing:(UISearchBar *)searchBar {
    isSearchOn = YES;
    canSelectRow = NO;
    self.tableView.scrollEnabled = NO;

    //---add the Done button at the top---
    self.navigationItem.rightBarButtonItem =
        [[[UIBarButtonItem alloc]
            initWithBarButtonSystemItem:UIBarButtonSystemItemDone
                                 target:self
                                 action:@selector(doneSearching:)]
            autorelease];
}

//---done with the searching---
- (void) doneSearching:(id)sender {
    isSearchOn = NO;
    canSelectRow = YES;
    self.tableView.scrollEnabled = YES;
    self.navigationItem.rightBarButtonItem = nil;

    //---hides the keyboard---
    [searchBar resignFirstResponder];

    //---refresh the TableView---
    [self.tableView reloadData];
}

//---fired when the user types something into the searchbar---
- (void)searchBar:(UISearchBar *)searchBar
    textDidChange:(NSString *)searchText {

    //---if there is something to search for---
    if ([searchText length] > 0) {
        isSearchOn = YES;
        canSelectRow = YES;
        self.tableView.scrollEnabled = YES;
        [self searchMoviesTableView];
    }
    else {
        //---nothing to search---
        isSearchOn = NO;
        canSelectRow = NO;
        self.tableView.scrollEnabled = NO;
    }
    [self.tableView reloadData];
}

//---performs the searching using the array of movies---
- (void) searchMoviesTableView {
    //---clears the search result---
    [searchResult removeAllObjects];

    for (NSString *str in listOfMovies) {
```

```
          NSRange titleResultsRange = [str rangeOfString:searchBar.text
                                          options:NSCaseInsensitiveSearch];
          if (titleResultsRange.length > 0)
             [searchResult addObject:str];
       }
   }

   //---fired when the user taps the Search button on the keyboard---
   - (void)searchBarSearchButtonClicked:(UISearchBar *)searchBar {
      [self searchMoviesTableView];
   }

   - (NSIndexPath *)tableView:(UITableView *)tableView
     willSelectRowAtIndexPath:(NSIndexPath *)indexPath {
        if (canSelectRow)
            return indexPath;
        else
            return nil;
   }
```

9. Modify the following methods in bold in the RootViewController.m file:

```
- (void)viewDidLoad {
    //---path to the property list file---
    NSString *path = [[NSBundle mainBundle] pathForResource:@"Movies"
                                            ofType:@"plist"];
    //---load the list into the dictionary---
    NSDictionary *dic = [[NSDictionary alloc] initWithContentsOfFile:path];

    //---save the dictionary object to the property---
    self.movieTitles = dic;
    [dic release];

    //---get all the keys in the dictionary object and sort them---
    NSArray *array =
        [[self.movieTitles allKeys]
            sortedArrayUsingSelector:@selector(compare:)];

    //---save the keys in the years property---
    self.years = array;

    //---Search---
    self.tableView.tableHeaderView = searchBar;
    self.searchBar.autocorrectionType = UITextAutocorrectionTypeYes;

    //---copy all the movie titles in the dictionary into
    // the listOfMovies array---
    listOfMovies = [[NSMutableArray alloc] init];
    for (NSString *year in array) {    //---get all the years---
        //---get all the movies for a particular year---
        NSArray *movies = [movieTitles objectForKey:year];
        for (NSString *title in movies) {
            [listOfMovies addObject:title];
        }
    }

    //---used for storing the search result---
```

```
    searchResult = [[NSMutableArray alloc] init];

    isSearchOn = NO;
    canSelectRow = YES;

    [super viewDidLoad];

    // Uncomment the following line to display an Edit button in the navigation
        bar for this view controller.
    // self.navigationItem.rightBarButtonItem = self.editButtonItem;
}


// Customize the number of sections in the table view.
- (NSInteger)numberOfSectionsInTableView:(UITableView *)tableView {
    //return 1;
    if (isSearchOn)
        return 1;
    else
        return [self.years count];
}

// Customize the number of rows in the table view.
- (NSInteger)tableView:(UITableView *)tableView
 numberOfRowsInSection:(NSInteger)section {
    //return 0;
    if (isSearchOn) {
        return [searchResult count];
    } else {
        //---check the current year based on the section index---
        NSString *year = [self.years objectAtIndex:section];

        //---returns the movies in that year as an array---
        NSArray *movieSection = [self.movieTitles objectForKey:year];

        //---return the number of movies for that year as the number
        // of rows in that section ---
        return [movieSection count];
    }
}


// Customize the appearance of table view cells.
- (UITableViewCell *)tableView:(UITableView *)tableView
        cellForRowAtIndexPath:(NSIndexPath *)indexPath {
    static NSString *CellIdentifier = @"Cell";

    UITableViewCell *cell =
        [tableView dequeueReusableCellWithIdentifier:CellIdentifier];
    if (cell == nil) {
        cell = [[[UITableViewCell alloc]
                    initWithStyle:UITableViewCellStyleDefault
                  reuseIdentifier:CellIdentifier]
                  autorelease];
    }

    // Configure the cell.
```

```
    if (isSearchOn) {
        NSString *cellValue = [searchResult objectAtIndex:indexPath.row];
        cell.textLabel.text = cellValue;
    } else {
        //---get the year---
        NSString *year = [self.years objectAtIndex:[indexPath section]];

        //---get the list of movies for that year---
        NSArray *movieSection = [self.movieTitles objectForKey:year];

        //---get the particular movie based on that row---
        cell.textLabel.text = [movieSection objectAtIndex:[indexPath row]];
    }
    return cell;
}

- (NSString *)tableView:(UITableView *)tableView
titleForHeaderInSection:(NSInteger)section {
    //---get the year as the section header---
    NSString *year = [self.years objectAtIndex:section];
    if (isSearchOn)
        return nil;
    else
        return year;
}

- (NSArray *)sectionIndexTitlesForTableView:(UITableView *)tableView {
    if (isSearchOn)
        return nil;
    else
        return self.years;
}

- (void)dealloc {
    [listOfMovies release];
    [searchResult release];
    [searchBar release];
    [movieTitles release];
    [years release];
    [super dealloc];
}
```

10. Press Command-R to test the application on the iPhone 4 Simulator.

11. Tap the Search Bar and the keyboard will appear. Observe the following:

➤   When the keyboard appears and the Search Bar has no text in it, the Table view contains the original list and the items are not selectable.

➤   As you type, the Table view displays the movies whose title contains the characters you are typing, as demonstrated in Figure 8-24, wherein "on" was typed into the search bar of the right-most image and movie titles containing "on" are now displayed. You can select a search result by tapping it.

➤   When you tap the Done button, the keyboard disappears and the original list appears.

FIGURE 8-24

How It Works

That was quite a bit of work, but it is actually quite easy to follow the details.

First, you add an outlet to connect to the Search Bar:

```
IBOutlet UISearchBar *searchBar;
```

You then define two Boolean variables so that you can track whether the search process is ongoing and whether the user can select the rows in the Table view:

```
BOOL isSearchOn;
BOOL canSelectRow;
```

You then define two NSMutableArray objects so that you can use one to store the list of movies and another to temporarily store the result of the search:

```
NSMutableArray *listOfMovies;
NSMutableArray *searchResult;
```

When the View window is first loaded, you first associate the Search Bar with the Table view and then copy the entire list of movie titles from the NSDictionary object into the NSMutableArray:

```
//---Search---
self.tableView.tableHeaderView = searchBar;
self.searchBar.autocorrectionType = UITextAutocorrectionTypeYes;

//---copy all the movie titles in the dictionary into
```

```
    // the listOfMovies array---
    listOfMovies = [[NSMutableArray alloc] init];
    for (NSString *year in array) {      //---get all the years---
        //---get all the movies for a particular year---
        NSArray *movies = [movieTitles objectForKey:year];
        for (NSString *title in movies) {
            [listOfMovies addObject:title];
        }
    }

    //---used for storing the search result---
    searchResult = [[NSMutableArray alloc] init];

    isSearchOn = NO;
    canSelectRow = YES;
```

When the user taps the Search Bar, the searchBarTextDidBeginEditing: event (one of the methods defined in the UISearchBarDelegate protocol) fires. In this method, you add a Done button to the top-right corner of the screen. When the Done button is tapped, the doneSearching: method is called (which you define next):

```
    //---fired when the user taps on the searchbar---
    - (void)searchBarTextDidBeginEditing:(UISearchBar *)searchBar {
        isSearchOn = YES;
        canSelectRow = NO;
        self.tableView.scrollEnabled = NO;

        //---add the Done button at the top---
        self.navigationItem.rightBarButtonItem =
            [[[UIBarButtonItem alloc]
                initWithBarButtonSystemItem:UIBarButtonSystemItemDone
                                    target:self
                                    action:@selector(doneSearching:)]
                                    autorelease];
    }
```

The doneSearching: method makes the Search Bar resign its First Responder status (thereby hiding the keyboard). At the same time, you reload the Table view by calling the reloadData method of the Table view. This causes the various events associated with the Table view to be fired again:

```
    //---done with the searching---
    - (void) doneSearching:(id)sender {
        isSearchOn = NO;
        canSelectRow = YES;
        self.tableView.scrollEnabled = YES;
        self.navigationItem.rightBarButtonItem = nil;

        //---hides the keyboard---
        [searchBar resignFirstResponder];

        //---refresh the TableView---
        [self.tableView reloadData];
    }
```

As the user types into the Search Bar, the `searchBar:textDidChange:` event is fired for each character entered. In this case, if the Search Bar has at least one character, the `searchMoviesTableView` method (which you define next) is called:

```
//---fired when the user types something into the searchbar---
- (void)searchBar:(UISearchBar *)searchBar
    textDidChange:(NSString *)searchText {

    //---if there is something to search for---
    if ([searchText length] > 0) {
        isSearchOn = YES;
        canSelectRow = YES;
        self.tableView.scrollEnabled = YES;
        [self searchMoviesTableView];
    }
    else {
        //---nothing to search---
        isSearchOn = NO;
        canSelectRow = NO;
        self.tableView.scrollEnabled = NO;
    }
    [self.tableView reloadData];
}
```

The `searchMoviesTableView` method performs the searching on the `listOfMovies` array. You use the `rangeOfString:options:` method of the `NSString` class to perform a case-insensitive search of each movie title using the specified string. The returned result is an `NSRange` object, which contains the location and length of the search string being searched. If the length is more than zero, then a match has been found, and hence you add it to the `searchResult` array:

```
//---performs the searching using the array of movies---
- (void) searchMoviesTableView {
    //---clears the search result---
    [searchResult removeAllObjects];

    for (NSString *str in listOfMovies) {
        NSRange titleResultsRange = [str rangeOfString:searchBar.text
                                        options:NSCaseInsensitiveSearch];
        if (titleResultsRange.length > 0)
            [searchResult addObject:str];
    }
}
```

When the user taps the Search button (on the keyboard), you make a call to the `searchMoviesTableView` method:

```
//---fired when the user taps the Search button on the keyboard---
- (void)searchBarSearchButtonClicked:(UISearchBar *)searchBar {
    [self searchMoviesTableView];
}
```

The rest of the methods are straightforward. If the search is currently active (as determined by the `isSearchOn` variable), then you display the list of titles contained in the `searchResult` array. If not, then you display the entire list of movies.

Disclosures and Check Marks

Because users often select rows in a Table view to view more detailed information, rows in a Table view often sport images such as an arrow or a checkmark. Figure 8-25 shows an example of such arrows.

FIGURE 8-25

There are three types of images that you can display:

➤ Checkmark

➤ Disclosure indicator

➤ Detail Disclosure button

To display a disclosure or a checkmark, insert the following statement that appears in bold in the `tableView:cellForRowAtIndexPath:` event:

```
// Customize the appearance of table view cells.
- (UITableViewCell *)tableView:(UITableView *)tableView
cellForRowAtIndexPath:(NSIndexPath *)indexPath {
    static NSString *CellIdentifier = @"Cell";

    UITableViewCell *cell =
        [tableView dequeueReusableCellWithIdentifier:CellIdentifier];
    if (cell == nil) {
        cell = [[[UITableViewCell alloc] initWithStyle:UITableViewCellStyleDefault
                                        reuseIdentifier:CellIdentifier]
                                        autorelease];
```

```
    }

    // Configure the cell.
    if (isSearchOn) {
        NSString *cellValue = [searchResult objectAtIndex:indexPath.row];
        cell.textLabel.text = cellValue;
    } else {
        //---get the year---
        NSString *year = [self.years objectAtIndex:[indexPath section]];

        //---get the list of movies for that year---
        NSArray *movieSection = [self.movieTitles objectForKey:year];

        //---get the particular movie based on that row---
        cell.textLabel.text = [movieSection objectAtIndex:[indexPath row]];

        //---set the accessory type---
        cell.accessoryType = UITableViewCellAccessoryDetailDisclosureButton;
    }
    return cell;
}
```

You can use the following constants for the accessoryType property:

➤ UITableViewCellAccessoryCheckmark

➤ UITableViewCellAccessoryDisclosureIndicator

➤ UITableViewCellAccessoryDetailDisclosureButton

Figure 8-26 shows the three different types of images corresponding to the preceding constants.

FIGURE 8-26

Of the three accessory types, only the UITableViewCellAccessoryDetailDisclosureButton can handle one additional user's tap event. To handle the additional event when the user taps the Disclosure button, you need to implement the tableView:accessoryButtonTappedForRowWithIndexPath: method:

```
- (void)tableView:(UITableView *)tableView
accessoryButtonTappedForRowWithIndexPath:(NSIndexPath *)indexPath {
    //---insert code here---
    // e.g. navigate to another view to display detailed information, etc
}
```

Figure 8-27 shows the two different events fired when a user taps the content of the cell, as well as the Disclosure button.

Commonly, you use the Disclosure button to display detailed information about the selected row.

Navigating to Another View

One of the features of a Navigation-based application is its ability to navigate from one View window to another. For example, the user may select an item from the Table view and the application will navigate to another View window showing the details of the item selected.

tableView:didSelectRowAtIndexPath:

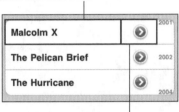

tableView:accessoryButtonTappedForRowWithIndexPath:

FIGURE 8-27

In the following Try It Out, you will modify the application that you have been building so that when the user selects a movie, the application displays the name of the movie selected in another View window.

TRY IT OUT　Displaying the Movie Selected

1. Using the project created in the previous section, right-click the Classes folder in Xcode and select Add ➪ New File.... Select Cocoa Touch Class (on the left) and then UIViewController subclass (check the "With XIB for user interface" option) and click Next (see Figure 8-28).

2. Name the file as **MovieDetailsViewController.m** and click Finish. There should now be three additional files in the Classes folder — MovieDetailsViewController.h, MovieDetailsViewController.m, and MovieDetailsViewController.xib

3. Double-click the MovieDetailsViewController.xib file to edit it in Interface Builder.

4. Populate the View window with a Label view (see Figure 8-29).

5. Add the following bold code in the MovieDetailsViewController.h file:

```
#import <UIKit/UIKit.h>

@interface MovieDetailsViewController : UIViewController {
    IBOutlet UILabel *label;
    NSString *movieSelected;
}

@property (nonatomic, retain) UILabel *label;
@property (nonatomic, retain) NSString *movieSelected;

@end
```

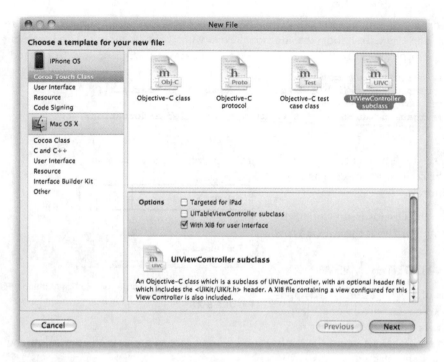

FIGURE 8-28

FIGURE 8-28

6. In Interface Builder, control-click the File's Owner item and drag and drop it over the Label view. Select `label`.

7. Add the following bold code in MovieDetailsViewController.m:

```
#import "MovieDetailsViewController.h"

@implementation MovieDetailsViewController

@synthesize label;
@synthesize movieSelected;

-(void) viewDidAppear:(BOOL)animated {
    label.text = self.movieSelected;
}

- (void)viewDidLoad {
    self.title = @"Movie Details";
    [super viewDidLoad];
}

- (void)dealloc {
    [movieSelected release];
    [label release];
    [super dealloc];
}
```

8. Add the following bold code in RootViewController.h:

```
#import <UIKit/UIKit.h>
#import "MovieDetailsViewController.h"

@interface RootViewController : UITableViewController
    <UISearchBarDelegate> {

    MovieDetailsViewController *detailsViewController;

    NSDictionary *movieTitles;
    NSArray *years;

    IBOutlet UISearchBar *searchBar;

    BOOL isSearchOn;
    BOOL canSelectRow;
    NSMutableArray *listOfMovies;
    NSMutableArray *searchResult;
}

@property (nonatomic, retain) NSDictionary *movieTitles;
@property (nonatomic, retain) NSArray *years;
@property (nonatomic, retain) UISearchBar *searchBar;

@property (nonatomic, retain) MovieDetailsViewController *detailsViewController;

- (void) doneSearching:(id)sender;
- (void) searchMoviesTableView;

@end
```

9. Add the following bold code in `RootViewController.m`:

```
#import "RootViewController.h"

@implementation RootViewController

@synthesize movieTitles;
@synthesize years;
@synthesize searchBar;

@synthesize detailsViewController;
```

10. In the `RootViewController.m` file, insert the following bold statement in the `viewDidLoad` method:

```
- (void)viewDidLoad {
    self.navigationItem.title = @"List of Movies";

    //---path to the property list file---
    NSString *path = [[NSBundle mainBundle] pathForResource:@"Movies"
                                                ofType:@"plist"];
    //---load the list into the dictionary---
    NSDictionary *dic = [[NSDictionary alloc] initWithContentsOfFile:path];

    //---save the dictionary object to the property---
    self.movieTitles = dic;
    [dic release];

    //---details omitted---
    //...
    //...
    [super viewDidLoad];
}
```

11. Code the `tableView:didSelectRowAtIndexPath:` method as follows:

```
- (void)tableView:(UITableView *)tableView
didSelectRowAtIndexPath:(NSIndexPath *)indexPath {
    NSString *year = [self.years objectAtIndex:[indexPath section]];
    NSArray *movieSection = [self.movieTitles objectForKey:year];
    NSString *movieTitle = [movieSection objectAtIndex:[indexPath row]];
    NSString *message = [[NSString alloc]
                        initWithFormat:@"You have selected %@",
                        movieTitle];

    //---Navigate to the details view---
    if (self.detailsViewController == nil) {
        MovieDetailsViewController *d = [[MovieDetailsViewController alloc]
                                        initWithNibName:@"MovieDetailsViewController"
                                        bundle:[NSBundle mainBundle]];
        self.detailsViewController = d;
        [d release];
    }

    //---set the movie selected in the method of the
    // MovieDetailsViewController---//
```

```
        self.detailsViewController.movieSelected = message;
        [self.navigationController pushViewController:self.detailsViewController
                                    animated:YES];
    }
```

12. Finally, add the following statement in bold to the `dealloc` method:

```
- (void)dealloc {
    [detailsViewController release];
    [listOfMovies release];
    [searchResult release];
    [searchBar release];
    [movieTitles release];
    [years release];
    [super dealloc];
}
```

13. Press Command-R to test the application on the iPhone 4 Simulator. Figure 8-30 shows that when you click one of the movies in the Table view, the application navigates to another View window, showing the name of the movie selected.

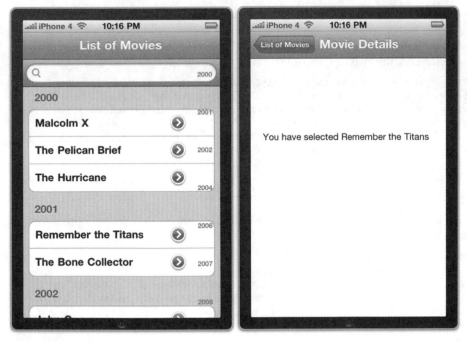

FIGURE 8-30

How It Works

In order to navigate to another View window, you first need to create a new View window with its corresponding View Controller. In order to pass the name of the movie selected from the

RootViewController to the MovieDetailsViewController, you expose a property named movieSelected on the MovieDetailsViewController:

```
#import <UIKit/UIKit.h>

@interface MovieDetailsViewController : UIViewController {
    IBOutlet UILabel *label;
    NSString *movieSelected;
}

@property (nonatomic, retain) UILabel *label;
@property (nonatomic, retain) NSString *movieSelected;

@end
```

The RootViewController class will use this property to pass the name of the movie selected.

The MovieDetailsViewController class displays the name of the movie selected in the Label view every time the View window appears:

```
-(void) viewDidAppear:(BOOL)animated {
    label.text = self.movieSelected;
}
```

When the user selects an item in the Table view, you first determine the name of the movie (in the tableView:didSelectRowAtIndexPath: method):

```
NSString *year = [self.years objectAtIndex:[indexPath section]];
NSArray *movieSection = [self.movieTitles objectForKey:year];
NSString *movieTitle = [movieSection objectAtIndex:[indexPath row]];
NSString *message = [[NSString alloc]
                        initWithFormat:@"You have selected %@",
                        movieTitle];
```

You then navigate to the MovieDetailsViewController class by instantiating a copy of it and then setting the movieSelected property to the name of the movie selected.

Finally, to navigate to the new View window, you use the pushViewController: method of the Navigation Controller:

```
//---Navigate to the details view---
if (self.detailsViewController == nil) {
    MovieDetailsViewController *d = [[MovieDetailsViewController alloc]
                                initWithNibName:@"MovieDetailsViewController"
                                bundle:[NSBundle mainBundle]];
    self.detailsViewController = d;
    [d release];
}

//---set the movie selected in the method of the
// MovieDetailsViewController---//
self.detailsViewController.movieSelected = message;
[self.navigationController pushViewController:self.detailsViewController
                                animated:YES];
```

SUMMARY

In this chapter, you had a good look at the Table view and learned how to customize it to display items in various formats. You also learned how to implement search functionality in the Table view, which is an essential function in real-world applications. In addition, you also saw how to move between View windows in a Navigation-based application.

EXERCISES

1. Name the two protocols to which your View Controller must conform when using the Table view in your view. Briefly describe their uses.

2. Which method should be implemented if you want to add an index in a Table view?

3. Name the three disclosure and checkmark images that you can use. Which one handles user taps?

Answers to Exercises can be found in Appendix E, on Wrox.com.

▶ WHAT YOU LEARNED IN THIS CHAPTER

TOPIC	KEY CONCEPTS
Adding items to a Table view	Handle the various events in the `UITableViewDataSource` protocol.
Allowing users to select rows in a Table view	Handle the various events in the `UITableViewDelegate` protocol.
Adding images to rows in a Table view	Use the image property of the `UITableViewCell` class and set it to an instance of the `UIImage` class containing an image.

Using a property list with a Table view	Use the following code snippet to locate the property list:
	
	`NSString *path = [[NSBundle mainBundle]`
	`pathForResource:@"Movies"`
	`ofType:@"plist"];`
	
	Then use a combination of `NSDictionary` and `NSArray` objects to retrieve the key/value pairs stored in the property list.

Grouping items in a Table view in sections	Implement the following methods:
	`numberOfSectionsInTableView:`
	`tableView:numberOfRowsInSection:`
	`tableView:titleForHeaderInSection:`

Adding an index to a Table view	Implement the `sectionIndexTitlesForTableView:` method.

Adding disclosure and checkmark images to a row in a Table view	Set the `accessoryType` property of an `UITableViewCell` object to one of the following:
	`UITableViewCellAccessoryDetailDisclosureButton`
	`UITableViewCellAccessoryCheckmark`
	`UITableViewCellAccessoryDisclosureIndicator`

Implementing a search in a Table view	Use the Search Bar view and handle the various events in the `UISearchBarDelegate` protocol.
Navigating to another View window	Use the `pushViewController:` method of the Navigation Controller

Application Preferences

WHAT YOU WILL LEARN IN THIS CHAPTER

➤ How to add application preferences to your application

➤ How to programmatically access the Settings values

➤ How to reset your application's preferences settings

If you are a relatively seasoned Mac OS X user, you're likely familiar with the concept of application preferences. Almost every Mac OS X application has application-specific settings that are used for configuring the application's appearance and behavior. These settings are known as the *application preferences.*

In the iPhone OS, applications also have application preferences. In contrast to Mac OS X applications, however, whose application preferences are an integral part of the application, iPhone preferences are centrally managed by an application called Settings (see Figure 9-1).

The Settings application displays the preferences of system applications as well as third-party applications. Tapping any setting displays the details, where you can configure the preferences of an application.

In this chapter, you learn how to incorporate application preferences into your application and modify them programmatically during runtime.

FIGURE 9-1

CREATING APPLICATION PREFERENCES

Creating application preferences for your iPhone application is a relatively straightforward process. It involves adding a resource called the Settings Bundle to your project, configuring a property list file, and then deploying your application. When your application is deployed, the application preferences are automatically created for you in the Settings application.

The following Try It Out shows how to add application preferences to your iPhone application project in Xcode.

TRY IT OUT   Adding Application Preferences

1.   Using Xcode, create a new View-based Application (iPhone) project and name it ApplicationSettings.

2.   Right-click the project name in Xcode and add a new file. Select the Resource template category and click Settings Bundle (see Figure 9-2). Click Next.

FIGURE 9-2

3.   When asked to name the file, use the default name of Settings.bundle and click Finish.

4.   The Settings.bundle item should now be part of your project. Click it and view the content of the Root.plist file using the default Property List editor (see Figure 9-3).

5.   Press Command-R to test the application on the iPhone 4 Simulator. When the application is loaded on the Simulator, press the Home key to return to the main screen of the iPhone. Click the Settings application. You can now see a new Settings entry, ApplicationSettings (see Figure 9-4). Click the ApplicationSettings entry to see the default settings created for you.

FIGURE 9-3

FIGURE 9-4

How It Works

It seems almost magical that without coding a single line, you have incorporated your application preferences into your application. The magic part is actually the `Settings.bundle` file that you have added to your project. It contains two files: `Root.plist` and `Root.strings`. The `Root.plist` file is an XML file that contains a collection of dictionary objects (key/value pairs). These key/value pairs are translated into the preferences entries you see in the Settings application.

Take a moment to review the use of the various keys used in the `Root.plist` file. There are two root-level keys in the `Root.plist` file:

➤ `StringsTable`, which contains the name of the strings file associated with this file. In this case, it is pointing to `Root.strings`. This file provides the localized content to display to the user for each of your preferences.

➤ `PreferenceSpecifiers`, which is of type `Array` and contains an array of dictionaries, with each item containing the information for a single preference.

Each preference is represented by an item (known as `PreferenceSpecifiers`), such as `Item 0`, `Item 1`, `Item 2`, and so on. Each item has a `Type` key, which indicates the type of data stored. Table 9-1 describes the preference specifiers.

TABLE 9-1: List of Preference Specifiers and Usage

ELEMENT TYPE	DESCRIPTION	USE FOR
PSTextFieldSpecifier	A text field preference. Displays an optional title and an editable text field.	Preferences that require the user to specify a custom string value
PSTitleValueSpecifier	A read-only string preference	Displaying preference values as formatted strings
PSToggleSwitchSpecifier	A toggle switch preference	Configuring a preference that can have only one of two values
PSSliderSpecifier	A slider preference	Preferences that represent a range of values. The value for this type is a real number whose minimum and maximum you specify.
PSMultiValueSpecifier	A multivalue preference	Preferences that support a set of mutually exclusive values
PSGroupSpecifier	A group item preference	Organizing groups of preferences on a single page
PSChildPaneSpecifier	A child pane preference	Linking to a new page of preferences

Each `PreferenceSpecifiers` key contains a list of subkeys that you can use. For example, the `PSTextFieldSpecifier` key provides `Type`, `Title`, `Key`, `DefaultValue`, `IsSecure`, `KeyBoardType`, `AutocapitalizationType`, and `AutocorrectionType` keys. You then set each key with its appropriate values.

Examine the `Root.plist` file in more detail. Note, for example, that `Item 2` has four keys under it: `Type`, `Title`, `Key`, and `DefaultValue`. The `Type` key specifies the type of information it is going to store. In this case, it is a `PSToggleSwitchSpecifier`, which means it will be represented visually as an On/Off switch. The `Title` key specifies the text that will be shown for this item (Item 2). The `Key` key is the identifier that uniquely identifies this key so that you can programmatically retrieve the value of this item in your application. Finally, the `DefaultValue` key specifies the default value of this item. In this case, it is checked, indicating that the value is On.

> **NOTE** *The key/value pair in the* `Root.plist` *file is case sensitive, so you need to be careful when modifying the entries. A typo can result in a nonfunctional application.*

In the next Try It Out, you modify the `Root.plist` file so that you can use it to store a user's credentials. This is very useful when you are writing an application that requires users to log in to a server. When users access your application for the first time, they will supply their login credentials, such as username and password. Your application can then store the credentials in the application preferences so that the next time a user accesses your application, the application can automatically retrieve the credentials without asking the user to supply them.

> **NOTE** *For more information on the use of each key, refer to Apple's "Settings Application Schema Reference" documentation. The easiest way to locate it is to do a Web search for the title. The full URL is* `http://developer.apple.com/iPhone/library/documentation/PreferenceSettings/Conceptual/SettingsApplicationSchemaReference/Introduction/Introduction.html.`

TRY IT OUT **Modifying the Application Preferences**

1. In Xcode (using the same project created in the previous section), select the `Root.plist` file and remove all four items under the `PreferenceSpecifiers` key. To do so, select individual items under the `PreferenceSpecifiers` key and then press the Delete key.

2. To add a new item under the `PreferenceSpecifiers` key, select the `PreferenceSpecifiers` key (see Figure 9-5) and click the Add Child button (the button on the bottom right).

Key	Type	Value
▼ Root	Dictionary	(2 items)
StringsTable	String	Root
▼ PreferenceSpecifiers	Array	(0 items)

FIGURE 9-5

3. A new item is added for you. To add additional items, click the Add Sibling button (see Figure 9-6; the button on the bottom right). Click the Add Sibling button three more times.

Key	Type	Value
▼ Root	Dictionary	(2 items)
StringsTable	String	Root
▼ PreferenceSpecifiers	Array	(1 item)
Item 0	String	

FIGURE 9-6

4. The `Root.plist` file should now look like Figure 9-7.

5. Change the Type of `Item 0` to Dictionary and expand it by clicking the arrow displayed to the left of it (see Figure 9-8). Click the Add Child button to add a child to `Item 0`.

Key	Type	Value
▼ Root	Dictionary	(2 items)
StringsTable	String	Root
▼ PreferenceSpecifiers	Array	(4 items)
Item 0	String	
Item 1	String	
Item 2	String	
Item 3	String	

FIGURE 9-7

6. A new item is added under `Item 0` (see Figure 9-9). Click the Add Sibling button to add another item under `Item 0`.

Remember that you use the Add Sibling button to add a new item within the same level. Use the Add Child button to add a new child item under the current level.

Key	Type	Value
▼ Root	Dictionary	(2 items)
StringsTable	String	Root
▼ PreferenceSpecifiers	Array	(4 items)
▼ Item 0	Dictionary	(0 items)
Item 1	String	
Item 2	String	
Item 3	String	

FIGURE 9-8

7. The `Root.plist` file should now look like Figure 9-10.

8. Modify the entire `Root.plist` file so that it looks like Figure 9-11. Ensure that the capitalization of each key and value pair is correct. Pay particular attention to the `Type` of each item.

Key	Type	Value
▼ Root	Dictionary	(2 items)
StringsTable	String	Root
▼ PreferenceSpecifiers	Array	(4 items)
▼ Item 0	Dictionary	(1 item)
New item	String	
Item 1	String	
Item 2	String	
Item 3	String	

FIGURE 9-9

9. Save the project and press Command-R to test the application on the iPhone 4 Simulator. Click the Home button and launch the Settings application again. Select the ApplicationSettings settings and observe the preferences shown (see Figure 9-12). Clicking the Favorite Color setting will display a page for choosing your favorite color (see Figure 9-13).

Key	Type	Value
▼ Root	Dictionary	(2 items)
StringsTable	String	Root
▼ PreferenceSpecifiers	Array	(4 items)
▼ Item 0	Dictionary	(2 items)
New item	String	
New item – 2	String	
Item 1	String	
Item 2	String	
Item 3	String	

FIGURE 9-10

10. Make some changes to the settings values and then press the Home button to return to the Home screen. The changes in the settings are automatically saved to the device. When you return to the Settings page again, the new values will be displayed.

How It Works

What you have done is basically modify the `Root.plist` file to store three preferences: Login Name, Password, and Favorite Color. For the Password field, you use the `IsSecure` key to indicate that the value must be masked when displaying it to the user. Of particular interest is the Favorite Color preference, for which you use the `Titles` and `Values` keys to display a list of selectable options and their corresponding values to store on the iPhone.

The following preference specifiers are used in this example:

➤ `PSGroupSpecifier` — Used to display a group for the settings. In this case, all the settings are grouped under the Account Information group.

➤ `PSTextFieldSpecifier` — Specifies a text field.

➤ `PSMultiValueSpecifier` — Specifies a list of selectable values. The `Titles` item contains a list of visible text from which users can select. The `Values` item is the corresponding value for the text selected by the user. For example, if a user selects Blue Color as the favorite color, the value `Blue` will be stored on the iPhone.

FIGURE 9-11

FIGURE 9-12

FIGURE 9-13

PROGRAMMATICALLY ACCESSING THE SETTINGS VALUES

The preferences settings are of little use if you can't programmatically access them from within your application. In the following sections, you modify the application so that you can load the preferences settings as well as make changes to them programmatically.

First, use the following Try It Out to prepare the UI by connecting the necessary outlets and actions.

TRY IT OUT Preparing the UI

1. Using the project created in the previous section, double-click the `ApplicationSettingsViewController.xib` file to edit it in Interface Builder.

2. Populate the View window with the following views (see Figure 9-14):

   ➤ Round Rect Button

   ➤ Label

   ➤ Text Field

   ➤ PickerView

3. In Xcode, insert the following code that appears in bold into the `ApplicationSettingsViewController.h` file:

```
#import <UIKit/UIKit.h>

@interface ApplicationSettingsViewController : UIViewController
    <UIPickerViewDataSource, UIPickerViewDelegate> {
    IBOutlet UITextField *loginName;
    IBOutlet UITextField *password;
    IBOutlet UIPickerView *favoriteColor;
}

@property (nonatomic, retain) UITextField *loginName;
@property (nonatomic, retain) UITextField *password;
@property (nonatomic, retain) UIPickerView *favoriteColor;

-(IBAction) loadSettings: (id) sender;
-(IBAction) saveSettings: (id) sender;
-(IBAction) doneEditing: (id) sender;

@end
```

4. In Interface Builder, connect the outlets and action to the various views. In the `ApplicationSettingsViewController.xib` window, do the following:

   ➤ Control-click and drag the File's Owner item to the first TextField view and select `loginName`.

   ➤ Control-click and drag the File's Owner item to the second TextField view and select `password`.

   ➤ Control-click and drag the File's Owner item to the Picker view and select `favoriteColor`.

   ➤ Control-click and drag the Picker view to the File's Owner item and select `dataSource`.

   ➤ Control-click and drag the Picker view to the File's Owner item and select `delegate`.

➤ Control-click and drag the Load Settings Value button to the File's Owner item and select `loadSettings:`.

➤ Control-click and drag the Save Settings Value button to the File's Owner item and select `saveSettings:`.

➤ Right-click the Load Settings Value button and connect the `Did End on Exit` event to the File's Owner item. Select `doneEditing:`.

➤ Right-click the Save Settings Value button and connect the `Did End on Exit` event to the File's Owner item. Select `doneEditing:`.

5. Right-click the File's Owner item to verify that all the connections are connected properly (see Figure 9-15).

FIGURE 9-14   FIGURE 9-15

6. Save the project in Interface Builder.

7. In Xcode, add the following bold code to the `ApplicationSettingsViewController.m` file:

```
#import "ApplicationSettingsViewController.h"

@implementation ApplicationSettingsViewController

@synthesize loginName;
@synthesize password;
@synthesize favoriteColor;

NSMutableArray *colors;
NSString *favoriteColorSelected;

-(IBAction) doneEditing:(id) sender {
```

```
        [sender resignFirstResponder];
    }

    - (void)viewDidLoad {
        //---create an array containing the colors values---
        colors = [[NSMutableArray alloc] init];
        [colors addObject:@"Red"];
        [colors addObject:@"Green"];
        [colors addObject:@"Blue"];
        [super viewDidLoad];
    }

    //---number of components in the Picker view---
    - (NSInteger)numberOfComponentsInPickerView:(UIPickerView *)thePickerView {
        return 1;
    }

    //---number of items(rows) in the Picker view---
    - (NSInteger)pickerView:(UIPickerView *)thePickerView
    numberOfRowsInComponent:(NSInteger)component {
        return [colors count];
    }

    //---populating the Picker view---
    - (NSString *)pickerView:(UIPickerView *)thePickerView
                titleForRow:(NSInteger)row
              forComponent:(NSInteger)component {
        return [colors objectAtIndex:row];
    }

    //---the item selected by the user---
    - (void)pickerView:(UIPickerView *)thePickerView
          didSelectRow:(NSInteger)row
           inComponent:(NSInteger)component {
        favoriteColorSelected = [colors objectAtIndex:row];
    }

    - (void)dealloc {
        [colors release];
        [favoriteColorSelected release];
        [loginName release];
        [password release];
        [favoriteColor release];
        [super dealloc];
    }
```

8. That's it! Press Command-R to test the application on the iPhone 4 Simulator. Figure 9-16 shows the Picker view loaded with the three colors.

 NOTE Clicking the buttons at this point will cause the application to crash, as they are not coded yet. You will do that in the next section.

FIGURE 9-16

How It Works

So far, all the work that has been done prepares the UI for displaying the values retrieved from the preferences settings. In particular, you need to prepare the Picker view to display a list of colors from which the user can choose.

To load the Picker view with the three colors, ensure that the ApplicationSettingsViewController class conforms to the UIPickerViewDataSource and UIPickerViewDelegate protocols:

```
@interface ApplicationSettingsViewController : UIViewController
    <UIPickerViewDataSource, UIPickerViewDelegate> {
```

The UIPickerViewDataSource protocol defines the methods to populate the Picker view with items, while the UIPickerViewDelegate protocol defines the methods to enable users to select an item from the Picker view.

In the ApplicationSettingsViewController.m file, you first create an NSMutableArray object to store the list of colors available for selection, in the viewDidLoad method:

```
- (void)viewDidLoad {
    //---create an array containing the colors values---
    colors = [[NSMutableArray alloc] init];
    [colors addObject:@"Red"];
    [colors addObject:@"Green"];
    [colors addObject:@"Blue"];
    [super viewDidLoad];
}
```

To set the number of components (columns) in the Picker view, implement the
`numberOfComponentsInPickerView:` method:

```
//---number of components in the Picker view---
- (NSInteger)numberOfComponentsInPickerView:(UIPickerView *)thePickerView {
    return 1;
}
```

To set the number of items (rows) you want to display in the Picker view, implement the
`pickerView:numberOfRowsInComponent:` method:

```
//---number of items(rows) in the Picker view---
- (NSInteger)pickerView:(UIPickerView *)thePickerView
numberOfRowsInComponent:(NSInteger)component {
    return [colors count];
}
```

To populate the Picker view with the three colors, implement the
`pickerView:titleForRow:forComponent:` method:

```
//---populating the Picker view---
- (NSString *)pickerView:(UIPickerView *)thePickerView
            titleForRow:(NSInteger)row
          forComponent:(NSInteger)component {
    return [colors objectAtIndex:row];
}
```

To save the color selected by the user in the Picker view, implement the
`pickerView:didSelectRow:inComponent:` method:

```
//---the item selected by the user---
- (void)pickerView:(UIPickerView *)thePickerView
      didSelectRow:(NSInteger)row
       inComponent:(NSInteger)component {
    favoriteColorSelected = [colors objectAtIndex:row];
}
```

The color selected will now be saved in the `favoriteColorSelected` object.

Loading the Settings Values

With the user interface of the application ready, it is now time to see how you can programmatically
load the values of the preferences settings and then display them in your application. This display is
useful because it gives users a chance to view the values of the settings without needing to go to the
Settings application.

TRY IT OUT Loading Settings Values

1. Using the project created in the previous section, modify the
`application:didFinishLaunchingWithOptions:` method in the
`ApplicationSettingsAppDelegate.m` file:

```
#import "ApplicationSettingsAppDelegate.h"
```

```objc
#import "ApplicationSettingsViewController.h"

@implementation ApplicationSettingsAppDelegate

@synthesize window;
@synthesize viewController;

- (BOOL)application:(UIApplication *)application
didFinishLaunchingWithOptions:(NSDictionary *)launchOptions {
    //-- initialize the settings value first;
    // if not all settings values will be null --
    NSUserDefaults *defaults = [NSUserDefaults standardUserDefaults];
    if (![defaults objectForKey:@"login_name"])
        [defaults setObject:@"login name" forKey:@"login_name"];

    if (![defaults objectForKey:@"password"])
        [defaults setObject:@"password" forKey:@"password"];

    if (![defaults objectForKey:@"color"])
        [defaults setObject:@"Green" forKey:@"color"];

    [defaults synchronize];

    // Override point for customization after application launch.

    // Add the view controller's view to the window and display.
    [window addSubview:viewController.view];
    [window makeKeyAndVisible];

    return YES;
}
```

2. Insert the following method into the ApplicationSettingsViewController.m file:

```objc
- (IBAction) loadSettings: (id) sender{
    NSUserDefaults *defaults = [NSUserDefaults standardUserDefaults];
    loginName.text = [defaults objectForKey:@"login_name"];
    password.text = [defaults objectForKey:@"password"];

    //---find the index of the array for the color saved---
    favoriteColorSelected = [[NSString alloc] initWithString:
                                [defaults objectForKey:@"color"]];

    int selIndex = [colors indexOfObject:favoriteColorSelected];

    //---display the saved color in the Picker view---
    [favoriteColor selectRow:selIndex inComponent:0 animated:YES];
}
```

3. Press Command-R to test the application on the iPhone 4 Simulator. When the application is loaded, click the Load Settings Values button. You should see the settings values displayed in the Text Field views and the Picker view (see Figure 9-17).

FIGURE 9-17

How It Works

To load the values of the preferences settings, you use a class known as NSUserDefaults:

```
NSUserDefaults *defaults = [NSUserDefaults standardUserDefaults];
```

The preceding statement returns the one instance of the NSUserDefaults class. Think of NSUserDefaults as a common database that you can use to store your application preferences settings.

When your application runs for the first time, you need to set the values of the settings *before* you can use them. Hence, the best place to initialize them is in the application delegate.

To retrieve the values of the preferences settings, you use the objectForKey: method to check whether each setting is null. If it is, the setting has not been initialized yet and hence you need to set it. To initialize the setting, use the setObject:forKey: method:

```
- (BOOL)application:(UIApplication *)application
didFinishLaunchingWithOptions:(NSDictionary *)launchOptions {
    //-- initialize the settings value first;
    // if not all settings values will be null --
    NSUserDefaults *defaults = [NSUserDefaults standardUserDefaults];
    if (![defaults objectForKey:@"login_name"])
        [defaults setObject:@"login name" forKey:@"login_name"];

    if (![defaults objectForKey:@"password"])
        [defaults setObject:@"password" forKey:@"password"];

    if (![defaults objectForKey:@"color"])
```

```
        [defaults setObject:@"Green" forKey:@"color"];

    [defaults synchronize];

    [window addSubview:viewController.view];
    [window makeKeyAndVisible];

    return YES;
}
```

Note that to immediately save the settings values to the Settings application, you should call the synchronize method of the NSUserDefaults instance.

To load the settings value, likewise you use the objectForKey: method, specifying the name of the preference setting you want to retrieve:

```
- (IBAction) loadSettings: (id) sender{
    NSUserDefaults *defaults = [NSUserDefaults standardUserDefaults];
    loginName.text = [defaults objectForKey:@"login_name"];
    password.text = [defaults objectForKey:@"password"];

    //---find the index of the array for the color saved---
    favoriteColorSelected = [[NSString alloc] initWithString:
                                [defaults objectForKey:@"color"]];

    int selIndex = [colors indexOfObject:favoriteColorSelected];

    //---display the saved color in the Picker view---
    [favoriteColor selectRow:selIndex inComponent:0 animated:YES];
}
```

Resetting the Preferences Settings Values

Sometimes you may want to reset the values of the preferences settings of your application. This is especially true if you have made an error in the Root.plist file and want to reset all the settings. The easiest way to do this is to remove the application from the device or Simulator. To do so, simply tap (or click the Simulator) and hold the application's icon, and when the icons start to wriggle, tap the X button to remove the application. The preferences settings associated with the application will also be removed.

Another way to clear the values of the preferences settings is to navigate to the folder containing your application (on the iPhone Simulator). The applications on the iPhone Simulator are stored in the following folder: ~/Library/Application Support/iPhone Simulator>/<version_no>/ Applications/ (note that the tilde symbol (~) represents your home directory and not your root directory). Inside this folder, you need to find the folder containing your application. Within the application folder is a Library/Preferences folder. Delete the file ending with <application_name> .plist (see Figure 9-18) and your preferences settings will be reset.

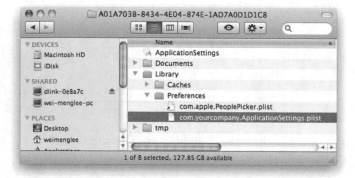

FIGURE 9-18

Saving the Settings Values

Now that you have seen how to load the values of preferences settings, the following Try It Out demonstrates how to save the values back to the preferences settings. This enables users to directly modify their preferences settings from within your application, instead of using the Settings application to do so.

TRY IT OUT **Saving Settings Values**

1. Using the same project created in the previous section, insert the following method in the `ApplicationSettingsViewController.m` file:

```
-(IBAction) saveSettings: (id) sender {
    NSUserDefaults *defaults = [NSUserDefaults standardUserDefaults];
    [defaults setObject:loginName.text forKey:@"login_name"];
    [defaults setObject:password.text forKey:@"password"];
    [defaults setObject:favoriteColorSelected forKey:@"color"];
    [defaults synchronize];

    UIAlertView *alert = [[UIAlertView alloc]
                          initWithTitle:@"Settings Value Saved"
                          message:@"Settings Saved"
                          delegate:nil
                          cancelButtonTitle:@"Done"
                          otherButtonTitles:nil];
    [alert show];
    [alert release];
}
```

2. Press Command-R to test the application on the iPhone 4 Simulator. Make some changes to the login name, password, and favorite color. When you click the Save Settings Value button, all the changes are made to the device (see Figure 9-19). When you check the Settings application, you will see the updated settings values (see Figure 9-20).

FIGURE 9-19

FIGURE 9-20

How It Works

To save the values back to the preferences settings, you use the same approach that you use to retrieve those settings — that is, you use the NSUserDefaults class:

```
NSUserDefaults *defaults = [NSUserDefaults standardUserDefaults];
[defaults setObject:loginName.text forKey:@"login_name"];
[defaults setObject:password.text forKey:@"password"];
[defaults setObject:favoriteColorSelected forKey:@"color"];
[defaults synchronize];
```

As usual, rather than use the objectForKey: method, you now use the setObject:forKey: method to save the values.

SUMMARY

This chapter explained how you can make use of the Application Preferences feature of the iPhone to save your application preferences to the Settings application. This enables you to delegate most of the mundane tasks of saving and loading an application's preferences settings to the OS. All you need to do is use the NSUserDefaults class to programmatically access the preferences settings.

EXERCISES

1. You have learned that you can use the NSUserDefaults class to access the preferences settings values for your application. What are the methods for retrieving and saving the values?

2. What are the two ways in which you can remove the preferences settings for an application?

3. What is the difference between the Add Child button and the Add Sibling button in the Property List editor?

Answers to the Exercises can be found in Appendix E, on Wrox.com.

▶ WHAT YOU LEARNED IN THIS CHAPTER

TOPIC	KEY CONCEPTS
Adding application preferences to your application	Add a Settings Bundle file to your project and modify the `Root.plist` file.

Loading the value of a preference setting	```NSUserDefaults *defaults =```
	``` [NSUserDefaults standardUserDefaults];```
	```loginName.text = [defaults```
	``` objectForKey:@"login_name"];```

Resetting preferences settings values	Either remove the entire application from the Home screen, or remove it via the iPhone Simulator folder on your Mac.

Saving the value of a preference setting	```NSUserDefaults *defaults = [NSUserDefaults```
	```standardUserDefaults];```
	```[defaults setObject:loginName.text```
	``` forKey:@"login_name"];```
	```[defaults synchronize];```

10

File Handling

WHAT YOU WILL LEARN IN THIS CHAPTER

➤ Where your applications are stored on the iPhone

➤ The various folders within your Applications folder

➤ How to read and write to files in the Documents and tmp folders

➤ How to use a property to store structured data

➤ How to programmatically retrieve values stored in a property list

➤ How to modify the values retrieved from a property list and save the changes to a file

➤ How to copy bundled resources to the application's folder during runtime

All the applications you have developed up to this point are pretty straightforward — the application starts, performs something interesting, and ends. In Chapter 9, you saw how you can make use of the application settings feature to save the preferences of your application to a central location managed by the Settings application. Sometimes, however, you simply need to save some data to your application's folder for use later. For example, rather than keep files you download from a remote server in memory, a more effective and memory-efficient method is to save them in a file so that you can use them later (even after the application has shut down and restarted).

In this chapter, you learn about the two available approaches to persisting data in your application so that you can access it later: saving the data as files or a property list. You also learn how to bundle resources such as text files and database files with your application so that when the application is installed on the user's device, the resources can be copied onto the local storage of the device and used from there.

UNDERSTANDING THE APPLICATION FOLDERS

Your applications are stored in the iPhone file system, so you'll find it useful to understand the folder structure of the iPhone.

On the desktop, the content of the iPhone Simulator is stored in the `~/Library/Application Support/iPhone Simulator>/<version_no>/` folder.

 NOTE *The ~ (tilde) represents the current user's directory. Specifically, the preceding directory is equivalent to the following:*

```
/Users/<username>/Library/Application Support/
iPhone Simulator>/<version_no>/
```

Within this folder are five subfolders:

➤ `Applications`

➤ `Library`

➤ `Media`

➤ `Root`

➤ `tmp`

The `Applications` folder contains all your installed applications (see Figure 10-1). Within it are several folders with long filenames. These filenames are generated by Xcode to uniquely identify each of your applications. Each application's folder holds your application's executable file (the `.app` file, which includes all embedded resources), together with a few other folders, such as `Documents`, `Library`, and `tmp`. On the iPhone, all applications run within their own sandboxed environments — that is, an application can access only the files stored within its own folder; it cannot access the folders of other applications.

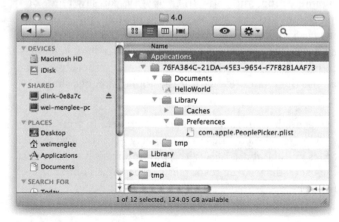

FIGURE 10-1

Using the Documents and Library Folders

The Documents folder is where you can store files used by your application, whereas the Library folder stores the application-specific settings. The tmp folder stores temporary data required by your application.

How you do write to these folders? The following Try It Out provides an example of doing just that. You can download the indicated code files to work through the project.

TRY IT OUT   Writing and Reading from Files

codefile FilesHandling.zip available for download at Wrox.com

1.   Using Xcode, create a new View-based Application project and name it FilesHandling.

2.   In the FilesHandlingViewController.h file, add the following bold statements:

```
#import <UIKit/UIKit.h>

@interface FilesHandlingViewController : UIViewController {

}

-(NSString *) documentsPath;
-(NSString *) readFromFile:(NSString *) filePath;
-(void) writeToFile:(NSString *) text
       withFileName:(NSString *) filePath;

@end
```

3.   In the FilesHandlingViewController.m file, add the following bold statements:

```
#import "FilesHandlingViewController.h"

@implementation FilesHandlingViewController

//---finds the path to the application's Documents directory---
-(NSString *) documentsPath {
    NSArray *paths =
        NSSearchPathForDirectoriesInDomains(
        NSDocumentDirectory, NSUserDomainMask, YES);
    NSString *documentsDir = [paths objectAtIndex:0];
    return documentsDir;
}

//---write content into a specified file path---
-(void) writeToFile:(NSString *) text
       withFileName:(NSString *) filePath {
    NSMutableArray *array = [[NSMutableArray alloc] init];
    [array addObject:text];
    [array writeToFile:filePath atomically:YES];
    [array release];
```

```objc
}

//---read content from a specified file path---
-(NSString *) readFromFile:(NSString *) filePath {
    //---check if file exists---
    if ([[NSFileManager defaultManager] fileExistsAtPath:filePath]) {
        NSArray *array =
            [[NSArray alloc] initWithContentsOfFile: filePath];
        NSString *data =
            [NSString stringWithFormat:@"%@",
                [array objectAtIndex:0]];
        [array release];
        return data;
    }
    else
        return nil;
}


- (void)viewDidLoad {
    //---formulate filename---
    NSString *fileName =
        [[self documentsPath] stringByAppendingPathComponent:@"data.txt"];

    //---write something to the file---
    [self writeToFile:@"a string of text" withFileName:fileName];

    //---read it back---
    NSString *fileContent = [self readFromFile:fileName];

    //---display the content read in the Debugger Console window---
    NSLog(@"%@", fileContent);
    [super viewDidLoad];
}
```

4. Press Command-R to test the application on the iPhone 4 Simulator.

5. Go to Finder and navigate to the Documents folder of your application. The data.txt file is now visible (see Figure 10-2).

6. When you deploy the application, the location of the file on the real device is /private/var/mobile/ Applications/<application_id>/ Documents/data.txt.

7. Double-click the data.txt file to see its contents as follows:

FIGURE 10-2

```xml
<?xml version="1.0" encoding="UTF-8"?>
<!DOCTYPE plist PUBLIC "-//Apple//DTD PLIST 1.0//EN"
    "http://www.apple.com/DTDs/PropertyList-1.0.dtd">
<plist version="1.0">
```

```
<array>
    <string>a string of text</string>
</array>
</plist>
```

8. Turn on the Debugger Console window (Shift-Command-R) and the application will print the string "a string of text."

How It Works

You first define the documentsPath method, which returns the path to the Documents directory:

```
//---finds the path to the application's Documents directory---
-(NSString *) documentsPath {
    NSArray *paths =
        NSSearchPathForDirectoriesInDomains(
        NSDocumentDirectory, NSUserDomainMask, YES);
    NSString *documentsDir = [paths objectAtIndex:0];
    return documentsDir;
}
```

Basically, you use the NSSearchPathForDirectoriesInDomains() function to create a list of directory search paths, indicating that you want to look for the Documents directory (using the NSDocumentDirectory constant). The NSUserDomainMask constant indicates that you want to search from the application's home directory, and the YES argument indicates that you want to obtain the full path of all the directories found.

To obtain the path to the Documents folder, simply extract the first item of the paths array (because there is only one Documents folder in an iPhone application's folder). In fact, this block of code is derived from the Mac OS X API, which might return multiple folders; but in the case of the iPhone, there can only be one Documents folder per application.

You next define the writeToFile:withFileName: method, which creates an NSMutableArray and adds the text to be written to the file to it:

```
//---write content into a specified file path---
-(void) writeToFile:(NSString *) text
        withFileName:(NSString *) filePath {
    NSMutableArray *array = [[NSMutableArray alloc] init];
    [array addObject:text];
    [array writeToFile:filePath atomically:YES];
    [array release];
}
```

To persist the content (a process known as *serialization*) of the NSMutableArray to a file, you use its writeToFile:atomically: method. The atomically: parameter indicates that the file should first be written to a temporary file before it is renamed to the filename specified. This approach guarantees that the file will never be corrupted, even if the system crashes during the writing process.

To read the content from a file, you define the readFromFile: method:

```
//---read content from a specified file path---
-(NSString *) readFromFile:(NSString *) filePath {
```

```
        //---check if file exists---
        if ([[NSFileManager defaultManager] fileExistsAtPath:filePath]) {
            NSArray *array =
                [[NSArray alloc] initWithContentsOfFile: filePath];
            NSString *data =
                [NSString stringWithFormat:@"%@",
                    [array objectAtIndex:0]];
            [array release];
            return data;
        }
        else
            return nil;
    }
```

You first use an instance of the `NSFileManager` class to determine whether the specified file exists. If it does, then you read the content of the file into an `NSArray` object. In this case, because you know that the file contains a single line of text, you extract the first element in the array.

With all the methods in place, you are ready to make use of them. When the view is loaded, you create the pathname for a file that you want to save. You then write a string of text into the file and immediately read it back and print it in the Debugger Console window:

```
- (void)viewDidLoad {
    //---formulate filename---
    NSString *fileName =
        [[self documentsPath] stringByAppendingPathComponent:@"data.txt"];

    //---write something to the file---
    [self writeToFile:@"a string of text" withFileName:fileName];

    //---read it back---
    NSString *fileContent = [self readFromFile:fileName];

    //---display the content read in the Debugger Console window---
    NSLog(@"%@", fileContent);
    [super viewDidLoad];
}
```

Storing Files in the Temporary Folder

In addition to storing files in the `Documents` directory, you can store temporary files in the `tmp` folder. Files stored in the `tmp` folder are not backed up by iTunes, so you need to find a permanent place for the files you want to be sure to keep. To get the path to the `tmp` folder, you can call the `NSTemporaryDirectory()` function, like this:

```
-(NSString *) tempPath{
    return NSTemporaryDirectory();
}
```

The following statement returns the path of a file (`"data.txt"`) to be stored in the `tmp` folder:

```
NSString *fileName =
    [[self tempPath] stringByAppendingPathComponent:@"data.txt"];
```

USING PROPERTY LISTS

In iPhone programming, you can use property lists to store structured data using key/value pairs. Property lists are stored as XML files and are highly transportable across file systems and networks. For example, you might want to store a list of App Store application titles in your application. Because applications in the App Store are organized by category, it would be natural to store this information using a property list employing the structure shown in the following table:

CATEGORY	TITLES
Games	"Animal Park", "Biology Quiz", "Calculus Test"
Entertainment	"Eye Balls - iBlower", "iBell", "iCards Birthday"
Utilities	"Battery Monitor", "iSystemInfo"

In Xcode, you can create and add a property list in the `Resources` folder of your application and populate it with items using the built-in Property List Editor. The property list is deployed together with the application. Programmatically, you can retrieve the values stored in a property list using the `NSDictionary` class. More important, if you need to make changes to a property list, you can write the changes to a file so that you can later refer to the file directly instead of the property list.

In the following Try It Out, you create a property list and populate it with some values. You then read the values from the property list during runtime, make some changes, and save the modified values to another property list file in the `Documents` directory.

 NOTE *To store application-specific settings that users can modify outside your application, consider using the* NSUserDefaults *class to store the settings in the Settings application. Application settings are discussed in Chapter 9.*

TRY IT OUT   Creating and Modifying a Property List

1. Using the same project created earlier, right-click the project name in Xcode and choose Add ➪ New File.

2. Select the Resource item on the left of the New File dialog and select the Property List template on the right of the dialog (see Figure 10-3).

3. Name the property list `Apps.plist`.

4. Populate `Apps.plist` as shown in Figure 10-4.

FIGURE 10-3

FIGURE 10-4

5. Add the following bold statements to the `viewDidLoad` method:

```
- (void)viewDidLoad {
    //---formulate filename---
    NSString *fileName =
        [[self documentsPath] stringByAppendingPathComponent:@"data.txt"];

    //---write something to the file---
    [self writeToFile:@"a string of text" withFileName:fileName];

    //---read it back---
    NSString *fileContent = [self readFromFile:fileName];

    //---display the content read in the Debugger Console window---
    NSLog(@"%@", fileContent);

    //---get the path to the property list file---
    NSString *plistFileName =
        [[self documentsPath]
            stringByAppendingPathComponent:@"Apps.plist"];

    //---if the property list file can be found---
    if ([[NSFileManager defaultManager] fileExistsAtPath:plistFileName]) {

        //---load the content of the property list file into a NSDictionary
        // object---
        NSDictionary *dict =
            [[NSDictionary alloc]
                initWithContentsOfFile:plistFileName];

        //---for each category---
        for (NSString *category in dict) {
            NSLog(@"%@", category);
            NSLog(@"========");

            //---return all titles in an array---
            NSArray *titles = [dict valueForKey:category];

            //---print out all the titles in that category---
            for (NSString *title in titles) {
                NSLog(@"%@", title);
            }
        }
        [dict release];
    }
    else {
        //---load the property list from the Resources folder---
        NSString *pListPath =
            [[NSBundle mainBundle] pathForResource:@"Apps"
```

```
                                         ofType:@"plist"];

    NSDictionary *dict =
        [[NSDictionary alloc] initWithContentsOfFile:pListPath];

    //---make a mutable copy of the dictionary object---
    NSMutableDictionary *copyOfDict = [dict mutableCopy];

    //---get all the different categories---
    NSArray *categoriesArray =
        [[copyOfDict allKeys]
            sortedArrayUsingSelector:@selector(compare:)];

    //---for each category---
    for (NSString *category in categoriesArray) {
        //---get all the app titles in that category---
        NSArray *titles = [dict valueForKey:category];

        //---make a mutable copy of the array---
        NSMutableArray *mutableTitles = [titles mutableCopy];

        //---add a new title to the category---
        [mutableTitles addObject:@"New App title"];

        //---set the array back to the dictionary object---
        [copyOfDict setObject:mutableTitles forKey:category];
        [mutableTitles release];
    }

    //---write the dictionary to file---
    fileName =
        [[self documentsPath]
            stringByAppendingPathComponent:@"Apps.plist"];
    [copyOfDict writeToFile:fileName atomically:YES];
    [dict release];
    [copyOfDict release];
    }
    [super viewDidLoad];
}
```

6. Press Command-R to test the application on the iPhone 4 Simulator.

7. When you first run the application, you'll see that it creates a new .plist file in the Documents directory. Double-click the .plist file to view it using the Property List Editor; you will see a new item named New App title for each category of applications (see Figure 10-5).

8. Run the application a second time. It prints the content of the .plist file in the Documents directory to the Debugger Console window (see Figure 10-6), proving the existence of the property list in the Documents folder.

FIGURE 10-5

FIGURE 10-6

How It Works

The first part of this example shows how you can add a property list file to your application. In the property list file, you add three keys representing the category of applications in the App Store: Entertainment, Games, and Utilities. Each category contains a list of application titles.

When the view is loaded, you look for a file named `Apps.plist` in the `Documents` directory of your application:

```
//---get the path to the property list file---
NSString *plistFileName =
    [[self documentsPath]
        stringByAppendingPathComponent:@"Apps.plist"];
```

If the file is found, you load its contents into an `NSDictionary` object:

```
//---if the property list file can be found---
if ([[NSFileManager defaultManager] fileExistsAtPath:plistFileName]) {

    //---load the content of the property list file into a NSDictionary
    // object---
    NSDictionary *dict =
        [[NSDictionary alloc]
            initWithContentsOfFile:plistFileName];

    //...
    //...
}
```

Next, you enumerate through all the keys in the dictionary object and print the title of each application in the Debugger Console window:

```
//---for each category---
for (NSString *category in dict) {
    NSLog(@"%@", category);
    NSLog(@"========");

    //---return all titles in an array---
    NSArray *titles = [dict valueForKey:category];

    //---print out all the titles in that category---
    for (NSString *title in titles) {
        NSLog(@"%@", title);
    }
}
[dict release];
```

When the application is run for the first time, the `Apps.plist` file is not available, so you load it from the `Resources` folder:

```
else {
    //---load the property list from the Resources folder---
    NSString *pListPath =
        [[NSBundle mainBundle] pathForResource:@"Apps"
                                        ofType:@"plist"];

    NSDictionary *dict =
        [[NSDictionary alloc] initWithContentsOfFile:pListPath];

    //...
    //...
}
```

Because you are making changes to the dictionary object, you need to make a mutable copy of it and assign it to an NSMutableDictionary object:

```
//---make a mutable copy of the dictionary object---
NSMutableDictionary *copyOfDict = [dict mutableCopy];
```

This step is important because the NSDictionary object is immutable, meaning that after the items are populated from the property list, you cannot add content to the dictionary object. Using the mutableCopy method of the NSDictionary class allows you to create a mutable instance of the dictionary object, which is NSMutableDictionary.

You then retrieve an array containing all the keys in the mutable dictionary object:

```
//---get all the different categories---
NSArray *categoriesArray =
    [[copyOfDict allKeys]
        sortedArrayUsingSelector:@selector(compare:)];
```

You use this array to loop through all the keys in the dictionary so that you can add some additional titles to each category:

```
//---for each category---
for (NSString *category in categoriesArray) {

}
```

Note that you cannot enumerate using the NSMutableDictionary object like this:

```
for (NSString *category in copyOfDict) {
    //...
}
```

That's because you cannot add items to the NSMutableDictionary object while it is being enumerated. Therefore, you need to loop using an NSArray object.

When you're inside the loop, you extract all the titles of the applications in each category and make a mutable copy of the array containing the titles of the applications:

```
//---get all the app titles in that category---
NSArray *titles = [dict valueForKey:category];

//---make a mutable copy of the array---
NSMutableArray *mutableTitles = [titles mutableCopy];
```

You can now add a new title to the mutable array containing the application titles:

```
//---add a new title to the category---
[mutableTitles addObject:@"New App title"];
```

After the additional item is added to the mutable array, you set it back to the mutable dictionary object:

```
//---set the array back to the dictionary object---
[copyOfDict setObject:mutableTitles forKey:category];
[mutableTitles release];
```

Finally, you write the mutable dictionary object to a file using the `writeToFile:atomically:` method:

```
//---write the dictionary to file---
fileName =
    [[self documentsPath]
        stringByAppendingPathComponent:@"Apps.plist"];
[copyOfDict writeToFile:fileName atomically:YES];
[dict release];
[copyOfDict release];
```

COPYING BUNDLED RESOURCES

In the previous section, you learned how to embed a property list file into your application and then programmatically recreate the property list and save it in the Documents folder during runtime. While that example showed the various ways to manipulate a property list, in general it is much easier to simply copy the resource (such as the property list) into the Documents folder directly.

All resources embedded within your application (commonly known as *bundled resources*) are read-only. If you need to make changes to them, you need to copy them into the application's folders, such as the Documents or tmp folders. You can do so by copying the resource when the application starts. The ideal location to perform this is in the application delegate. Using the preceding example, you could define the following `copyFileInBundleToDocumentsFolder:withExtension:` method in the FilesHandlingAppDelegate.m file:

```
- (void) copyFileInBundleToDocumentsFolder:(NSString *) fileName
                          withExtension:(NSString *) ext {

    //---get the path of the Documents folder---
    NSArray *paths = NSSearchPathForDirectoriesInDomains(
        NSDocumentDirectory, NSUserDomainMask, YES);

    NSString *documentsDirectory = [paths objectAtIndex:0];

    //---get the path to the file you want to copy in the Documents folder---
    NSString *filePath =
        [documentsDirectory
            stringByAppendingPathComponent:
            [NSString stringWithString:fileName]];

    filePath = [filePath stringByAppendingString:@"."];
    filePath = [filePath stringByAppendingString:ext];

    //---check if file is already in Documents folder,
    // if not, copy it from the bundle---
    NSFileManager *fileManager = [NSFileManager defaultManager];
```

```
if (![fileManager fileExistsAtPath:filePath]) {

    //---get the path of the file in the bundle---
    NSString *pathToFileInBundle =
    [[NSBundle mainBundle] pathForResource:fileName ofType:ext];

    //---copy the file in the bundle to the Documents folder---
    NSError *error = nil;
    bool success =
    [fileManager copyItemAtPath:pathToFileInBundle
                         toPath:filePath error:&error];

    if (success) {
        NSLog(@"File copied");
    }
    else {
        NSLog(@"%@", [error localizedDescription]);
    }
}
}
```

This method simply copies the specified file to the Documents folder if it is not already there.

To copy the property list when the application is starting, call the `copyFileInBundleToDocumentsFolder:withExtension:` method in the `application:didFinishLaunchingWithOptions:` event:

```
- (BOOL)application:(UIApplication *)application
didFinishLaunchingWithOptions:(NSDictionary *)launchOptions {

    //---copy the txt files to the Documents folder---
    [self copyFileInBundleToDocumentsFolder:@"Apps"
                              withExtension:@"plist"];

    // Override point for customization after application launch.

    // Add the view controller's view to the window and display.
    [window addSubview:viewController.view];
    [window makeKeyAndVisible];

    return YES;
}
```

Doing so ensures that the property list is always copied to the Documents folder when the application begins running.

SUMMARY

This chapter demonstrated how to write a file to the file system of the iPhone and how to read it back. In addition, you saw how structured data can be represented using a property list and how you can programmatically work with a property list using a dictionary object. The next chapter shows you how to use databases to store more complex data.

EXERCISES

1. Describe the uses of the various folders within an application's folder.

2. What is the difference between the `NSDictionary` and `NSMutableDictionary` classes?

3. Name the paths of the `Documents` and `tmp` folders on a real device.

Answers to exercises can be found in Appendix E, on Wrox.com.

▶ **WHAT YOU LEARNED IN THIS CHAPTER**

TOPIC	KEY CONCEPTS
Subdirectories in each of the applications folders	Documents, Library, and tmp

Getting the path of the Documents **directory**	```NSArray *paths =```
	``` NSSearchPathForDirectoriesInDomains(```
	``` NSDocumentDirectory, NSUserDomainMask, YES);```
	```NSString *documentsDir = [paths objectAtIndex:0];```

Getting the path of the tmp **directory**	```-(NSString *) tempPath{```
	``` return NSTemporaryDirectory();```
	```}```

Checking whether a file exists	```if ([[NSFileManager defaultManager]```
	``` fileExistsAtPath:filePath]) {```
	```}```

Loading a property list from the Resources **folder**	```NSString *pListPath =```
	``` [[NSBundle mainBundle]```
	``` pathForResource:@"Apps"```
	``` ofType:@"plist"];```

Creating a mutable copy of an NSDictionary **object**	```NSDictionary *dict =```
	``` [[NSDictionary alloc]```
	``` initWithContentsOfFile:plistFileName];```
	```NSMutableDictionary *copyOfDict = [dict mutableCopy];```

Using bundled resources in your application	Copy the resources onto the application's folders, such as Documents or tmp. You should copy the resources in the application's delegate when the application has just finished launching.

11

Database Storage Using SQLite3

WHAT YOU WILL LEARN IN THIS CHAPTER

➤ How to use the SQLite3 database in your Xcode project

➤ How to create and open a SQLite3 database

➤ How to use the various SQLite3 functions to execute SQL strings

➤ How to use bind variables to insert values into a SQL string

➤ How to bundle a pre-built SQLite database with your application

As you continue on your iPhone development journey, you will soon realize that your application needs to find a way to save data. For example, you may want to save the text that the user is entering into a Text Field, or in an RSS application the last item that the user has read.

For simple applications, you can write the data you want to persist to a simple text file. For more structured data, you can use a property list. For large and complex data, it is more efficient to store it using a database. The iPhone comes with the SQLite3 database library, which you can use to store your data. With your data stored in a database, your application can populate a Table view or store a large amount of data in a structured manner.

 NOTE *Besides using SQLite for data storage, developers can also use another framework for storage: Core Data. Core Data is part of the Cocoa API, which was first introduced in the iPhone SDK 3.0. It is basically a framework for manipulating data without worrying about the details of storage and retrieval. A discussion of Core Data is beyond the scope of this book.*

This chapter shows you how to use the embedded SQLite3 database library in your applications.

USING SQLITE3

To use a SQLite3 database in your application, you first need to add the `libsqlite3.dylib` library to your Xcode project. Use the following Try It Out to find out how. You will need to download the code files indicated for this and the rest of the Try It Out features in this chapter.

TRY IT OUT   Preparing Your Project to Use SQLite3

codefile Databases.zip available for download at Wrox.com

1. Using Xcode, create a new View-based Application project and name it `Databases`.

2. Right-click the `Frameworks` folder in your project and add the `libsqlite3.dylib` library to it (see Figure 11-1).

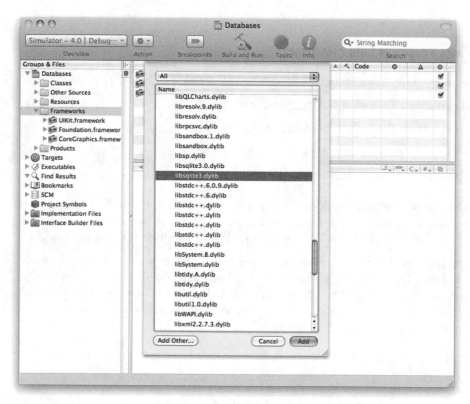

FIGURE 11-1

3. In the `DatabasesViewController.h` file, declare a variable of type `sqlite3` as well as a method named `filePath` (see the code in bold):

```
#import <UIKit/UIKit.h>
#import "sqlite3.h"

@interface DatabasesViewController : UIViewController {
```

```
        sqlite3 *db;
}

-(NSString *) filePath;

@end
```

4. In the `DatabasesViewController.m` file, define the `filePath` method as shown in bold:

```
#import "DatabasesViewController.h"

@implementation DatabasesViewController

-(NSString *) filePath {
    NSArray *paths = NSSearchPathForDirectoriesInDomains(
                        NSDocumentDirectory,
                        NSUserDomainMask,
                        YES);

    NSString *documentsDir = [paths objectAtIndex:0];
    return [documentsDir stringByAppendingPathComponent:@"database.sql"];
}
```

How It Works

To work with SQLite3, you must link your application to a dynamic library called `libsqlite3.dylib`. The `libsqlite3.dylib` that you selected is an alias to the latest version of the SQLite3 library. On an actual iPhone device, the `libsqlite3.dylib` is located in the `/usr/lib/` directory.

To use a SQLite database, you need to create an object of type `sqlite3`:

```
        sqlite3 *db;
```

The `filePath` method returns the full path to the SQLite database that will be created in the `Documents` directory on your iPhone (within your application's sandbox):

```
    -(NSString *) filePath {
        NSArray *paths = NSSearchPathForDirectoriesInDomains(
                            NSDocumentDirectory,
                            NSUserDomainMask,
                            YES);

        NSString *documentsDir = [paths objectAtIndex:0];
        return [documentsDir stringByAppendingPathComponent:@"database.sql"];
    }
```

NOTE *Chapter 10 discusses the various folders that you can access within your application's sandbox.*

CREATING AND OPENING A DATABASE

After the necessary library is added to the project, you can open a database for usage. You use the various C functions included with SQLite3 to create or open a database, as demonstrated in the following one-step Try It Out.

TRY IT OUT   **Opening a Database**

1.   Using the Databases project created previously, define the openDB method in the DatabasesViewController.m file:

```
-(void) openDB {
    //---create database---
    if (sqlite3_open([[self filePath] UTF8String], &db) != SQLITE_OK ) {
        sqlite3_close(db);
        NSAssert(0, @"Database failed to open.");
    }
}

- (void)viewDidLoad {
    [self openDB];
    [super viewDidLoad];
}
```

How It Works

The sqlite3_open() C function opens a SQLite database whose filename is specified as the first argument:

```
[self filePath] UTF8String]
```

In this case, the filename of the database is specified as a C string using the UTF8String method of the NSString class because the sqlite3_open() C function does not understand an NSString object.

The second argument contains a handle to the sqlite3 object, which in this case is db.

If the database is available, it is opened. If the specified database is not found, a new database is created. If the database is successfully opened, the function will return a value of 0 (represented using the SQLITE_OK constant).

The following list from www.sqlite.org/c3ref/c_abort.html shows the result codes returned by the various SQLite functions:

```
#define SQLITE_OK           0    /* Successful result */
#define SQLITE_ERROR        1    /* SQL error or missing database */
#define SQLITE_INTERNAL     2    /* Internal logic error in SQLite */
#define SQLITE_PERM         3    /* Access permission denied */
#define SQLITE_ABORT        4    /* Callback routine requested an abort */
#define SQLITE_BUSY         5    /* The database file is locked */
#define SQLITE_LOCKED       6    /* A table in the database is locked */
#define SQLITE_NOMEM        7    /* A malloc() failed */
#define SQLITE_READONLY     8    /* Attempt to write a readonly database */
#define SQLITE_INTERRUPT    9    /* Operation terminated by sqlite3_interrupt()*/
#define SQLITE_IOERR       10    /* Some kind of disk I/O error occurred */
```

```
#define SQLITE_CORRUPT      11   /* The database disk image is malformed */
#define SQLITE_NOTFOUND     12   /* NOT USED. Table or record not found */
#define SQLITE_FULL         13   /* Insertion failed because database is full */
#define SQLITE_CANTOPEN     14   /* Unable to open the database file */
#define SQLITE_PROTOCOL     15   /* NOT USED. Database lock protocol error */
#define SQLITE_EMPTY        16   /* Database is empty */
#define SQLITE_SCHEMA       17   /* The database schema changed */
#define SQLITE_TOOBIG       18   /* String or BLOB exceeds size limit */
#define SQLITE_CONSTRAINT   19   /* Abort due to constraint violation */
#define SQLITE_MISMATCH     20   /* Data type mismatch */
#define SQLITE_MISUSE       21   /* Library used incorrectly */
#define SQLITE_NOLFS        22   /* Uses OS features not supported on host */
#define SQLITE_AUTH         23   /* Authorization denied */
#define SQLITE_FORMAT       24   /* Auxiliary database format error */
#define SQLITE_RANGE        25   /* 2nd parameter to sqlite3_bind out of range */
#define SQLITE_NOTADB       26   /* File opened that is not a database file */
#define SQLITE_ROW          100  /* sqlite3_step() has another row ready */
#define SQLITE_DONE         101  /* sqlite3_step() has finished executing */
```

Examining the Database Created

If the database is created successfully, it can be found in the Documents folder of your application's sandbox on the iPhone 4 Simulator in the ~/Library/Application Support/iPhone Simulator/4.0/ Applications/<App_ID>/Documents/ folder. Figure 11-2 shows the database.sql file.

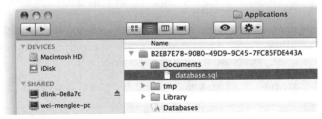

FIGURE 11-2

Creating a Table

After the database is created, you can create a table to store some data. The following one-step Try It Out demonstrates how to create a table with two text fields. For illustration purposes, create a table named Contacts, with two fields called email and name.

TRY IT OUT Creating a Table

1. Using the same Databases project, define the createTableNamed:with-Field1:withField2: method in the DatabasesViewController.m file as follows:

```
-(void) createTableNamed:(NSString *) tableName
         withField1:(NSString *) field1
```

```
                    withField2:(NSString *) field2 {

        char *err;
        NSString *sql = [NSString stringWithFormat:
                            @"CREATE TABLE IF NOT EXISTS '%@' ('%@'
                            TEXT PRIMARY KEY, '%@' TEXT);",
                            tableName, field1, field2];
        //---the above SQL statement to be typed in a single line---

        if (sqlite3_exec(db, [sql UTF8String], NULL, NULL, &err)
            != SQLITE_OK) {
            sqlite3_close(db);
            NSAssert(0, @"Tabled failed to create.");
        }
    }

    - (void)viewDidLoad {
        [self openDB];
        [self createTableNamed:@"Contacts"
                    withField1:@"email"
                    withField2:@"name"];
        [super viewDidLoad];
    }
```

How It Works

The createTableNamed:withField1:withField2: method takes three parameters: tableName, field1, and field2.

Using these parameters, you first formulate a SQL string and then create a table using the sqlite3_exec() C function, with the important arguments to this function being the sqlite3 object, the SQL query string, and a pointer to a variable for error messages. If an error occurs in creating the database, you use the NSAssert method to halt the application and close the database connection.

If the operation is successful, a table named Contacts with two fields (email and name) is created.

 NOTE *For a jump start in the SQL language, check out the SQL tutorial at* http://w3schools.com/sql/default.asp.

Inserting Records

After the table is created, you can insert some records into it. The following Try It Out shows you how to write three rows of records in the table created in the previous section.

TRY IT OUT   Inserting Records

1.   In the Databases project, define the
insertRecordIntoTableNamed:withField1:field1Value:andField2:field2Value: method in the
DatabasesViewController.m file as follows and modify the viewDidLoad method as shown in bold:

```
-(void) insertRecordIntoTableNamed:(NSString *) tableName
                  withField1:(NSString *) field1
                  field1Value:(NSString *) field1Value
                  andField2:(NSString *) field2
                  field2Value:(NSString *) field2Value {

    NSString *sql = [NSString stringWithFormat:
                @"INSERT OR REPLACE INTO '%@' ('%@', '%@')
                    VALUES ('%@','%@')", tableName, field1, field2,
                    field1Value, field2Value];
    //---the above SQL statement to be typed in a single line---

    char *err;
    if (sqlite3_exec(db, [sql UTF8String], NULL, NULL, &err)
        != SQLITE_OK) {
        sqlite3_close(db);
        NSAssert(0, @"Error updating table.");
    }
}

- (void)viewDidLoad {
    [self openDB];
    [self createTableNamed:@"Contacts"
              withField1:@"email"
              withField2:@"name"];
    for (int i=0; i<=2; i++) {
        NSString *email = [[NSString alloc] initWithFormat:
                      @"user%d@learn2develop.net",i];

        NSString *name = [[NSString alloc] initWithFormat: @"user %d",i];
        [self insertRecordIntoTableNamed:@"Contacts"
                          withField1:@"email" field1Value:email
                            andField2:@"name" field2Value:name];

        [email release];
        [name release];
    }
    [super viewDidLoad];
}
```

How It Works

The code in this example is similar to that of the previous one; you formulate a SQL string and use the
sqlite3_exec() C function to insert a record into the database:

```
NSString *sql = [NSString stringWithFormat:
            @"INSERT OR REPLACE INTO '%@' ('%@', '%@')
                VALUES ('%@','%@')", tableName, field1, field2,
```

```
                              field1Value, field2Value];
        //---the above SQL statement to be typed in a single line---

        char *err;
        if (sqlite3_exec(db, [sql UTF8String], NULL, NULL, &err)
            != SQLITE_OK) {
            sqlite3_close(db);
            NSAssert(0, @"Error updating table.");
        }
```

In the `viewDidLoad` method, you insert three records into the database by calling the `insertRecordIntoTableNamed:withField1:field1Value:andField2:field2Value:` method:

```
        for (int i=0; i<=2; i++) {
            NSString *email = [[NSString alloc] initWithFormat:
                              @"user%d@learn2develop.net",i];

            NSString *name = [[NSString alloc] initWithFormat: @"user %d",i];
            [self insertRecordIntoTableNamed:@"Contacts"
                              withField1:@"email" field1Value:email
                                andField2:@"name" field2Value:name];

            [email release];
            [name release];
        }
```

Bind Variables

When formulating SQL strings, you often need to insert values into the query string and ensure that the string is well formulated and contains no invalid characters. In the preceding section, you saw that to insert a row into the database, you had to formulate your SQL statement like this:

```
        NSString *sql = [NSString stringWithFormat:
                        @"INSERT OR REPLACE INTO '%@' ('%@', '%@')
                          VALUES ('%@','%@')", tableName, field1, field2,
                          field1Value, field2Value];
        //---the above SQL statement to be typed in a single line---

        char *err;
        if (sqlite3_exec(db, [sql UTF8String], NULL, NULL, &err)
            != SQLITE_OK) {
            sqlite3_close(db);
            NSAssert(0, @"Error updating table.");
        }
```

SQLite supports a feature known as *bind variables* to help you formulate your SQL string. For example, the preceding SQL string can be formulated as follows using bind variables:

```
        NSString *sqlStr = [NSString stringWithFormat:
                           @"INSERT OR REPLACE INTO '%@' ('%@', '%@')
                             VALUES (?,?)", tableName, field1, field2];
                    const char *sql = [sqlStr UTF8String];
```

Here, the ? is a placeholder for you to replace with the actual value of the query. In the preceding statement, assuming that `tableName` is `Contacts`, `field1` is `email`, and `field2` is `name`, the `sql` is now as follows:

```
INSERT OR REPLACE INTO Contacts ('email', 'name') VALUES (?,?)
```

> **NOTE** The ? can be inserted only into the *VALUES* and *WHERE* section of the SQL statement; you cannot insert it into a table name, for example. The following statement would be invalid:
>
> ```
> INSERT OR REPLACE INTO ? ('email', 'name') VALUES (?,?)
> ```

To substitute the values for the ?, create a `sqlite3_stmt` object and use the `sqlite3_prepare_v2()` function to compile the SQL string into a binary form and then insert the placeholder values using the `sqlite3_bind_text()` function, like this:

```
sqlite3_stmt *statement;

if (sqlite3_prepare_v2(db, sql, -1, &statement, nil) == SQLITE_OK) {
    sqlite3_bind_text(statement, 1, [field1Value UTF8String],
                      -1, NULL);
    sqlite3_bind_text(statement, 2, [field2Value UTF8String],
                      -1, NULL);
}
```

> **NOTE** To bind integer values, use the `sqlite3_bind_int()` *function.*

After the preceding call, the SQL string looks like this:

```
INSERT OR REPLACE INTO Contacts ('email', 'name') VALUES
('user0@learn2develop.net', 'user0')
```

To execute the SQL statement, you use the `sqlite3_step()` function, followed by the `sqlite3_finalize()` function to delete the prepared SQL statement:

```
if (sqlite3_step(statement) != SQLITE_DONE)
    NSAssert(0, @"Error updating table.");
sqlite3_finalize(statement);
```

Using bind variables, the `insertRecordIntoTableNamed:withField1:field1Value:andField2:field2Value:` method could now be rewritten as follows:

```
-(void) insertRecordIntoTableNamed:(NSString *) tableName
                        withField1:(NSString *) field1
                       field1Value:(NSString *) field1Value
                         andField2:(NSString *) field2
```

```
                            field2Value:(NSString *) field2Value {

    NSString *sqlStr = [NSString stringWithFormat:
                        @"INSERT OR REPLACE INTO '%@' ('%@', '%@')
                          VALUES (?,?)", tableName, field1, field2];
    //---the above SQL statement to be typed in a single line---

    const char *sql = [sqlStr UTF8String];
    sqlite3_stmt *statement;
    if (sqlite3_prepare_v2(db, sql, -1, &statement, nil) == SQLITE_OK) {
        sqlite3_bind_text(statement, 1, [field1Value UTF8String],
                          -1, NULL);
        sqlite3_bind_text(statement, 2, [field2Value UTF8String],
                          -1, NULL);
    }

    if (sqlite3_step(statement) != SQLITE_DONE)
        NSAssert(0, @"Error updating table.");

    sqlite3_finalize(statement);
}
```

 NOTE In the Inserting Records section, you used the `sqlite3_exec()` function to execute SQL statements. In this example, you actually use a combination of the `sqlite3_prepare()`, `sqlite3_step()`, and `sqlite3_finalize()` functions to do the same thing. In fact, the `sqlite3_exec()` function is actually a wrapper for these three functions. For non-query SQL statements (such as for creating tables, inserting rows, and so on), it is always better to use the `sqlite3_exec()` function.

Retrieving Records

Now that the records have been successfully inserted into the table, it is time to retrieve them. This is a good way to ensure that they have actually been saved. The following Try It Out shows you how to retrieve your records.

TRY IT OUT   Retrieving the Records from the Table

1. In the `Databases` project, define the `getAllRowsFromTableNamed:` method in the `DatabasesViewController.m` file as follows and modify the `viewDidLoad` method as shown in bold:

```
-(void) getAllRowsFromTableNamed: (NSString *) tableName {
    //---retrieve rows---
    NSString *qsql = [NSString stringWithFormat:@"SELECT * FROM %@",
                      tableName];

    sqlite3_stmt *statement;
```

```objc
    if (sqlite3_prepare_v2( db, [qsql UTF8String], -1,
        &statement, nil) == SQLITE_OK) {
        while (sqlite3_step(statement) == SQLITE_ROW) {
            char *field1 = (char *) sqlite3_column_text(statement, 0);
            NSString *field1Str =
                [[NSString alloc] initWithUTF8String: field1];

            char *field2 = (char *) sqlite3_column_text(statement, 1);
            NSString *field2Str =
                [[NSString alloc] initWithUTF8String: field2];

            NSString *str = [[NSString alloc] initWithFormat:@"%@ - %@",
                                field1Str, field2Str];
            NSLog(@"%@", str);

            [field1Str release];
            [field2Str release];
            [str release];
        }

        //---deletes the compiled statement from memory---
        sqlite3_finalize(statement);
    }
}

- (void)viewDidLoad {
    [self openDB];
    [self createTableNamed:@"Contacts"
                withField1:@"email"
                withField2:@"name"];

    for (int i=0; i<=2; i++) {
        NSString *email = [[NSString alloc] initWithFormat:
                            @"user%d@learn2develop.net",i];

        NSString *name = [[NSString alloc] initWithFormat: @"user %d",i];
        [self insertRecordIntoTableNamed:@"Contacts"
                            withField1:@"email" field1Value:email
                              andField2:@"name" field2Value:name];
        [email release];
        [name release];
    }

    [self getAllRowsFromTableNamed:@"Contacts"];
    sqlite3_close(db);
    [super viewDidLoad];
}
```

2. Press Command-R to test the application. In Xcode, press Command-Shift-R to display the Debugger Console window. When the application has loaded, the Debugger Console displays the records (see Figure 11-3), proving that the rows are indeed in the table.

FIGURE 11-3

How It Works

To retrieve the records from the table, you first prepare the SQL statement and then use the `sqlite3_step()` function to execute the prepared statement. The `sqlite3_step()` function returns a value of 100 (represented by the `SQLITE_ROW` constant) if another row is ready. In this case, you call the `sqlite3_step()` function using a `while` loop, continuing as long as it returns a `SQLITE_ROW`:

```
if (sqlite3_prepare_v2( db, [qsql UTF8String], -1,
    &statement, nil) == SQLITE_OK) {
    while (sqlite3_step(statement) == SQLITE_ROW) {
        char *field1 = (char *) sqlite3_column_text(statement, 0);
        NSString *field1Str =
            [[NSString alloc] initWithUTF8String: field1];

        char *field2 = (char *) sqlite3_column_text(statement, 1);
        NSString *field2Str =
            [[NSString alloc] initWithUTF8String: field2];

        NSString *str = [[NSString alloc] initWithFormat:@"%@ - %@",
                            field1Str, field2Str];
        NSLog(@"%@", str);

        [field1Str release];
        [field2Str release];
        [str release];
    }

    //---deletes the compiled statement from memory---
    sqlite3_finalize(statement);
}
```

To retrieve the value for the first field in the row, you use the `sqlite3_column_text()` function by passing it the `sqlite3_stmt` object as well as the index of the field you are retrieving. For example, you use the following to retrieve the first field of the returned row:

```
char *field1 = (char *) sqlite3_column_text(statement, 0);
```

To retrieve an integer column (field), use the `sqlite3_column_int()` function.

BUNDLING SQLITE DATABASES WITH YOUR APPLICATION

While programmatically creating a SQLite database and using it during runtime is very flexible, most of the time you just need to create the database file during the designing stage of your development, and bundle the database with your application so that it can be used during runtime. Therefore, instead of creating the database file using code, you need to create it in Mac OS X.

Fortunately, you can easily create a SQLite database file in Mac OS X by using the `sqlite3` application in Terminal. Figure 11-4 shows the command that you need to create a database named `mydata.sql`, containing a table named `Contacts` with two fields: `email` and `name`. It also inserts a row into the table and then retrieves it to verify that it is inserted properly.

FIGURE 11-4

The commands are as follows:

➤ `sqlite3 mydata.sql`

➤ `CREATE TABLE IF NOT EXISTS Contacts (email TEXT PRIMARY KEY, name TEXT);`

➤ `INSERT INTO Contacts (email, name) VALUES ('weimenglee@gmail.com', 'weimenglee');`

➤ `SELECT * FROM Contacts`

 NOTE *Remember to end each command with a semicolon (;). Also, by default, when you launch Terminal, you are in your home directory. Hence, running the* `sqlite3` *application will save your database file in your home directory.*

Even though you could use the `sqlite3` application to insert records into the database, it would be much easier to use a graphical tool to do that. You can use the SQLite Database Browser (see

Figure 11-5), which you can download free from `http://sourceforge.net/projects/` `sqlitebrowser/`. Using the SQLite Database Browser, you can perform a wide variety of functions with the database file.

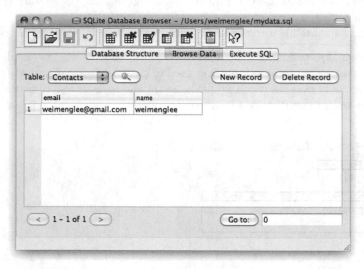

FIGURE 11-5

SUMMARY

This chapter provided a brief introduction to the SQLite3 database used in the iPhone. With SQLite3, you can now store all your structured data in an efficient manner and perform complex aggregations on your data. To learn more about SQLite, visit its official page at: `www.sqlite.org/`.

EXERCISES

1. Explain the difference between the `sqlite3_exec()` function and the three functions `sqlite3_prepare()`, `sqlite3_step()`, and `sqlite3_finalize()`.

2. How do you obtain a C-style string from an `NSString` object?

3. Write the code segment to retrieve a set of rows from a table.

Answers to the Exercises can be found in Appendix E, on Wrox.com.

► **WHAT YOU LEARNED IN THIS CHAPTER**

TOPIC	KEY CONCEPTS
Using a SQLite3 database in your application	Add a reference to the `libsqlite3.dylib` library to your project.
Obtaining a C-style string from an `NSString` object	Use the `UTF8String` method of the `NSString` class.
Creating and opening a SQLite3 database	Use the `sqlite3_open()` C function.
Executing a SQL query	Use the `sqlite3_exec()` C function.
Closing a database connection	Use the `sqlite3_close()` C function.
Using bind variables	Create a `sqlite3_stmt` object.
	Use the `sqlite3_prepare_v2()` C function to prepare the statement.
	Use the `sqlite3_bind_text()` (or `sqlite3_bind_int()`, and so on) C function to insert the values into the statement.
	Use the `sqlite3_step()` C function to execute the statement.
	Use the `sqlite3_finalize()` C function to delete the statement from memory.
Retrieving records	Use the `sqlite3_step()` C function to retrieve each individual row.
Retrieving columns from a row	Use the `sqlite3_column_text()` (or `sqlite3_column_int()`, and so on) C function.

PART III
Advanced iOS 4 Programming Techniques

12

Simple Animations and Video Playback

WHAT YOU WILL LEARN IN THIS CHAPTER

➤ How to use the NSTimer class to create timers that call methods at regular intervals

➤ How to perform simple animations using the NSTimer class

➤ How to perform affine transformation on an Image View

➤ How to animate a series of images using Image View

➤ How to play back videos in your iPhone application

Up to this point, the applications you have written have all made use of the standard views provided by the iPhone SDK. As Apple has reiterated, the iPhone is not just for serious work; it is also a gaming platform.

In this chapter, you have some fun creating something visual. You learn how to perform some simple animations using a timer object and then perform some transformations on a view. Although it is beyond the scope of this book to show you how to create animations using OpenGL ES, this chapter does demonstrate some interesting techniques that you can use to make your applications come alive. In addition, you will also learn how to play back a video in your iPhone application.

USING THE NSTIMER CLASS

One of the easiest ways to get started with animation is to use the NSTimer class. The NSTimer class creates timer objects, which enable you to call a method at a regular time interval. Using an NSTimer object, you can update an image at regular time intervals, thereby creating an impression that it is being animated.

In the following Try It Out, you learn how to display a bouncing ball on the screen using the NSTimer class. When the ball touches the sides of the screen, it bounces off in the opposite direction. You also learn how to control the frequency with which the ball animates. Download the code files indicated here for this and other Try It Out features within this chapter.

TRY IT OUT   Animating a Ball

codefile Animation.zip is available for download at Wrox.com

1.   Using Xcode, create a new View-based Application (iPhone) project and name it Animation.

2.   Drag and drop an image named tennisball.jpg to the Resources folder in Xcode. When the Add dialog appears, check the Copy Item into the Destination Group's Folder (If Needed) option so that the image is copied into the project (see Figure 12-1).

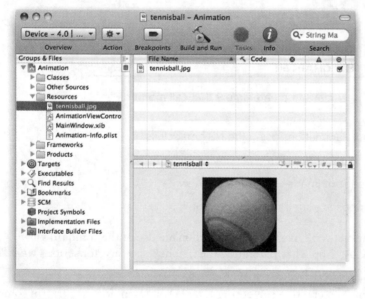

FIGURE 12-1

3.   Double-click the AnimationViewController.xib file to edit it in Interface Builder.

4.   Drag and drop an Image View onto the View window and set its Image property to tennisball.jpg (see Figure 12-2).

Ensure that the size of the Image View fits the entire tennis ball image. Later, you will move the Image View on the screen, so it is important not to fill the entire screen with the Image View.

5.   Select the View (outside the Image View) and change the background color to black (see Figure 12-3).

FIGURE 12-2

FIGURE 12-3

6. Add a Label and a Slider view from the Library onto the View window (see the lower-left corner of Figure 12-4). Set the `Initial` property of the Slider view to `0.01`.

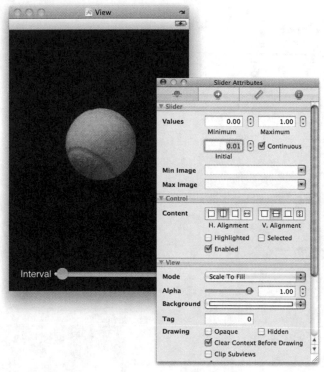

FIGURE 12-4

7. In the `AnimationViewController.h` file, declare the following outlets, fields, and actions (shown in bold):

```objc
#import <UIKit/UIKit.h>

@interface AnimationViewController : UIViewController {
    IBOutlet UIImageView *imageView;
    IBOutlet UISlider *slider;

    CGPoint delta;
    NSTimer *timer;
    float ballRadius;
}

@property (nonatomic, retain) UIImageView *imageView;
@property (nonatomic, retain) UISlider *slider;

-(IBAction) sliderMoved:(id) sender;

@end
```

8. Back in Interface Builder, connect the outlets and actions as follows (see Figure 12-5 for the connections after all the outlets and actions are connected):

➤ Control-click and drag the File's Owner item to the Image View and select `imageView`.

➤ Control-click and drag the File's Owner item to the Slider view and select `slider`.

➤ Control-click and drag the Slider view to the File's Owner item and select `sliderMoved:`.

FIGURE 12-5

9. Add the following bold statements to the `AnimationViewController.m` file:

```objc
#import "AnimationViewController.h"

@implementation AnimationViewController

@synthesize imageView;
@synthesize slider;

-(void) onTimer {
    imageView.center = CGPointMake(imageView.center.x + delta.x,
                                   imageView.center.y + delta.y);

    if (imageView.center.x > self.view.bounds.size.width - ballRadius ||
        imageView.center.x < ballRadius)
        delta.x = -delta.x;

    if (imageView.center.y > self.view.bounds.size.height - ballRadius ||
        imageView.center.y < ballRadius)
        delta.y = -delta.y;
}

- (void) viewDidLoad {
    ballRadius = imageView.frame.size.width / 2;
    [slider setShowValue:YES];
    delta = CGPointMake(12.0,4.0);
    timer = [NSTimer scheduledTimerWithTimeInterval:slider.value
                                target:self
                                selector:@selector(onTimer)
```

```
                                                    userInfo:nil
                                                     repeats:YES];

        [super viewDidLoad];
}

-(IBAction) sliderMoved:(id) sender {
    [timer invalidate];
    timer = [NSTimer scheduledTimerWithTimeInterval:slider.value
                                             target:self
                                           selector:@selector(onTimer)
                                           userInfo:nil
                                            repeats:YES];
}

- (void)dealloc {
    [timer invalidate];
    [imageView release];
    [slider release];
    [super dealloc];
}
```

10. Press Command-R to test the application on the iPhone 4 Simulator. The tennis ball should now be animated on the screen (see Figure 12-6). Vary the speed of the animation by moving the slider — to the right to slow it down and to the left to speed it up.

FIGURE 12-6

How It Works

When the view is loaded, the first thing you do is get the radius of the tennis ball, which in this case is half the width of the image:

```
ballRadius = imageView.frame.size.width / 2;
```

This value is used during the animation to check whether the tennis ball has touched the edges of the screen.

To set the slider to show its value, you use the setShowValue: method:

```
[slider setShowValue:YES];
```

 NOTE The setShowValue: *method is undocumented, hence the compiler will sound a warning. Be forewarned that using any undocumented methods may result in your application being rejected when you submit it to Apple for approval. In general, use undocumented methods only for debugging purposes.*

You also initialize the delta variable:

```
delta = CGPointMake(12.0,4.0);
```

The delta variable is used to specify how many pixels the image must move every time the timer fires. The preceding code tells it to move 12 pixels horizontally and 4 pixels vertically.

You next call the scheduledTimerWithTimeInterval:target:selector:userInfo:repeats: class method of the NSTimer class to create a new instance of the NSTimer object:

```
timer = [NSTimer scheduledTimerWithTimeInterval:slider.value
                                         target:self
                                       selector:
                                           @selector(onTimer)
                                       userInfo:nil
                                        repeats:YES];
```

The scheduledTimerWithTimeInterval: parameter specifies the number of seconds between firings of the timer. Here, you set it to the value of the Slider view, which accepts a value from 0.0 to 1.0. For example, if the slider's value is 0.5, the timer object will fire every half-second.

The selector: parameter specifies the method to call when the timer fires, and the repeats: parameter indicates whether the timer object will repeatedly reschedule itself. In this case, when the timer fires, it calls the onTimer method, which you define next.

In the onTimer method, you change the position of the Image View by setting its center property to a new value. After repositioning, you check whether the image has touched the edges of the screen; if it has, the value of the delta variable is negated:

```
-(void) onTimer {
```

```
    imageView.center = CGPointMake(imageView.center.x + delta.x,
                                   imageView.center.y + delta.y);
    if (imageView.center.x >
            self.view.bounds.size.width - ballRadius ||
        imageView.center.x < ballRadius)
        delta.x = -delta.x;

    if (imageView.center.y >
            self.view.bounds.size.height - ballRadius ||
        imageView.center.y < ballRadius)
        delta.y = -delta.y;
}
```

When you move the slider, the `sliderMoved:` method is called. In this method, first invalidate the timer object and then create another instance of the `NSTimer` class:

```
-(IBAction) sliderMoved:(id) sender {
    [timer invalidate];
    timer = [NSTimer scheduledTimerWithTimeInterval:slider.value
                                    target:self
                                    selector:
                                       @selector(onTimer)
                                    userInfo:nil
                                     repeats:YES];
}
```

Moving the slider enables you to change the frequency at which the image is animated.

 NOTE *After an* `NSTimer` *object is started, you cannot change its firing interval. Therefore, the only way to change the interval is to invalidate the current one and create a new* `NSTimer` *object.*

Animating the Visual Change

You may have noticed that as you move the slider toward the right, the animation slows and becomes choppy.

To make the animation smoother, you can animate the visual changes by using an *animation block*. The start of the animation block is defined by the `beginAnimations:context:` class method of the `UIView` class:

```
[UIView beginAnimations:@"my_own_animation" context:nil];

//---animate for the duration of the slider value (time interval)---
[UIView setAnimationDuration:slider.value];
```

```
//---set the animation curve type---
[UIView setAnimationCurve:UIViewAnimationCurveLinear];

imageView.center = CGPointMake(imageView.center.x + delta.x,
                              imageView.center.y + delta.y);


//---committing the animations--
[UIView commitAnimations];
```

To end an animation block, you call the commitAnimations class method of the UIView class. The preceding code animates the Image View when it moves from one position to another. This results in a much smoother animation.

TRANSFORMING VIEWS

You can use the NSTimer class to simulate a simple animation by continuously changing the position of the Image View, but you can use the transformation techniques supported by the iPhone SDK to achieve the same effect.

Transforms are defined in Core Graphics (a C-based API that is based on the Quartz advanced drawing engine; you use this framework to handle things such as drawings, transformations, image creation, etc.), and the iPhone SDK supports standard affine 2D transforms. You can use the iPhone SDK to perform the following affine 2D transforms:

➤ **Translation** — Moves the origin of the view by the amount specified using the x and y axes.

➤ **Rotation** — Moves the view by the angle specified.

➤ **Scaling** — Changes the scale of the view by the x and y factors specified.

> **NOTE** An affine transformation *is a linear transformation that preserves co-linearity and ratio of distances. This means that all the points lying on a line initially will remain in a line after the transformation, with the respective distance ratios between them maintained.*

Figure 12-7 shows the effects of the various transformations.

Translation

To perform an affine transform on a view, simply use its transform property. Recall that in the previous example, you set the new position of the view through its center property:

```
imageView.center = CGPointMake(imageView.center.x + delta.x,
                              imageView.center.y + delta.y);
```

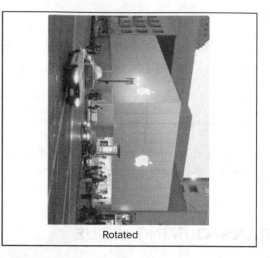

Rotated

Scaled

FIGURE 12-7

Using 2D transformation, you can use its transform property and set it to a CGAffineTransform data structure returned by the CGAffineTransformMakeTranslation() function, like this:

```
//--add the following bold line in the AnimationViewController.h file--
#import <UIKit/UIKit.h>

@interface AnimationViewController : UIViewController {
    IBOutlet UIImageView *imageView;
    IBOutlet UISlider *slider;
    CGPoint delta;
    NSTimer *timer;
    float ballRadius;

    //--add this line--
    CGPoint translation;
}

@property (nonatomic, retain) UIImageView *imageView;
```

```
@property (nonatomic, retain) UISlider *slider;

-(IBAction) sliderMoved:(id) sender;

@end
```

```
//--add the following bold line in the AnimationViewController.m file--
- (void)viewDidLoad {
    ballRadius = imageView.frame.size.width / 2;
    [slider setShowValue:YES];
    delta = CGPointMake(12.0,4.0);

    translation = CGPointMake(0.0,0.0);

    timer = [NSTimer scheduledTimerWithTimeInterval:slider.value
                                             target:self
                                           selector:@selector(onTimer)
                                           userInfo:nil
                                            repeats:YES];
    [super viewDidLoad];
}

-(void) onTimer {
    [UIView beginAnimations:@"my_own_animation" context:nil];

    //---animate for the duration of the slider value (time interval)---
    [UIView setAnimationDuration:slider.value];

    //---set the animation curve type---
    [UIView setAnimationCurve:UIViewAnimationCurveLinear];

    imageView.transform =
        CGAffineTransformMakeTranslation(translation.x, translation.y);

    [UIView commitAnimations];

    translation.x += delta.x;
    translation.y += delta.y;

    if (imageView.center.x + translation.x >
        self.view.bounds.size.width - ballRadius ||
        imageView.center.x + translation.x < ballRadius)
        delta.x = -delta.x;

    if (imageView.center.y + translation.y >
        self.view.bounds.size.height - ballRadius ||
        imageView.center.y + translation.y < ballRadius)
        delta.y = -delta.y;
}
```

The `CGAffineTransformMakeTranslation()` function takes two arguments: the value to move for the *x* axis and the value to move for the *y* axis.

The preceding code achieves the same effect as setting the `center` property of Image View.

Rotation

The rotation transformation enables you to rotate a view using the angle you specify. In the following Try It Out, you modify the code from the previous example so that the tennis ball rotates as it bounces across the screen.

TRY IT OUT   Rotating the Tennis Ball

1. In the `AnimationViewController.h` file, add the declaration for the `angle` variable as shown in bold:

```
#import <UIKit/UIKit.h>

@interface AnimationViewController : UIViewController {
    IBOutlet UIImageView *imageView;
    IBOutlet UISlider *slider;
    CGPoint delta;
    NSTimer *timer;
    float ballRadius;

    CGPoint translation;

    //--add this line--
    float angle;
}

@property (nonatomic, retain) UIImageView *imageView;
@property (nonatomic, retain) UISlider *slider;

-(IBAction) sliderMoved:(id) sender;

@end
```

2. In the `AnimationViewController.m` file, add the following bold statements:

```
- (void)viewDidLoad {

    //---set the angle to 0---
    angle = 0;

    ballRadius = imageView.frame.size.width / 2;
    [slider setShowValue:YES];
    delta = CGPointMake(12.0,4.0);

    translation = CGPointMake(0.0,0.0);

    timer = [NSTimer scheduledTimerWithTimeInterval:slider.value
                                             target:self
                                           selector:@selector(onTimer)
                                           userInfo:nil
                                            repeats:YES];
    [super viewDidLoad];
```

```
}

-(void) onTimer {
    //---rotation---
    [UIView beginAnimations:@"my_own_animation" context:nil];

    //---animate for the duration of the slider value (time interval)---
    [UIView setAnimationDuration:slider.value];

    //---set the animation curve type---
    [UIView setAnimationCurve:UIViewAnimationCurveLinear];

    imageView.transform = CGAffineTransformMakeRotation(angle);

    [UIView commitAnimations];

    angle += 0.02;
    if (angle>6.2857) angle = 0;

    imageView.center = CGPointMake(imageView.center.x + delta.x,
                                   imageView.center.y + delta.y);

    if (imageView.center.x > self.view.bounds.size.width - ballRadius ||
        imageView.center.x < ballRadius)
        delta.x = -delta.x;

    if (imageView.center.y > self.view.bounds.size.height - ballRadius ||
        imageView.center.y < ballRadius)
        delta.y = -delta.y;
}
```

3. Press Command-R to test the application. The tennis ball now rotates as it bounces across the screen.

How It Works

To rotate a view, set its `transform` property using a `CGAffineTransform` data structure returned by the `CGAffineTransformMakeRotation()` function. The `CGAffineTransformMakeRotation()` function takes a single argument, which contains the angle to rotate (in radians). After each rotation, you increment the angle by 0.02:

```
//---rotation---
imageView.transform = CGAffineTransformMakeRotation(angle);
...
angle += 0.02;
```

A full rotation takes 360 degrees, which works out to be 2PI radians (recall that PI is equal to 22/7, which is approximately 3.142857). If the angle exceeds 6.2857 (=2*3.142857), you reset `angle` to 0:

```
if (angle>6.2857) angle = 0;
```

Scaling

For scaling of views, you use the `CGAffineTransformMakeScale()` function to return a `CGAffineTransform` data structure and set it to the `transform` property of the view:

```
imageView.transform = CGAffineTransformMakeScale(angle,angle);
```

`CGAffineTransformMakeScale()` takes two arguments: the factor to scale for the x axis and the factor to scale for the y axis.

If you modify the previous Try It Out with the preceding statement, the tennis ball gets bigger as it bounces on the screen (see Figure 12-8). It then resets back to its original size and grows again.

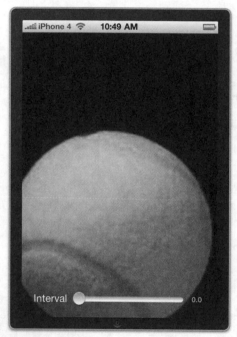

FIGURE 12-8

ANIMATING A SERIES OF IMAGES

So far, you have seen that you can use an Image View to display a static image. In addition, you can use it to display a series of images and then alternate between them.

The following Try It Out shows how this is done using an Image View.

TRY IT OUT Displaying a Series of Images

codefile Animations2.zip is available for download at Wrox.com

1. Using Xcode, create a new View-based Application (iPhone) project and name it **Animations2**.

2. Add a series of images to the Resources folder by dragging and dropping them into the Resources folder in Xcode. When the Add dialog appears, check the Copy Item into Destination Group's Folder (If Needed) option so that each of the images will be copied into the project. Figure 12-9 shows the images added.

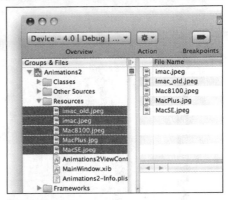

FIGURE 12-9

3. In the Animations2ViewController.m file, add the following bold statements:

```
- (void)viewDidLoad {
    NSArray *images = [NSArray arrayWithObjects:
                       [UIImage imageNamed:@"MacSE.jpeg"],
                       [UIImage imageNamed:@"imac.jpeg"],
                       [UIImage imageNamed:@"MacPlus.jpg"],
                       [UIImage imageNamed:@"imac_old.jpeg"],
                       [UIImage imageNamed:@"Mac8100.jpeg"],
                       nil];

    CGRect frame = CGRectMake(0,0,320,460);
    UIImageView *imageView = [[UIImageView alloc] initWithFrame:frame];
    imageView.animationImages = images;
    imageView.contentMode = UIViewContentModeScaleAspectFit;

    //---seconds to complete one set of animation---
    imageView.animationDuration = 3;

    //---continuous---
    imageView.animationRepeatCount = 0;

    //--start the animation---
    [imageView startAnimating];

    //--add the image view to the View window---
    [self.view addSubview:imageView];

    [imageView release];
    [super viewDidLoad];
}
```

4. Press Command-R to view the series of images on the iPhone 4 Simulator. The images are displayed in the Image View (see Figure 12-10), one at a time.

FIGURE 12-10

How It Works

You first create an NSArray object and initialize it with a few UIImage objects:

```
NSArray *images = [NSArray arrayWithObjects:
                      [UIImage imageNamed:@"MacSE.jpeg"],
                      [UIImage imageNamed:@"imac.jpeg"],
                      [UIImage imageNamed:@"MacPlus.jpg"],
                      [UIImage imageNamed:@"imac_old.jpeg"],
                      [UIImage imageNamed:@"Mac8100.jpeg"],
                      nil];
```

You then instantiate a UIImageView object:

```
CGRect frame = CGRectMake(0,0,320,460);
UIImageView *imageView = [[UIImageView alloc] initWithFrame:frame];
```

To get the Image View to display the series of images, set its animationImages property to the images object. You also set the display mode of the Image View:

```
imageView.animationImages = images;
imageView.contentMode = UIViewContentModeScaleAspectFit;
```

To control how fast the images are displayed, you set the animationDuration property to a value. This value indicates the number of seconds that the Image View will take to display one complete set of images. The `animationRepeatCount` property enables you to specify how many times you want the animation to occur. Set it to 0 if you want it to be displayed indefinitely:

```
//---seconds to complete one set of animation---
imageView.animationDuration = 3;

//---continuous---
imageView.animationRepeatCount = 0;
```

Finally, you start the animation by calling the `startAnimating` method. You also need to add the Image View to the View window by calling the `addSubView:` method:

```
//--start the animation---
[imageView startAnimating];

//--add the image view to the View window---
[self.view addSubview:imageView];
```

Note that the animation technique described in this section is suitable for a moderate number of animating objects. For more complex animation, you might want to explore OpenGL ES.

PLAYING VIDEO ON THE IPHONE

Playing videos is one of the most commonly performed tasks on the iPhone. Prior to iOS 4 for the iPhone, all videos must be played full-screen. However, on the iOS 4, this rule has been relaxed – you can now embed videos within your iPhone applications. This makes it possible for you to embed more than one video in any View window. This section shows you how to enable video playback in your iPhone applications.

TRY IT OUT   Enabling Video Playback

codefile PlayVideo.zip is available for download at Wrox.com

1. Using Xcode, create a new View-based Application (iPhone) project and name it **PlayVideo**.

2. Drag a sample video into the `Resources` folder of your Xcode project (see Figure 12-11).

3. Right-click the Frameworks folder and add the `MediaPlayer.framework` to your project (see Figure 12-12).

FIGURE 12-11

FIGURE 12-12

4. In the `PlayVideoViewController.h` file, code the following in bold:

```
#import <UIKit/UIKit.h>
#import <MediaPlayer/MediaPlayer.h>

@interface PlayVideoViewController : UIViewController {
    MPMoviePlayerController *player;
}

@end
```

5. In the `PlayVideoViewController.m` file, code the following in bold:

```
#import "PlayVideoViewController.h"

@implementation PlayVideoViewController

- (void)viewDidLoad {
    NSString *url = [[NSBundle mainBundle]
                     pathForResource:@"Trailer"
                     ofType:@"m4v"];

    player = [[MPMoviePlayerController alloc]
              initWithContentURL:[NSURL fileURLWithPath:url]];

    [[NSNotificationCenter defaultCenter]
```

```
        addObserver:self
            selector:@selector(movieFinishedCallback:)
                name:MPMoviePlayerPlaybackDidFinishNotification
              object:player];

    //--set the size of the movie view and then add it to the View window--
    player.view.frame = CGRectMake(10, 10, 300, 300);
    [self.view addSubview:player.view];

    //--play movie--
    [player play];
    [super viewDidLoad];
}

//--called when the movie is done playing--
- (void) movieFinishedCallback:(NSNotification*) aNotification {
    MPMoviePlayerController *moviePlayer = [aNotification object];
    [[NSNotificationCenter defaultCenter]
        removeObserver:self
                  name:MPMoviePlayerPlaybackDidFinishNotification
                object:moviePlayer];
    [moviePlayer.view removeFromSuperview];
    [player release];
}
```

6. To test the application on the iPhone 4 Simulator, press Command-R. Figure 12-13 shows the movie playing on the iPhone 4 Simulator.

FIGURE 12-13

7. Click the movie and you will be able to display the movie full-screen. Figure 12-14 shows two different scenes from the same movie; one shown full-screen width.

FIGURE 12-14

How It Works

Basically, you use the MPMoviePlayerController class to control the playback of a video:

```
player = [[MPMoviePlayerController alloc]
            initWithContentURL:[NSURL fileURLWithPath:url]];
```

You then use the NSNotificationCenter class to register a notification so that when the movie is done playing (i.e., it ends), the movieFinishedCallback: method can be called:

```
[[NSNotificationCenter defaultCenter]
    addObserver:self
       selector:@selector(movieFinishedCallback:)
           name:MPMoviePlayerPlaybackDidFinishNotification
         object:player];
```

To display the movie on the View window, you set the size of the movie and then add its view property to the View window and then play it:

```
//--set the size of the movie view and then add it to the View window--
player.view.frame = CGRectMake(10, 10, 300, 300);
[self.view addSubview:player.view];

//--play movie--
[player play];
```

When the movie stops playing, you should unregister the notification, remove the movie, and then release the `player` object:

```
//--called when the movie is done playing--
- (void) movieFinishedCallback:(NSNotification*) aNotification {
    MPMoviePlayerController *moviePlayer = [aNotification object];
    [[NSNotificationCenter defaultCenter]
        removeObserver:self
                  name:MPMoviePlayerPlaybackDidFinishNotification
                object:moviePlayer];
    [moviePlayer.view removeFromSuperview];
    [player release];
}
```

SUMMARY

In this chapter, you have seen the usefulness of the NSTimer class and how it can help you perform some simple animations. You have also learned about the various affine transformations supported by the iPhone SDK. Next, you learned how the Image View enables you to animate a series of images at a regular time interval. Last, but not least, you learned how to play back a video in your iPhone application.

EXERCISES

1. Name the three affine transformations supported by the iPhone SDK.

2. How do you pause an NSTimer object and then resume it?

3. What is the purpose of enclosing your block of code with the beginAnimations and commitAnimations methods of the UIView class, as shown in the following code snippet?

```
[UIView beginAnimations:@"my_own_animation" context:nil];
//---code to effect visual change---
[UIView commitAnimations];
```

4. Name the class that you can use for video playback.

Answers to the Exercises can be found in Appendix E, on Wrox.com.

▶ **WHAT YOU LEARNED IN THIS CHAPTER**

TOPIC	KEY CONCEPTS
Using the NSTimer **object to create timers**	Create a timer object that will call the onTimer method every half-second: ```\ntimer = [NSTimer scheduledTimerWithTimeInterval: 0.5\n target:self\n selector:@selector(onTimer)\n userInfo:nil\n repeats:YES];\n```
Stopping the NSTimer **object**	`[timer invalidate];`

Animating visual changes	`[UIView beginAnimations:@"my_own_animation" context:nil];`
	
	`//---code to effect visual change---`
	`[UIView commitAnimations];`

Performing affine transformations	Use the transform property of the view.
Translation	Use the CGAffineTransformMakeTranslation() function to return a CGAffineTransform data structure and set it to the transform property.
Rotation	Use the CGAffineTransformMakeRotation() function to return a CGAffineTransform data structure and set it to the transform property.
Scaling	Use the CGAffineTransformMakeScale() function to return a CGAffineTransform data structure and set it to the transform property.
Animating a series of images using Image View	Set the animationImages property to an array containing UIImage objects. Set the animationDuration property. Set the animationRepeatCount property. Call the startAnimating method.
Playing back a video	Use the MPMoviePlayerController class.

13
Accessing Built-In Applications

WHAT YOU WILL LEARN IN THIS CHAPTER

➤ How to send e-mails from within your application

➤ Invoking Safari from within your application

➤ How to invoke the phone from within your application

➤ How to send SMS messages from within your application

➤ Accessing the camera and Photo Library

The iPhone comes with a number of built-in applications that make it one of the most popular mobile devices of all time. Some of these applications are Mail, Phone, Safari, SMS, and Calendar. These applications perform most of the tasks you would expect from a mobile phone. As an iPhone developer, you can also programmatically invoke these applications from within your application using the various APIs provided by the iPhone SDK.

In this chapter, you learn how to invoke some of the built-in applications that are bundled with the iPhone, as well as how to interact with them from within your iPhone application.

SENDING E-MAILS

Sending e-mails is one of the many tasks performed by iPhone users. Sending e-mails on the iPhone is accomplished using the built-in Mail application, which is a rich HTML mail client that supports POP3, IMAP, and Exchange e-mail systems, and most web-based e-mails such as Yahoo! and Gmail.

There are times where you need to allow your user to send an e-mail in your iPhone application. A good example is embedding a feedback button in your application that users can click to send feedback to you directly. You have two ways to send e-mails programmatically:

➤ Build your own e-mail client and implement all the necessary protocols necessary to communicate with an e-mail server.

➤ Invoke the built-in Mail application and ask it to send the e-mail for you.

Unless you are well versed in network communications and familiar with all the e-mail protocols, your most logical choice is the second option — invoke the Mail application to do the job. The following Try It Out shows you how (you need to download the code files indicated here to work through this example).

TRY IT OUT   Sending E-mails Using the Mail Application

Codefile [Emails.zip] is available for download at Wrox.com

1. Using Xcode, create a View-based Application project and name it Emails.

2. Double-click the EmailsViewController.xib file to edit it in Interface Builder.

3. Populate the View window with the following views (see Figure 13-1):

➤ Label

➤ TextField

➤ TextView (remember to delete the sample text inside the view)

➤ Button

FIGURE 13-1

4. Insert the following statements in bold into the EmailsViewController.h file:

```
#import <UIKit/UIKit.h>

@interface EmailsViewController : UIViewController {
    IBOutlet UITextField *to;
    IBOutlet UITextField *subject;
    IBOutlet UITextView *body;
}

@property (nonatomic, retain) UITextField *to;
@property (nonatomic, retain) UITextField *subject;
```

```
@property (nonatomic, retain) UITextView *body;

-(IBAction) btnSend: (id) sender;

@end
```

5. Back in Interface Builder, Control-click and drag the File's Owner item to each of the three Text Field and Text View views and select to, subject, and body, respectively.

6. Control-click and drag the Button view to the File's Owner item and select btnSend:.

7. Insert the following code in bold into the EmailsViewController.m file:

```
#import "EmailsViewController.h"

@implementation EmailsViewController

@synthesize to, subject, body;

- (void) sendEmailTo:(NSString *) toStr
        withSubject:(NSString *) subjectStr
          withBody:(NSString *) bodyStr {

    NSString *emailString =
        [[NSString alloc]
            initWithFormat:@"mailto:?to=%@&subject=%@&body=%@",
            [toStr
                stringByAddingPercentEscapesUsingEncoding:
                NSASCIIStringEncoding],
            [subjectStr
                stringByAddingPercentEscapesUsingEncoding:
                NSASCIIStringEncoding],
            [bodyStr
                stringByAddingPercentEscapesUsingEncoding:
                NSASCIIStringEncoding]];
    [[UIApplication sharedApplication] openURL:[NSURL URLWithString:emailString]];
    [emailString release];
}

-(IBAction) btnSend: (id) sender{
    [self sendEmailTo:to.text withSubject:subject.text withBody:body.text];
}

- (void)dealloc {
    [to release];
    [subject release];
    [body release];
    [super dealloc];
}
```

8. Press Command-R to test the application on a real iPhone. Figure 13-2 shows the application in action. After you have filled in the Text Field and Text View views with the necessary information, click the Send button to invoke the Mail application and fill it with all the information you have typed in your application. Clicking the Send button in Mail sends the e-mail.

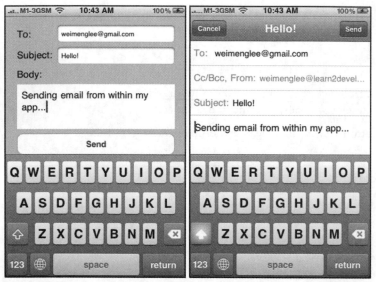

FIGURE 13-2

How It Works

The magic of invoking the Mail application lies in the string that you create in the
`sendEmailTo:withSubject:withBody:` method that you have defined:

```
NSString *emailString =
    [[NSString alloc]
        initWithFormat:@"mailto:?to=%@&subject=%@&body=%@",
            [toStr
                stringByAddingPercentEscapesUsingEncoding:
                NSASCIIStringEncoding],
            [subjectStr
                stringByAddingPercentEscapesUsingEncoding:
                NSASCIIStringEncoding],
            [bodyStr
                stringByAddingPercentEscapesUsingEncoding:
                NSASCIIStringEncoding]];
```

Basically, this is a URL string with the `mailto:` protocol indicated. The various parameters, such as
`to`, `subject`, and `body`, are inserted into the string. Note that you use the
`stringByAddingPercentEscapesUsingEncoding:` method of the `NSString` class to encode the various
parameters with the correct percent escapes so that the result is a valid URL string.

To invoke the Mail application, simply call the `sharedApplication` method to return the singleton
application instance and then use the `openURL:` method to invoke the Mail application:

```
[[UIApplication sharedApplication] openURL:[NSURL URLWithString:emailString]];
```

NOTE *Remember that this example works only on a real device. Testing it on the iPhone 4 Simulator will not work. Appendix A discusses how to prepare your iPhone for testing.*

The downside of using this approach is that when you tap the Send button, the application is pushed to the background when the Mail application takes over. When the e-mail is sent, you have to manually bring the application to the foreground again; otherwise, it will not appear. To compose the e-mail from within your application and then get the Mail application to send it for you, you can use the `MFMailComposeViewController` class. The following Try It Out shows how this can be done.

TRY IT OUT Sending E-mails without Leaving the Application

1. Using the same project created in the previous Try It Out, add a new Round Rect button to the `EmailViewController.xib` file (see Figure 13-3).

2. In Xcode, right-click the Frameworks folder and add the `MessageUI.framework` file (see Figure 13-4).

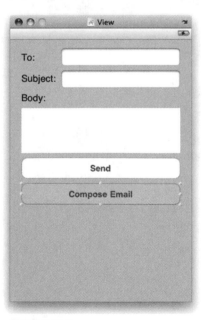

FIGURE 13-3

FIGURE 13-4

3. Add the following statement in bold to the `EmailsViewController.h` file:

```
#import <UIKit/UIKit.h>
#import <MessageUI/MFMailComposeViewController.h>

@interface EmailsViewController : UIViewController
    <MFMailComposeViewControllerDelegate> {
    IBOutlet UITextField *to;
    IBOutlet UITextField *subject;
    IBOutlet UITextView *body;
}

@property (nonatomic, retain) UITextField *to;
@property (nonatomic, retain) UITextField *subject;
@property (nonatomic, retain) UITextView *body;

-(IBAction) btnSend: (id) sender;
-(IBAction) btnComposeEmail: (id) sender;

@end
```

4. In Interface Builder, Control-click and drag the Compose E-mail button over the File's Owner item. Select `btnComposeEmail:`.

5. Add the following statement in bold to the `EmailsViewController.m` file:

```
#import "EmailsViewController.h"

@implementation EmailsViewController

@synthesize to, subject, body;

-(IBAction) btnComposeEmail: (id) sender {
    MFMailComposeViewController *picker =
        [[MFMailComposeViewController alloc] init];
    picker.mailComposeDelegate = self;

    [picker setSubject:@"Email subject here"];
    [picker setMessageBody:@"Email body here" isHTML:NO];
    [self presentModalViewController:picker animated:YES];
    [picker release];
}

- (void)mailComposeController:(MFMailComposeViewController*)controller
          didFinishWithResult:(MFMailComposeResult)result
                        error:(NSError*)error {
    [controller dismissModalViewControllerAnimated:YES];
}
```

6. Press Command-R to test the application on a real iPhone. Like the previous Try It Out, you will see the Mail application's compose screen (see Figure 13-5). However, unlike the previous example, when the e-mail is sent, control is returned to the application.

How It Works

The MFMailComposeViewController class presents the window for composing a message modally and does not cause the current application to go into the background. This is very useful when you want to resume with the current application after the e-mail has been sent.

FIGURE 13-5

Invoking Safari

If you want to invoke the Safari Web browser on your iPhone, you can also make use of a URL string and then use the openURL: method of the application instance, like this:

```
[[UIApplication sharedApplication]
    openURL:[NSURL URLWithString: @"http://www.apple.com"]];
```

The preceding code snippet invokes Safari to open the www.apple.com page (see Figure 13-6).

Invoking the Phone

To make a phone call using the iPhone's phone dialer, use the following URL string:

```
[[UIApplication sharedApplication]
    openURL:[NSURL URLWithString: @"tel:96924065"]];
```

The preceding statement invokes the dialer of the iPhone using the phone number specified.

 NOTE *The preceding statement works only for the iPhone, and not the iPod touch, of course, because the iPod touch does not have phone capabilities. Also, you would need to use a real device to test this out; the code does not have an effect on the iPhone Simulator. Appendix A discusses how to prepare your iPhone for testing.*

Invoking SMS

You can also use a URL string to send SMS messages using the SMS application:

```
[[UIApplication sharedApplication]
    openURL:[NSURL URLWithString: @"sms:96924065"]];
```

The preceding statement invokes the SMS application (see Figure 13-7). Note that the current application will be sent to the background.

FIGURE 13-6

FIGURE 13-7

 NOTE *As noted in the preceding section, this statement works only for iPhone, and not iPod touch, because the iPod touch does not have a phone, and therefore messaging, capabilities. Also, you would need to use a real device to test this out; the code does not have an effect on the iPhone Simulator. Appendix A discusses how to prepare your iPhone for testing.*

In the iPhone SDK 4, you can also send SMS messages directly from within your application. The following Try It Out shows how to do this.

TRY IT OUT Sending SMS Messages without Leaving Your Application

1. Using the previous project – Emails, add the following statements in bold to the EmailsViewController.h file:

```
#import <UIKit/UIKit.h>
#import <MessageUI/MFMailComposeViewController.h>
#import <MessageUI/MFMessageComposeViewController.h>

@interface EmailsViewController : UIViewController
```

```
        <MFMailComposeViewControllerDelegate,
        MFMessageComposeViewControllerDelegate> {
        IBOutlet UITextField *to;
        IBOutlet UITextField *subject;
        IBOutlet UITextView *body;
    }

    @property (nonatomic, retain) UITextField *to;
    @property (nonatomic, retain) UITextField *subject;
    @property (nonatomic, retain) UITextView *body;

    -(IBAction) btnSend: (id) sender;
    -(IBAction) btnComposeEmail: (id) sender;

    @end
```

2.   Add the following statements in bold to the `EmailsViewController.m` file

```
-(IBAction) btnComposeEmail: (id) sender {
    MFMessageComposeViewController *picker =
        [[MFMessageComposeViewController alloc] init];
    picker.messageComposeDelegate = self;

    [picker setBody:@"This message sent from the application."];
    [self presentModalViewController:picker animated:YES];
    [picker release];
}

- (void)messageComposeViewController:(MFMessageComposeViewController *)controller
              didFinishWithResult:(MessageComposeResult)result {
    [controller    dismissModalViewControllerAnimated:YES];
}
```

3.   Press Command-R to test the application on an iPhone device. You will be able to compose your SMS message (see Figure 13-8). When the message is sent, control is returned to your application.

How It Works

The `MFMessageComposeViewController` class is one of the new APIs in the iPhone 4 SDK. It presents the SMS composer window modally and does not cause the current application to go into the background. This is very useful when you want to resume with the current application after the SMS message has been sent.

FIGURE 13-8

INTERCEPTING SMS MESSAGES

One of the most frequently requested features of the iPhone SDK is the capability to intercept incoming SMS messages from within an iPhone application. Unfortunately, the current version of the SDK does not provide a means to do this.

Likewise, you cannot send SMS messages directly from within your application; the messages must be sent from the built-in SMS application itself. This requirement prevents rogue applications from sending SMS messages without the user's knowledge.

ACCESSING THE CAMERA AND THE PHOTO LIBRARY

The iPhone has a camera (the iPhone 4 has two – one front facing and one rear facing) that enables users to both take pictures and record videos. These pictures and videos are saved in the Photos application. As a developer, you have two options to manipulate the camera and to access the pictures and videos stored in the Photos application:

➤ You can invoke the camera to take pictures or record a video.

➤ You can invoke the Photos application to allow users to select a picture or video from the photo albums. You can then use the picture or video selected in your application.

Accessing the Photo Library

Every iPhone and iPod touch device includes the Photos application, in which any pictures and videos are stored. Using the iPhone SDK, you can use the UIImagePickerController class to programmatically display a UI that enables users to select pictures and videos from the Photos application. The following Try It Out demonstrates how you can do that in your application.

TRY IT OUT   Accessing the Photos in the Photo Library

Codefile [PhotoLibrary.zip] is available for download at Wrox.com

1. Using Xcode, create a View-based Application project and name it PhotoLibrary.

2. Double-click the PhotoLibraryViewController.xib file to edit it in Interface Builder.

3. Populate the View window with the following views (see Figure 13-9):

➤ Round Rect Button

➤ ImageView

4. In the Attributes Inspector window for the ImageView view, set the Mode to Aspect Fit (see Figure 13-10).

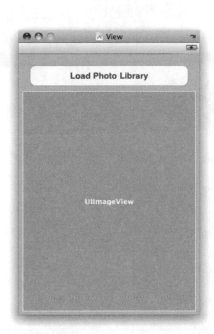

FIGURE 13-9

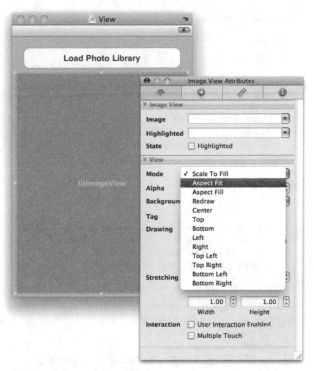

FIGURE 13-10

5. In the `PhotoLibraryViewController.h` file, insert the following statements that appear in bold:

```
#import <UIKit/UIKit.h>

@interface PhotoLibraryViewController : UIViewController
    <UINavigationControllerDelegate,
     UIImagePickerControllerDelegate>{

    IBOutlet UIImageView *imageView;
    UIImagePickerController *imagePicker;
}

@property (nonatomic, retain) UIImageView *imageView;

-(IBAction) btnClicked: (id) sender;

@end
```

6. Back in Interface Builder, Control-click and drag the File's Owner item to the ImageView view and select `imageView`.

7. Control-click and drag the Button view to the File's Owner item and select `btnClicked:`.

8. In the `PhotoLibraryViewController.m` file, insert the following statements that appear in bold:

```
#import "PhotoLibraryViewController.h"

@implementation PhotoLibraryViewController

@synthesize imageView;

- (void)viewDidLoad {
    imagePicker = [[UIImagePickerController alloc] init];
    [super viewDidLoad];
}

- (IBAction) btnClicked: (id) sender{
    imagePicker.delegate = self;
    imagePicker.sourceType =
        UIImagePickerControllerSourceTypePhotoLibrary;

    //---show the Image Picker---
    [self presentModalViewController:imagePicker animated:YES];
}

- (void)imagePickerController:(UIImagePickerController *)picker
didFinishPickingMediaWithInfo:(NSDictionary *)info {
    UIImage *image;
    NSURL *mediaUrl;
    mediaUrl = (NSURL *)[info valueForKey:
                         UIImagePickerControllerMediaURL];

    if (mediaUrl == nil) {
        image = (UIImage *) [info valueForKey:
                            UIImagePickerControllerEditedImage];
        if (image == nil) {
            //---original image selected---
            image = (UIImage *)
            [info valueForKey:UIImagePickerControllerOriginalImage];

            //---display the image---
            imageView.image = image;
        }
        else { //---edited image picked---
            //---get the cropping rectangle applied to the image---
            CGRect rect =
                [[info valueForKey:UIImagePickerControllerCropRect]
                  CGRectValue];

            //---display the image---
            imageView.image = image;
        }
    }
    else {
        //---video picked---
        // -- implement this later --
    }
    //---hide the Image Picker---
    [picker dismissModalViewControllerAnimated:YES];
```

```
}

- (void)imagePickerControllerDidCancel:(UIImagePickerController *)picker {
    //---user did not select image/video; hide the Image Picker---
    [picker dismissModalViewControllerAnimated:YES];
}

- (void)dealloc {
    [imageView release];
    [imagePicker release];
    [super dealloc];
}
```

9. Press Command-R to test the application on the iPhone 4 Simulator.

10. When the application is loaded, tap the Load Photo Library button. The Photo Albums on the iPhone 4 Simulator appear. Select a particular album (see Figure 13-11), and then select a picture. The selected picture is then displayed on the ImageView view (see Figure 13-12).

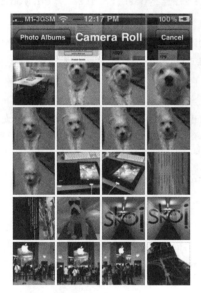
FIGURE 13-11

FIGURE 13-12

How It Works

Access to the Photo Library is provided by the UIImagePickerController class, which provides the UI for choosing and taking pictures and videos on your iPhone. All you need to do is create an instance of this class and provide a delegate that conforms to the UIImagePickerControllerDelegate protocol. In addition, your delegate must conform to the UINavigationControllerDelegate protocol because the UIImagePickerController class uses the navigation controller to enable users to select photos from the Photo Library. Therefore, you first need to specify the protocols in PhotoLibraryViewController.h:

```
@interface PhotoLibraryViewController : UIViewController
    <UINavigationControllerDelegate,
    UIImagePickerControllerDelegate> {
. . .
```

When the Load Library button is clicked, you set the type of picker interface displayed by the `UIImagePickerController` class and then display it modally:

```
- (IBAction) btnClicked: (id) sender{
    imagePicker.delegate = self;

    imagePicker.sourceType =
        UIImagePickerControllerSourceTypePhotoLibrary;

    //---show the Image Picker---
    [self presentModalViewController:imagePicker animated:YES];
}
```

Note that if you want the picture to be editable when the user chooses the picture, you can add the following statement:

```
imagePicker.allowsEditing = YES;
```

By default, the source type is always `UIImagePickerControllerSourceTypePhotoLibrary`, but you can change it to one of the following:

➤ `UIImagePickerControllerSourceTypeCamera` — for taking photos directly with the camera

➤ `UIImagePickerControllerSourceTypeSavedPhotosAlbum` — for directly going to the Photo Albums application

When a picture/video has been selected by the user, the `imagePickerController:didFinishPickingMediaWithInfo:` event fires, which you handle by checking the type of media selected by the user:

```
- (void)imagePickerController:(UIImagePickerController *)picker
didFinishPickingMediaWithInfo:(NSDictionary *)info {

    UIImage *image;
    NSURL *mediaUrl;
    mediaUrl = (NSURL *)[info valueForKey:UIImagePickerControllerMediaURL];

    if (mediaUrl == nil) {
        image = (UIImage *) [info valueForKey:UIImagePickerControllerEditedImage];
        if (image == nil) {
            //---original image selected---
            image = (UIImage *)
            [info valueForKey:UIImagePickerControllerOriginalImage];

            //---display the image---
            imageView.image = image;
        }
        else { //---edited image picked---
            //---get the cropping rectangle applied to the image---
            CGRect rect =
                [[info valueForKey:UIImagePickerControllerCropRect]
                  CGRectValue];

            //---display the image---
            imageView.image = image;
```

```
            }
        }
        else {
            //---video picked---
            // -- implement this later --
        }
        //---hide the Image Picker---
        [picker dismissModalViewControllerAnimated:YES];
    }
```

The type of media selected by the user is encapsulated in the `info:` parameter. You use the `valueForKey:` method to extract the appropriate media type and then typecast it to the respective type:

```
    mediaUrl = (NSURL *)[info valueForKey:UIImagePickerControllerMediaURL];
```

If the user cancels the selection, the `imagePickerControllerDidCancel:` event fires. In this case, you simply dismiss the Image Picker:

```
- (void)imagePickerControllerDidCancel:(UIImagePickerController *)picker {
    //---user did not select image/video; hide the Image Picker---
    [picker dismissModalViewControllerAnimated:YES];
}
```

Notice that in the preceding example, the user can see only the photos in the Photo Library. What if the user wants to access videos? The following Try It Out shows you how to enable users to select a video from the Photo Library and then play it in the application.

TRY IT OUT Accessing the Videos in the Photo Library

1. Using the same project, add the `MediaPlayer.framework` and `MobileCoreServices.framework` files to the `Frameworks` folder of the Xcode project (see Figure 13-13).

2. In the `PhotoLibraryViewController.h` file, insert the following statements that appear in bold:

```
#import <UIKit/UIKit.h>
#import <MediaPlayer/MediaPlayer.h>
#import <MobileCoreServices/MobileCoreServices.h>

@interface PhotoLibraryViewController : UIViewController
    <UINavigationControllerDelegate, UIImagePickerControllerDelegate>{

    IBOutlet UIImageView *imageView;
    UIImagePickerController *imagePicker;
}

@property (nonatomic, retain) UIImageView *imageView;

-(IBAction) btnClicked: (id) sender;

@end
```

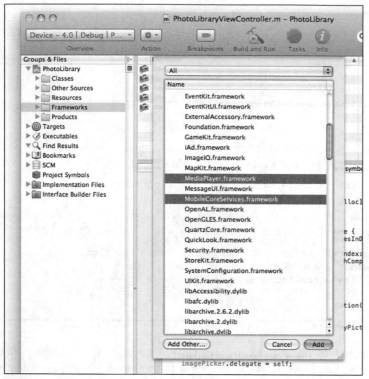

FIGURE 13-13

3. In the `PhotoLibraryViewController.m` file, insert the following statements that appear in bold:

```
- (IBAction) btnClicked: (id) sender{
    imagePicker.delegate = self;

    imagePicker.sourceType = UIImagePickerControllerSourceTypePhotoLibrary;

    NSArray *mediaTypes =
        [NSArray arrayWithObjects:kUTTypeImage, kUTTypeMovie, nil];
    imagePicker.mediaTypes = mediaTypes;

    //---show the Image Picker---
    [self presentModalViewController:imagePicker animated:YES];
}

- (void)imagePickerController:(UIImagePickerController *)picker
didFinishPickingMediaWithInfo:(NSDictionary *)info {
    UIImage *image;
    NSURL *mediaUrl;
    mediaUrl = (NSURL *)[info valueForKey:UIImagePickerControllerMediaURL];
    if (mediaUrl == nil) {
        image = (UIImage *) [info valueForKey:UIImagePickerControllerEditedImage];
        if (image == nil) {
```

```
                    //---original image selected---
                    image = (UIImage *)
                    [info valueForKey:UIImagePickerControllerOriginalImage];

                    //---display the image---
                    imageView.image = image;
                }
            else { //---edited image picked---
                //---get the cropping rectangle applied to the image---
                CGRect rect =
                    [[info valueForKey:UIImagePickerControllerCropRect]
                        CGRectValue];

                //---display the image---
                imageView.image = image;
            }
        }
        else {
            //---video picked---
            MPMoviePlayerController *player =
                [[MPMoviePlayerController alloc]
                    initWithContentURL:mediaUrl];

            [[NSNotificationCenter defaultCenter]
                addObserver:self
                    selector:@selector(movieFinishedCallback:)
                        name:MPMoviePlayerPlaybackDidFinishNotification
                    object:player];

            //---play partial screen---
            player.view.frame = CGRectMake(0, 0, 320, 460);
            [self.view addSubview:player.view];

            [player play];
        }
        //---hide the Image Picker---
        [picker dismissModalViewControllerAnimated:YES];
}

- (void) movieFinishedCallback:(NSNotification*) aNotification {
    MPMoviePlayerController *player = [aNotification object];
    [[NSNotificationCenter defaultCenter]
        removeObserver:self
                name:MPMoviePlayerPlaybackDidFinishNotification
            object:player];

    [player.view removeFromSuperview];
    [player autorelease];
}
```

4. Press Command-R to test the application on the iPhone 4 Simulator. You can now select a video and then click the Choose button (see Figure 13-14). The video will be compressed and then played in the application.

FIGURE 13-14

How It Works

By default, the `UIImagePickerController` object always displays images. To allow movies to be displayed and selected, you need to set the `mediaTypes` property of the `UIImagePickerController` object. This property takes an `NSArray` object containing the types of media you want to display. Here, you set the media types to be `kUTTypeImage` and `kUTTypeMovie`:

```
imagePicker.sourceType = UIImagePickerControllerSourceTypePhotoLibrary;

NSArray *mediaTypes =
    [NSArray arrayWithObjects:kUTTypeImage, kUTTypeMovie, nil];
imagePicker.mediaTypes = mediaTypes;

//---show the Image Picker---
[self presentModalViewController:imagePicker animated:YES];
```

When a movie is selected, you will then play it using the `MPMoviePlayerController` class:

```
if (mediaUrl == nil) {
    //...
    //...
} else {
    //---video picked---
    MPMoviePlayerController *player =
        [[MPMoviePlayerController alloc]
            initWithContentURL:mediaUrl];

    [[NSNotificationCenter defaultCenter]
        addObserver:self
            selector:@selector(movieFinishedCallback:)
                name:MPMoviePlayerPlaybackDidFinishNotification
```

```
                                object:player];

                //---play partial screen---
                player.view.frame = CGRectMake(0, 0, 320, 460);
                [self.view addSubview:player.view];

                [player play];
        }
        //---hide the Image Picker---
        [picker dismissModalViewControllerAnimated:YES];
    }
```

When the movie has finished playing, simply remove it from the View window:

```
- (void) movieFinishedCallback:(NSNotification*) aNotification {
    MPMoviePlayerController *player = [aNotification object];
    [[NSNotificationCenter defaultCenter]
        removeObserver:self
                  name:MPMoviePlayerPlaybackDidFinishNotification
                object:player];

    [player.view removeFromSuperview];
    [player autorelease];
}
```

Accessing the Camera

Besides accessing the Photo Library, you can also access the camera on your iPhone. Although accessing the hardware is the focus of the next chapter, you take a look here at how to access the camera because it is also accomplished using the UIImagePickerController class.

In the following Try It Out, you modify the existing project created in the previous section. There isn't much to modify because most of the code you have written still applies.

TRY IT OUT **Activating the Camera**

1. Using the same project created in the previous section, edit the PhotoLibraryViewController.m file by changing the source type of the Image Picker to camera (see code highlighted in bold):

```
- (IBAction) btnClicked: (id) sender{
    imagePicker.delegate = self;

    //---comment this out---
    /*
    imagePicker.sourceType = UIImagePickerControllerSourceTypePhotoLibrary;
    NSArray *mediaTypes =
        [NSArray arrayWithObjects:kUTTypeImage, kUTTypeMovie, nil];
    imagePicker.mediaTypes = mediaTypes;
    */

    //---invoke the camera---
    imagePicker.sourceType = UIImagePickerControllerSourceTypeCamera;
    NSArray *mediaTypes =
        [NSArray arrayWithObjects:kUTTypeImage, kUTTypeMovie, nil];
```

```
        imagePicker.mediaTypes = mediaTypes;

        imagePicker.cameraCaptureMode = UIImagePickerControllerCameraCaptureModeVideo;
        imagePicker.allowsEditing = YES;

        //---show the Image Picker---
        [self presentModalViewController:imagePicker animated:YES];
    }
```

2. In the `PhotoLibraryViewController.m` file, define the following two methods:

```
- (NSString *) filePath: (NSString *) fileName {
    NSArray *paths =
        NSSearchPathForDirectoriesInDomains(
            NSDocumentDirectory, NSUserDomainMask, YES);
    NSString *documentsDir = [paths objectAtIndex:0];
    return [documentsDir stringByAppendingPathComponent:fileName];
}

- (void) saveImage{
    //---get the date from the ImageView---
    NSData *imageData =
    [NSData dataWithData:UIImagePNGRepresentation(imageView.image)];

    //---write the date to file---
    [imageData writeToFile:[self filePath:@"MyPicture.png"] atomically:YES];
}
```

3. Insert the following statements that appear in bold:

```
- (void)imagePickerController:(UIImagePickerController *)picker
didFinishPickingMediaWithInfo:(NSDictionary *)info {
    UIImage *image;
    NSURL *mediaUrl;
    mediaUrl = (NSURL *)[info valueForKey:UIImagePickerControllerMediaURL];

    if (mediaUrl == nil) {
        image = (UIImage *) [info valueForKey:UIImagePickerControllerEditedImage];
        if (image == nil) {
            //---original image selected---
            image = (UIImage *)
            [info valueForKey:UIImagePickerControllerOriginalImage];

            //---display the image---
            imageView.image = image;

            //---save the image captured---
            [self saveImage];
        }
        else { //---edited image picked---

            //---get the cropping rectangle applied to the image---
            CGRect rect =
                [[info valueForKey:UIImagePickerControllerCropRect]
                    CGRectValue];

            //---display the image---
```

```
            imageView.image = image;

            //---save the image captured---
            [self saveImage];
        }
    }
    else {
        //---video picked---
        MPMoviePlayerController *player =
            [[MPMoviePlayerController alloc]
                initWithContentURL:mediaUrl];

        [[NSNotificationCenter defaultCenter]
            addObserver:self
              selector:@selector(movieFinishedCallback:)
                  name:MPMoviePlayerPlaybackDidFinishNotification
                object:player];

        //---play partial screen---
        player.view.frame = CGRectMake(0, 0, 320, 460);
        [self.view addSubview:player.view];

        [player play];
    }
    //---hide the Image Picker---
    [picker dismissModalViewControllerAnimated:YES];
}
```

4. Press Command-R to test the application on a real iPhone.

5. Tap the Load Photo Library button. You can now use your iPhone's camera to take photos and videos. If you use it to take a picture (see Figure 13-15), the picture is saved to the Documents folder of your application. If you take a video, the video can be played back using the media player on your device (see Figure 13-16).

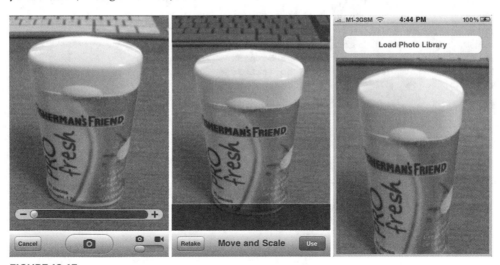

FIGURE 13-15

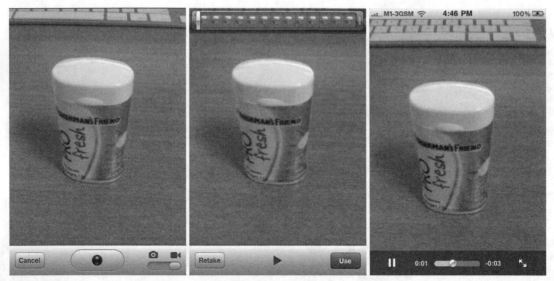

FIGURE 13-16

How It Works

In this exercise you modified the source type of the Image Picker to camera:

```
imagePicker.sourceType = UIImagePickerControllerSourceTypeCamera;
```

When the camera takes a picture, the picture is passed back in the
`imagePickerController:didFinishPickingMediaWithInfo:` method and displayed in the ImageView
view. However, it is your responsibility to manually save the image to a location on the phone. In this
case, you defined the `filePath:` method to save the picture to the Documents folder of your application:

```
- (NSString *) filePath: (NSString *) fileName {
    NSArray *paths =
        NSSearchPathForDirectoriesInDomains(
            NSDocumentDirectory, NSUserDomainMask, YES);
    NSString *documentsDir = [paths objectAtIndex:0];
    return [documentsDir stringByAppendingPathComponent:fileName];
}
```

The `saveImage:` method extracts the image data on the ImageView view and then calls the `filePath:`
method to save the data into a file named `MyPicture.png`:

```
- (void) saveImage{
    //---get the date from the ImageView---
    NSData *imageData =
    [NSData dataWithData:UIImagePNGRepresentation(imageView.image)];

    //---write the date to file---
    [imageData writeToFile:[self filePath:@"MyPicture.png"] atomically:YES];
}
```

For video recording, the video captured by the iPhone's camera is saved on the device and returned as a URL. You can use the MPMoviePlayerController class (available in the MediaPlayer framework) to play back the video.

> **NOTE** *By default on the iPhone 4, the rear camera is always activated when you use the* UIImagePickerController *class. If you want to activate the front camera instead, you can set the* cameraDevice *property of the* UIImagePickerController *class, which can be one of the following values:* UIImagePickerControllerCameraDeviceRear *(default), or* UIImagePickerControllerCameraDeviceFront.

> **NOTE** *Appendix A discusses how to prepare your iPhone for testing.*

SUMMARY

In this chapter, you learned how you can easily integrate the various built-in applications into your own iPhone applications. In particular, you saw how you can invoke the built-in SMS, Mail, Safari, and Phone simply by using a URL string. In addition, you learned how to send SMS and e-mail messages without leaving your application. You also learned about accessing the Photo Library applications using the classes provided by the iPhone SDK.

EXERCISES

1. Name the various URL strings for invoking the Safari, Mail, SMS, and Phone applications.

2. What is the class name for invoking the Image Picker UI in the iPhone?

3. What is the class name for invoking the Mail Composer UI in the iPhone?

4. What is the class name for invoking the Message Composer UI in the iPhone?

Answers to the Exercises can be found in Appendix E, on Wrox.com.

▶ **WHAT YOU LEARNED IN THIS CHAPTER**

TOPIC	KEY CONCEPTS

Sending e-mail from within your application	`NSString *emailString =`
	`    @"mailto:?to=user@email.com&subject=Subject&body=Body";`
	`[[UIApplication sharedApplication] openURL:[NSURL`
	`                                URLWithString:emailString]];`

Invoking Safari	`[[UIApplication sharedApplication]` `    openURL:[NSURL URLWithString: @"http://www.apple.com"]];`
Invoking the Phone	`[[UIApplication sharedApplication]` `    openURL:[NSURL URLWithString: @"tel:96924065"]];`
Invoking SMS	`[[UIApplication sharedApplication]` `    openURL:[NSURL URLWithString: @"sms:96924065"]];`
Accessing the Photo Library	Use the `UIImagePickerController` class and ensure that your View Controller conforms to the `UINavigationControllerDelegate` protocol.
Invoking the Mail Composer UI	Use the `MFMailComposeViewController` class.
Invoking the Message Composer UI	Use the `MFMessageComposeViewController` class.

14

Recognizing Gestures

WHAT YOU WILL LEARN IN THIS CHAPTER

➤ How to use the six gesture recognizers to recognize commonly used gestures

➤ How to detect touches in your application

➤ How to differentiate between single and double taps

➤ How to implement the pinch gesture

➤ How to implement the drag gesture

One of the most important selling points of the iPhone is its screen, which can detect multiple points of input. Multi-touch inputs allow for very natural interaction between users and your applications. Because of multi-touch, the mobile Safari Web browser is easily one of the most user-friendly Web browsers available on a smart phone. The iPhone recognizes various multi-touch sequences, known as *gestures*, and performs the appropriate action associated with each.

In this chapter, you learn how to recognize gestures in your application and then implement some cool features that improve the interaction between the user and the application, such as a jigsaw puzzle application. By detecting touches, your application enables users to rearrange the locations of the onscreen images, as well as change the size of the images using the pinching gesture.

RECOGNIZING GESTURES

Beginning with version 3.2 of the iPhone SDK, Apple introduced a new set of classes known as *gesture recognizers*. Gesture recognizers enable you to easily detect gestures performed by the user. For example, the user may use two fingers to pinch the screen, indicating an intention to zoom in and out of an image. Instead of writing the code to detect the fingers movement, gesture recognizers provide an easy way to detect the various gestures supported by the iPhone.

 NOTE *The various gesture recognizers only work for devices running iOS 3.2 or above, so if your application uses them it won't be able to run on pre-iPhone 3.2 devices.*

The iPhone SDK 3.2/4.0 supports six gesture recognizers:

➤ `UITapGestureRecognizer` — Detects tap(s) on a view.

➤ `UIPinchGestureRecognizer` — Detects pinching in and out of a view.

➤ `UIPanGestureRecognizer` — Detects panning or dragging of a view.

➤ `UISwipeGestureRecognizer` — Detects swiping of a view.

➤ `UIRotationGestureRecognizer` — Detects rotation of a view.

➤ `UILongPressGestureRecognizer` — Detects long presses on a view (also known as "touch and hold").

All six gesture recognizers inherit from the `UIGestureRecognizer` base class. To get started with gesture recognizers, let's build an application that detects taps on a view, and then progressively detects other gestures.

Tapping

To use a gesture recognizer, all you need to do is create an instance of the appropriate gesture recognizer, configure it accordingly, and then connect it to an event handler that will perform the required action when the gesture is recognized. The following Try It Out shows you how to detect taps on the iPhone screen.

TRY IT OUT Recognizing Tapping

codefile Gestures.zip is available for download at Wrox.com

1. Using Xcode, create a new View-based Application (iPhone) project and name it `Gestures`.

2. Drag and drop the image named `architecture.jpg` onto the `Resources` folder of the Xcode project. When the Add dialog appears, check the Copy Item into the Destination Group's Folder (If Needed) option so that the image is copied into the project (see Figure 14-1).

3. Double-click the `GesturesViewController.xib` file located in the `Resources` folder to edit it in Interface Builder.

4. Add an ImageView from the Library to the View window.

5. Select the ImageView and view its Attributes Inspector window (Tools ⇨ Attributes Inspector). Set its properties as follows (see Figure 14-2):

➤ **Image** — `architecture.jpg`

➤ **Mode** — Aspect Fit

➤ Check the User Interaction Enabled option.

➤ Check the Multiple Touch option.

6. Save the file in Interface Builder.

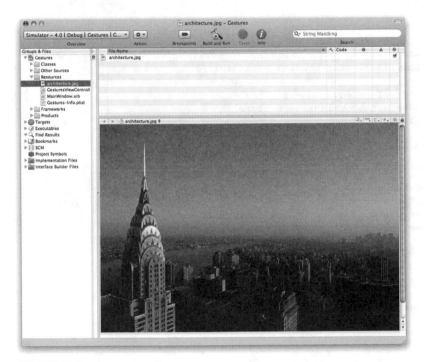

FIGURE 14-1

7. Back in Xcode, edit the `GesturesViewController.h` file by adding the following bold statements:

```
#import <UIKit/UIKit.h>

@interface GesturesViewController : UIViewController {
    IBOutlet UIImageView *imageView;
}

@property (nonatomic, retain) UIImageView *imageView;

@end
```

8. In Interface Builder, connect the `imageView` outlet to the ImageView by control-clicking and dragging the File's Owner item over the ImageView. Select `imageView`.

9. In Xcode, edit the `GesturesViewController.m` file and add the following bold statements:

```
#import "GesturesViewController.h"

@implementation GesturesViewController

@synthesize imageView;

- (void)viewDidLoad {
    //---tap gesture---
    UITapGestureRecognizer *tapGesture =
    [[UITapGestureRecognizer alloc]
        initWithTarget:self
                action:@selector(handleTapGesture:)];

    tapGesture.numberOfTapsRequired = 2;
    [imageView addGestureRecognizer:tapGesture];
    [tapGesture release];

    [super viewDidLoad];
}

//---handle tap gesture---
-(IBAction) handleTapGesture:(UIGestureRecognizer *) sender {
    if (sender.view.contentMode == UIViewContentModeScaleAspectFit)
        sender.view.contentMode = UIViewContentModeCenter;
    else
        sender.view.contentMode = UIViewContentModeScaleAspectFit;
}

- (void)dealloc {
    [imageView release];
    [super dealloc];
}
```

10. To test the application on the iPhone 4 Simulator, press Command-R.

11. Figure 14-3 shows the image displayed on the iPhone 4 Simulator. When you double-click the image (which is double-tap on a real device), it is enlarged. When you double-click the image again, it switches back to its original size.

How It Works

To detect taps on a view, you first create an instance of the `UITapGestureRecognizer` class:

```
UITapGestureRecognizer *tapGesture =
[[UITapGestureRecognizer alloc]
    initWithTarget:self
            action:@selector(handleTapGesture:)];
```

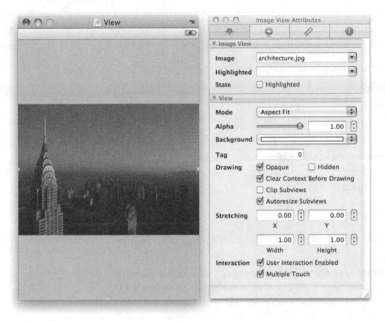

FIGURE 14-2

FIGURE 14-3

You set the current View Controller (`self`) to be the target of the gesture recognizer (which means you will handle all the messages sent when a gesture is detected in this current View Controller). The `action:` parameter specifies a selector that identifies the method name to handle the recognized gesture.

To recognize double-taps, set the `numberOfTapsRequired` property to `2`:

```
tapGesture.numberOfTapsRequired = 2;
```

To attach the gesture recognizer to a view, in this case `imageView`, pass the `tapGesture` object to the `addGestureRecognizer:` method:

```
[imageView addGestureRecognizer:tapGesture];
```

Finally, release the `tapGesture` recognizer object:

```
[tapGesture release];
```

When a double-tap is detected by the application, the `handleTapGesture:` method will be invoked:

```
//---handle tap gesture---
-(IBAction) handleTapGesture:(UIGestureRecognizer *) sender {
    if (sender.view.contentMode == UIViewContentModeScaleAspectFit)
        sender.view.contentMode = UIViewContentModeCenter;
    else
        sender.view.contentMode = UIViewContentModeScaleAspectFit;
}
```

In `handleTapGesture:`, you can reference the view that has recognized the gesture, in this case `imageView`, by the `sender.view` object (alternatively, you can directly refer to the ImageView via `self.imageView`). This method is useful, as you may have multiple views attached to the same gesture handler and `sender.view` will automatically refer to the view that recognized the gesture.

In this gesture handler, you toggle the image between the `UIViewContentModeScaleAspectFit` and `UIViewContentModeCenter` modes.

DISCRETE GESTURES AND CONTINUOUS GESTURES

There are two types of gestures: discrete and continuous. A *discrete gesture* sends a single message to the target when the gesture is recognized. For example, when you double-tap on a view and the gesture is detected, the target (the method handling the gesture) is only invoked once. A *continuous gesture*, conversely, sends multiple messages to the target until the gesture ends. An example of a continuous gesture is the pinch gesture. As you put your fingers on the screen and pinch on a view, the target is called repeatedly until you lift your fingers off your screen.

The `UITapGestureRecognizer`, `UISwipeGestureRecognizer`, and `UILongPressGestureRecognizer` are all discrete gesture recognizers. The `UIPinchGestureRecognizer`, `UIPanGestureRecognizer`, and `UIRotationGestureRecognizer` are all continuous gesture recognizers.

Pinching

The pinch gesture is very popular on the iPhone (and on the iPad). In the pinch gesture, you place two fingers on the screen and move them either apart or closer together to indicate your intention to zoom in or out of a view. The following Try It Out shows you how to recognize the pinch gesture in your application to change the size of an ImageView. Note that all the Try It Outs in this chapter use source code and images from the zip file you downloaded for the first Try It Out.

TRY IT OUT Recognizing Pinching

1. Using the same project created in the previous Try It Out, edit the GesturesViewController.m file by adding the following bold statements:

```
#import "GesturesViewController.h"

@implementation GesturesViewController

@synthesize imageView;

CGFloat lastScaleFactor = 1;

- (void)viewDidLoad {
    //---tap gesture---
    UITapGestureRecognizer *tapGesture =
    [[UITapGestureRecognizer alloc]
        initWithTarget:self
                action:@selector(handleTapGesture:)];

    tapGesture.numberOfTapsRequired = 2;
    [imageView addGestureRecognizer:tapGesture];
    [tapGesture release];

    //---pinch gesture---
    UIPinchGestureRecognizer *pinchGesture =
    [[UIPinchGestureRecognizer alloc]
        initWithTarget:self
                action:@selector(handlePinchGesture:)];

    [imageView addGestureRecognizer:pinchGesture];
    [pinchGesture release];

    [super viewDidLoad];
}

//---handle pinch gesture---
-(IBAction) handlePinchGesture:(UIGestureRecognizer *) sender {
    CGFloat factor = [(UIPinchGestureRecognizer *) sender scale];

    if (factor > 1) {
        //---zooming in---
        sender.view.transform = CGAffineTransformMakeScale(
                                    lastScaleFactor + (factor-1),
```

```
                                         lastScaleFactor + (factor-1));
        } else {
            //---zooming out---
            sender.view.transform = CGAffineTransformMakeScale(
                                         lastScaleFactor * factor,
                                         lastScaleFactor * factor);
        }

        if (sender.state == UIGestureRecognizerStateEnded){
            if (factor > 1) {
                lastScaleFactor += (factor-1);
            } else {
                lastScaleFactor *= factor;
            }
        }
    }
}
```

2. To test the application on the iPhone 4 Simulator, press Command-R.

3. Press the Option button and you will be able to simulate the touch of two fingers on the screen. You will see two translucent white circle dots on the simulator. Click and drag the mouse to move them apart. Observe that the size of the image changes as you move the mouse (see Figure 14-4).

FIGURE 14-4

How It Works

As with the UITapGestureRecognizer, you first create an instance of the UIPinchGestureRecognizer and then connect it to a gesture handler:

```
//---pinch gesture---
UIPinchGestureRecognizer *pinchGesture =
[[UIPinchGestureRecognizer alloc]
    initWithTarget:self
            action:@selector(handlePinchGesture:)];

[imageView addGestureRecognizer:pinchGesture];
[pinchGesture release];
```

When a pinch gesture is recognized, the handlePinchGesture: method is invoked to handle it. Recall that the pinch gesture is a continuous gesture, and hence the handlePinchGesture: method will be called repeatedly as long as the fingers are on the screen.

To know whether this is a "zoom in" or "zoom out" gesture, you examine the scale property of the UIPinchGestureRecognizer object:

```
CGFloat factor = [(UIPinchGestureRecognizer *) sender scale];
```

If the fingers are moving apart, the value of scale is 1 or greater. If the fingers are moving closer, the value is smaller than 1. Every time you perform a pinch gesture, your application needs to remember the scale factor so that the next time you perform the gesture, you can resize the image based on its last drawn size. This is done when the pinch gesture ends (when the fingers are lifted off the screen). You examine the sender.state to determine whether the gesture has ended and then proceed to save the last scale factor:

```
if (sender.state == UIGestureRecognizerStateEnded){
    if (factor > 1) {
        lastScaleFactor += (factor-1);
    } else {
        lastScaleFactor *= factor;
    }
}
```

You change the size of the ImageView using the CGAffineTransformMakeScale() method.

```
if (factor > 1) {
    //---zooming in---
    sender.view.transform = CGAffineTransformMakeScale(
                                lastScaleFactor + (factor-1),
                                lastScaleFactor + (factor-1));
} else {
    //---zooming out---
    sender.view.transform = CGAffineTransformMakeScale(
                                lastScaleFactor * factor,
                                lastScaleFactor * factor);
}
```

Rotation

Another gesture that is supported by the iPhone SDK 3.2/4.0 is rotation. In the rotation gesture, you place two fingers on the screen and rotate them in a circular fashion. The following Try It Out shows how to use the `UIRotationGestureRecognizer` class to rotate the ImageView.

TRY IT OUT Recognizing Rotation

1. Using the same project created in the previous Try It Out, edit the `GesturesViewController.m` file by adding the following bold statements:

```
#import "GesturesViewController.h"

@implementation GesturesViewController

@synthesize imageView;

CGFloat lastScaleFactor = 1;

CGFloat netRotation;

- (void)viewDidLoad {
    //---tap gesture---
    UITapGestureRecognizer *tapGesture =
    [[UITapGestureRecognizer alloc]
        initWithTarget:self
                action:@selector(handleTapGesture:)];

    tapGesture.numberOfTapsRequired = 2;
    [imageView addGestureRecognizer:tapGesture];
    [tapGesture release];

    //---pinch gesture---
    UIPinchGestureRecognizer *pinchGesture =
    [[UIPinchGestureRecognizer alloc]
        initWithTarget:self
                action:@selector(handlePinchGesture:)];

    [imageView addGestureRecognizer:pinchGesture];
    [pinchGesture release];

    //---rotate gesture---
    UIRotationGestureRecognizer *rotateGesture =
    [[UIRotationGestureRecognizer alloc]
        initWithTarget:self
                action:@selector(handleRotateGesture:)];

    [imageView addGestureRecognizer:rotateGesture];
```

```
    [rotateGesture release];

    [super viewDidLoad];
}

//---handle rotate gesture---
-(IBAction) handleRotateGesture:(UIGestureRecognizer *) sender {
    CGFloat rotation = [(UIRotationGestureRecognizer *) sender rotation];
    CGAffineTransform transform = CGAffineTransformMakeRotation(
                                        rotation + netRotation);
    sender.view.transform = transform;

    if (sender.state == UIGestureRecognizerStateEnded){
        netRotation += rotation;
    }
}
```

2. To test the application on the iPhone 4 Simulator, press Command-R.

3. Press the Option button to simulate two fingers touching the screen. Click and drag the mouse in either a clockwise or a counterclockwise direction. Observe that the ImageView rotates (see Figure 14-5).

FIGURE 14-5

How It Works

As usual, you create an instance of the UIRotationGestureRecognizer class and connect it to a handler method:

```
//---rotate gesture---
UIRotationGestureRecognizer *rotateGesture =
[[UIRotationGestureRecognizer alloc]
    initWithTarget:self
            action:@selector(handleRotateGesture:)];

[imageView addGestureRecognizer:rotateGesture];
[rotateGesture release];
```

When a rotation gesture is recognized, the handleRotateGesture: method is invoked. Because the rotation gesture is a continuous gesture, this method is called repeatedly.

To obtain the amount of rotation, you examine the rotation property of the UIRotationGestureRecognizer object:

```
CGFloat rotation = [(UIRotationGestureRecognizer *) sender rotation];
```

The amount to rotate is represented in radians. To ensure that the ImageView rotates based on its last position, you save the angle of rotation when the rotation gesture is completed:

```
if (sender.state == UIGestureRecognizerStateEnded){
    netRotation += rotation;
}
```

Finally, you perform the rotation using the CGAffineTransformMakeRotation() method:

```
CGAffineTransform transform = CGAffineTransformMakeRotation(
                                    rotation + netRotation);
sender.view.transform = transform;
```

Panning (or Dragging)

A very common gesture that most iPhone users will encounter is the pan (or drag) gesture. Panning involves using the finger to touch a view on the screen and then moving it while the finger is still on the screen. In the following Try It Out, you will use the UIPanGestureRecognizer to move the ImageView.

TRY IT OUT Recognizing Panning

1. Using the same project created in the previous Try It Out, edit the GesturesViewController.m file by adding the following bold statements:

```
#import "GesturesViewController.h"

@implementation GesturesViewController

@synthesize imageView;

CGFloat lastScaleFactor = 1;

CGFloat netRotation;

CGPoint netTranslation;

- (void)viewDidLoad {
    //---tap gesture---
    UITapGestureRecognizer *tapGesture =
    [[UITapGestureRecognizer alloc]
        initWithTarget:self
                action:@selector(handleTapGesture:)];

    tapGesture.numberOfTapsRequired = 2;
    [imageView addGestureRecognizer:tapGesture];
    [tapGesture release];

    //---pinch gesture---
    UIPinchGestureRecognizer *pinchGesture =
    [[UIPinchGestureRecognizer alloc]
        initWithTarget:self
                action:@selector(handlePinchGesture:)];

    [imageView addGestureRecognizer:pinchGesture];
    [pinchGesture release];

    //---rotate gesture---
    UIRotationGestureRecognizer *rotateGesture =
    [[UIRotationGestureRecognizer alloc]
        initWithTarget:self
                action:@selector(handleRotateGesture:)];

    [imageView addGestureRecognizer:rotateGesture];
    [rotateGesture release];

    //---pan gesture---
    UIPanGestureRecognizer *panGesture =
    [[UIPanGestureRecognizer alloc]
        initWithTarget:self
                action:@selector(handlePanGesture:)];

    [imageView addGestureRecognizer:panGesture];
    [panGesture release];

    [super viewDidLoad];
```

```
    }

    //---handle pan gesture---
    -(IBAction) handlePanGesture:(UIGestureRecognizer *) sender {
        CGPoint translation =
            [(UIPanGestureRecognizer *) sender translationInView:imageView];

        sender.view.transform = CGAffineTransformMakeTranslation(
                                    netTranslation.x + translation.x,
                                    netTranslation.y + translation.y);

        if (sender.state == UIGestureRecognizerStateEnded){
            netTranslation.x += translation.x;
            netTranslation.y += translation.y;
        }
    }
```

2. To test the application on the iPhone 4 Simulator, press Command-R.

3. Click the ImageView and move the mouse. Observe that the ImageView moves with your mouse (see Figure 14-6).

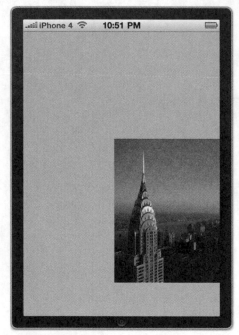

FIGURE 14-6

How It Works

You create an instance of the UIPanGestureRecognizer class and connect it to a handler method:

```
//---pan gesture---
UIPanGestureRecognizer *panGesture =
[[UIPanGestureRecognizer alloc]
    initWithTarget:self
            action:@selector(handlePanGesture:)];

[imageView addGestureRecognizer:panGesture];
[panGesture release];
```

When a panning gesture is recognized, the `handlePanGesture:` method is invoked. Panning is a continuous gesture, so this method is called repeatedly.

To obtain the amount of panning, you examine the `translation` property of the `UIPanGestureRecognizer` object:

```
CGPoint translation =
    [(UIPanGestureRecognizer *) sender translationInView:imageView];
```

To ensure that the ImageView can be moved from its last drawn position, you save the current panning amount when the gesture ends:

```
if (sender.state == UIGestureRecognizerStateEnded){
    netTranslation.x += translation.x;
    netTranslation.y += translation.y;
}
```

Finally, you move the ImageView using the `CGAffineTransformMakeTranslation()` method:

```
sender.view.transform = CGAffineTransformMakeTranslation(
                            netTranslation.x + translation.x,
                            netTranslation.y + translation.y);
```

Swiping

Another common gesture that you will encounter is the swipe. Using the swipe gesture, a user touches the screen with a finger, moves it in a particular direction, and then lifts it off the screen. The swipe gesture is commonly used for switching between views (such as viewing a series of photos in the Photos application).

The following Try It Out illustrates how to use the `UISwipeGestureRecognizer` to recognize the swipe gesture and then display different images in the ImageView.

TRY IT OUT Recognizing Swiping

1. Using the same project created in the previous Try It Out, drag and drop the two images named `Buildings.jpeg` and `Bridge.jpeg` onto the `Resources` folder of the Xcode project. When the Add dialog appears, check the Copy Item into Destination Group's Folder (If Needed) option so that each image is copied into the project (see Figure 14-7).

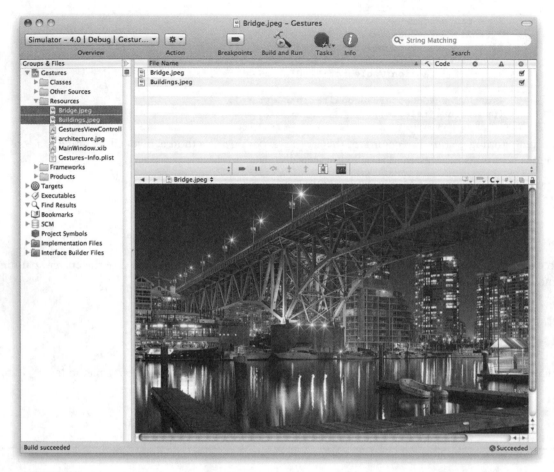

FIGURE 14-7

2. Edit the `GesturesViewController.m` file by adding the following bold statements:

```
#import "GesturesViewController.h"

@implementation GesturesViewController

@synthesize imageView;

CGFloat lastScaleFactor = 1;

CGFloat netRotation;

CGPoint netTranslation;

NSArray *images;
int imageIndex = 0;

- (void)viewDidLoad {
```

```
//---tap gesture---
UITapGestureRecognizer *tapGesture =
[[UITapGestureRecognizer alloc]
    initWithTarget:self
           action:@selector(handleTapGesture:)];

tapGesture.numberOfTapsRequired = 2;
[imageView addGestureRecognizer:tapGesture];
[tapGesture release];

//---pinch gesture---
UIPinchGestureRecognizer *pinchGesture =
[[UIPinchGestureRecognizer alloc]
    initWithTarget:self
           action:@selector(handlePinchGesture:)];

[imageView addGestureRecognizer:pinchGesture];
[pinchGesture release];

//---rotate gesture---
UIRotationGestureRecognizer *rotateGesture =
[[UIRotationGestureRecognizer alloc]
    initWithTarget:self
           action:@selector(handleRotateGesture:)];

[imageView addGestureRecognizer:rotateGesture];
[rotateGesture release];

//---pan gesture---
UIPanGestureRecognizer *panGesture =
[[UIPanGestureRecognizer alloc]
    initWithTarget:self
           action:@selector(handlePanGesture:)];

//---comment out this line---
//[imageView addGestureRecognizer:panGesture];

[panGesture release];

//---swipe gesture---
images = [[NSArray alloc] initWithObjects:
           @"architecture.jpg",
           @"Buildings.jpeg",
           @"Bridge.jpeg", nil];

//---right swipe (default)---
UISwipeGestureRecognizer *swipeGesture =
[[UISwipeGestureRecognizer alloc]
    initWithTarget:self
           action:@selector(handleSwipeGesture:)];

[imageView addGestureRecognizer:swipeGesture];
[swipeGesture release];

//---left swipe---
```

```objectivec
        UISwipeGestureRecognizer *swipeLeftGesture =
        [[UISwipeGestureRecognizer alloc]
            initWithTarget:self
                    action:@selector(handleSwipeGesture:)];
        swipeLeftGesture.direction = UISwipeGestureRecognizerDirectionLeft;

        [imageView addGestureRecognizer:swipeLeftGesture];
        [swipeLeftGesture release];

        [super viewDidLoad];
    }

//---handle swipe gesture---
-(IBAction) handleSwipeGesture:(UIGestureRecognizer *) sender {
        UISwipeGestureRecognizerDirection direction =
            [(UISwipeGestureRecognizer *) sender direction];

        switch (direction) {
            case UISwipeGestureRecognizerDirectionUp:
                NSLog(@"up");
                break;
            case UISwipeGestureRecognizerDirectionDown:
                NSLog(@"down");
                break;
            case UISwipeGestureRecognizerDirectionLeft:
                imageIndex++;
                break;
            case UISwipeGestureRecognizerDirectionRight:
                imageIndex--;
                break;
            default:
                break;
        }
        imageIndex = (imageIndex < 0) ? ([images count] - 1):
        imageIndex % [images count];
        imageView.image = [UIImage imageNamed:
                                [images objectAtIndex:imageIndex]];
    }

- (void)dealloc {
        [images release];
        [imageView release];
        [super dealloc];
    }
```

3. Test the application on the iPhone 4 Simulator by pressing Command-R.

4. Click the ImageView and drag the mouse from left to right and then from right to left. The ImageView changes its image as you swipe it with your mouse (see Figure 14-8).

FIGURE 14-8

How It Works

You first instantiate the `images` `NSArray` object with the names of the three images:

```
//---swipe gesture---
images = [[NSArray alloc] initWithObjects:
            @"architecture.jpg",
            @"Buildings.jpeg",
            @"Bridge.jpeg", nil];
```

By default, the `UISwipeGestureRecognizer` only recognizes right swipes (swiping from left to right). Hence, to recognize right swipes, you create an instance of the `UISwipeGestureRecognizer` class:

```
//---right swipe (default)---
UISwipeGestureRecognizer *swipeGesture =
[[UISwipeGestureRecognizer alloc]
    initWithTarget:self
            action:@selector(handleSwipeGesture:)];

[imageView addGestureRecognizer:swipeGesture];
[swipeGesture release];
```

To recognize left swipes (swiping from right to left), you need to create another instance of the `UISwipeGestureRecognizer` class and configure its `direction` property, like this:

```
//---left swipe---
UISwipeGestureRecognizer *swipeLeftGesture =
[[UISwipeGestureRecognizer alloc]
    initWithTarget:self
            action:@selector(handleSwipeGesture:)];
swipeLeftGesture.direction = UISwipeGestureRecognizerDirectionLeft;

[imageView addGestureRecognizer:swipeLeftGesture];
[swipeLeftGesture release];
```

When the swipe gestures are recognized, the `handleSwipeGesture:` method is invoked. Here, you examine the `direction` property of the `UISwipeGestureRecognizer` object to obtain the direction of the swipe:

```
UISwipeGestureRecognizerDirection direction =
    [(UISwipeGestureRecognizer *) sender direction];
```

Depending on the swipe direction, the image in the ImageView changes accordingly:

```
switch (direction) {
    case UISwipeGestureRecognizerDirectionUp:
        NSLog(@"up");
        break;
    case UISwipeGestureRecognizerDirectionDown:
        NSLog(@"down");
        break;
    case UISwipeGestureRecognizerDirectionLeft:
        imageIndex++;
        break;
    case UISwipeGestureRecognizerDirectionRight:
        imageIndex -- ;
        break;
    default:
        break;
}
imageIndex = (imageIndex < 0) ? ([images count] - 1):
imageIndex % [images count];
imageView.image = [UIImage imageNamed:
                        [images objectAtIndex:imageIndex]];
```

NOTE *Remember to comment out the statements for the pan gesture recognizer. The swipe gesture recognizer will not work with the pan gesture recognizer.*

Long Press

Use the long press gesture recognizer to detect whether the user is touching a view and then holding onto it. A very common use of the long press gesture is when you want to save an image in the mobile Safari Web browser. When you long press on an image, an action sheet pops up, enabling you to save or copy that image.

The following Try It Out shows you how to recognize a long press using the `UILongPressGestureRecognizer`.

TRY IT OUT Recognizing Long Presses

1. Using the same project created in the previous Try It Out, edit the `GesturesViewController.m` file by adding the following bold statements:

```
#import "GesturesViewController.h"

@implementation GesturesViewController

@synthesize imageView;

CGFloat lastScaleFactor = 1;

CGFloat netRotation;

CGPoint netTranslation;

NSArray *images;
int imageIndex = 0;

- (void)viewDidLoad {
    //---tap gesture---
    UITapGestureRecognizer *tapGesture =
    [[UITapGestureRecognizer alloc]
        initWithTarget:self
                action:@selector(handleTapGesture:)];

    tapGesture.numberOfTapsRequired = 2;
    [imageView addGestureRecognizer:tapGesture];
    [tapGesture release];

    //---pinch gesture---
    UIPinchGestureRecognizer *pinchGesture =
    [[UIPinchGestureRecognizer alloc]
        initWithTarget:self
                action:@selector(handlePinchGesture:)];

    [imageView addGestureRecognizer:pinchGesture];
    [pinchGesture release];

    //---rotate gesture---
    UIRotationGestureRecognizer *rotateGesture =
    [[UIRotationGestureRecognizer alloc]
        initWithTarget:self
```

```
               action:@selector(handleRotateGesture:)];

[imageView addGestureRecognizer:rotateGesture];
[rotateGesture release];

//---pan gesture---
UIPanGestureRecognizer *panGesture =
[[UIPanGestureRecognizer alloc]
    initWithTarget:self
           action:@selector(handlePanGesture:)];

//---comment this out---
//[imageView addGestureRecognizer:panGesture];

[panGesture release];

//---swipe gesture---
images = [[NSArray alloc] initWithObjects:
              @"architecture.jpg",
              @"Buildings.jpeg",
              @"Bridge.jpeg", nil];

//---right swipe (default)---
UISwipeGestureRecognizer *swipeGesture =
[[UISwipeGestureRecognizer alloc]
    initWithTarget:self
           action:@selector(handleSwipeGesture:)];

[imageView addGestureRecognizer:swipeGesture];
[swipeGesture release];

//---left swipe---
UISwipeGestureRecognizer *swipeLeftGesture =
[[UISwipeGestureRecognizer alloc]
    initWithTarget:self
           action:@selector(handleSwipeGesture:)];
swipeLeftGesture.direction = UISwipeGestureRecognizerDirectionLeft;

[imageView addGestureRecognizer:swipeLeftGesture];
[swipeLeftGesture release];

//---long press gesture---
UILongPressGestureRecognizer *longpressGesture =
[[UILongPressGestureRecognizer alloc]
    initWithTarget:self
           action:@selector(handleLongpressGesture:)];

longpressGesture.minimumPressDuration = 1;
longpressGesture.allowableMovement = 15;
longpressGesture.numberOfTouchesRequired = 1;

[imageView addGestureRecognizer:longpressGesture];
```

```
    [longpressGesture release];

    [super viewDidLoad];
}

//---handle long press gesture---
-(IBAction) handleLongpressGesture:(UIGestureRecognizer *) sender {
    UIActionSheet *actionSheet = [[UIActionSheet alloc]
                                    initWithTitle:@"Image options"
                                         delegate:self
                                cancelButtonTitle:nil
                           destructiveButtonTitle:nil
                                otherButtonTitles:
                                  @"Save Image", @"Copy", nil];
    //---remember to implement the UIActionSheetDelegate protocol in your
    // view controller---
    [actionSheet showInView:self.view];
    [actionSheet release];
}
```

2. To test the application on the iPhone 4 Simulator, press Command-R.

3. Click the ImageView and hold it there. Observe that an action sheet pops up, asking you to either save the image or copy it (see Figure 14-9).

FIGURE 14-9

How It Works

As usual, you create an instance of the `UIPanGestureRecognizer` class and connect it to a handler method:

```
//---long press gesture---
UILongPressGestureRecognizer *longpressGesture =
[[UILongPressGestureRecognizer alloc]
    initWithTarget:self
            action:@selector(handleLongpressGesture:)];
```

You configure the recognizer so that it recognizes the long press only when the user has touched the view using one finger, for one second, and does not move that finger more than 15 pixels from the original point of contact:

```
longpressGesture.minimumPressDuration = 1;
longpressGesture.allowableMovement = 15;
longpressGesture.numberOfTouchesRequired = 1;
```

You then attach the recognizer to the ImageView:

```
[imageView addGestureRecognizer:longpressGesture];
[longpressGesture release];
```

When a long press is detected, the `handleLongpressGesture:` method is invoked. Here, you simply display an action sheet:

```
//---handle long press gesture---
-(IBAction) handleLongpressGesture:(UIGestureRecognizer *) sender {
    UIActionSheet *actionSheet = [[UIActionSheet alloc]
                                initWithTitle:@"Image options"
                                      delegate:self
                              cancelButtonTitle:nil
                         destructiveButtonTitle:nil
                              otherButtonTitles:
                                @"Save Image", @"Copy", nil];
    //---remember to implement the UIActionSheetDelegate protocol in your
    // view controller---
    [actionSheet showInView:self.view];
    [actionSheet release];
}
```

NOTE You need to implement the necessary action to perform when the user clicks a button in your action sheet. The implementation details are not shown in this example. Remember to implement the `UIActionSheetControllerDelegate` protocol in your View Controller, though.

DETECTING TOUCHES

While the gesture recognizers greatly simplify your life in detecting gestures, sometimes you simply want to detect touches on the screen and perform some custom action (such as writing a doodle application that enables users to use their fingers to make a sketch).

To detect touches on the screen of the iPhone, you need to acquaint yourself with a few events that handle the detection of touches. Through these events, you will know whether users have single-tapped, double-tapped, or moved their fingers on your application, and react accordingly. These events are as follows:

➤ `touchesBegan:withEvent:` — Fires when one or more fingers touch in a view or window.

➤ `touchesMoved:withEvent:` — Fires when one or more fingers move within a view or window.

➤ `touchesEnded:withEvent:` — Fires when one or more fingers are raised from a view or window.

➤ `touchesCancelled:withEvent:` — Fires when a system event (such as a low-memory warning) cancels the touch event.

These events are defined in the `UIResponder` class, which is the superclass of `UIApplication`, `UIView`, and its subclasses. Hence, you can implement event handlers for these events in your View Controller.

NOTE *The four touch events are the foundation events used by the gesture recognizers described earlier in this chapter. To create custom gesture recognizers to recognize your own gestures (such as a figure-eight gesture), you need to implement your own event handlers for these four events. Creating your own custom gesture recognizer is beyond the scope of this book.*

Detecting Single Touch

Time to get the engine rolling! Make sure you download the code indicated here so you can work through the following Try It Out activity, in which you'll see how to detect when the user is tapping on the screen.

TRY IT OUT Detecting Taps

codefile MultiTouch.zip is available for download at Wrox.com

1. Using Xcode, create a new View-based Application (iPhone) project and name it `MultiTouch`.

2. Drag and drop an image into the `Resources` folder. Figure 14-10 shows an image named `apple.jpeg` located in the `Resources` folder.

3. Double-click the `MultiTouchViewController.xib` file to edit it in Interface Builder.

4. Populate the View window with an ImageView. Ensure that the ImageView covers the entire View window.

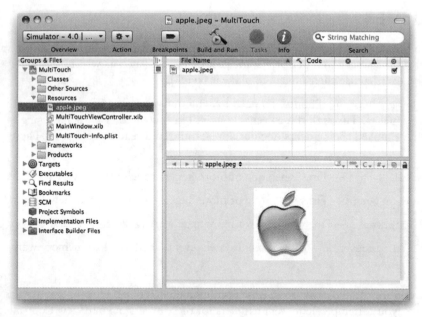

FIGURE 14-10

5. Select the ImageView and view its Attributes Inspector window (see Figure 14-11). Set its Image property to apple.jpeg.

FIGURE 14-11

6. In the `MultiTouchViewController.h` file, add the following statements that appear in bold:

```
#import <UIKit/UIKit.h>

@interface MultiTouchViewController : UIViewController {
    IBOutlet UIImageView *imageView;
}

@property (nonatomic, retain) UIImageView *imageView;

@end
```

7. Back in Interface Builder, Control-click and drag the File's Owner item to the ImageView. Select ImageView.

8. In the `MultiTouchViewController.m` file, add the following statements that appear in bold:

```
#import "MultiTouchViewController.h"

@implementation MultiTouchViewController

@synthesize imageView;

//---fired when the user finger(s) touches the screen---
-(void) touchesBegan: (NSSet *) touches withEvent: (UIEvent *) event {
    //---get all touches on the screen---
    NSSet *allTouches = [event allTouches];

    //---compare the number of touches on the screen---
    switch ([allTouches count])
    {
        //---single touch---
        case 1: {
            //---get info of the touch---
            UITouch *touch = [[allTouches allObjects] objectAtIndex:0];

            //---compare the taps---
            switch ([touch tapCount])
            {
                //---single tap---
                case 1: {
                    imageView.contentMode =
                        UIViewContentModeScaleAspectFit;
                } break;

                //---double tap---
                case 2: {
                    imageView.contentMode = UIViewContentModeCenter;
                } break;
            }
        } break;
    }
```

```
    }

- (void)dealloc {
    [imageView release];
    [super dealloc];
    }
```

9. Press Command-R to test the application on the iPhone 4 Simulator.

10. Single-tap the apple icon to enlarge it (see Figure 14-12). Double-tap it to return it to its original size.

FIGURE 14-12

How It Works

This application works by sensing the user's touch on the screen of the iPhone. When the user touches the screen, the View or View Controller fires a series of events that you can handle. There are four such events:

➤   `touchesBegan:withEvent:`

➤   `touchesEnded:withEvent:`

➤   `touchesMoved:withEvent:`

➤   `touchesCancelled:withEvent:`

Take a closer look at the first event. The touchesBegan:withEvent: event is fired when at least one touch is sensed on the screen. In this event, you can determine how many fingers are on the screen by calling the allTouches method of the UIEvent object (event):

```
//---get all touches on the screen---
NSSet *allTouches = [event allTouches];
```

The allTouches method returns an NSSet object containing a set of UITouch objects. To determine how many fingers are on the screen, simply count the number of UITouch objects in the NSSet object using the count method. In this case, you are currently interested only in a single touch, therefore you implement only the case for one touch:

```
//---compare the number of touches on the screen---
switch ([allTouches count])
{
    //---single touch---
    case 1: {
        //---get info of the touch---
        UITouch *touch = [[allTouches allObjects] objectAtIndex:0];

        //---compare the taps---
        switch ([touch tapCount])
        {
            //---single tap---
            case 1: {
                imageView.contentMode =
                    UIViewContentModeScaleAspectFit;
            } break;

            //---double tap---
            case 2: {
                imageView.contentMode = UIViewContentModeCenter;
            } break;
        }
    } break;
}
```

You extract details of the first touch by using the allObjects method of the NSSet object to return an NSArray object. You then use the objectAtIndex: method to obtain the first array item.

The UITouch object (touch) contains the tapCount property, which indicates whether the user has single-tapped the screen or performed a double-tap (or more). If the user single-tapped the screen, you resize the image to fit the entire ImageView view using the UIViewContentModeScaleAspectFit constant. If it is a double-tap, you restore it to its original size using the UIViewContentModeCenter constant.

The other three events are not discussed in this section. The touchesEnded:withEvent: event is fired when the user's finger or fingers are lifted from the screen. The touchesMoved:withEvent: event is fired continuously when the user's finger or fingers are touching and moving on the screen. Finally, if the application is interrupted while the user's finger is on the screen, the touchesCancelled:withEvent: event is fired.

NOTE *In addition to detecting taps in the* `touchesBegan:withEvent:` *event, you can also detect them in the* `touchesEnded:withEvent:` *event.*

In the next section, you learn how to detect multi-touches in your application.

UNDERSTANDING MULTI-TAPPING

When a user performs a multi-tap on the screen, your application will fire the `touchesBegan:` and `touchesEnded:` events multiple times. For example, if the user taps on the screen once, the `touchesBegan:` and `touchesEnded:` events will be fired once, with the `tapCount` property of the `UITouch` object returning a value of 1. However, if the user taps the screen twice (in quick succession), then the `touchesBegan:` and `touchesEnded:` events will be fired twice; the first time these events are fired, the `tapCount` property will be 1, the second time the `tapCount` property will be 2.

Understanding the way multi-taps are detected is important because if you are detecting double-taps, your application might redundantly execute blocks of code that are designed for single-tap. For example, in the preceding Try It Out, double-tapping on the image will first try to change the mode of the image to `UIViewContentModeScaleAspectFit` (which is what single-tap is supposed to do; in this case, because the image is already in the `UIViewContentModeScaleAspectFit` mode, the user won't notice any difference), then it changes back to the `UIViewContentModeCenter` mode (which is what double-tap is supposed to do). Ideally, it should not need to execute the block of code for single-tap.

To solve this problem, you have to write some code to check whether a second tap is indeed coming:

➤ When a single-tap is detected, use a timer using an `NSTimer` object.

➤ When a double-tap is detected, stop the timer and check whether the time difference between the second tap and the first tap is small enough (such as a fraction of a second) to constitute a double-tap. If it is, execute the code for double-tap. If it isn't, execute the code for single-tap.

If you are simply detecting for multi-taps in your application, the easiest method is to use the `UITapGestureRecognizer`, illustrated earlier.

Detecting Multi-Touches

Detecting multi-touches is very simple once you understand the concepts in the previous section. The capability to detect for multi-touches is very useful because you can use that to zoom in on views in your application.

The following Try It Out demonstrates how to detect multi-touches.

Detecting Multi-Touches

1. Using the same project created in the previous section, modify the `touchesBegan:withEvent:` method by adding the following statements that appear in bold:

```objectivec
//---fired when the user finger(s) touches the screen---
-(void) touchesBegan: (NSSet *) touches withEvent: (UIEvent *) event {
    //---get all touches on the screen---
    NSSet *allTouches = [event allTouches];

    //---compare the number of touches on the screen---
    switch ([allTouches count])
    {
        //---single touch---
        case 1: {
            //---get info of the touch---
            UITouch *touch = [[allTouches allObjects] objectAtIndex:0];

            //---compare the taps---
            switch ([touch tapCount])
            {
                //---single tap---
                case 1: {
                    imageView.contentMode =
                        UIViewContentModeScaleAspectFit;
                } break;

                //---double tap---
                case 2: {
                    imageView.contentMode = UIViewContentModeCenter;
                } break;
            }
        } break;

        //---double-touch---
        case 2: {
            //---get info of first touch---
            UITouch *touch1 = [[allTouches allObjects] objectAtIndex:0];

            //---get info of second touch---
            UITouch *touch2 = [[allTouches allObjects] objectAtIndex:1];

            //---get the points touched---
            CGPoint touch1PT = [touch1 locationInView:[self view]];
            CGPoint touch2PT = [touch2 locationInView:[self view]];

            NSLog(@"Touch1: %.0f, %.0f", touch1PT.x, touch1PT.y);
            NSLog(@"Touch2: %.0f, %.0f", touch2PT.x, touch2PT.y);
        } break;
    }
}
```

2. Press Command-R to test the application on the iPhone 4 Simulator.

3. In the iPhone 4 Simulator, press the Option key, and two circles should appear. Clicking the screen simulates two fingers touching the screen of the device.

4. Open the Debugger Console window (press Command-Shift-R) and observe the output as you Option-click the screen of the iPhone 4 Simulator multiple times (see Figure 14-13).

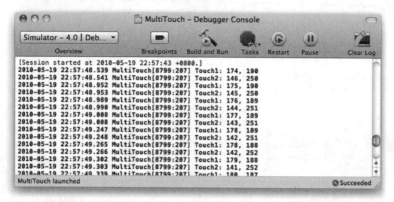

FIGURE 14-13

How It Works

As you do when detecting for single-touch, you check for multi-touches in the `touchesBegan:withEvent:` event. Rather than receive information about the first touch, you now obtain information for both the first touch and the second touch:

```
//---get info of first touch---
UITouch *touch1 = [[allTouches allObjects] objectAtIndex:0];

//---get info of second touch---
UITouch *touch2 = [[allTouches allObjects] objectAtIndex:1];
```

To get the coordinates (represented as a `CGPoint` structure) of each touch, you use the `locationInView:` method of the `UITouch` class and pass it the view whose coordinate system in which you want the touch located:

```
//---get the points touched---
CGPoint touch1PT = [touch1 locationInView:[self view]];
CGPoint touch2PT = [touch2 locationInView:[self view]];
```

The coordinates returned by the `locationInView:` method are relative to the view specified. In the preceding snippet, the coordinates displayed are relative to the main View window.

The x and y coordinates of a `CGPoint` structure are represented using the `CGFloat` type, so you need to use the `%f` format specifier when printing them in the Debugger Console window:

```
NSLog(@"Touch1: %.0f, %.0f", touch1PT.x, touch1PT.y);
NSLog(@"Touch2: %.0f, %.0f", touch2PT.x, touch2PT.y);
```

To detect more than two touches, you simply extend the preceding code to get information about the third touch, fourth touch, and so on.

 NOTE *Using the iPhone 4 Simulator, the coordinates for the two touches are often interchanged as you Option-click the same spot on the screen of the Simulator.*

Implementing the Pinch Gesture

You can combine the `UIPinchGestureRecognizer`, which you used earlier in this chapter, with what you've just learned about detecting for multi-touches to implement your own pinch gesture recognizer.

In the earlier pinch gesture example, you used the `CGAffineTransformMakeScale()` method to alter the size of the image. In this example, you will see another technique for changing the size of an image in the ImageView — you will alter the size of the image as it is being pinched.

In the following Try It Out, you learn how to implement the pinch gesture to zoom the image in and out in the ImageView.

TRY IT OUT **Zooming In and Out**

1. Using the same project created in the previous section, add the following statement that appears in bold to the `MultiTouchViewController.h` file:

```
#import <UIKit/UIKit.h>

@interface MultiTouchViewController : UIViewController {
    IBOutlet UIImageView *imageView;
}

@property (nonatomic, retain) UIImageView *imageView;

-(CGFloat) distanceBetweenTwoPoints:(CGPoint)fromPoint
                            toPoint:(CGPoint)toPoint;

@end
```

2. In the `MultiTouchViewController.m` file, implement the `distanceBetweenTwoPoints:toPoint:` and `touchesMoved:withEvent:` methods and add the statements that appear in bold to the `touchesBegan:withEvent:` method:

```
#import "MultiTouchViewController.h"

@implementation MultiTouchViewController

@synthesize imageView;
```

```objc
CGFloat originalDistance;

-(CGFloat) distanceBetweenTwoPoints:(CGPoint)fromPoint
                            toPoint:(CGPoint)toPoint {
    float lengthX = fromPoint.x - toPoint.x;
    float lengthY = fromPoint.y - toPoint.y;
    return sqrt((lengthX * lengthX) + (lengthY * lengthY));
}

//---fired when the user finger(s) touches the screen---
-(void) touchesBegan: (NSSet *) touches withEvent: (UIEvent *) event {
    //---get all touches on the screen---
    NSSet *allTouches = [event allTouches];

    //---compare the number of touches on the screen---
    switch ([allTouches count])
    {
        //---single touch---
        case 1: {
            //---get info of the touch---
            UITouch *touch = [[allTouches allObjects] objectAtIndex:0];

            //---compare the taps---
            switch ([touch tapCount])
            {
                //---single tap---
                case 1: {
                    imageView.contentMode =
                        UIViewContentModeScaleAspectFit;
                } break;
                //---double tap---
                case 2: {
                    imageView.contentMode = UIViewContentModeCenter;
                } break;
            }
        } break;

        //---double-touch---
        case 2: {
            //---get info of first touch---
            UITouch *touch1 = [[allTouches allObjects] objectAtIndex:0];

            //---get info of second touch---
            UITouch *touch2 = [[allTouches allObjects] objectAtIndex:1];

            //---get the points touched---
            CGPoint touch1PT = [touch1 locationInView:[self view]];
            CGPoint touch2PT = [touch2 locationInView:[self view]];

            NSLog(@"Touch1: %.0f, %.0f", touch1PT.x, touch1PT.y);
            NSLog(@"Touch2: %.0f, %.0f", touch2PT.x, touch2PT.y);

            //---record the distance made by the two touches---
            originalDistance = [self distanceBetweenTwoPoints:touch1PT
```

```
                                                  toPoint:touch2PT];

        } break;

    }
}

//---fired when the user moved his finger(s) on the screen---
-(void) touchesMoved: (NSSet *) touches withEvent: (UIEvent *) event {
    //---get all touches on the screen---
    NSSet *allTouches = [event allTouches];

    //---compare the number of touches on the screen---
    switch ([allTouches count])
    {
        //---single touch---
        case 1: {
        } break;

        //---double-touch---
        case 2: {
            //---get info of first touch---
            UITouch *touch1 = [[allTouches allObjects] objectAtIndex:0];

            //---get info of second touch---
            UITouch *touch2 = [[allTouches allObjects] objectAtIndex:1];

            //---get the points touched---
            CGPoint touch1PT = [touch1 locationInView:[self view]];
            CGPoint touch2PT = [touch2 locationInView:[self view]];

            NSLog(@"Touch1: %.0f, %.0f", touch1PT.x, touch1PT.y);
            NSLog(@"Touch2: %.0f, %.0f", touch2PT.x, touch2PT.y);

            CGFloat currentDistance =
                [self distanceBetweenTwoPoints:touch1PT
                                       toPoint:touch2PT];

            //---zoom in---
            if (currentDistance > originalDistance) {
                imageView.frame = CGRectMake(
                                imageView.frame.origin.x - 2,
                                imageView.frame.origin.y - 2,
                                imageView.frame.size.width + 4,
                                imageView.frame.size.height + 4);
            }
            else {
                //---zoom out---
                imageView.frame = CGRectMake(
                                imageView.frame.origin.x + 2,
                                imageView.frame.origin.y + 2,
                                imageView.frame.size.width - 4,
                                imageView.frame.size.height - 4);
            }
            originalDistance = currentDistance;
```

```
        } break;
    }
}
```

3. Press Command-R to test the application on the iPhone 4 Simulator.

4. Single-tap the ImageView to enlarge it. To zoom the image in and out, Option-click the image (see Figure 14-14).

 NOTE *To use the pinch gesture on an image, you need to enlarge the image first. That's because the image can only be resized if its display mode is set to* `UIViewContentModeScaleAspectFit`*. Hence, in this case, you need to single-tap on the image (which actually sets the image mode to* `UIViewContentModeScaleAspectFit`*) before you can try the pinching effect.*

FIGURE 14-14

How It Works

To detect for the pinch gesture, you find the distance between the two fingers and constantly compare that distance so that you know whether the two fingers are moving toward or away from each other.

To find the distance between two fingers, you define the `distanceBetweenTwoPoints:toPoint:` method:

```
-(CGFloat) distanceBetweenTwoPoints:(CGPoint)fromPoint
                         toPoint:(CGPoint)toPoint {
    float lengthX = fromPoint.x - toPoint.x;
    float lengthY = fromPoint.y - toPoint.y;
    return sqrt((lengthX * lengthX) + (lengthY * lengthY));
}
```

This method takes two `CGPoint` structures and then calculates the distance between them. No rocket science here — just the Pythagorean theorem in action.

When the two fingers first touch the screen, you record their distance in the `touchesBegan:withEvent:` method (see the code in bold):

```
//---fired when the user finger(s) touches the screen---
-(void) touchesBegan: (NSSet *) touches
          withEvent: (UIEvent *) event {
    //---get all touches on the screen---
    NSSet *allTouches = [event allTouches];

    //---compare the number of touches on the screen---
    switch ([allTouches count])
    {
        //---single touch---
        case 1: {
            //---get info of the touch---
            //...
            //...
        } break;

        //---double-touch---
        case 2: {
            //---get info of first touch---
            UITouch *touch1 =
                [[allTouches allObjects] objectAtIndex:0];

            //---get info of second touch---
            UITouch *touch2 =
                [[allTouches allObjects] objectAtIndex:1];

            //---get the points touched---
            CGPoint touch1PT =
                [touch1 locationInView:[self view]];
            CGPoint touch2PT =
                [touch2 locationInView:[self view]];

            NSLog(@"Touch1: %.0f, %.0f", touch1PT.x, touch1PT.y);
            NSLog(@"Touch2: %.0f, %.0f", touch2PT.x, touch2PT.y);

            //---record the distance made by the two touches---
            originalDistance =
                [self distanceBetweenTwoPoints:touch1PT
```

```
                                        toPoint:touch2PT];
        } break;
    }
}
```

As the two fingers move on the screen, you constantly compare their current distance with the original distance. If the current distance is greater than the original distance, this is a zoom-in gesture. If not, it is a zoom-out gesture:

```
//---fired when the user moved his finger(s) on the screen---
-(void) touchesMoved: (NSSet *) touches
        withEvent: (UIEvent *) event {

    //---get all touches on the screen---
    NSSet *allTouches = [event allTouches];

    //---compare the number of touches on the screen---
    switch ([allTouches count])
    {
        //---single touch---
        case 1: {
        } break;

        //---double-touch---
        case 2: {
            //---get info of first touch---
            UITouch *touch1 =
                [[allTouches allObjects] objectAtIndex:0];

            //---get info of second touch---
            UITouch *touch2 =
                [[allTouches allObjects] objectAtIndex:1];

            //---get the points touched---
            CGPoint touch1PT =
                [touch1 locationInView:[self view]];
            CGPoint touch2PT =
                [touch2 locationInView:[self view]];

            NSLog(@"Touch1: %.0f, %.0f", touch1PT.x, touch1PT.y);
            NSLog(@"Touch2: %.0f, %.0f", touch2PT.x, touch2PT.y);

            CGFloat currentDistance =
                [self distanceBetweenTwoPoints:touch1PT
                                       toPoint:touch2PT];

            //---zoom in---
            if (currentDistance > originalDistance) {
                imageView.frame =
                    CGRectMake(
                        imageView.frame.origin.x - 2,
                        imageView.frame.origin.y - 2,
                        imageView.frame.size.width + 4,
                        imageView.frame.size.height + 4);
```

```
        }
        else {
            //---zoom out---
            imageView.frame =
                CGRectMake(
                    imageView.frame.origin.x + 2,
                    imageView.frame.origin.y + 2,
                    imageView.frame.size.width - 4,
                    imageView.frame.size.height - 4);
        }
        originalDistance = currentDistance;
    } break;
    }
}
```

Implementing the Drag Gesture

Another gesture that you can implement is the drag, which is touching an item on the screen and then dragging it by moving the finger. In the following Try It Out, you learn how to drag an ImageView on the screen by implementing the drag gesture.

TRY IT OUT   Dragging the ImageView

1.   Using the MultiTouch project created earlier, resize the ImageView so that it fits the size of the image (see Figure 14-15).

2.   Add the following statements that appear in bold to the touchesMoved:withEvent: method:

```
//---fired when the user moved his finger(s) on the screen---
-(void) touchesMoved: (NSSet *) touches withEvent: (UIEvent *) event {
    //---get all touches on the screen---
    NSSet *allTouches = [event allTouches];

    //---compare the number of touches on the screen---
    switch ([allTouches count])
    {
        //---single touch---
        case 1: {
            //---get info of the touch---
            UITouch *touch = [[allTouches allObjects] objectAtIndex:0];

            //---check to see if the image is being touched---
            CGPoint touchPoint = [touch locationInView:[self view]];

            if (touchPoint.x > imageView.frame.origin.x &&
                touchPoint.x < imageView.frame.origin.x +
                imageView.frame.size.width &&
                touchPoint.y > imageView.frame.origin.y &&
                touchPoint.y <imageView.frame.origin.y +
                imageView.frame.size.height) {
                [imageView setCenter:touchPoint];
```

```
            }
        } break;

        //---double-touch---
        case 2: {
            //---get info of first touch---
            UITouch *touch1 = [[allTouches allObjects] objectAtIndex:0];

            //---get info of second touch---
            UITouch *touch2 = [[allTouches allObjects] objectAtIndex:1];

            //...
            //...
        } break;
    }
}
```

3. Press Command-R to test the application on the iPhone 4 Simulator.

4. You can now tap the ImageView and then move the image anywhere on the screen simply by moving your finger (see Figure 14-16).

FIGURE 14-15

FIGURE 14-16

How It Works

The concept for this example is very simple. When a finger taps the screen, you check whether the position of the finger falls within the range of the ImageView:

```
//---check to see if the image is being touched---
CGPoint touchPoint = [touch locationInView:[self view]];

if (touchPoint.x > imageView.frame.origin.x &&
    touchPoint.x < imageView.frame.origin.x +
    imageView.frame.size.width &&
    touchPoint.y > imageView.frame.origin.y &&
    touchPoint.y <imageView.frame.origin.y +
    imageView.frame.size.height) {
    [imageView setCenter:touchPoint];
}
```

If it does, then you simply reposition the ImageView by calling its `setCenter` property.

Using this technique, you can easily write a jigsaw puzzle application that enables users to rearrange the different pieces of the jigsaw puzzle simply by dragging them on the screen.

SUMMARY

In this chapter, you saw the use of the various gesture recognizers included in the iPhone SDK 3.2/4.0 that enable you to easily recognize the gestures commonly performed on an iPhone. In addition, you have seen the various events that you can handle if you want to perform your own tracking of the user's touch. Using these events, you can write your own routine to detect multiple touches in your application and use this knowledge to create some really interesting applications.

EXERCISES

1. Name the six gesture recognizers included in the iPhone SDK 3.2/4.0.

2. Name the gestures that are discrete and those that are continuous.

3. Name the four events for detecting touches in your application.

4. What is the difference between multi-taps and multi-touches?

5. How do you simulate multi-touch on the iPhone Simulator?

Answers to the exercises can be found in Appendix E, on Wrox.com.

▶ WHAT YOU LEARNED IN THIS CHAPTER

TOPIC	KEY CONCEPTS

New gesture recognizers	`UITapGestureRecognizer`
	`UIPinchGestureRecognizer`
	`UIPanGestureRecognizer`
	`UISwipeGestureRecognizer`
	`UIRotationGestureRecognizer`
	`UILongPressGestureRecognizer`

Discrete gesture	A discrete gesture sends a single message to the target when the gesture is recognized.
Continuous gesture	A continuous gesture sends multiple messages to the target until the gesture ends.

Detect touches on the view	Handle the following events in the view or View Controller:
	`touchesBegan:withEvent:`
	`touchesEnded:withEvent:`
	`touchesMoved:withEvent:`
	`touchesCancelled:withEvent:`

Detect for taps (single, double, and so on)	You can detect for taps in either the `touchesBegan:withEvent:` or `touchesEnded:withEvent:` method.
Implement pinch gesture	Compare the distance made by the two touch points to determine whether the gesture is zoom in or zoom out.
Implement drag gesture	Ensure that the touch point falls within the area occupied by the view in question.

15

Accessing the Accelerometer

WHAT YOU WILL LEARN IN THIS CHAPTER

➤ How to obtain accelerometer data from your iPhone

➤ How to detect shakes to your device

iPhone's built-in accelerometer enables your program to detect the orientation of the device and adapt the content to suit the new orientation. For example, when you rotate your device sideways, the Safari Web browser automatically switches the screen to landscape mode to provide a wider viewing space.

In this chapter, you learn how to access the accelerometer and use the Shake API to detect shakes to your iPhone.

USING THE ACCELEROMETER

The accelerometer in iPhone measures the acceleration of the device relative to freefall. A value of 1 indicates that the device is experiencing 1 g of force exerted on it (1 g of force being the gravitational pull of the earth, which your device experiences when it is stationary). The accelerometer measures the acceleration of the device in three different axes: x, y and z. Figure 15-1 shows the different axes measured by the accelerometer.

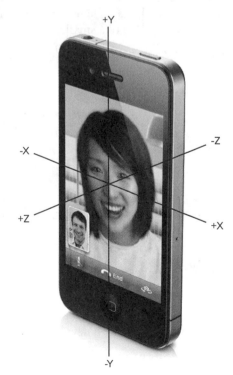

FIGURE 15-1

Table 15-1 shows example readings of the three axes when the device is in the various positions. Bear in mind that you won't see the exact same values as these, because they are always fluctuating due to the accelerometer's sensitivity.

TABLE 15-1: Example Readings of the X, Y, and Z Axes

POSITION	X	Y	Z
Vertical upright position	0.0	-1.0	0.0
Landscape left	1.0	0.0	0.0
Landscape right	-1.0	0.0	0.0
Upside down	0.0	1.0	0.0
Flat up	0.0	0.0	-1.0
Flat down	0.0	0.0	1.0

If the iPhone is held upright and moved to the right quickly, the value of the x-axis will increase from 0 to a positive value. If it is moved to the left quickly, the value of the x-axis will decrease from 0 to a negative value. If the device is moved upward quickly, the value of the y-axis will increase from -1.0 to a larger value. If the device is moved downward quickly, the value of the y-axis will decrease from -1.0 to a smaller value.

If the device is horizontal and then moved downward, the value of the z-axis will decrease from -1.0 to a smaller number. If it is moved upward, the value of the z-axis will increase from -1.0 to a bigger number.

 NOTE *The accelerometer used on the iPhone gives a maximum reading of about +/- 2.3 g, with a resolution of about 0.018 g.*

In the following Try it Out, you programmatically access the data returned by the accelerometer. Obtaining the accelerometer data enables you to build very interesting applications, such as a spirit level, as well as games that depend on motion detection.

TRY IT OUT   Accessing the Accelerometer Data

codefile Accelerometer.zip available for download at Wrox.com

1. Using Xcode, create a new View-based Application (iPhone) project and name it `Accelerometer`.

2. In the `AccelerometerViewController.h` file, add the following statements that appear in bold:

```
#import <UIKit/UIKit.h>

@interface AccelerometerViewController : UIViewController
```

```
    <UIAccelerometerDelegate> {
}

@end
```

3. In the `AccelerometerViewController.m` file, add the following statements that appear in bold:

```
#import "AccelerometerViewController.h"

@implementation AccelerometerViewController

- (void)viewDidLoad {
    UIAccelerometer *accel = [UIAccelerometer sharedAccelerometer];
    accel.delegate = self;
    accel.updateInterval = 1.0f/60.0f;

    [super viewDidLoad];
}

- (void)accelerometer:(UIAccelerometer *)acel
        didAccelerate:(UIAcceleration *)acceleration {
    NSLog(@"x: %g", acceleration.x);
    NSLog(@"y: %g", acceleration.y);
    NSLog(@"z: %g", acceleration.z);
}
```

4. Press Command-R to test the application on a real iPhone device. Figure 15-2 shows example data displayed by the application when my iPhone is held in my hand.

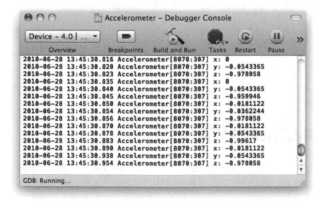

FIGURE 15-2

 NOTE For accelerometer data, you need a real device; the iPhone Simulator does not return any readings for accelerometer data.

How It Works

To use the accelerometer in your iPhone, you implement the `UIAccelerometerDelegate` protocol in your delegate (such as the View Controller):

```
@interface AccelerometerViewController : UIViewController
    <UIAccelerometerDelegate> {
```

When the view is loaded, you first obtain a single instance of the `UIAccelerometer` class using the `sharedAccelerometer` method. You then specify the delegate of the instance and the update interval for which you want to obtain accelerometer data:

```
- (void)viewDidLoad {
    UIAccelerometer *accel =
        [UIAccelerometer sharedAccelerometer];
    accel.delegate = self;
    accel.updateInterval = 1.0f/60.0f;

    [super viewDidLoad];
}
```

The `updateInterval` property specifies the interval in seconds — that is, the number of seconds between updates. In this case, you want the accelerometer data to be updated 60 times a second.

The `UIAccelerometerDelegate` protocol defines a single method that you need to implement to obtain accelerometer data: `accelerometer:didAccelerate:`. You then extract the values of the three axes and display them in the Debugger Console window:

```
- (void)accelerometer:(UIAccelerometer *)acel
        didAccelerate:(UIAcceleration *)acceleration {
    NSLog(@"x: %g", acceleration.x);
    NSLog(@"y: %g", acceleration.y);
    NSLog(@"z: %g", acceleration.z);
}
```

VISUALIZING THE ACCELEROMETER DATA

Printing out the raw values of the accelerometer data is not very exciting. Instead, the following Try It Out shows you how to modify the application so that you can use the accelerometer data to move a tennis ball on the screen.

TRY IT OUT   Visualizing the Accelerometer Data

1. Using the same project created in the previous section, add an image of a tennis ball to the Resources folder as shown in Figure 15-3.

2. Double-click the `AccelerometerViewController.xib` file to edit it in Interface Builder.

3. Add an Image View to the View window and set its `Image` attribute to `tennisball.jpg` (see Figure 15-4). Also, set the background color of the View window to black (see Figure 15-5).

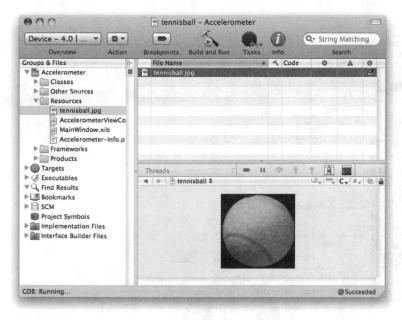

FIGURE 15-3

FIGURE 15-4

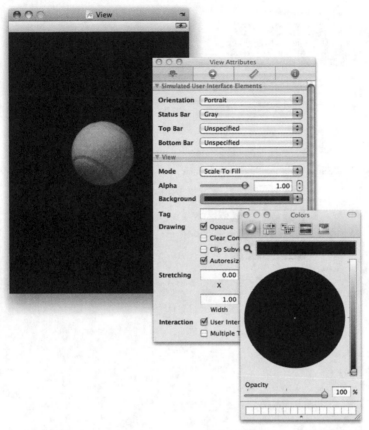

FIGURE 15-5

4. In the `AccelerometerViewController.h` file, add the following code in bold:

```
#import <UIKit/UIKit.h>

@interface AccelerometerViewController : UIViewController
    <UIAccelerometerDelegate> {
    IBOutlet UIImageView *imageView;
    CGPoint delta;
    CGPoint translation;
    float ballRadius;
}

@property (nonatomic, retain) UIImageView *imageView;

@end
```

5. In Interface Builder, Control-click and drag the File's Owner item over the Image View. Select `imageView`.

6. In the `AcceleromenterViewController.m` file, add the following code in bold:

```
#import "AccelerometerViewController.h"

@implementation AccelerometerViewController

@synthesize imageView;

- (void)viewDidLoad {
    UIAccelerometer *accel = [UIAccelerometer sharedAccelerometer];
    accel.delegate = self;
    accel.updateInterval = 1.0f/60.0f;

    ballRadius = imageView.frame.size.width / 2;
    delta = CGPointMake(12.0,4.0);
    translation = CGPointMake(0.0,0.0);

    [super viewDidLoad];
}

- (void)accelerometer:(UIAccelerometer *)acel
        didAccelerate:(UIAcceleration *)acceleration {

    //--Comment this out--
    // NSLog(@"x: %g", acceleration.x);
    // NSLog(@"y: %g", acceleration.y);
    // NSLog(@"z: %g", acceleration.z);

    if (acceleration.x>0) delta.x = 2; else delta.x = -2;
    if (acceleration.y>0) delta.y = -2; else delta.y = 2;

    [UIView beginAnimations:@"translate" context:nil];

    imageView.transform =
        CGAffineTransformMakeTranslation(translation.x, translation.y);
    translation.x = translation.x + delta.x;
    translation.y = translation.y + delta.y;

    [UIView commitAnimations];

    if (imageView.center.x + translation.x > 320 - ballRadius ||
        imageView.center.x + translation.x < ballRadius) {
        translation.x -= delta.x;
    }

    if (imageView.center.y + translation.y > 460 - ballRadius ||
        imageView.center.y + translation.y < ballRadius) {
        translation.y -= delta.y;
    }
}

- (void)dealloc {
    [imageView release];
    [super dealloc];
}
```

7. Press Command-R to test the application on a real iPhone device. Observe that as you move the device, the tennis ball moves in the same direction as your hand (see Figure 15-6).

FIGURE 15-6

 NOTE *Remember to comment out the three* `NSLog()` *statements. If you don't, the application will be too busy trying to output the accelerometer data and this will affect the animation of the image.*

How It Works

This exercise enables you to visually examine the data reported by the accelerometer. In this case, only the data from the x and y axes is used. The `delta` variable represents the amount to move, both in the x-axis and the y-axis.

To move the image, you apply a translation via the Image View's `transform` property:

```
[UIView beginAnimations:@"translate" context:nil];

imageView.transform =
    CGAffineTransformMakeTranslation(
        translation.x, translation.y);
translation.x = translation.x + delta.x;
translation.y = translation.y + delta.y;

[UIView commitAnimations];
```

The `translation` variable keeps track of the current translation so that the image will animate smoothly.

USING THE SHAKE API TO DETECT SHAKES

Beginning with the iPhone OS 3.0, Apple introduced the Shake API, which helps your application to detect shakes to the device. In reality, this API comes in the form of three events that you can handle in your code:

➤ `motionBegan:`

➤ `motionEnded:`

➤ `motionCancelled:`

These three events are defined in the `UIResponder` class, which is the superclass of `UIApplication`, `UIView`, and its subclasses (including `UIWindow`). The following Try It Out shows you how to detect shakes to your device using these three events.

TRY IT OUT Using the Shake API

codefile Shake.zip available for download at Wrox.com

1. Using Xcode, create a new View-based Application (iPhone) project and name it `Shake`.

2. Double-click the `ShakeViewController.xib` file to edit it in Interface Builder.

3. Populate the View window with the following views, and you'll see Figure 15-7:

   ➤ TextField

   ➤ DatePicker

FIGURE 15-7

4. Insert the following statements that appear in bold into the `ShakeViewController.h` file:

```
#import <UIKit/UIKit.h>

@interface ShakeViewController : UIViewController {
    IBOutlet UITextField *textField;
    IBOutlet UIDatePicker *datePicker;
}

@property (nonatomic, retain) UITextField *textField;
@property (nonatomic, retain) UIDatePicker *datePicker;

-(IBAction) doneEditing: (id) sender;

@end
```

5. In Interface Builder:

➤ Control-click and drag the File's Owner item to the TextField view and select `textField`.

➤ Control-click and drag the File's Owner item to the DatePicker view and select `datePicker`.

➤ Right-click the TextField view and connect its `Did End on Exit` event to the File's Owner item. Select `doneEditing:`.

6. Insert the following statements that appear in bold to the `ShakeViewController.m` file:

```
#import "ShakeViewController.h"

@implementation ShakeViewController

@synthesize textField, datePicker;

- (void) viewDidAppear:(BOOL)animated {
    [self.view becomeFirstResponder];
    [super viewDidAppear:animated];
}

- (IBAction) doneEditing: (id) sender {
    //---when keyboard is hidden, make the view
    // the first responder
    // or else the Shake API will not work---
    [self.view becomeFirstResponder];
}

- (void)motionBegan:(UIEventSubtype)motion
        withEvent:(UIEvent *)event {
    if (event.subtype == UIEventSubtypeMotionShake) {
        NSLog(@"motionBegan:");
    }
}

- (void)motionCancelled:(UIEventSubtype)motion
            withEvent:(UIEvent *)event {

    if (event.subtype == UIEventSubtypeMotionShake) {
        NSLog(@"motionCancelled:");
    }
```

```
    }

- (void)motionEnded:(UIEventSubtype)motion
          withEvent:(UIEvent *)event {
    if (event.subtype == UIEventSubtypeMotionShake) {
        NSLog(@"motionEnded:");
    }
}

- (void)dealloc {
    [textField release];
    [datePicker release];
    [super dealloc];
}
```

7. Right-click the Classes group in Xcode and choose Add ➪ New File. Choose the Cocoa Touch Class item on the left and select the Objective-C class template. Choose the UIView subclass (see Figure 15-8) and click Next. Name the file `ShakeView.m`.

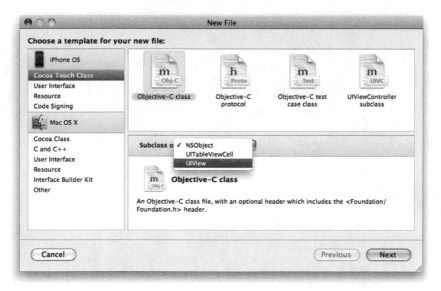

FIGURE 15-8

8. Insert the following statements in bold in `ShakeView.m`:

```
#import "ShakeView.h"

@implementation ShakeView

- (id)initWithFrame:(CGRect)frame {
    if ((self = [super initWithFrame:frame])) {
        // Initialization code
    }
    return self;
}

/*
```

```
// Only override drawRect: if you perform custom drawing.
// An empty implementation adversely affects performance during animation.
- (void)drawRect:(CGRect)rect {
    // Drawing code
}
*/

- (void)dealloc {
    [super dealloc];
}

- (BOOL)canBecomeFirstResponder {
    return YES;
}

@end
```

9. In Interface Builder, select the View item in the ShakeViewController.xib window and view its Identity Inspector window. Set `ShakeView` as its class name (see Figure 15-9).

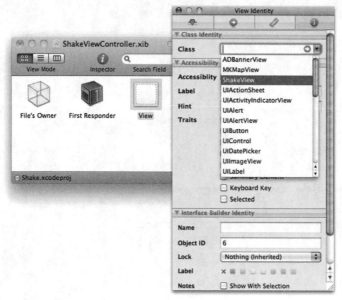

FIGURE 15-9

10. Save the file in Interface Builder.

11. Press Command-R to test the application on the iPhone 4 Simulator. Open the Debugger Console window by pressing Command-Shift-R in Xcode.

12. With the application in the iPhone 4 Simulator, choose Hardware ➪ Shake Gesture to simulate shaking the device. Observe the information printed in the Debugger Console window (see Figure 15-10).

13. Tap the TextField view to make the keyboard appear. Choose Hardware ➪ Shake Gesture to simulate shaking the device again. Observe the values printed in the Debugger Console window.

FIGURE 15-10

14. Close the keyboard by clicking the return key on the keyboard. Simulate shaking the device again and observe the output on the Debugger Console window.

How It Works

Be aware that the three events used for monitoring shakes are fired only when there is a first responder in your View. Hence, the first thing you do when your View appears is set it to become the first responder (in the ShakeViewController.m file):

```
- (void) viewDidAppear:(BOOL)animated {
    [self.view becomeFirstResponder];
    [super viewDidAppear:animated];
}
```

However, by default, the View cannot be a first responder, so you need to create a UIView subclass (ShakeView.m) so that you can override the default canBecomeFirstResponder method to return a YES:

```
- (BOOL)canBecomeFirstResponder {
    return YES;
}
```

Doing so allows your View to become a first responder. By default, Interface Builder wires your View with the UIView base class (with which you need not do anything most of the time). You now need to tell Interface Builder to use the newly created ShakeView subclass.

Next, you handle the three events in the ShakeViewController.m file:

```
- (void)motionBegan:(UIEventSubtype)motion
```

```
          withEvent:(UIEvent *)event {
    if (event.subtype == UIEventSubtypeMotionShake) {
        NSLog(@"motionBegan:");
    }
}

- (void)motionCancelled:(UIEventSubtype)motion
           withEvent:(UIEvent *)event {

    if (event.subtype == UIEventSubtypeMotionShake) {
        NSLog(@"motionCancelled:");
    }
}

- (void)motionEnded:(UIEventSubtype)motion
        withEvent:(UIEvent *)event {
    if (event.subtype == UIEventSubtypeMotionShake) {
        NSLog(@"motionEnded:");
    }
}
```

For each event, you first check that the motion is indeed a shake; then, print a debugging statement in the Debugger Console.

In the `doneEditing:` method (which is fired when the user dismisses the keyboard by tapping the return key), you make the View the first responder:

```
- (IBAction) doneEditing: (id) sender {
    //---when keyboard is hidden, make the view
    // the first responder
    // or else the Shake API will not work---
    [self.view becomeFirstResponder];
}
```

If you don't do this, the three motion-sensing events are not fired. The key point to remember is that something must be the first responder.

The `motionBegan:` event is fired when the OS suspects that the device is being shaken. If eventually the OS determines that the action is not a shake, the `motionCancelled:` event is fired. When the OS finally determines that the action is a shake action, the `motionEnded:` event is fired.

Performing an Action When the Device Is Shaken

Now modify your project so that when the iPhone is shaken, the DatePicker view is reset to the current date.

TRY IT OUT   Resetting the DatePicker When Shaken

1. In the `ShakeViewController.m` file, add the following statements that appear in bold:

```
- (void)ResetDatePicker {
    [datePicker setDate:[NSDate date]];
```

```
    }
- (void)motionEnded:(UIEventSubtype)motion
         withEvent:(UIEvent *)event {
    if (event.subtype == UIEventSubtypeMotionShake) {
        NSLog(@"motionEnded:");
        [self ResetDatePicker];
    }
}
```

2. Press Command-R to test the application on the iPhone Simulator. Set the DatePicker view to some date. Choose Hardware ⇨ Shake Gesture to simulate shaking the device. Notice that the DatePicker view resets to the current date.

How It Works

In this example, you first added a ResetDatePicker method to reset the DatePicker view to the current date:

```
- (void)ResetDatePicker {
    [datePicker setDate:[NSDate date]];
}
```

When the device is shaken, you called the ResetDatePicker method to reset the DatePicker view to the current date:

```
- (void)motionEnded:(UIEventSubtype)motion
         withEvent:(UIEvent *)event {
    if (event.subtype == UIEventSubtypeMotionShake) {
        NSLog(@"motionEnded:");
        [self ResetDatePicker];
    }
}
```

SUMMARY

In this chapter, you have seen how to obtain the accelerometer data of your iPhone. You also saw how to use the Shake API to help you determine whether your device is being shaken. Combining this knowledge enables you to create very compelling applications.

EXERCISES

1. Name the protocol that your delegate needs to conform to in order to use the accelerometer on your iPhone.

2. Name the three events in the Shake API in the iPhone SDK 3.0.

Answers to the Exercises can be found in Appendix E, on Wrox.com.

▶ **WHAT YOU LEARNED IN THIS CHAPTER**

TOPIC	KEY CONCEPTS
Accessing the accelerometer	Ensure that your View Controller conforms to the `UIAccelerometerDelegate` protocol and create an instance of the `UIAccelerometer` class.
	To listen to changes in acceleration, implement the `accelerometer:didAccelerate:` method.
Detecting shakes	You can use either the accelerometer data or the new Shake API in the iPhone OS 3.0. For the Shake API, handle the following events: `motionBegan:`, `motionEnded:`, and `motionCancelled:`.

PART IV
Network Programming Techniques

16

Web Services

WHAT YOU WILL LEARN IN THIS CHAPTER

➤ Understanding the various ways to consume Web services in your iPhone applications

➤ How to communicate with a Web service using SOAP

➤ How to parse the result of a Web service call using the NSXMLParser class

Communicating with the outside world is one of the ways to make your iPhone applications interesting and useful. This is especially true today when so many Web services provide such useful functionality. However, consuming Web services in an iPhone is not for the fainthearted. Unlike other development tools (such as Microsoft Visual Studio), Xcode does not have built-in tools that make consuming Web services easy. Everything must be done by hand, and you need to know how to form the relevant XML messages to send to the Web services and then parse the returning XML result.

This chapter explains how to communicate with XML Web services from within your iPhone application. Working through the examples in this chapter will give you a solid foundation for consuming other Web services that you will need in your own projects.

 NOTE *For an introduction to XML Web services, check out this link:* www.w3schools .com/webservices/ws_intro.asp.

BASICS OF CONSUMING XML WEB SERVICES

Before you create an Xcode project to consume a Web service, it is good to examine a real Web service to see the different ways you can consume it. My favorite example is to use an ASMX XML Web service created using .NET. For the purposes of this discussion, we'll look at a Web service called IPToCountry, which enables you to supply an IP address and then returns the country to which the IP address belongs.

The IPToCountry Web service is located at www.ecubicle.net/iptocountry.asmx. If you use Safari to load this URL, you will see that it exposes two Web methods, as shown in Figure 16-1.

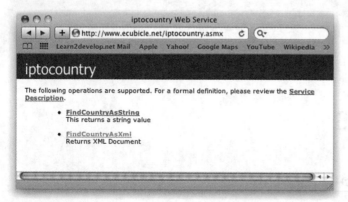

FIGURE 16-1

For this example, use the FindCountryAsXml method, which returns the result (the country) as an XML string. Clicking the FindCountryAsXml link reveals the page shown in Figure 16-2.

FIGURE 16-2

The important parts are the sections following the Test section shown on the page. They detail the various ways in which you can consume the Web service — SOAP, and optionally, HTTP GET and HTTP POST. In the .NET world, accessing the Web service is a pretty straightforward affair — Visual Studio provides a built-in tool to create a Web proxy service object for the Web service simply by downloading the WSDL document. For iPhone development, you need to get your hands dirty, so you must understand the underlying mechanics of how to consume a Web service.

Using SOAP 1.1

The most common method to consume a Web service is using SOAP (Simple Object Access Protocol). When using SOAP, you need to use the POST method to send the following request to the Web service:

```
POST /iptocountry.asmx HTTP/1.1
Host: www.ecubicle.net
Content-Type: text/xml; charset=utf-8
Content-Length: length
SOAPAction: "http://www.ecubicle.net/webservices/FindCountryAsXml"

<?xml version="1.0" encoding="utf-8"?>
<soap:Envelope xmlns:xsi="http://www.w3.org/2001/XMLSchema-instance"
xmlns:xsd=http://www.w3.org/2001/XMLSchema
xmlns:soap="http://schemas.xmlsoap.org/soap/envelope/">
  <soap:Body>
    <FindCountryAsXml xmlns="http://www.ecubicle.net/webservices/">
      <V4IPAddress>string</V4IPAddress>
    </FindCountryAsXml>
  </soap:Body>
</soap:Envelope>
```

The bold italic word in the code is the placeholder where you need to substitute the actual value. Note a few important things in this example:

➤ The URL for the Web service is `http://www.ecubicle.net/iptocountry.asmx`. This is the URL as shown in Figure 16-1.

➤ The URL for the `SOAPAction` is `http://www.ecubicle.net/webservices/FindCountryAsXml`.

➤ The `Content-Type` for the request is `text/xml; charset=utf-8`.

➤ The `HTTP` method is POST.

➤ The SOAP request is as follows:

```
<?xml version="1.0" encoding="utf-8"?>
<soap:Envelope xmlns:xsi="http://www.w3.org/2001/XMLSchema-instance"
xmlns:xsd="http://www.w3.org/2001/XMLSchema"
xmlns:soap="http://schemas.xmlsoap.org/soap/envelope/">
  <soap:Body>
    <FindCountryAsXml xmlns="http://www.ecubicle.net/webservices/">
      <V4IPAddress>string</V4IPAddress>
    </FindCountryAsXml>
  </soap:Body>
</soap:Envelope>
```

➤ The `Content-Length` of the SOAP request is the total number of characters in the request.

➤ The Web service will return the following response:

```
HTTP/1.1 200 OK
Content-Type: text/xml; charset=utf-8
Content-Length: length

<?xml version="1.0" encoding="utf-8"?>
<soap:Envelope xmlns:xsi="http://www.w3.org/2001/XMLSchema-instance"
xmlns:xsd="http://www.w3.org/2001/XMLSchema"
xmlns:soap="http://schemas.xmlsoap.org/soap/envelope/">
  <soap:Body>
    <FindCountryAsXmlResponse xmlns="http://www.ecubicle.net/webservices/">
      <FindCountryAsXmlResult>xml result</FindCountryAsXmlResult>
    </FindCountryAsXmlResponse>
  </soap:Body>
</soap:Envelope>
```

The result (country) will be enclosed within the block of XML results (shown in bold above). You would need to extract it from the XML result.

Using SOAP 1.2

Using SOAP 1.2 is very similar to using SOAP 1.1. The following shows the SOAP request for SOAP 1.2:

```
POST /iptocountry.asmx HTTP/1.1
Host: www.ecubicle.net
Content-Type: application/soap+xml; charset=utf-8
Content-Length: length

<?xml version="1.0" encoding="utf-8"?>
<soap12:Envelope xmlns:xsi="http://www.w3.org/2001/XMLSchema-instance"
xmlns:xsd="http://www.w3.org/2001/XMLSchema"
xmlns:soap12="http://www.w3.org/2003/05/soap-envelope">
  <soap12:Body>
    <FindCountryAsXml xmlns="http://www.ecubicle.net/webservices/">
      <V4IPAddress>string</V4IPAddress>
    </FindCountryAsXml>
  </soap12:Body>
</soap12:Envelope>
```

The SOAP response for SOAP 1.2 would be as follows:

```
HTTP/1.1 200 OK
Content-Type: application/soap+xml; charset=utf-8
Content-Length: length

<?xml version="1.0" encoding="utf-8"?>
<soap12:Envelope xmlns:xsi="http://www.w3.org/2001/XMLSchema-instance"
xmlns:xsd="http://www.w3.org/2001/XMLSchema"
xmlns:soap12="http://www.w3.org/2003/05/soap-envelope">
  <soap12:Body>
    <FindCountryAsXmlResponse xmlns="http://www.ecubicle.net/webservices/">
```

```
    <FindCountryAsXmlResult>xml result</FindCountryAsXmlResult>
  </FindCountryAsXmlResponse>
 </soap12:Body>
</soap12:Envelope>
```

CONSUMING WEB SERVICES USING SOAP, HTTP GET, AND HTTP POST

Besides using SOAP to communicate with a Web service, two more methods are available: HTTP and HTTP POST. Using HTTP GET (the simplest), all the information you need to pass to the Web service can be sent through the query string. For example, you can invoke a Web service through the query string like this: www.somewebservice.com/webservice.asmx?key1=value1&key2=value2. However, the query string has a limit on its length, and is hence not suitable if you need to pass a lot of data to the Web service.

An alternative to this would be to use the HTTP POST method, which allows more data to be sent. Using the example just used, instead of passing all the keys and their values through the URL, you would send them through the HTTP headers. However, HTTP POST has its limitations as well. As with HTTP GET, the data to be sent must be formatted as key/value pairs but each key/value pair is limited in size to 1024 characters. The most versatile method is to use the SOAP method, which allows complex data types to be sent to the Web service through the SOAP request.

As not all Web services support HTTP GET and HTTP POST, this chapter will not discuss them in detail. Readers who are interested in learning more about how to consume Web services using HTTP GET and HTTP POST can refer to my online article at www.devx.com/wireless/Article/43209.

CONSUMING A WEB SERVICE IN YOUR IPHONE APPLICATION

Now you're ready to tackle the exciting task of consuming a Web service in your iPhone application! In the following Try It Out, you learn how to communicate with the Web service using the SOAP method.

TRY IT OUT   Consuming Web Services Using SOAP

1. Using Xcode, create a View-based Application (iPhone) project and name it **WebServices**.

2. Double-click the WebServicesViewController.xib file to edit it in Interface Builder.

3. Double-click the View item and populate the View window with the views as follows (see also Figure 16-3):

   ➤ Label (name it IP **Address**)

   ➤ Text Field

➤ Round Rect Button (name it **Find Country**)

➤ Activity Indicator

4. Select the Activity Indicator view and display its Attributes Inspector window. Check the Hide When Stopped attribute (see Figure 16-4).

5. In Xcode, edit the `WebServicesViewController.h` file by adding the following bold statements:

```
#import <UIKit/UIKit.h>

@interface WebServicesViewController : UIViewController {
    IBOutlet UITextField *ipAddress;
    IBOutlet UIActivityIndicatorView *activityIndicator;

    NSMutableData *webData;
    NSMutableString *soapResults;
    NSURLConnection *conn;
}

@property (nonatomic, retain) UITextField *ipAddress;
@property (nonatomic, retain) UIActivityIndicatorView *activityIndicator;

-(IBAction) btnFindCountry:(id)sender;

@end
```

6. Save the file and return to Interface Builder.

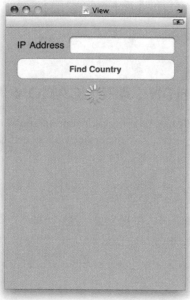

FIGURE 16-3

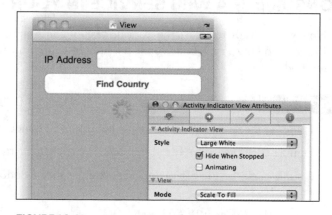

FIGURE 16-4

7. Perform the following actions:

➤ Control-click the File's Owner item and drag it over the Text Field view. Select `ipAddress`.

➤ Control-click the File's Owner item and drag it over the Activity Indicator view. Select `activityIndicator`.

➤ Control-click the Round Rect Button view and drag it over the File's Owner item. Select `btnFindCountry:`.

8. Right-click the File's Owner item now and you should see the connections as shown in Figure 16-5.

9. In the `WebServicesViewController.m` file, add the following bold statements:

FIGURE 16-5

```
#import "WebServicesViewController.h"

@implementation WebServicesViewController

@synthesize ipAddress;
@synthesize activityIndicator;

- (IBAction)btnFindCountry:(id)sender {
    NSString *soapMsg =
        [NSString stringWithFormat:
        @"<?xml version=\"1.0\" encoding=\"utf-8\"?>"
        "<soap:Envelope xmlns:xsi="
        "\"http://www.w3.org/2001/XMLSchema-instance\" "
        "xmlns:xsd=\"http://www.w3.org/2001/XMLSchema\" "
        "xmlns:soap=\"http://schemas.xmlsoap.org/soap/envelope/\">"
        "<soap:Body>"
        "<FindCountryAsXml xmlns=\"http://www.ecubicle.net/webservices/\">"
        "<V4IPAddress>%@</V4IPAddress>"
        "</FindCountryAsXml>"
        "</soap:Body>"
        "</soap:Envelope>", ipAddress.text];

    //---print it to the Debugger Console for verification---
    NSLog(@"%@",soapMsg);
    NSURL *url = [NSURL URLWithString:
                    @"http://www.ecubicle.net/iptocountry.asmx"];
    NSMutableURLRequest *req = [NSMutableURLRequest requestWithURL:url];

    //---set the various headers---
    NSString *msgLength = [NSString stringWithFormat:@"%d",
                                [soapMsg length]];
    [req addValue:@"text/xml; charset=utf-8"
        forHTTPHeaderField:@"Content-Type"];
    [req addValue:@"http://www.ecubicle.net/webservices/FindCountryAsXml"
        forHTTPHeaderField:@"SOAPAction"];
```

```objectivec
    [req addValue:msgLength forHTTPHeaderField:@"Content-Length"];

    //---set the HTTP method and body---
    [req setHTTPMethod:@"POST"];
    [req setHTTPBody:[soapMsg dataUsingEncoding:NSUTF8StringEncoding]];

    //---start animating--
    [activityIndicator startAnimating];

    conn = [[NSURLConnection alloc] initWithRequest:req
                                            delegate:self];
    if (conn) {
        webData = [[NSMutableData data] retain];
    }
}

-(void) connection:(NSURLConnection *) connection
didReceiveResponse:(NSURLResponse *) response {
    [webData setLength: 0];
}

-(void) connection:(NSURLConnection *) connection
    didReceiveData:(NSData *) data {
    [webData appendData:data];
}

-(void) connection:(NSURLConnection *) connection
  didFailWithError:(NSError *) error {
    [webData release];
    [connection release];
}

-(void) connectionDidFinishLoading:(NSURLConnection *) connection {
    NSLog(@"DONE. Received Bytes: %d", [webData length]);
    NSString *theXML = [[NSString alloc]
                         initWithBytes:[webData mutableBytes]
                               length:[webData length]
                             encoding:NSUTF8StringEncoding];

    //---shows the XML---
    NSLog(@"%@",theXML);
    [theXML release];

    //---stop animating---
    [activityIndicator stopAnimating];

    [connection release];
    [webData release];
}

- (void)dealloc {
    [ipAddress release];
    [activityIndicator release];
    [super dealloc];
}
```

10. Press Command-R to test the application on the iPhone 4 Simulator. Enter the IP address `3.4.5.6` in the Text Field, and click the Find Country button.

11. In Xcode, press Shift-Command-R to open the Debugger Console window. Observe that the following was sent to the Web service:

```
<?xml version="1.0" encoding="utf-8"?>
<soap:Envelope
    xmlns:xsi="http://www.w3.org/2001/XMLSchema-instance"
    xmlns:xsd="http://www.w3.org/2001/XMLSchema"
    xmlns:soap="http://schemas.xmlsoap.org/soap/envelope/">
    <soap:Body>
        <FindCountryAsXml xmlns="http://www.ecubicle.net/webservices/">
            <V4IPAddress>3.4.5.6</V4IPAddress>
        </FindCountryAsXml>
    </soap:Body>
</soap:Envelope>
```

12. The Web service responded with the following:

```
<?xml version="1.0" encoding="utf-8"?>
<soap:Envelope
    xmlns:soap="http://schemas.xmlsoap.org/soap/envelope/"
    xmlns:xsi="http://www.w3.org/2001/XMLSchema-instance"
    xmlns:xsd="http://www.w3.org/2001/XMLSchema">
    <soap:Body>
        <FindCountryAsXmlResponse
            xmlns="http://www.ecubicle.net/webservices/">
            <FindCountryAsXmlResult>
                <IPCountryService xmlns="">
                    <Country>United States</Country>
                </IPCountryService>
            </FindCountryAsXmlResult>
        </FindCountryAsXmlResponse>
    </soap:Body>
</soap:Envelope>
```

The response from the Web service indicates that you have managed to communicate with it. The challenge now is how to parse the XML to extract the relevant result that you want. In this case, the result you want is encapsulated in the <Country> element. In the next section you'll learn how to parse the XML response.

How It Works

Let's spend some time examining what you just did. First, you create the SOAP request packet:

```
NSString *soapMsg =
    [NSString stringWithFormat:
    @"<?xml version=\"1.0\" encoding=\"utf-8\"?>"
    "<soap:Envelope xmlns:xsi="
    "\"http://www.w3.org/2001/XMLSchema-instance\" "
    "xmlns:xsd=\"http://www.w3.org/2001/XMLSchema\" "
    "xmlns:soap=\"http://schemas.xmlsoap.org/soap/envelope/\">"
    "<soap:Body>"
    "<FindCountryAsXml xmlns=\"http://www.ecubicle.net/webservices/\">"
```

```
            "<V4IPAddress>%@</V4IPAddress>"
            "</FindCountryAsXml>"
            "</soap:Body>"
            "</soap:Envelope>", ipAddress.text];
```

Next, you create a URL load request object using an instance of the NSMutableURLRequest and NSURL objects:

```
NSURL *url = [NSURL URLWithString:
                @"http://www.ecubicle.net/iptocountry.asmx"];
NSMutableURLRequest *req = [NSMutableURLRequest requestWithURL:url];
```

You then populate the request object with the various headers, such as Content-Type, SOAPAction, and Content-Length. You also set the HTTP method and HTTP body:

```
//---set the various headers---
NSString *msgLength = [NSString stringWithFormat:@"%d",
                        [soapMsg length]];
[req addValue:@"text/xml; charset=utf-8"
    forHTTPHeaderField:@"Content-Type"];
[req addValue:@"http://www.ecubicle.net/webservices/FindCountryAsXml"
    forHTTPHeaderField:@"SOAPAction"];
[req addValue:msgLength forHTTPHeaderField:@"Content-Length"];
//---set the HTTP method and body---
[req setHTTPMethod:@"POST"];
[req setHTTPBody:[soapMsg dataUsingEncoding:NSUTF8StringEncoding]];
```

Before you make the actual request to the Web service, you get the Activity Indicator view to start animating, providing a visual feedback to the user that the application is waiting for a response from the Web service:

```
//---start animating --
[activityIndicator startAnimating];
```

To establish the connection with the Web service, you use the NSURLConnection class together with the request object just created:

```
conn = [[NSURLConnection alloc] initWithRequest:req
                                delegate:self];
if (conn) {
    webData = [[NSMutableData data] retain];
}
```

The NSURLConnection object will now proceed to send the request to the Web service and asynchronously call the various methods (which you will define next) when responses are received from the Web service. The data method of the NSMutableData class returns an empty data object. The NSMutableData object represents a wrapper for byte buffers, which you will use to receive incoming data from the Web service.

When data starts streaming in from the Web service, the connection:didReceiveResponse: method is called, which you need to implement here:

```
-(void) connection:(NSURLConnection *) connection
didReceiveResponse:(NSURLResponse *) response {
    [webData setLength: 0];
}
```

Here, you initialize the length of webData to zero.

As the data progressively comes in from the Web service, the connection:didReceiveData: method is called. Here, you append the data received to the webData object:

```
-(void) connection:(NSURLConnection *) connection
    didReceiveData:(NSData *) data {
    [webData appendData:data];
}
```

If there is an error during the transmission, the connection:didFailWithError: method is called:

```
-(void) connection:(NSURLConnection *) connection
  didFailWithError:(NSError *) error {
    [webData release];
    [connection release];
}
```

It is important that you handle a communication failure gracefully so that the user can try again later.

When the connection has finished and successfully downloaded the response, the connectionDidFinishLoading: method is called:

```
-(void) connectionDidFinishLoading:(NSURLConnection *) connection {
    NSLog(@"DONE. Received Bytes: %d", [webData length]);
    NSString *theXML = [[NSString alloc]
                            initWithBytes:[webData mutableBytes]
                                   length:[webData length]
                                 encoding:NSUTF8StringEncoding];

    //---shows the XML---
    NSLog(@"%@",theXML);
    [theXML release];

    //---stop animating --
    [activityIndicator stopAnimating];

    [connection release];
    [webData release];
}
```

Here, you simply print the XML response received from the Web service to the Debugger Console window and then stop the Activity Indicator view from animating.

PARSING THE XML RESPONSE

In the iPhone SDK, you can use the NSXMLParser object to parse an XML response returned by the Web service. The NSXMLParser class is an implementation of the Simple API for the XML (SAX) mechanism, which parses an XML document serially.

An NSXMLParser object reads an XML document, scanning it from beginning to end. As it encounters the various items in the document (such as elements, attributes, comments, and so on), it notifies its delegates so that appropriate actions can be taken (such as extracting the value of an element, etc.).

In the following Try It Out, you will parse the XML result returned by the Web service so that you can display the country of the IP address that you have sent to the Web service.

TRY IT OUT   **Parsing the XML Result Returned by the Web Service**

1.   Using the WebServices project created in the previous section, add the following statements to the WebServicesViewController.h file to parse the response from the Web service:

```
#import <UIKit/UIKit.h>

@interface WebServicesViewController : UIViewController
    <NSXMLParserDelegate> {

    IBOutlet UITextField *ipAddress;
    IBOutlet UIActivityIndicatorView *activityIndicator;

    NSMutableData *webData;
    NSMutableString *soapResults;
    NSURLConnection *conn;

    NSXMLParser *xmlParser;
    BOOL elementFound;
}

@property (nonatomic, retain) UITextField *ipAddress;
@property (nonatomic, retain) UIActivityIndicatorView *activityIndicator;

- (IBAction) btnFindCountry:(id)sender;

@end
```

2.   In the WebServicesViewController.m file, add the following bold statements to the connectionDidFinishLoading: method:

```
-(void) connectionDidFinishLoading:(NSURLConnection *) connection {
    NSLog(@"DONE. Received Bytes: %d", [webData length]);
    NSString *theXML = [[NSString alloc]
                        initWithBytes:[webData mutableBytes]
                            length:[webData length]
                        encoding:NSUTF8StringEncoding];

    //---shows the XML---
    NSLog(@"%@",theXML);
    [theXML release];

    //---stop animating---
    [activityIndicator stopAnimating];

    if (xmlParser) {
        [xmlParser release];
```

```
    }

    xmlParser = [[NSXMLParser alloc] initWithData: webData];
    [xmlParser setDelegate:self];
    [xmlParser setShouldResolveExternalEntities:YES];
    [xmlParser parse];

    [connection release];
    [webData release];
}
```

3. In the `WebServicesViewController.m` file, add the following methods:

```
//---when the start of an element is found---
-(void) parser:(NSXMLParser *) parser
didStartElement:(NSString *) elementName
  namespaceURI:(NSString *) namespaceURI
 qualifiedName:(NSString *) qName
    attributes:(NSDictionary *) attributeDict {

    if ([elementName isEqualToString:@"Country"]) {
        if (!soapResults) {
            soapResults = [[NSMutableString alloc] init];
        }
        elementFound = YES;
    }
}

//---when the text in an element is found---
-(void)parser:(NSXMLParser *) parser
foundCharacters:(NSString *)string {
    if (elementFound) {
        [soapResults appendString: string];
    }
}

//---when the end of element is found---
-(void)parser:(NSXMLParser *)parser
didEndElement:(NSString *)elementName
 namespaceURI:(NSString *)namespaceURI
qualifiedName:(NSString *)qName {

    if ([elementName isEqualToString:@"Country"]) {
        //---displays the country---
        NSLog(@"%@", soapResults);
        UIAlertView *alert = [[UIAlertView alloc]
                                    initWithTitle:@"Country found!"
                                          message:soapResults
                                         delegate:self
                                cancelButtonTitle:@"OK"
                                otherButtonTitles:nil];

        [alert show];
        [alert release];
        [soapResults setString:@""];
        elementFound = FALSE;
```

```
        }
    }

    - (void)dealloc {
        [soapResults release];

        [ipAddress release];
        [activityIndicator release];
        [super dealloc];
    }
```

4. Test the application on the iPhone 4 Simulator by pressing Command-R. Enter an IP address and click the Find Country button. The application displays the result, as shown in Figure 16-6.

FIGURE 16-6

How It Works

To parse the XML result, you create an instance of the NSXMLParser class and then initialize it with the response returned by the Web service. The NSXMLParser is an implementation of the Simple API for the XML (SAX) parser. It parses an XML document sequentially, in an event-driven manner. As the parser encounters the various elements, attributes, and so forth, in an XML document, it raises events where you can insert your own event handlers to do your processing.

As the NSXMLParser object encounters the various items in the XML document, it fires off several methods, which you need to define:

➤ `parser:didStartElement:namespaceURI:qualifiedName:attributes:` — Fired when the start tag of an element is found:

```
//---when the start of an element is found---
-(void) parser:(NSXMLParser *) parser
didStartElement:(NSString *) elementName
  namespaceURI:(NSString *) namespaceURI
 qualifiedName:(NSString *) qName
    attributes:(NSDictionary *) attributeDict {

    if ([elementName isEqualToString:@"Country"]) {
        if (!soapResults) {
            soapResults = [[NSMutableString alloc] init];
        }
        elementFound = YES;
    }
}
```

Here, you check to see whether the tag is <Country>. If it is, you set the Boolean variable `elementFound` to YES.

➤ `parser:foundCharacters:` — Fired when the text of an element is found:

```
//---when the text in an element is found---
-(void)parser:(NSXMLParser *) parser
foundCharacters:(NSString *)string {
    if (elementFound) {
        [soapResults appendString: string];
    }
}
```

Here, if the <Country> tag is found, you start to extract the value of the Country element into the soapResults object.

➤ `parser:didEndElement:namespaceURI:qualifiedName:` — Fired when the end of an element is found:

```
//---when the end of element is found---
-(void)parser:(NSXMLParser *)parser
didEndElement:(NSString *)elementName
 namespaceURI:(NSString *)namespaceURI
qualifiedName:(NSString *)qName {

    if ([elementName isEqualToString:@"Country"]) {
        //---displays the country---
        NSLog(@"%@", soapResults);
        UIAlertView *alert = [[UIAlertView alloc]
                                    initWithTitle:@"Country found!"
                                          message:soapResults
                                         delegate:self
                                cancelButtonTitle:@"OK"
                                otherButtonTitles:nil];

        [alert show];
        [alert release];
```

```
            [soapResults setString:@""];
            elementFound = FALSE;
        }
    }
```

Here, you simply look for the `</Country>` tag to confirm that the value of the `Country` element has been correctly extracted. You then print out the value using a `UIAlertView` object.

SUMMARY

This chapter explored the various ways you can consume a Web service in your iPhone applications — SOAP, HTTP GET, and HTTP POST. You also learned how to extract data from an XML document. It is hoped that you now have a good idea of what is involved in consuming Web services.

EXERCISES

1. Name the three ways in which you can consume a Web service in your iPhone applications.

2. Name the three key events you need to handle when using the `NSURLConnection` class.

3. Describe the steps by which the `NSXMLParser` class parses the content of an XML document.

Answers to the Exercises can be found in Appendix E, on Wrox.com.

▶ **WHAT YOU LEARNED IN THIS CHAPTER**

TOPIC	KEY CONCEPTS
Ways to consume a Web service	SOAP 1.1/1.2, HTTP GET, and HTTP POST
Formulating a URL request	Use the `NSMutableURLRequest` class.
Establishing a URL connection	Use the `NSURLConnection` class.
Class for storing byte buffers	Use the `NSMutableData` class.

Events fired by the `NSURLConnection` **class**	`connection:didReceiveResponse:`
	`connection:didReceiveData:`
	`connection:didFailWithError:`
	`connectionDidFinishLoading:`

Parsing XML content	Use the `NSXMLParser` class.

Events fired by the `NSXMLParser` **class**	`parser:didStartElement:namespaceURI:qualifiedName:attributes:`
	`parser:foundCharacters:`
	`parser:didEndElement:namespaceURI:qualifiedName:`

17
Bluetooth Programming

WHAT YOU WILL LEARN IN THIS CHAPTER

➤ How to use the various APIs within the Game Kit framework for Bluetooth communications

➤ How to look for peer Bluetooth devices using the GKPeerPickerController class

➤ How to send and receive data from a connected device

➤ How to implement Bluetooth voice chat

The iPhone comes with built-in Bluetooth functionality, enabling it to communicate with other Bluetooth devices, such as Bluetooth headsets, iPhone, iPod touch, and iPad. This chapter shows you how to write iPhone applications that use Bluetooth to communicate with another device, performing tasks such as sending and receiving text messages, as well as voice chatting. Daunting as it may sound, Bluetooth programming is actually quite simple using the iPhone SDK. All the Bluetooth functionalities are encapsulated within the Game Kit framework.

 NOTE *To test the concepts covered in this chapter, you need two devices: iPads, iPhones (4, 3G or 3GS), or iPod touches (second generation or later) running iPhone OS 3.0 or later.*

USING THE GAME KIT FRAMEWORK

One of the neat features available in the iPhone SDK is the Game Kit framework, which contains APIs that enable communications over a Bluetooth network. You can use these APIs to create peer-to-peer games and applications with ease. Unlike other mobile platforms, using

Bluetooth as a communication channel in the iPhone is much easier than you might expect. In this section, you will learn how to build a simple application that enables two iPhone (or iPad and iPod touch) devices to communicate with each other.

Searching for Peer Devices

Before any exchanges of data can take place, the first step to Bluetooth communication is for the devices to locate each other. The following Try It Out shows you how to use the Game Kit framework to locate your Bluetooth peer.

TRY IT OUT   Looking for Peer Devices

codefile Bluetooth.zip available for download at Wrox.com

1. Using Xcode, create a new View-based Application project and name it **Bluetooth**.

2. Add the `GameKit.framework` to your project (see Figure 17-1).

FIGURE 17-1

3. Double-click `BluetoothViewController.xib` to edit it in Interface Builder. As shown in Figure 17-2, add the following views to the View window:

➤ Round Rect buttons (name them **Connect, Disconnect,** and **Send**)

➤ Label (name it "Enter message here")

➤ Text Field

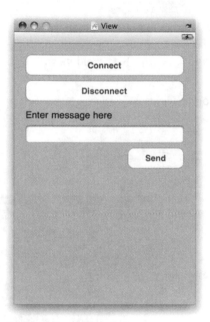

FIGURE 17-2

4. In the `BluetoothViewController.h` file, add the following statements shown in bold:

```
#import <UIKit/UIKit.h>
#import <GameKit/GameKit.h>

@interface BluetoothViewController : UIViewController
    <GKSessionDelegate,
    GKPeerPickerControllerDelegate> {

    GKSession *currentSession;
    GKPeerPickerController *picker;

    IBOutlet UITextField *txtMessage;
    IBOutlet UIButton *connect;
    IBOutlet UIButton *disconnect;
}

@property (nonatomic, retain) GKSession *currentSession;
```

```
@property (nonatomic, retain) UITextField *txtMessage;
@property (nonatomic, retain) UIButton *connect;
@property (nonatomic, retain) UIButton *disconnect;

-(IBAction) btnSend:(id) sender;
-(IBAction) btnConnect:(id) sender;
-(IBAction) btnDisconnect:(id) sender;

@end
```

5. Back in Interface Builder, perform the following actions:

➤ Control-click the File's Owner item and drag and drop it over the Text Field view. Select `txtMessage`.

➤ Control-click the File's Owner item and drag and drop it over the Connect button. Select `connect`.

➤ Control-click the File's Owner item and drag and drop it over the Disconnect button. Select `disconnect`.

➤ Control-click the Send button and drag and drop it over the File's Owner item. Select `btnSend:`.

➤ Control-click the Connect button and drag and drop it over the File's Owner item. Select `btnConnect:`.

➤ Control-click the Disconnect button and drag and drop it over the File's Owner item. Select `btnDisconnect:`.

FIGURE 17-3

6. Right-click on the File's Owner item to verify that all the connections are made correctly (see Figure 17-3).

7. In the `BluetoothViewController.m` file, add the following statements in bold:

```
#import "BluetoothViewController.h"

@implementation BluetoothViewController

@synthesize currentSession;
@synthesize txtMessage;
@synthesize connect;
@synthesize disconnect;

- (void)viewDidLoad {
    [connect setHidden:NO];
    [disconnect setHidden:YES];
    [super viewDidLoad];
}

//---select a nearby Bluetooth device---
```

```objc
-(IBAction) btnConnect:(id) sender {
    picker = [[GKPeerPickerController alloc] init];
    picker.delegate = self;
    picker.connectionTypesMask = GKPeerPickerConnectionTypeNearby;

    [connect setHidden:YES];
    [disconnect setHidden:NO];
    [picker show];
}

//---did connect to a peer---
-(void)peerPickerController:(GKPeerPickerController *)pk
            didConnectPeer:(NSString *)peerID
                  toSession:(GKSession *)session {
    self.currentSession = session;
    session.delegate = self;
    [session setDataReceiveHandler:self withContext:nil];
    picker.delegate = nil;
    [picker dismiss];
    [picker autorelease];
}

-(void)peerPickerControllerDidCancel:(GKPeerPickerController *)pk {
    picker.delegate = nil;
    [picker autorelease];
    [connect setHidden:NO];
    [disconnect setHidden:YES];
}

//---connection was cancelled---
-(IBAction) btnDisconnect:(id) sender {
    [self.currentSession disconnectFromAllPeers];
    [self.currentSession release];
    currentSession = nil;
    [connect setHidden:NO];
    [disconnect setHidden:YES];
}

//---session state changed---
-(void)session:(GKSession *)session
          peer:(NSString *)peerID
didChangeState:(GKPeerConnectionState)state {

    switch (state) {
        case GKPeerStateConnected:
            NSLog(@"connected");
            break;

        case GKPeerStateDisconnected:
            NSLog(@"disconnected");
            [self.currentSession release];
            currentSession = nil;
            [connect setHidden:NO];
            [disconnect setHidden:YES];
            break;
    }
```

```
    }

    //---session failed with error---
    -(void)session:(GKSession *)session
    didFailWithError:(NSError *)error {
        NSLog(@"%@",[error description]);
    }

    - (void)dealloc {
        [txtMessage release];
        [currentSession release];
        [connect release];
        [disconnect release];

        [super dealloc];
    }
```

8. Deploy the application onto two devices (either iPhone, iPad, or iPod touch).

9. Once the application is deployed onto two devices, launch the application on both devices. If Bluetooth is not turned on, you will be asked to turn it on (see Figure 17-4). Tap the Connect button on each device. You will see the standard UI to discover other devices (see Figure 17-5).

10. After a few seconds, both devices should be able to find each other (see Figure 17-6). Tap the name of the found device and the application will attempt to connect to it.

11. When another device tries to connect to your device, a popup is displayed, as shown in Figure 17-7. Tap Accept to connect or tap Decline to decline the connection.

FIGURE 17-4

FIGURE 17-5

FIGURE 17-6

FIGURE 17-7

How It Works

The GKSession object is used to represent a session between two connected Bluetooth devices. You use it to send and receive data between the two devices. Hence, you first create a variable of type GKSession:

```
GKSession *currentSession;
```

The GKPeerPickerController class provides a standard UI to enable your application to discover and connect to another Bluetooth device. This is the easiest way to connect to another Bluetooth device.

To discover and connect to another Bluetooth device, implement the btnConnect: method as follows:

```
-(IBAction) btnConnect:(id) sender {
    picker = [[GKPeerPickerController alloc] init];
    picker.delegate = self;
    picker.connectionTypesMask = GKPeerPickerConnectionTypeNearby;

    [connect setHidden:YES];
    [disconnect setHidden:NO];
    [picker show];
}
```

The connectionTypesMask property indicates the types of connections from which the user can choose. There are two types available: GKPeerPickerConnectionTypeNearby and GKPeerPickerConnectionTypeOnline. For Bluetooth communication, use the GKPeerPickerConnectionTypeNearby constant. The GKPeerPickerConnectionTypeOnline constant indicates an Internet-based connection.

When remote Bluetooth devices are detected and the user has selected and connected to one of them, the peerPickerController:didConnectPeer:toSession: method is called. It is implemented as follows:

```
-(void)peerPickerController:(GKPeerPickerController *)pk
```

```
            didConnectPeer:(NSString *)peerID
                   toSession:(GKSession *)session {
    self.currentSession = session;
    session.delegate = self;
    [session setDataReceiveHandler:self withContext:nil];
    picker.delegate = nil;
    [picker dismiss];
    [picker autorelease];
}
```

When the user has connected to the peer Bluetooth device, you save the GKSession object to the currentSession property. This enables you to use the GKSession object to communicate with the remote device.

If the user cancels the Bluetooth Picker, the peerPickerControllerDidCancel: method is called. It's defined as follows:

```
-(void)peerPickerControllerDidCancel:(GKPeerPickerController *)pk {
    picker.delegate = nil;
    [picker autorelease];
    [connect setHidden:NO];
    [disconnect setHidden:YES];
}
```

To disconnect from a connected device, use the disconnectFromAllPeers method from the GKSession object:

```
-(IBAction) btnDisconnect:(id) sender {
    [self.currentSession disconnectFromAllPeers];
    [self.currentSession release];
    currentSession = nil;
    [connect setHidden:NO];
    [disconnect setHidden:YES];
}
```

When a device is connected or disconnected, the session:peer:didChangeState: method is called:

```
-(void)session:(GKSession *)session
          peer:(NSString *)peerID
didChangeState:(GKPeerConnectionState)state {

    switch (state) {
        case GKPeerStateConnected:
            NSLog(@"connected");
            break;

        case GKPeerStateDisconnected:
            NSLog(@"disconnected");
            [self.currentSession release];
            currentSession = nil;
            [connect setHidden:NO];
            [disconnect setHidden:YES];
            break;
    }
}
```

Handling this event enables you to determine when a connection is established or ended. For example, when the connection is established, you might want to immediately start sending data to the other device.

Sending and Receiving Data

Once two devices are connected via Bluetooth, you can begin to send data between them. The data is transmitted using the NSData object (which is actually a bytes buffer), so you are free to define your own data format to send any types of data (such as images, text files, binary files, and so on).

The following Try It Out shows how to send a simple text message to another Bluetooth-connected device.

TRY IT OUT Sending Text to Another Device

1. Using the project created in the previous section, add the following methods to the BluetoothViewController.m file:

```
//---send data to peer---
- (void) mySendDataToPeers:(NSData *) data {
    if (currentSession)
        [self.currentSession sendDataToAllPeers:data
                               withDataMode:GKSendDataReliable
                                      error:nil];
}

-(IBAction) btnSend:(id) sender {
    //---convert an NSString object to NSData---
    NSData* data;
    NSString *str = [NSString stringWithString:txtMessage.text];
    data = [str dataUsingEncoding: NSASCIIStringEncoding];
    [self mySendDataToPeers:data];
}

//---data received from peer---
- (void) receiveData:(NSData *)data
            fromPeer:(NSString *)peer
           inSession:(GKSession *)session
             context:(void *)context {
    //---convert the NSData to NSString---
    NSString* str;
    str = [[NSString alloc] initWithData:data
                                encoding:NSASCIIStringEncoding];

    UIAlertView *alert = [[UIAlertView alloc]
                          initWithTitle:@"Data received"
                                message:str
                               delegate:self
                      cancelButtonTitle:@"OK"
                      otherButtonTitles:nil];
    [alert show];
    [alert release];
```

```
        [str release];
}
```

2. Deploy the application onto two devices. Connect the devices using Bluetooth. Now enter some
    text and start sending to the other device. Data received from another device is shown in an Alert
    view (see Figure 17-8).

FIGURE 17-8

How It Works

To send data to the connected Bluetooth device, use the `mysendDataToAllPeers:` method of the
`GKSession` object. The data that you send is transmitted via an `NSData` object.

The `mySendDataToAllPeers:` method is defined as follows:

```
- (void) mySendDataToPeers:(NSData *) data {
    if (currentSession)
        [self.currentSession sendDataToAllPeers:data
                            withDataMode:GKSendDataReliable
                                      error:nil];
}
```

 NOTE Note the use of the `GKSendDataReliable` constant. This constant means
that the `GKSession` object continues to send the data until it is successfully transmitted or the connection times out. The data is delivered in the order it is sent.
Use this constant when you need to ensure guaranteed delivery. Conversely, the
`GKSendDataUnreliable` constant indicates that the `GKSession` object sends the
data once and does not retry if an error occurs. The data sent can be received
out of order by recipients. Use this constant for small packets of data that must
arrive quickly in order to be useful to the recipient.

The btnSend: method enables text entered by the user to be sent to the remote device:

```
-(IBAction) btnSend:(id) sender {
    //---convert an NSString object to NSData---
    NSData* data;
    NSString *str = [NSString stringWithString:txtMessage.text];
    data = [str dataUsingEncoding: NSASCIIStringEncoding];
    [self mySendDataToPeers:data];
}
```

When data is received from the other device, the receiveData:fromPeer:inSession:context: method is called:

```
- (void) receiveData:(NSData *)data
            fromPeer:(NSString *)peer
           inSession:(GKSession *)session
             context:(void *)context {
    //---convert the NSData to NSString---
    NSString* str;
    str = [[NSString alloc] initWithData:data
                               encoding:NSASCIIStringEncoding];

    UIAlertView *alert = [[UIAlertView alloc]
                          initWithTitle:@"Data received"
                                message:str
                               delegate:self
                      cancelButtonTitle:@"OK"
                      otherButtonTitles:nil];
    [alert show];
    [alert release];
    [str release];
}
```

Here, the received data is in the NSData format. To display it using the UIAlertView class, you convert it to an NSString object.

IMPLEMENTING VOICE CHATTING

Another cool feature of the Game Kit framework is its support for voice chat.

The Voice Chat service in the Game Kit enables two devices to establish a voice chat. The voice chat takes place over either an Internet connection or a Bluetooth connection. This section shows you how to implement voice chatting over a Bluetooth communication channel.

TRY IT OUT   Bluetooth Voice Chatting

codefile BluetoothChat.zip available for download at Wrox.com

1.   Using Xcode, create a new View-based Application project and name it BluetoothChat.

2. Add the `GameKit` and `AVFoundation` frameworks to the `Frameworks` folder of the project (see Figure 17-9).

3. Drag and drop a WAV file onto the `Resources` folder in Xcode (see Figure 17-10).

FIGURE 17-9　　　　　　　　　　**FIGURE 17-10**

4. Double-click the `BluetoothViewController.xib` file to edit it in Interface Builder.

5. Populate the View window with three Round Rect Button views (see Figure 17-11). Name them **MUTE**, **Disconnect**, and **Connect**.

6. Add the following bold statements to the `BluetoothChatViewController.h` file:

```
#import <UIKit/UIKit.h>

#import <GameKit/GameKit.h>
#import <AVFoundation/AVFoundation.h>

@interface BluetoothChatViewController : UIViewController
    <GKVoiceChatClient,
    GKPeerPickerControllerDelegate,
    GKSessionDelegate> {

    GKSession *currentSession;
    IBOutlet UIButton *connect;
    IBOutlet UIButton *disconnect;
    GKPeerPickerController *picker;
}

@property (nonatomic, retain) GKSession *currentSession;
@property (nonatomic, retain) UIButton *connect;
@property (nonatomic, retain) UIButton *disconnect;

-(IBAction)btnMute:(id) sender;
-(IBAction)btnUnmute:(id) sender;
-(IBAction)btnConnect:(id) sender;
-(IBAction)btnDisconnect:(id) sender;

@end
```

7. In the `BluetoothViewController.xib` window, perform the following connections:

> Control-click the File's Owner item and drag and drop it over the Connect button. Select `connect`.

> Control-click the File's Owner item and drag and drop it over the Disconnect button. Select `disconnect`.

> Control-click the Connect button and drag and drop it over the File's Owner item. Select `btnConnect:`.

> Control-click the Disconnect button and drag and drop it over the File's Owner item. Select `btnDisconnect:`.

> Right-click the Mute button and connect the Touch Down event to the File's Owner item. Select `btnMute:`.

> Right-click the Mute button and connect the Touch Up Inside event to the File's Owner item. Select `btnUnmute:`.

FIGURE 17-11

8. To verify that all the connections are made correctly, right-click the File's Owner item and view its connections (see Figure 17-12).

FIGURE 17-12

9. Add the following bold statements to the `BluetoothViewController.m` file:

```
#import "BluetoothChatViewController.h"

@implementation BluetoothChatViewController

@synthesize currentSession;
@synthesize connect;
```

```objc
@synthesize disconnect;

NSString *recorderFilePath;
AVAudioPlayer *audioPlayer;

- (void)viewDidLoad {
    [connect setHidden:NO];
    [disconnect setHidden:YES];
    [super viewDidLoad];
}

//---select a nearby Bluetooth device---
-(IBAction) btnConnect:(id) sender {
    picker = [[GKPeerPickerController alloc] init];
    picker.delegate = self;
    picker.connectionTypesMask = GKPeerPickerConnectionTypeNearby;

    [connect setHidden:YES];
    [disconnect setHidden:NO];
    [picker show];
}

//---disconnect from the other device---
-(IBAction) btnDisconnect:(id) sender {
    [self.currentSession disconnectFromAllPeers];
    [self.currentSession release];
    currentSession = nil;

    [connect setHidden:NO];
    [disconnect setHidden:YES];
}


//---did connect to a peer---
-(void) peerPickerController:(GKPeerPickerController *)pk
            didConnectPeer:(NSString *)peerID
                 toSession:(GKSession *) session {
    self.currentSession = session;
    session.delegate = self;
    [session setDataReceiveHandler:self withContext:nil];
    picker.delegate = nil;

    [picker dismiss];
    [picker autorelease];
}


//---connection was cancelled---
-(void) peerPickerControllerDidCancel:(GKPeerPickerController *)pk {
    picker.delegate = nil;
    [picker autorelease];

    [connect setHidden:NO];
    [disconnect setHidden:YES];
}

//---mute the voice chat---
```

```objc
-(IBAction) btnMute:(id) sender {
    [GKVoiceChatService defaultVoiceChatService].microphoneMuted = YES;
}

//---unmute the voice chat---
-(IBAction) btnUnmute:(id) sender {
    [GKVoiceChatService defaultVoiceChatService].microphoneMuted = NO;
}

//---returns a unique ID that identifies the local user---
-(NSString *) participantID {
    return currentSession.peerID;
}

//---sends voice chat configuration data to the other party---
-(void) voiceChatService:(GKVoiceChatService *) voiceChatService
                sendData:(NSData *) data
          toParticipantID:(NSString *) participantID {

    [currentSession sendData:data toPeers:
    [NSArray arrayWithObject:participantID]
                withDataMode:GKSendDataReliable error:nil];
}

//---session state changed---
-(void) session:(GKSession *)session
           peer:(NSString *)peerID
 didChangeState:(GKPeerConnectionState)state {
    switch (state) {
        case GKPeerStateConnected: {
            //---plays an audio file---
            NSString *soundFilePath = [[NSBundle mainBundle]
                                        pathForResource:@"beep"
                                        ofType:@"wav"];

            NSURL *fileURL = [[NSURL alloc]
                              initFileURLWithPath:soundFilePath];

            AVAudioPlayer *audioPlayer =
            [[AVAudioPlayer alloc] initWithContentsOfURL:fileURL
                                                   error:nil];

            [fileURL release];
            [audioPlayer play];

            NSError *error;
            AVAudioSession *audioSession = [AVAudioSession sharedInstance];

            if (![audioSession
                  setCategory:AVAudioSessionCategoryPlayAndRecord
                  error:&error]) {
                NSLog(@"Error setting category: %@",
                      [error localizedDescription]);
            }

            if (![audioSession setActive:YES error:&error]) {
```

```objc
                    NSLog(@"Error activating audioSession: %@",
                        [error description]);
            }

            [GKVoiceChatService defaultVoiceChatService].client = self;

            //---initiating the voice chat---
            if (![[GKVoiceChatService defaultVoiceChatService]
                startVoiceChatWithParticipantID:peerID error:&error]) {
                NSLog(@"Error starting startVoiceChatWithParticipantID:%@",
                    [error userInfo]);
            }
        } break;

        case GKPeerStateDisconnected: {
            [[GKVoiceChatService defaultVoiceChatService]
             stopVoiceChatWithParticipantID:peerID];

            [self.currentSession release];
            currentSession = nil;

            [connect setHidden:NO];
            [disconnect setHidden:YES];
        } break;
    }
}


//---data received from the other party---
-(void) receiveData:(NSData *)data
         fromPeer:(NSString *)peer
        inSession:(GKSession *)session
          context:(void *)context {

    //---start the voice chat when initiated by the client---
    [[GKVoiceChatService defaultVoiceChatService]
     receivedData:data fromParticipantID:peer];
}

//---session failed with error---
-(void) session:(GKSession *)session
didFailWithError:(NSError *)error {
    NSLog(@"%@",[error description]);
}


- (void)dealloc {
    if (currentSession) [currentSession release];
    [connect release];
    [disconnect release];
    [super dealloc];
}
```

10. To test the application, deploy it onto two devices. (For the iPod touch, you need to connect it to an external microphone, as it does not include one.) Then run the application and press the Connect button to use Bluetooth to connect the two devices. As soon as the two devices are connected, you can start chatting! To temporarily mute the conversation, press and hold the MUTE button. When it is released, the conversation resumes. Have fun!

How It Works

When two Bluetooth devices are connected, you first play the beep sound and start the audio session (via the `session:peer:didChangeState:` method):

```
//---plays an audio file---
NSString *soundFilePath = [[NSBundle mainBundle]
                            pathForResource:@"beep"
                            ofType:@"wav"];

NSURL *fileURL = [[NSURL alloc]
                    initFileURLWithPath:soundFilePath];

AVAudioPlayer *audioPlayer =
[[AVAudioPlayer alloc] initWithContentsOfURL:fileURL
                                        error:nil];

[fileURL release];
[audioPlayer play];

NSError *error;
AVAudioSession *audioSession = [AVAudioSession sharedInstance];

if (![audioSession
      setCategory:AVAudioSessionCategoryPlayAndRecord
      error:&error]) {
    NSLog(@"Error setting category: %@",
        [error localizedDescription]);
}

if (![audioSession setActive:YES error:&error]) {
    NSLog(@"Error activating audioSession: %@",
        [error description]);
}

[GKVoiceChatService defaultVoiceChatService].client = self;
```

 WARNING *If you do not start the audio player, the voice chat might not work.*

You then retrieve a singleton instance of the `GKVoiceChatService` class and call its `startVoiceChatWithParticipantID:error:` method to start the voice chat:

```
//---initiating the voice chat---
if (![[GKVoiceChatService defaultVoiceChatService]
    startVoiceChatWithParticipantID:peerID
                        error:&error]) {
    NSLog(@"Error starting startVoiceChatWithParticipantID:%@",
```

```
                    [error userInfo]);
    }
```

Calling the `startVoiceChatWithParticipantID:error:` method invokes the
`voiceChatService:sendData:toParticipantID:` method (defined in the `GKVoiceChatClient` protocol),
which makes use of the current Bluetooth session to send the configuration data to the other connected
device:

```
//---sends voice chat configuration data to the other party---
-(void) voiceChatService:(GKVoiceChatService *) voiceChatService
            sendData:(NSData *) data
      toParticipantID:(NSString *) participantID {

    [currentSession sendData:data toPeers:
    [NSArray arrayWithObject:participantID]
            withDataMode:GKSendDataReliable error:nil];
}
```

When it has received the configuration data, the other device starts the Voice Chat service by calling
the `receivedData:fromParticipantID:` method (also defined in the `GKVoiceChatClient` protocol):

```
//---data received from the other party---
-(void) receiveData:(NSData *)data
        fromPeer:(NSString *)peer
       inSession:(GKSession *)session
         context:(void *)context {

    //---start the voice chat when initiated by the client---
    [[GKVoiceChatService defaultVoiceChatService]
      receivedData:data fromParticipantID:peer];
}
```

The `GKVoiceChatService` uses the configuration information that was exchanged between the two
devices and creates its own connection to transfer voice data.

You can mute the microphone by setting the `microphoneMuted` property to YES:

```
[GKVoiceChatService defaultVoiceChatService].microphoneMuted = YES;
```

SUMMARY

This chapter has demonstrated how easy it is to connect two iPhones (or iPads and iPod
touches) using Bluetooth. Using the concepts shown in this chapter, you can build networked games
and other interesting applications easily. You also saw how the Game Kit framework provides the
`GKVoiceChatService` class, which makes voice communication between two devices seamless. It is
not necessary to understand how the voices are transported between two devices — all you need
to know is how to call the relevant methods to initialize the chat. However, there is one important
thing you should know: Voice chat works not only over Bluetooth, but over any communication
channel. In fact, if you have two devices connected using TCP/IP, you can stream the voices over
the wire.

EXERCISES

1. What class can you use to locate peer Bluetooth devices?

2. Name the object that is responsible for managing the session between two connected Bluetooth devices.

3. Name the method from the `GKVoiceChatService` class that you need to call to establish a voice chat.

4. Name the two methods defined in the `GKVoiceChatClient` protocol that establish a voice chat channel.

Answers to the Exercises can be found in Appendix E, on Wrox.com.

▶ **WHAT YOU LEARNED IN THIS CHAPTER**

TOPIC	KEY CONCEPTS
Looking for peer Bluetooth devices	Use the `GKPeerPickerController` class.
Communicating between two Bluetooth devices	Use the `GKSession` class.
Establishing a voice chat	Call the `startVoiceChatWithParticipantID:error:` method from the `GKVoiceChatService` class. On the initiator, call the `voiceChatService:sendData:toParticipantID:` method defined in the `GKVoiceChatClient` protocol. On the receiver, call the `receivedData:fromParticipantID:` method defined in the `GKVoiceChatClient` protocol.
Muting the microphone	`[GKVoiceChatService defaultVoiceChatService].microphoneMuted = YES;`

18

Bonjour Programming

WHAT YOU WILL LEARN IN THIS CHAPTER

➤   How to publish a service on the network using the NSNetService class

➤   How to discover services on the network using the
    NSNetServiceBrowser class

➤   How to resolve the IP addresses of services on the network

Bonjour is Apple's implementation of the Zeroconf protocol, which enables the automatic discovery of computers, devices, and services on an IP network. In this chapter, you will learn how to implement Bonjour on the iPhone by using the NSNetService class to publish a service. You will also use the NSNetServiceBrowser class to discover services that have been published.

CREATING THE APPLICATION

In this section, you will create the user interface for the application. You'll use a Table view to display the users that you have discovered on the network. As users are discovered, they will be added to the Table view.

TRY IT OUT   Creating the Application's UI

1.   Using Xcode, create a View-based Application (iPhone) project and name it **Bonjour**.

2.   Double-click the BonjourViewController.xib file to edit it in Interface Builder. Populate the View window with the following views (see Figure 18-1):

➤   Label (set its text to **Discovered Users**)

➤   Table View

➤   Text View

FIGURE 18-1

3.   In the `BonjourViewController.h` file, add the following bold statements:

```
#import <UIKit/UIKit.h>

@interface BonjourViewController : UIViewController
    <UITableViewDelegate,
    UITableViewDataSource> {
    //---outlets---
    IBOutlet UITableView *tbView;
    IBOutlet UITextView *debug;
}

//---expose the outlets as properties---
@property (nonatomic, retain) UITableView *tbView;
@property (nonatomic, retain) UITextView *debug;

@end
```

4.   In the `BonjourViewController.xib` window, perform the following connections:

   ➤   Control-click the File's Owner item and drag and drop it over the Table view. Select `tbView`.

   ➤   Control-click the File's Owner item and drag and drop it over the Text View. Select `debug`.

   ➤   Right-click the Table view and connect the `dataSource` outlet to the File's Owner item.

   ➤   Right-click the Table view and connect the `delegate` outlet to the File's Owner item.

5. To verify that all the connections are made correctly, right-click the File's Owner item and view its connections (see Figure 18-2).

How It Works

Because you'll use the Table view to display the list of users discovered on the network, you need to set the `dataSource` and `delegate` outlets to the File's Owner item. The Text View will be used to show the various things happening in the background. This is very useful for debugging your application and understanding what happens as services are discovered on the network.

FIGURE 18-2

PUBLISHING A SERVICE

With all the views and outlets wired up, you can publish a service using the `NSNetService` class. The following Try It Out shows you how.

TRY IT OUT Publishing a Service on the Network

1. Using the same project created in the previous section, add the following bold statements to the `BonjourAppDelegate.h` file:

```objc
#import <UIKit/UIKit.h>

@class BonjourViewController;

@interface BonjourAppDelegate : NSObject
    <UIApplicationDelegate,
    NSNetServiceDelegate> {

    UIWindow *window;
    BonjourViewController *viewController;

    //---use this to publish a service---
    NSNetService *netService;
}

@property (nonatomic, retain) IBOutlet UIWindow *window;
@property (nonatomic, retain) IBOutlet BonjourViewController
    *viewController;

@end
```

2. In the `BonjourAppDelegate.m` file, add the following statements in bold:

```objc
#import "BonjourAppDelegate.h"
#import "BonjourViewController.h"

@implementation BonjourAppDelegate

@synthesize window;
@synthesize viewController;

- (BOOL)application:(UIApplication *)application
didFinishLaunchingWithOptions:(NSDictionary *)launchOptions {

    // Add the view controller's view to the window and display.
    [window addSubview:viewController.view];
    [window makeKeyAndVisible];

    //---publish the service---
    netService = [[NSNetService alloc] initWithDomain:@""
                                        type:@"_MyService._tcp."
                                        name:@""
                                        port:9876];

    netService.delegate = self;
    [netService publish];

    return YES;
}

-(void)netService:(NSNetService *)aNetService
    didNotPublish:(NSDictionary *)dict {
    NSLog(@"Service did not publish: %@", dict);
}

- (void)applicationWillTerminate:(UIApplication *)application {
    //---stop the service when the application is terminated---
    [netService stop];
}

- (void)applicationDidEnterBackground:(UIApplication *)application {
    //---stop the service when the application is paused---
    [netService stop];
}

- (void)applicationWillEnterForeground:(UIApplication *)application {
    [netService publish];
}

- (void)dealloc {
    [netService release];
    [viewController release];
    [window release];
    [super dealloc];
}
```

How It Works

To publish a service on the network, you use the NSNetService class to advertise your presence on the network:

```
//---use this to publish a service---
NSNetService *netService;
```

Here, you advertise your presence on the network by publishing a network service when your application has finished launching (application:DidFinishLaunchingWithOptions:). You publish a network service first by instantiating it with several parameters to the NSNetService class:

```
//---publish the service---
netService = [[NSNetService alloc] initWithDomain:@""
                                    type:@"_MyService._tcp."
                                    name:@""
                                    port:9876];
```

The first argument specifies the domain for the service. You use @"" to denote the default domain. The second argument indicates the service type and transport layer. In this example, you named the service as MyService and it uses TCP as the protocol. Note that you need to prefix the service name and protocol with an underscore (_) and end the protocol with a period (.). The third argument specifies the name of the service — you have used an empty string in this case. Finally, you specify the port number on which the service is published via the fourth argument.

To publish the service, you use the publish method of the NSNetService class:

```
netService.delegate = self;
[netService publish];
```

You also implemented the netService:didNotPublish: method so that in the event that the service is not published successfully, you write a message to the Debugger Console window (or perhaps display an alert to the user):

```
-(void)netService:(NSNetService *)aNetService
    didNotPublish:(NSDictionary *)dict {
    NSLog(@"Service did not publish: %@", dict);
}
```

When the application exits (applicationWillTerminate:) or goes into background mode (applicationDidEnterBackground:) you stop publishing the service:

```
- (void)applicationWillTerminate:(UIApplication *)application {
    //---stop the service when the application is terminated---
    [netService stop];
}

- (void)applicationDidEnterBackground:(UIApplication *)application {
    //---stop the service when the application is paused---
    [netService stop];
}
```

When the application returns to the foreground (`applicationWillEnterForeground:`), you publish the service again:

```
- (void)applicationWillEnterForeground:(UIApplication *)application {
    [netService publish];
}
```

BROWSING FOR SERVICES

Now that you have seen how to publish a service, this section demonstrates how you can browse for services that have been published on the network. You will use the `NSNetServiceBrowser` class to discover services published on the network.

TRY IT OUT   Browsing for Services on the Network

1. Using the `Bonjour` project from the previous Try it Out, add the following bold statements to the `BonjourViewController.h` file:

```
#import <UIKit/UIKit.h>

@interface BonjourViewController : UIViewController
    <UITableViewDelegate,
    UITableViewDataSource,
    NSNetServiceDelegate,
    NSNetServiceBrowserDelegate> {

    //---outlets---
    IBOutlet UITableView *tbView;
    IBOutlet UITextView *debug;

    //---use for browsing services---
    NSNetServiceBrowser *browser;
    NSMutableArray *services;
}

-(void) resolveIPAddress:(NSNetService *)service;
-(void) browseServices;

//---expose the outlets as properties---
@property (nonatomic, retain) UITableView *tbView;
@property (nonatomic, retain) UITextView *debug;

@property (readwrite, retain) NSNetServiceBrowser *browser;
@property (readwrite, retain) NSMutableArray *services;


@end
```

2. In the `BonjourViewController.m` file, add the following bold statements:

```
#import "BonjourViewController.h"

#import <netinet/in.h>
#import <arpa/inet.h>

@implementation BonjourViewController

@synthesize tbView;
@synthesize debug;
@synthesize browser;
@synthesize services;

//---set the number of rows in the TableView---
- (NSInteger)tableView:(UITableView *)tableView
 numberOfRowsInSection:(NSInteger)section {
    return [services count];
}

//---display the individual rows in the TableView---
- (UITableViewCell *)tableView:(UITableView *)tableView
         cellForRowAtIndexPath:(NSIndexPath *)indexPath {

    static NSString *CellIdentifier = @"Cell";
    UITableViewCell *cell =
        [tableView dequeueReusableCellWithIdentifier:CellIdentifier];

    if (cell == nil) {
        cell = [[[UITableViewCell alloc]
                initWithStyle:UITableViewCellStyleDefault
                reuseIdentifier:CellIdentifier] autorelease];
    }

    //---display the hostname of each service---
    cell.textLabel.text =
        [[services objectAtIndex:indexPath.row] hostName];

    return cell;
}

//---browse for services---
-(void) browseServices {
    services = [NSMutableArray new];
    self.browser = [[NSNetServiceBrowser new] autorelease];
    self.browser.delegate = self;
    [self.browser searchForServicesOfType:@"_MyService._tcp."
                                  inDomain:@""];
}

//---browse for services when the View is loaded---
-(void) viewDidLoad {
    debug.text = @"";
```

```objc
    [self browseServices];
    [super viewDidLoad];
}


//---services found---
-(void)netServiceBrowser:(NSNetServiceBrowser *)aBrowser
         didFindService:(NSNetService *)aService
             moreComing:(BOOL)more {

    [services addObject:aService];
    debug.text = [debug.text stringByAppendingString:
                 @"Found service. Resolving address...\n"];
    [self resolveIPAddress:aService];
}


//---services removed from the network---
-(void)netServiceBrowser:(NSNetServiceBrowser *)aBrowser
       didRemoveService:(NSNetService *)aService
             moreComing:(BOOL)more {

    [services removeObject:aService];
    debug.text = [debug.text stringByAppendingFormat:@"Removed: %@\n",
                     [aService hostName]];

    [self.tbView reloadData];
}


//---resolve the IP address(es) of a service---
-(void)resolveIPAddress:(NSNetService *)service {
    NSNetService *remoteService = service;
    remoteService.delegate = self;
    [remoteService resolveWithTimeout:0];
}


//---managed to resolve---
-(void)netServiceDidResolveAddress:(NSNetService *)service {
    NSData            *address = nil;
    struct sockaddr_in *socketAddress = nil;
    NSString          *ipString = nil;
    int               port;

    //---get the IP address(es) of a service---
    for(int i=0;i < [[service addresses] count]; i++ ) {
        address = [[service addresses] objectAtIndex: i];
        socketAddress = (struct sockaddr_in *) [address bytes];
        ipString = [NSString stringWithFormat: @"%s",
                   inet_ntoa(socketAddress->sin_addr)];

        port = socketAddress->sin_port;
        debug.text = [debug.text stringByAppendingFormat:
                        @"Resolved: %@ -- >%@:%hu\n",
                        [service hostName], ipString, port];
    }
    //---reload the table view---
    [self.tbView reloadData];
```

```
    }

    //---did not manage to resolve---
    -(void)netService:(NSNetService *)service
        didNotResolve:(NSDictionary *)errorDict {
        debug.text = [debug.text stringByAppendingFormat:
                        @"Could not resolve: %@\n", errorDict];
    }

    - (void)dealloc {
        [tbView release];
        [debug release];
        [browser release];
        [services release];
        [super dealloc];
    }
```

3. That's it! Deploy the application onto at least two devices (one on the iPhone 4 Simulator and one on a real device). When the application is running, it will search for all services published on the same network. As services are discovered, their names appear in the Table view. Figure 18-3 shows the Table view displaying the hostname of the devices it has discovered. In this example:

➤ "Wei-Meng-Lees-iMac.local" refers to the iPhone Simulator running the application.

➤ "Wei-Meng-Lees-iPhone.local" refers to my iPhone running the application.

➤ "Wei-Meng-Lees-iPod.local" refers to my iPod touch running the application.

FIGURE 18-3

How It Works

There is quite a bit of coding involved here, so let's take a more detailed look.

First, you defined the browseServices method, which uses the NSNetServiceBrowser class to search for the service named "_MyService._tcp." in the default domain:

```
    //---browse for services---
    -(void) browseServices {
        services = [NSMutableArray new];
        self.browser = [[NSNetServiceBrowser new] autorelease];
        self.browser.delegate = self;
        [self.browser searchForServicesOfType:@"_MyService._tcp."
                                     inDomain:@""];
    }
```

As services are discovered, the netServiceBrowser:didFindService:moreComing: method will be called. In this method, you add all the discovered services to the services mutable array:

```
//---services found---
-(void)netServiceBrowser:(NSNetServiceBrowser *)aBrowser
        didFindService:(NSNetService *)aService
            moreComing:(BOOL)more {

    [services addObject:aService];
    debug.text = [debug.text stringByAppendingString:
                    @"Found service. Resolving address...\n"];
    [self resolveIPAddress:aService];
}
```

You also try to resolve the IP address of the discovered service by calling the resolveIPhonedress: method, which you will define.

The resolveIPAddress: method uses the resolveWithTimeout: method of the NSNetService instance (representing the service that was discovered) to obtain its IP addresses:

```
//---resolve the IP address(es) of a service---
-(void)resolveIPAddress:(NSNetService *)service {
    NSNetService *remoteService = service;
    remoteService.delegate = self;
    [remoteService resolveWithTimeout:0];
}
```

If it managed to resolve the IP addresses of the service, the netServiceDidResolveAddress: method is called. If it did not manage to resolve the IP address, the netService:didNotResolve: method is called.

In the netServiceDidResolveAddress: method, you extract all the available IP addresses of the service and display them on the TextView. You then try to reload the Table view using the reloadData method of the UITableView class:

```
//---managed to resolve---
-(void)netServiceDidResolveAddress:(NSNetService *)service {
    NSData             *address = nil;
    struct sockaddr_in *socketAddress = nil;
    NSString           *ipString = nil;
    int                port;

    //---get the IP address(es) of a service---
    for(int i=0;i < [[service addresses] count]; i++ ) {
        address = [[service addresses] objectAtIndex: i];
        socketAddress = (struct sockaddr_in *) [address bytes];
        ipString = [NSString stringWithFormat: @"%s",
                    inet_ntoa(socketAddress->sin_addr)];

        port = socketAddress->sin_port;
        debug.text = [debug.text stringByAppendingFormat:
                        @"Resolved: %@ -- >%@:%hu\n",
```

```
                            [service hostName], ipString, port];
    }
    //---reload the table view---
    [self.tbView reloadData];
}
```

When services are removed from the network, the netServiceBrowser:didRemoveService: method is
called; therefore, in this method you remove the service from the services mutable array:

```
//---services removed from the network---
-(void)netServiceBrowser:(NSNetServiceBrowser *)aBrowser
        didRemoveService:(NSNetService *)aService
              moreComing:(BOOL)more {

    [services removeObject:aService];
    debug.text = [debug.text stringByAppendingFormat:@"Removed: %@\n",
                     [aService hostName]];

    [self.tbView reloadData];
}
```

The rest of the code involves loading the Table view with the hostname of the services that have been
discovered. In particular, you display the host name of each service in the Table view:

```
//---set the number of rows in the TableView---
- (NSInteger)tableView:(UITableView *)tableView
 numberOfRowsInSection:(NSInteger)section {
    return [services count];
}

//---display the individual rows in the TableView---
- (UITableViewCell *)tableView:(UITableView *)tableView
        cellForRowAtIndexPath:(NSIndexPath *)indexPath {

    static NSString *CellIdentifier = @"Cell";
    UITableViewCell *cell =
        [tableView dequeueReusableCellWithIdentifier:CellIdentifier];

    if (cell == nil) {
        cell = [[[UITableViewCell alloc]
                initWithStyle:UITableViewCellStyleDefault
                reuseIdentifier:CellIdentifier] autorelease];
    }

    //---display the hostname of each service---
    cell.textLabel.text =
        [[services objectAtIndex:indexPath.row] hostName];

    return cell;
}
```

DOING MORE WITH TCP/IP

With peers on the network discovered, what can you do next? You can use TCP/IP to connect with your peers on the network and send messages to them. Using TCP/IP for networking is beyond the scope of this book. However, interested users can download a working application from the author's website — http://www.learn2develop.net — that illustrates how to build a chat application using Bonjour.

SUMMARY

This chapter explained how to publish a service on the network using the NSNetService class and how to discover services on the local network using the NSNetServiceBrowser class. Once peers are discovered on the network, you can connect to them and initiate a peer-to-peer communication. A chat application is a good example of a Bonjour application.

EXERCISES

1. What class can you use to publish a service on the network?

2. What class can you use to discover services on the network?

3. Name the method that is called when a service is discovered.

4. Name the method that is called when a service is removed.

Answers to the Exercises can be found in Appendix E, on Wrox.com.

▶ **WHAT YOU LEARNED IN THIS CHAPTER**

TOPIC	KEY CONCEPTS
Publishing a service	Use the NSNetService class.
Discovering services	Use the NSNetServiceBrowser class.
Resolving the IP addresses of a service	Use the resolveWithTimeout: method of an NSNetService object.
Getting the IP addresses of a service	Use the addresses method of an NSNetService object.
Method that is called when a service is discovered	netServiceBrowser:didFindService:moreComing:
Method that is called when a service is removed	netServiceBrowser:didRemoveService:moreComing:

19

Apple Push Notification Service

WHAT YOU WILL LEARN IN THIS CHAPTER

➤ How to use the Apple Push Notification service

➤ Generating a certificate request

➤ Generating a development certificate

➤ How to create an App ID

➤ How to configure an App ID for push notification

➤ Creating a provisioning profile

➤ How to provision a device

➤ How to deploy an iPhone application onto a device

➤ Using a push notification provider application

One of the key limitations of the iPhone is its constraint on running applications in the background, which means that applications requiring a constant state of connectivity (such as social networking applications) will not be able to receive timely updates when the user switches to another application.

 NOTE *Chapter 21 discusses the new multi-tasking feature of iOS 4. While you now have the ability to run your application in the background, the types of applications that are allowed to do so are limited. Also, applications running in the background are not allowed to have any network connectivity.*

To overcome this limitation, Apple released the Apple Push Notification service (APNs). The APNs enable your device to remain connected to Apple's push notification server (PNS). When you want to send a push notification to an application installed on the users' devices, you (the provider) can contact the APNs so that it can deliver a push message to the particular application installed on the intended device.

When your iPhone application uses the Apple Push Notification service, the device remains connected to the APNs server using an open TCP/IP connection. To send notifications to your application running on iPhone devices, you need to write a *provider application* that communicates with that server. Your provider application will send messages to the APNs server, which in turn relays the message to the various devices running your application by pushing the message to these devices through the TCP/IP connection.

While the steps for using the APNs are straightforward, you need to be aware of several details in order to enable messages to be pushed successfully to the devices. In this chapter, you learn how to create an iPhone application using the APNs. The following sections take you through the steps for APNs programming in more detail.

GENERATING A CERTIFICATE REQUEST

The first step to using the APNs is to generate a *certificate request file* so that you can request two development certificates — one for code-signing your application and one to be used by your provider to send notifications to the APNs server. The following Try It Out shows you how to generate the certificate request.

TRY IT OUT Generating a Certificate Request

1. Launch the Keychain Access application (an application in Mac OS X that manages your security credentials) in your Mac OS X (you can do so by typing **Keychain** in Spotlight).

2. Select Keychain Access ⇨ Certificate Assistant ⇨ Request a Certificate From a Certificate Authority (see Figure 19-1).

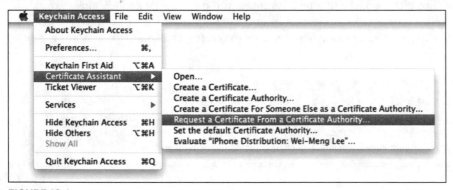

FIGURE 19-1

3. Enter the information required, select the Saved to disk option, and click Continue (see Figure 19-2).

FIGURE 19-2

4. Save the certificate request using the suggested name and click Save (see Figure 19-3). Click Done in the next screen.

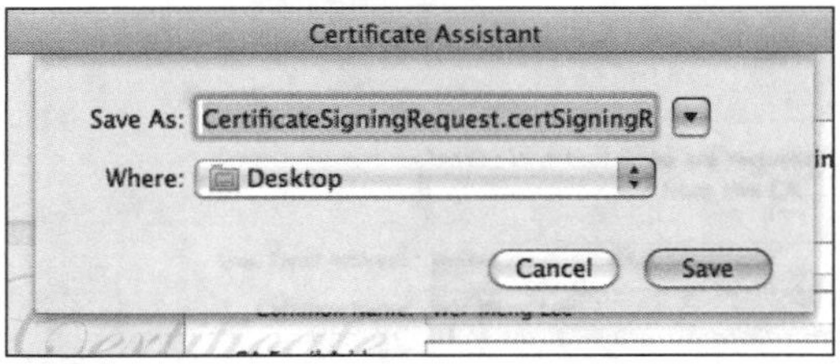

FIGURE 19-3

How It Works

This part is straightforward — use the Keychain Access application to generate a certificate request so that you can send it to Apple later to request certificates.

GENERATING A DEVELOPMENT CERTIFICATE

Once the certificate request is generated, you use it to request a development certificate from Apple. The development certificate is used for code-signing your application so that you can deploy it on a real device.

TRY IT OUT Generating a Development Certificate

1. Sign in to the iPhone Developer Program at `http://developer.apple.com/iphone`. Click the iPhone Provisioning Portal on the right side of the page (see Figure 19-4). The welcome page opens (see Figure 19-5).

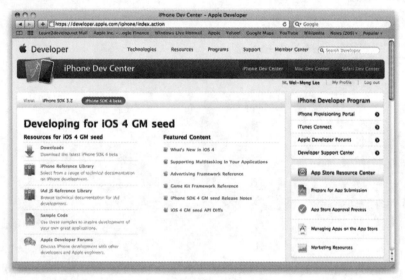

FIGURE 19-4

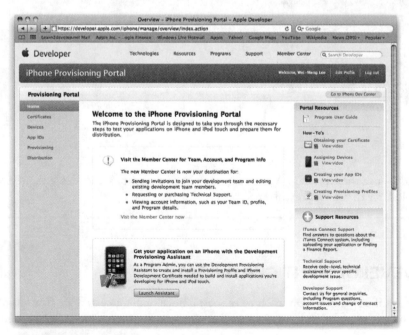

FIGURE 19-5

2. Click the Certificates tab on the left. The page shown in Figure 19-6 opens.

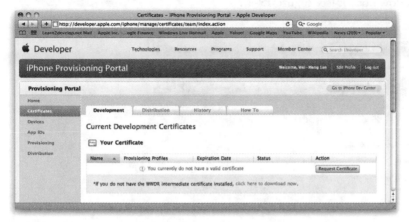

FIGURE 19-6

3. Click the Request Certificate button in the lower-right corner. The page shown in Figure 19-7 opens. Click the Choose File button and select the certificate request file that you created in the previous section, and then click Submit.

FIGURE 19-7

4. Your certificate is now pending approval. Refresh the page. After a few seconds the certificate will be ready and you can download it (see Figure 19-8).

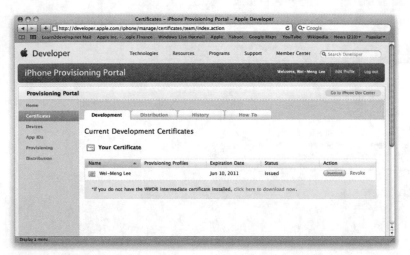

FIGURE 19-8

5. Once the certificate is downloaded, double-click it to install it in the Keychain Access application. Figure 19-9 shows the development certificate installed in the Keychain Access application.

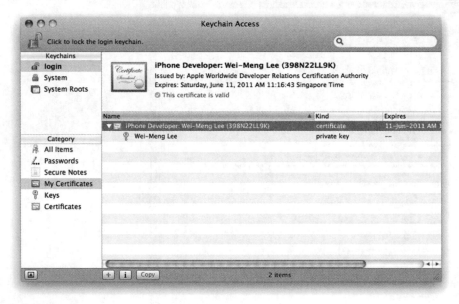

FIGURE 19-9

How It Works

This Try It Out generates the development certificate that you need to code-sign your application so that it can be deployed to a real iPhone for testing. The certificate installed in the Keychain Access application contains the private and public key pair. It is a good idea to back up the certificate at this juncture so that in the event that you need to shift your development work to another computer, you can simply restore the certificate from the backup. Downloading the certificate from the iPhone Development Portal and installing the certificate to another computer will not work because the certificate downloaded from Apple contains only the public key, not the private key.

CREATING AN APPLICATION ID

Each iPhone application that uses the APNs must have a unique application ID that identifies itself. In the following Try It Out, you create an App ID for push notification.

TRY IT OUT Creating an App ID for Your Application

1. In the iPhone Provisioning Portal, click the App IDs tab on the left and then click the New App ID button (see Figure 19-10).

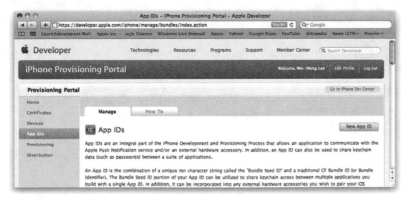

FIGURE 19-10

2. As shown in Figure 19-11, enter **PushAppID** for the Description and select Generate New for the Bundle Seed ID. For the Bundle Identifier, enter **net.learn2develop.MyPushApp**. When you are done, click Submit.

> **NOTE** *App IDs are globally universal, even amongst developers. So in this step, instead of entering* `net.learn2develop.MyPushApp` *for the Bundle Identifier, you should enter your own unique Bundle Identifier. A good recommendation is to use your reverse domain name, such as* `com.yourcompany.MyPushApp`*.*

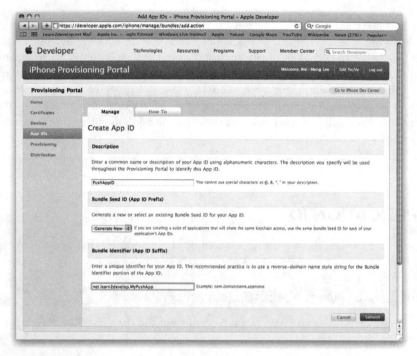

FIGURE 19-11

3. You should now see the App ID that you have created, together with any you may have previously created (see Figure 19-12).

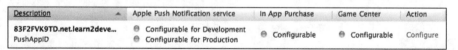

FIGURE 19-12

How It Works

For applications using the APNs, you need to specifically create an App ID to uniquely identify the application. The next section demonstrates how to configure the new App ID for push notifications.

Configuring an App ID for Push Notifications

Once an App ID is created, you need to configure it for push notifications. The following Try It Out shows you how to do this.

TRY IT OUT   Configuring an App ID for Push Notifications

1. To configure an App ID for push notification, click the Configure link displayed to the right of the App ID (see Figure 19-12). The Configure option (see Figure 19-13) becomes available.

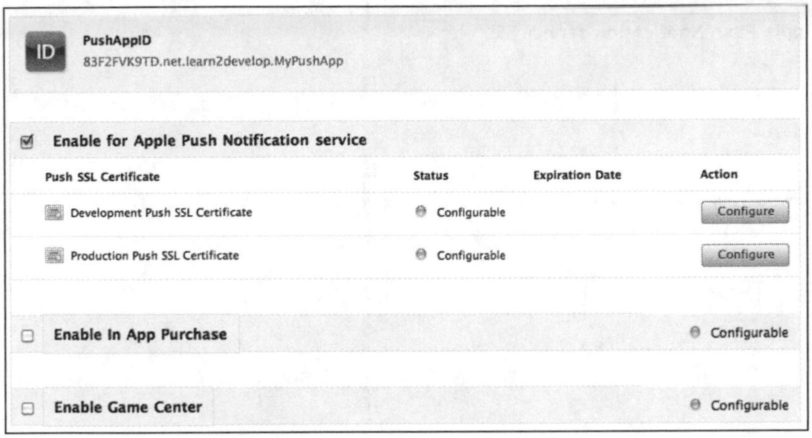

FIGURE 19-13

2. Check the Enable for Apple Push Notification service option and click the Configure button on the right of the Development Push SSL Certificate.

3. The Apple Push Notification service SSL Certificate Assistant screen opens (see Figure 19-14). Click Continue.

4. Click the Choose File button to locate the certificate request file that you saved earlier, and then click Generate.

FIGURE 19-14

5. Your SSL certificate will now be generated. Click Continue (see Figure 19-15).

FIGURE 19-15

6. Click the Download Now button to download the SSL certificate, and then click Done (see Figure 19-16).

FIGURE 19-16

7. The SSL certificate you download is named `aps.developer.identity.cer`. Double-click it to install it in the Keychain Access application (see Figure 19-17). The SSL certificate is used by your provider application in order to contact the APNs to send push notifications to your applications.

FIGURE 19-17

How It Works

When the App ID is configured for push notifications, you need to upload the certificate signing request that you generated earlier to Apple so that you can obtain an SSL certificate for your provider application. Once the SSL certificate is downloaded, you install it into your Keychain Access application.

Creating a Provisioning Profile

Next, you create a provisioning profile so that your application can be installed onto a real iPhone device.

TRY IT OUT Creating a Provisioning Profile

1. In the iPhone Provisioning Portal, select the Provisioning tab on the left and click the New Profile button (see Figure 19-18).

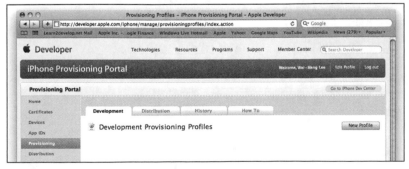

FIGURE 19-18

2. Enter **PushAppProfile** as the profile name, and select PushAppID as the App ID (see Figure 19-19). Finally, check all the devices that you want to provision (you can register these devices with the iPhone Provisioning Portal through the Devices tab). When you are done, click Submit.

 NOTE *Appendix A describes how to register your devices through the iPhone Provisioning Portal.*

3. The provisioning profile is now pending approval. After a few seconds, it appears (just refresh the browser if it is not ready). Click the Download button to download the provisioning profile (see Figure 19-20).The downloaded provisioning profile is named `PushAppProfile.mobileprovision`.

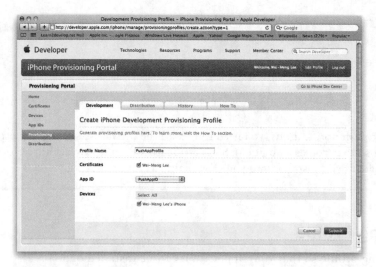

FIGURE 19-19

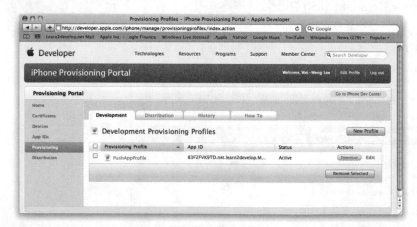

FIGURE 19-20

How It Works

The provisioning profile associates one or more development certificates with one or more devices and an App ID so that you can install your signed iPhone application on a real iPhone.

Provisioning a Device

With the provision profile created, you will now install it onto a real device. Once a device is provisioned, your signed iPhone application will be able to run on your iPhone.

TRY IT OUT   Provisioning a Device

1. Connect your iPhone to your Mac.

2. Drag and drop the downloaded `MyDevicesProfile.mobileprovision` file onto the Xcode icon on the Dock.

3. Launch the Organizer application from within Xcode and select the device currently connected to your Mac. You should see the `MyDevicesProfile` installed on the device.

How It Works

Any devices on which you want to test your application must be provisioned. If a device is not provisioned, you will not be able to install your application on it.

CREATING THE IPHONE APPLICATION

Finally, you can write your iPhone application to receive push notifications. The following Try It Out shows how you can programmatically receive notifications received from the APNs server.

TRY IT OUT   Creating an iPhone Application

1. In Xcode, create a new View-based Application project and name it **ApplePushNotification**.

2. Drag and drop a WAV file (shown as `beep.wav` in this example) onto the Resources folder in Xcode (see Figure 19-21).

3. Expand the Targets item in Xcode and double-click the `ApplePushNotification` item. In the info window, click the Properties tab (see Figure 19-22).

4. In the Identifier textbox, type **net.learn2develop.MyPushApp** (which is the Bundle Identifier you set in Figure 19-11; change this to match the Bundle Identifier you set earlier).

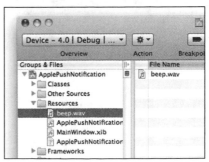

FIGURE 19-21

FIGURE 19-22

5. Click the Build tab and locate the Code Signing Identity setting. In the Any iPhone OS Device item (located under the Code Signing Identity setting), select the PushAppProfile as shown in Figure 19-23.

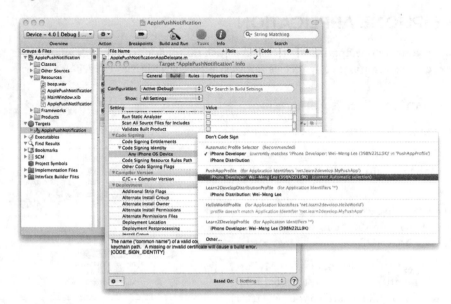

FIGURE 19-23

6. In the `ApplePushNotificationAppDelegate.m` file, type the following bold code:

```objc
#import "ApplePushNotificationAppDelegate.h"
#import "ApplePushNotificationViewController.h"

@implementation ApplePushNotificationAppDelegate

@synthesize window;
@synthesize viewController;

#pragma mark -
#pragma mark Application lifecycle

- (BOOL)application:(UIApplication *)application
didFinishLaunchingWithOptions:(NSDictionary *)launchOptions {

    // Override point for customization after application launch.

    // Add the view controller's view to the window and display.
    [window addSubview:viewController.view];
    [window makeKeyAndVisible];

    NSLog(@"Registering for push notifications...");
    [[UIApplication sharedApplication]
        registerForRemoteNotificationTypes:
        (UIRemoteNotificationTypeAlert |
         UIRemoteNotificationTypeBadge |
         UIRemoteNotificationTypeSound)];

    return YES;
}

- (void)application:(UIApplication *)app
didRegisterForRemoteNotificationsWithDeviceToken:(NSData *)deviceToken {
    NSString *str =
        [NSString stringWithFormat:@"Device Token=%@",deviceToken];
    NSLog(@"%@", str);
}

- (void)application:(UIApplication *)app
didFailToRegisterForRemoteNotificationsWithError:(NSError *)err {
    NSString *str = [NSString stringWithFormat: @"Error: %@", err];
    NSLog(@"%@", str);
}

- (void)application:(UIApplication *)application
didReceiveRemoteNotification:(NSDictionary *)userInfo {
    for (id key in userInfo) {
        NSLog(@"key: %@, value: %@", key, [userInfo objectForKey:key]);
    }
}
```

7. Press Command-R to test the application on a real device. When the application is loaded, you will be asked to turn on Push Notification so that your application can receive notifications. Tap the Settings button to turn on notifications.

8. Press Shift-Command-R in Xcode to display the Debugger Console window. Carefully observe the device token that is printed. The device token is of the format: xxxxxxxx xxxxxxxx xxxxxxxx xxxxxxx xxxxxxxx xxxxxxxx xxxxxxxx xxxxxxxx. Record this device token (you might want to cut and paste it into a text file). You will need it later so your provider application can uniquely identify the devices that will receive push notifications.

How It Works

To receive push notifications, you first need to configure your application with the App ID that you created earlier. You then configure your application so it is signed with the correct provisioning profile associated with your development certificate.

To register your application for push notification, you use the `registerForRemoteNotificationTypes:` method of the `UIApplication` class:

```
[[UIApplication sharedApplication]
    registerForRemoteNotificationTypes:
    (UIRemoteNotificationTypeAlert |
    UIRemoteNotificationTypeBadge |
    UIRemoteNotificationTypeSound)];
```

This registers your application for the three types of notifications — alert, badge, and sound.

If the registration is successful, the `application:didRegisterForRemoteNotificationsWithDeviceToken:` event will be called:

```
- (void)application:(UIApplication *)app
didRegisterForRemoteNotificationsWithDeviceToken:(NSData *)deviceToken {
    NSString *str =
        [NSString stringWithFormat:@"Device Token=%@",deviceToken];
    NSLog(@"%@", str);
}
```

At this juncture, you print out the device token. In a real application, you should programmatically send the device token back to the provider application so that it can maintain a list of devices that need to be sent the notifications. In fact, Apple recommends that every time your application starts up, you send the device token to the provider application to inform the provider that the application is still in use.

If the registration fails, the `application:didFailToRegisterForRemoteNotificationsWithError:` event is called:

```
- (void)application:(UIApplication *)app
didFailToRegisterForRemoteNotificationsWithError:(NSError *)err {
    NSString *str = [NSString stringWithFormat: @"Error: %@", err];
    NSLog(@"%@", str);
}
```

If the application is running when it receives a push notification, the
`application:didReceiveRemoteNotification:` event is called:

```
- (void)application:(UIApplication *)application
didReceiveRemoteNotification:(NSDictionary *)userInfo {
    for (id key in userInfo) {
        NSLog(@"key: %@, value: %@", key, [userInfo objectForKey:key]);
    }
}
```

Here, you can examine the content of the message received. If the application is not running when it receives a push notification, the user is
prompted with an alert (see Figure 19-24).

Clicking the View button launches the application and fires the
`application:didReceiveRemoteNotification:` event.

FIGURE 19-24

CREATING THE PUSH NOTIFICATION PROVIDER

A *push notification provider* is an application written by the application's developer to send push
notifications to the iPhone application through the APNs.

Here are the basic steps to send push notifications to your applications via the APNs server:

1. Communicate with the APNs server using the SSL Certificate you created earlier.

2. Construct the payload for the message you want to send.

3. Send the push notification containing the payload to the APNs.

The APNs is a stream TCP socket that your provider can communicate with using a SSL secured
communication channel. You send the push notification (containing the payload) as a binary stream.
Once you are connected to the APNs, you can send as many push notifications as you want within
the duration of the connection.

 NOTE *Refrain from opening and closing the connections to the APNs for each
push notification that you want to send. Rapid opening and closing of connections to the APNs will be deemed a denial-of-service (DOS) attack and may prevent your provider from sending push notifications to your applications.*

The format of a push notification message looks like Figure 19-25 (taken from Apple's
documentation).

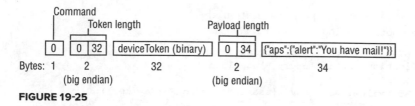

FIGURE 19-25

NOTE *For more details on APNs, refer to the* Apple Push Notification Service Programming Guide. *The full path to this guide is* `http://developer.apple.com/iphone/library/documentation/NetworkingInternet/Conceptual/RemoteNotificationsPG/Introduction/Introduction.html.`

The payload is a JSON-formatted string (maximum 256 bytes) carrying the information you want to send to your application. An example of a payload looks like the following:

```
{
    "aps":
    {
        "alert":"You got a new message!",
        "badge":5,
        "sound":"beep.wav"
    },
    "acme1":"bar",
    "acme2":42
}
```

To save yourself the trouble of developing a push notification provider from scratch, you can use the `PushMeBaby` application (for Mac OS X) written by Stefan Hafeneger (available at `http://stefan.hafeneger.name/download/PushMeBabySource.zip`).

The following Try It Out shows how to modify the `PushMeBaby` application to send a notification to your application.

TRY IT OUT | **Modifying the Provider Application**

1. Download the source of the `PushMeBaby` application and then open it in Xcode.

2. Right-click the Resources folder in Xcode and select Add Existing Files. Select the `aps_developer_identity.cer` file that you downloaded earlier (see Figure 19-26).

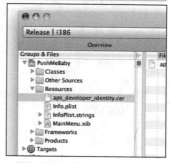

FIGURE 19-26

3. In the `ApplicationDelegate.m` file, modify the code as shown in bold, replacing the xxxxxxxx xxxxxxxx xxxxxxxx xxxxxxx xxxxxxxx xxxxxxxx xxxxxxxx xxxxxxxx with the actual device token you obtained earlier:

```
- (id)init {
    self = [super init];
    if (self != nil) {
        self.deviceToken = @"xxxxxxxx xxxxxxxx xxxxxxxx xxxxxxxx
xxxxxxxx xxxxxxxx xxxxxxxx xxxxxxxx";
        //---the above statement all in a single line--

        self.payload = @"{\"aps\":{\"alert\":\"You got a new
message!\",\"badge\":5,\"sound\":\"beep.wav\"},
\"acme1\":\"bar\",\"acme2\":42}";
        //---the above statement all in a single line--

        self.certificate = [[NSBundle mainBundle]
            pathForResource:@"aps_developer_identity" ofType:@"cer"];
    }
    return self;
}
```

4. Press Command-R to test the application. You will be asked to grant access to the certificate. Click Always Allow (see Figure 19-27).

FIGURE 19-27

5. On the iPhone, ensure that the `ApplePushNotification` application is not running. To send a message to the device, click the Push button. The server essentially sends the following message to the APNs:

```
{
    "aps":
    {
        "alert":"You got a new message!",
        "badge":5,
        "sound":"beep.wav"
    },
    "acme1":"bar",
    "acme2":42
}
```

6.   If the message is pushed correctly, you will see the notification as shown in Figure 19-28.

FIGURE 19-28

7.   Debug the `ApplePushNotification` application by pressing Command-R and send a push message from the `PushMeBaby` application; the Debugger Console window will display the following output:

```
2010-06-30 23:03:38.876 ApplePushNotification[408:307] key: aps, value: {
    alert = "You got a new message!";
    badge = 5;
    sound = "beep.wav";
}
2010-06-30 23:03:38.879 ApplePushNotification[408:307] key: acme1, value: bar
2010-06-30 23:03:38.881 ApplePushNotification[408:307] key: acme2, value: 42
```

How It Works

Basically, the role of the provider is to send notifications to the APNs server for relaying to the devices. Hence, you are sending a message of the following format:

```
{
    "aps":
    {
        "alert":"You got a new message!",
        "badge":5,
        "sound":"beep.wav"
    },
    "acme1":"bar",
    "acme2":42
}
```

The `beep.wav` filename indicates to the client to play the `beep.wav` file when the notification is received.

SUMMARY

In this chapter, you have seen the various steps required to build an iPhone application that utilizes the Apple Push Notification service. Take some time to go through the steps to obtain your development certificates and provisioning profile, for they commonly trip up a developer. Once you get the service working, however, the effort is well worth it!

EXERCISES

1. Name the two certificates that you need to generate in order to use the Apple Push Notification service.

2. Why is it recommended that you back up the development certificate in the Keychain Access application?

3. Name the method used for registering for push notifications.

4. What is the use of the device token?

5. Name the event where you can obtain the notification pushed to your device.

Answers to the Exercises can be found in Appendix E, on Wrox.com.

▶ **WHAT YOU LEARNED IN THIS CHAPTER**

TOPIC	KEY CONCEPTS
Steps to using APNs	Generate a Certificate Request.
	Generate a Development certificate.
	Create an App ID.
	Configure App ID for Push Notification.
	Create a Provisioning Profile.
	Provision a device.
	Create the iPhone application.
	Deploy the application onto a device.
	Create the Push Notification Provider application.
Development certificate	The certificate you download from Apple contains only the public key; the private key is saved in Keychain Access when you generated the certificate request.
	It is recommended that you backup the development certificate.
Provisioning profile	Specifies which devices can be allowed to deploy your applications.
Registering for push notification	Use the `registerForRemoteNotificationTypes:` method of the `UIApplication` class.
Obtaining the device token	Obtainable from the `application:didRegisterForRemoteNotificationsWithDeviceToken:` event
Obtaining the push notification sent to the device	Obtainable from the `application:didReceiveRemoteNotification:` event

20

Displaying Maps

WHAT YOU WILL LEARN IN THIS CHAPTER

➤ How to display Google Maps using the Map Kit framework

➤ How to obtain geographical data using the Core Location framework

➤ How to obtain directional data to rotate a map

➤ How to add annotations to a map

➤ How to perform reverse geocoding to obtain an address

With the advent of mobile devices, users have become accustomed to having access to locale information at their fingertips. In this chapter, you will learn how to use the Map Kit to give users that information quickly and easily.

DISPLAYING MAPS AND MONITORING CHANGES USING THE MAP KIT

The iPhone SDK 4.0 ships with the Map Kit framework, a set of libraries that work with the Google Mobile Maps Service. You can use the Map Kit to display maps within your iPhone application, as well as to display your current location. In fact, you can enable the Map Kit to track your current location simply by setting a single property, and Map Kit will then automatically display your current location as you move.

In the following Try It Out, you will get started with the Map Kit. In particular, you will use **Map Kit** to display your current location on the map.

TRY IT OUT Getting Started with Map Kit

codefile Maps.zip available for download at Wrox.com

1. Using Xcode, create a View-based Application project and name it Maps.

2. Add the `MapKit.framework` to the Frameworks folder of the project (see Figure 20-1).

FIGURE 20-1

3. Double-click the `MapsViewController.xib` file to edit it in Interface Builder.

4. Populate the View window with the following views (see Figure 20-2):

➤ Map View

➤ Round Rect Button (label it as Show My Location; be sure to label this correctly, including the capitalization)

5. In the `MapsViewController.h` file, add the following bold statements:

```
#import <UIKit/UIKit.h>
#import <MapKit/MapKit.h>

@interface MapsViewController : UIViewController {
    IBOutlet UIButton *btnShowLocation;
```

```
    IBOutlet MKMapView *mapView;
}

@property (nonatomic, retain) UIButton *btnShowLocation;
@property (nonatomic, retain) MKMapView *mapView;

-(IBAction) showLocation:(id) sender;

@end
```

FIGURE 20-2

6. In Interface Builder, perform the following actions:

➤ Control-click and drag the File's Owner item and drop it over the Map View. Select `mapView`.

➤ Control-click and drag the File's Owner item and drop it over the Show My Location button. Select `btnShowLocation`.

➤ Control-click and drag the Show My Location button and drop it over the File's Owner item. Select `showLocation:`.

7. In the `MapsViewController.m` file, add the following bold statements:

```
#import "MapsViewController.h"

@implementation MapsViewController

@synthesize btnShowLocation;
```

```
@synthesize mapView;

-(IBAction) showLocation:(id) sender {
    if ([[btnShowLocation titleForState:UIControlStateNormal]
         isEqualToString:@"Show My Location"]) {
        [btnShowLocation setTitle:@"Hide My Location"
                         forState:UIControlStateNormal];
        mapView.showsUserLocation = YES;
    } else {
        [btnShowLocation setTitle:@"Show My Location"
                         forState:UIControlStateNormal];
        mapView.showsUserLocation = NO;
    }
}

- (void)dealloc {
    [mapView release];
    [btnShowLocation release];
    [super dealloc];
}
```

8. Press Command-R to test the application on the iPhone 4 Simulator. You should now be able to see the map. Click the Show My Location button to view your current location (see Figure 20-3). You can also zoom out of the map by pinching it, and zoom in by spreading your two fingers apart on the screen.

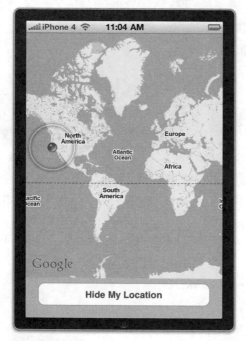

FIGURE 20-3

NOTE *The map may take up to 20 seconds to locate your current location. In addition, the location displayed in the iPhone 4 Simulator is locked on Apple's headquarters in Cupertino, CA, not your actual location.*

How It Works

To show your current location on the map, you simply set the showsUserLocation of the MKMapView object to YES:

```
mapView.showsUserLocation = YES;
```

The map will automatically obtain the device's location using the Core Location framework (discussed in the second part of this chapter). As long as the showsUserLocation property is set to YES, the map will continually update to display the user's location.

Note that this property merely specifies whether the user's location is displayed on the map (represented as a throbbing blue circle); it does not center the map to display the user's location. Hence, if you are viewing the map of another location, your current location indicator may not be visible on the map.

Observe that as you pinch the map to zoom it in or out, it is important to keep track of the zoom level of the map so that when the user restarts the application, you can display the map using the previous zoom level.

In the following Try It Out, you keep track of the map zoom level as the user changes it.

TRY IT OUT   Printing Out the Map's Zoom Level

1. Using the Maps project created in the previous section, edit the MapsViewController.h file by adding the following bold statement:

```
#import <UIKit/UIKit.h>
#import <MapKit/MapKit.h>

@interface MapsViewController : UIViewController
    <MKMapViewDelegate> {
    IBOutlet UIButton *btnShowLocation;
    IBOutlet MKMapView *mapView;
}

@property (nonatomic, retain) UIButton *btnShowLocation;
@property (nonatomic, retain) MKMapView *mapView;

-(IBAction) showLocation:(id) sender;

@end
```

2. In the `MapsViewController.m` file, add the following bold statements:

```
- (void)viewDidLoad {
    //---connect the delegate of the MKMapView object to
    // this view controller programmatically; you can also connect
    // it via Interface Builder---
    mapView.delegate = self;
    mapView.mapType = MKMapTypeHybrid;
    [super viewDidLoad];
}

-(void)mapView:(MKMapView *)mv regionWillChangeAnimated:(BOOL)animated {
    //---print out the region span - aka zoom level---
    MKCoordinateRegion region = mapView.region;
    NSLog(@"%f",region.span.latitudeDelta);
    NSLog(@"%f",region.span.longitudeDelta);
}
```

3. Press Command-R to test the application on the iPhone 4 Simulator. Zoom in and out of the map and observe the values displayed on the Debugger Console window (see Figure 20-4).

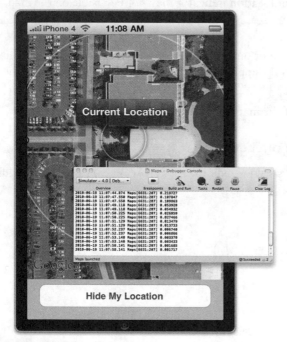

FIGURE 20-4

How It Works

Whenever the zoom level of the map changes, the `mapView:regionWillChangeAnimated:` event is fired. Hence, implement the event handler for this event if you want to know when a map is pinched.

The `mapView:regionWillChangeAnimated:` event is defined in the `MKMapViewDelegate` protocol, so you need to implement this protocol in the View Controller:

```
@interface MapsViewController : UIViewController
    <MKMapViewDelegate> {
```

The region displayed by the map is defined by the `region` property, which is a structure of type `MKCoordinateRegion`:

```
//---print out the region span - aka zoom level---
MKCoordinateRegion region = mapView.region;
```

The `MKCoordinateRegion` structure contains a member called `center` (of type `CLLocationCoordinate2D`) and another member called `span`, of type `MKCoordinateSpan`. The `MKCoordinateSpan` structure in turn contains two members: `latitudeDelta` and `longitudeDelta` (both of type `CLLocationDegrees`, which is a `double`):

```
NSLog([NSString stringWithFormat:@"%f",
    region.span.latitudeDelta]);
NSLog([NSString stringWithFormat:@"%f",
    region.span.longitudeDelta]);
```

Both members define the amount of distance to display for the map:

➤ `latitudeDelta` — One degree of latitude is approximately 111 kilometers (69 miles).

➤ `longitudeDelta` — One degree of longitude spans a distance of approximately 111 kilometers (69 miles) at the equator but shrinks to 0 kilometers at the poles.

Examine the value of these two structures as you zoom in and out of the map — they are a good indicator of the map's zoom level.

GETTING LOCATION DATA

Nowadays, mobile devices are commonly equipped with GPS receivers. Because of the many satellites orbiting the earth, courtesy of the U.S. government, you can use a GPS receiver to find your location easily. However, GPS requires a clear sky to work and hence does not always work indoors or where satellites can't penetrate (such as a tunnel through a mountain).

Another effective way to locate your position is through cell tower triangulation. When a mobile phone is switched on, it is constantly in contact with base stations surrounding it. By knowing the identity of cell towers, it is possible to correlate this information into a physical location through the use of various databases containing the cell towers' identities and their exact geographical locations. Cell tower triangulation has its advantages over GPS because it works indoors, without the need to obtain information from satellites. However, it is not as precise as GPS because its accuracy depends on the area you are in. Cell tower triangulation works best in densely populated areas where the cell towers are closely located.

A third method of locating your position is to rely on Wi-Fi triangulation. Rather than connect to cell towers, the device connects to a Wi-Fi network and checks the service provider against databases to determine the location serviced by the provider. Of the three methods described here, Wi-Fi triangulation is the least accurate.

On the iPhone, Apple provides the Core Location framework to help you determine your physical location. The beauty of this framework is that it makes use of all three approaches, and whichever method it uses is totally transparent to the developer. You simply specify the accuracy you need, and Core Location determines the best way to obtain the results for you.

Sound amazing? It is. The following Try It Out shows you how this is done in code.

TRY IT OUT   Obtaining Location Coordinates

codefile LBS.zip available for download at Wrox.com

1. Using Xcode, create a View-based Application project and name it LBS.

2. Add the `CoreLocation.framework` to the Frameworks folder (see Figure 20-5).

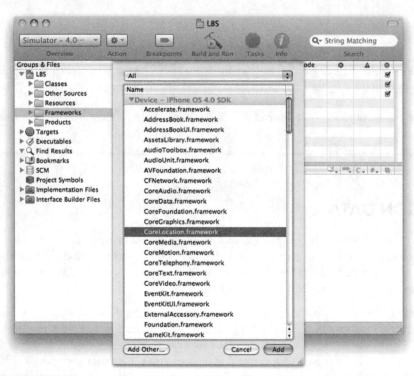

FIGURE 20-5

3. Double-click `LBSViewController.xib` to edit it in Interface Builder. Populate the View window with the following views (see Figure 20-6):

➤ Label (name them **Latitude, Longitude,** and **Accuracy**)

➤ Text Field

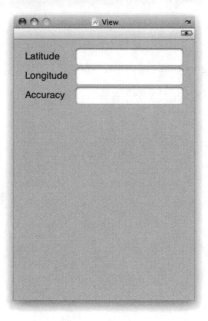

FIGURE 20-6

4. In the `LBSViewController.h` file, add the following statements that appear in bold:

```
#import <UIKit/UIKit.h>
#import <CoreLocation/CoreLocation.h>

@interface LBSViewController : UIViewController
    <CLLocationManagerDelegate> {
    IBOutlet UITextField *accuracyTextField;
    IBOutlet UITextField *latitudeTextField;
    IBOutlet UITextField *longitudeTextField;
    CLLocationManager *lm;
}

@property (retain, nonatomic) CLLocationManager *lm;
@property (retain, nonatomic) UITextField *accuracyTextField;
@property (retain, nonatomic) UITextField *latitudeTextField;
@property (retain, nonatomic) UITextField *longitudeTextField;

@end
```

5. In Interface Builder, perform the following actions:

➤ Control-click and drag the File's Owner item and drop it over the first Text Field view. Select `latitudeTextField`.

➤ Control-click and drag the File's Owner item and drop it over the second Text Field view. Select `longitudeTextField`.

➤ Control-click and drag the File's Owner item and drop it over the third Text Field view. Select `accuracyTextField`.

6. In the `LBSViewController.m` file, add the following statements that appear in bold:

```objc
#import "LBSViewController.h"

@implementation LBSViewController

@synthesize lm;
@synthesize latitudeTextField;
@synthesize longitudeTextField;
@synthesize accuracyTextField;

- (void)viewDidLoad {
    self.lm = [[CLLocationManager alloc] init];
    lm.delegate = self;
    lm.desiredAccuracy = kCLLocationAccuracyBest;
    lm.distanceFilter = kCLDistanceFilterNone;
    [lm startUpdatingLocation];
    [super viewDidLoad];
}

- (void) locationManager:(CLLocationManager *) manager
      didUpdateToLocation:(CLLocation *) newLocation
             fromLocation:(CLLocation *) oldLocation {

    //---display latitude---
    NSString *lat = [[NSString alloc] initWithFormat:@"%f",
                        newLocation.coordinate.latitude];
    latitudeTextField.text = lat;

    //---display longitude---
    NSString *lng = [[NSString alloc] initWithFormat:@"%f",
                        newLocation.coordinate.longitude];
    longitudeTextField.text = lng;

    //---display accuracy---
    NSString *acc = [[NSString alloc] initWithFormat:@"%f",
                        newLocation.horizontalAccuracy];
    accuracyTextField.text = acc;

    [acc release];
    [lat release];
    [lng release];
```

```
}

- (void) locationManager:(CLLocationManager *) manager
        didFailWithError:(NSError *) error {
    NSString *msg = [[NSString alloc]
                       initWithString:@"Error obtaining location"];
    UIAlertView *alert = [[UIAlertView alloc] initWithTitle:@"Error"
                                                    message:msg
                                                   delegate:nil
                                          cancelButtonTitle:@"Done"
                                          otherButtonTitles:nil];

    [alert show];
    [msg release];
    [alert release];
}

- (void)dealloc {
    [lm release];
    [latitudeTextField release];
    [longitudeTextField release];
    [accuracyTextField release];
    [super dealloc];
}
```

7. Press Command-R to test the application on the iPhone 4 Simulator. Observe the latitude, longitude, and accuracy reported (see Figure 20-7). The accuracy indicates the radius of uncertainty for the location, measured in meters.

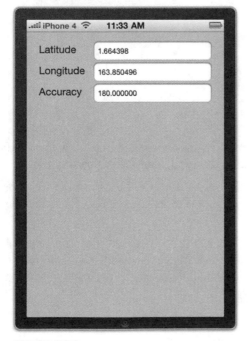

FIGURE 20-7

NOTE *If you test the application on the iPhone 4 Simulator, the application will report the location of your Mac.*

How It Works

First, to use the `CLLocationManager` class, you need to implement the `CLLocationManagerDelegate` protocol in your View Controller:

```
@interface LBSViewController : UIViewController
    <CLLocationManagerDelegate> {
```

When the View is loaded, you create an instance of the `CLLocationManager` class:

```
- (void)viewDidLoad {
    self.lm = [[CLLocationManager alloc] init];
    lm.delegate = self;
    lm.desiredAccuracy = kCLLocationAccuracyBest;
    lm.distanceFilter = kCLDistanceFilterNone;
    [lm startUpdatingLocation];
    [super viewDidLoad];
}
```

You then proceed to specify the desired accuracy using the `desiredAccuracy` property. You can use the following constants to specify the accuracy that you want:

➤ `kCLLocationAccuracyBestForNavigation`

➤ `kCLLocationAccuracyBest`

➤ `kCLLocationAccuracyNearestTenMeters`

➤ `kCLLocationAccuracyHundredMeters`

➤ `kCLLocationAccuracyKilometer`

➤ `kCLLocationAccuracyThreeKilometers`

While you can specify the accuracy that you want, the actual accuracy is not guaranteed. Also, specifying a location with greater accuracy takes a significant amount of time and your device's battery power.

The `distanceFilter` property enables you to specify the distance a device must move laterally before an update is generated. The unit for this property is in meters, relative to its last position. To be notified of all movements, use the `kCLDistanceFilterNone` constant.

Finally, you start the location manager using the `startUpdatingLocation` method. The user can enable/disable location services in the Settings application. If the service is not enabled and you go ahead with the location update, the application will ask the user if he or she would like to enable the location services.

To obtain location information, you need to handle two events:

➤ `locationManager:didUpdateToLocation:fromLocation:`

➤ `locationManager:didFailWithError:`

When a new location value is available, the `locationManager:didUpdateToLocation:fromLocation:` event is fired. If the location manager cannot determine the location, it fires the `locationManager:didFailWithError:` event.

When a location value is obtained, you display its latitude and longitude along with its accuracy using the `CLLocation` object:

```
- (void) locationManager:(CLLocationManager *) manager
      didUpdateToLocation:(CLLocation *) newLocation
             fromLocation:(CLLocation *) oldLocation {

    //---display latitude---
    NSString *lat = [[NSString alloc] initWithFormat:@"%f",
                        newLocation.coordinate.latitude];
    latitudeTextField.text = lat;

    //---display longitude---
    NSString *lng = [[NSString alloc] initWithFormat:@"%f",
                        newLocation.coordinate.longitude];
    longitudeTextField.text = lng;

    //---display accuracy---
    NSString *acc = [[NSString alloc] initWithFormat:@"%f",
                        newLocation.horizontalAccuracy];
    accuracyTextField.text = acc;

    [acc release];
    [lat release];
    [lng release];
}
```

The `horizontalAccuracy` property of the `CLLocation` object specifies the radius of accuracy, in meters.

Displaying Location Using a Map

Obtaining the location value of a position is interesting, but it isn't very useful if you can't visually locate it on a map. Hence, the most ideal situation would be to use the location information to display the location on a map. In the following Try It Out, you will use the Map Kit that you learned how to use in the first part of this chapter to display the map of the location coordinates returned by the Core Location framework. You will also learn how to create the map programmatically, instead of creating it in Interface Builder.

TRY IT OUT   Displaying the Location Using a Map

1. Using the LBS project that you just created, add the `MapKit.framework` to the Frameworks folder (see Figure 20-8).

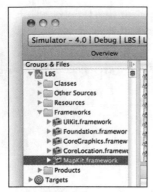

FIGURE 20-8

2. Add the following bold statements to the `LBSViewController.h` file:

```
#import <UIKit/UIKit.h>
#import <CoreLocation/CoreLocation.h>
#import <MapKit/MapKit.h>

@interface LBSViewController : UIViewController
    <CLLocationManagerDelegate,
    MKMapViewDelegate> {
    IBOutlet UITextField *accuracyTextField;
    IBOutlet UITextField *latitudeTextField;
    IBOutlet UITextField *longitudeTextField;
    CLLocationManager *lm;

    MKMapView *mapView;
}

@property (retain, nonatomic) CLLocationManager *lm;
@property (retain, nonatomic) UITextField *accuracyTextField;
@property (retain, nonatomic) UITextField *latitudeTextField;
@property (retain, nonatomic) UITextField *longitudeTextField;

@end
```

3. In the `LBSViewController.m` file, add the following bold statements:

```
#import "LBSViewController.h"

@implementation LBSViewController

@synthesize lm;
@synthesize latitudeTextField;
@synthesize longitudeTextField;
@synthesize accuracyTextField;

- (void)viewDidLoad {
    self.lm = [[CLLocationManager alloc] init];
    lm.delegate = self;
    lm.desiredAccuracy = kCLLocationAccuracyBest;
```

```objc
        lm.distanceFilter = kCLDistanceFilterNone;
        [lm startUpdatingLocation];

        //---display the map in a region---
        mapView = [[MKMapView alloc]
                    initWithFrame:CGRectMake(0, 120, 320, 340)];
        mapView.delegate = self;
        mapView.mapType = MKMapTypeHybrid;
        [self.view addSubview:mapView];

        [super viewDidLoad];
    }

- (void) locationManager:(CLLocationManager *) manager
        didUpdateToLocation:(CLLocation *) newLocation
            fromLocation:(CLLocation *) oldLocation {

        //---display latitude---
        NSString *lat = [[NSString alloc] initWithFormat:@"%f",
                            newLocation.coordinate.latitude];
        latitudeTextField.text = lat;

        //---display longitude---
        NSString *lng = [[NSString alloc] initWithFormat:@"%f",
                            newLocation.coordinate.longitude];
        longitudeTextField.text = lng;

        //---display accuracy---
        NSString *acc = [[NSString alloc] initWithFormat:@"%f",
                            newLocation.horizontalAccuracy];
        accuracyTextField.text = acc;

        [acc release];
        [lat release];
        [lng release];

        //---update the map---
        MKCoordinateSpan span;
        span.latitudeDelta = .001;
        span.longitudeDelta = .001;
        MKCoordinateRegion region;
        region.center = newLocation.coordinate;
        region.span = span;
        [mapView setRegion:region animated:TRUE];
    }

- (void)dealloc {
        [mapView release];
        [lm release];
        [latitudeTextField release];
        [longitudeTextField release];
        [accuracyTextField release];
        [super dealloc];
    }
```

4. Press Command-R to test the application on the iPhone 4 Simulator. Observe the map displaying the location reported by the location manager (see Figure 20-9). The center of the map is the location reported.

FIGURE 20-9

 NOTE *If you test the application on an actual iPhone device, you will see that the map updates itself dynamically when you move about.*

How It Works

To use the Map Kit in your application, you first need to add the `MapKit.framework` to your project.

Then, you implement the `MKMapViewDelegate` protocol in the View Controller to handle the various methods associated with the MapView:

```
@interface LBSViewController : UIViewController
    <CLLocationManagerDelegate,
    MKMapViewDelegate> {
```

When the view has loaded, you create an instance of the `MKMapView` class and set the map type (hybrid — map and satellite) to display:

```
//---display the map in a region---
```

```
mapView = [[MKMapView alloc]
            initWithFrame:CGRectMake(0, 120, 320, 340)];
mapView.delegate = self;
mapView.mapType = MKMapTypeHybrid;
[self.view addSubview:mapView];
```

In this case, you specify the size of the map to display. You set the `delegate` property to `self` so that the View Controller can implement the methods declared in the `MKMapViewDelegate` protocol.

When the location information is updated, you zoom into the location using the `setRegion:` method of the `mapView` object:

```
//---update the map---
MKCoordinateSpan span;
span.latitudeDelta=.001;
span.longitudeDelta=.001;
MKCoordinateRegion region;
region.center = newLocation.coordinate;
region.span = span;
[mapView setRegion:region animated:TRUE];
```

> **NOTE** For more information on the `MKMapView` class, refer to Apple's documentation at `http://developer.apple.com/iphone/library/navigation/Frameworks/CocoaTouch/MapKit/index.html`.

Getting Directional Information

The iPhone comes with a built-in compass. The following Try It Out shows you how to programmatically obtain directional information using this new feature.

TRY IT OUT Incorporating a Compass

You will need a real device (iPhone) to test this application.

1. Using the LBS project, add an image named `Compass.gif` to the `Resources` folder of the project (see Figure 20-10).

2. In Interface Builder, drag and drop an ImageView to the View window and set its `Image` attribute to `Compass.gif` in the Attributes Inspector window as follows (see Figure 20-11).

3. Add a Label view to the View window (see Figure 20-12).

4. Set the background color of the View window to white (see Figure 20-13).

FIGURE 20-10

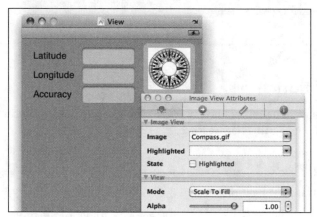

FIGURE 20-11

5. In the `LBSViewController.h` file, add the following bold statements:

```
#import <UIKit/UIKit.h>
#import <CoreLocation/CoreLocation.h>

#import <MapKit/MapKit.h>

@interface LBSViewController : UIViewController
```

```
        <CLLocationManagerDelegate,
         MKMapViewDelegate> {
        IBOutlet UITextField *accuracyTextField;
        IBOutlet UITextField *latitudeTextField;
        IBOutlet UITextField *longitudeTextField;
        CLLocationManager *lm;

        MKMapView *mapView;

        IBOutlet UIImageView *compass;
        IBOutlet UILabel *heading;
}

@property (retain, nonatomic) CLLocationManager *lm;
@property (retain, nonatomic) UITextField *accuracyTextField;
@property (retain, nonatomic) UITextField *latitudeTextField;
@property (retain, nonatomic) UITextField *longitudeTextField;

@property (nonatomic, retain) UIImageView *compass;
@property (nonatomic, retain) UILabel *heading;

@end
```

FIGURE 20-12

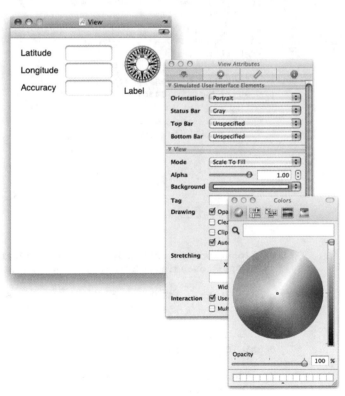

FIGURE 20-13

6. In Interface Builder, perform the following actions:

➤ Control-click and drag the File's Owner item and drop it over the ImageView. Select `compass`.

➤ Control-click and drag the File's Owner item and drop it over the Label view. Select `heading`.

7. In the `LBSViewController.m` file, add the following bold statements:

```objc
#import "LBSViewController.h"

@implementation LBSViewController

@synthesize lm;
@synthesize latitudeTextField;
@synthesize longitudeTextField;
@synthesize accuracyTextField;

@synthesize compass;
@synthesize heading;

- (void)viewDidLoad {
    self.lm = [[CLLocationManager alloc] init];
    lm.delegate = self;
    lm.desiredAccuracy = kCLLocationAccuracyBest;
    lm.distanceFilter = kCLDistanceFilterNone;
    [lm startUpdatingLocation];

    //---get the compass readings---
    [lm startUpdatingHeading];

    //---display the map in a region---
    mapView = [[MKMapView alloc]
                initWithFrame:CGRectMake(0, 120, 320, 340)];
    mapView.delegate = self;
    mapView.mapType = MKMapTypeHybrid;
    [self.view addSubview:mapView];

    [super viewDidLoad];
}

- (void)locationManager:(CLLocationManager *)manager
        didUpdateHeading:(CLHeading *)newHeading {

    heading.text = [NSString stringWithFormat:@"%.2f degrees",
                        newHeading.magneticHeading];

    // -- -- headings is in degrees -- --
    double d = newHeading.magneticHeading;

    //---convert degrees to radians---
    double radians = d / 57.2957795;

    compass.transform = CGAffineTransformMakeRotation(-radians);
```

```
}

- (void)dealloc {
    [compass release];
    [heading release];
    [mapView release];
    [lm release];
    [latitudeTextField release];
    [longitudeTextField release];
    [accuracyTextField release];
    [super dealloc];
}
```

8. Press Command-R to test the application on an actual iPhone. Observe the image as you turn the device (see Figure 20-14).

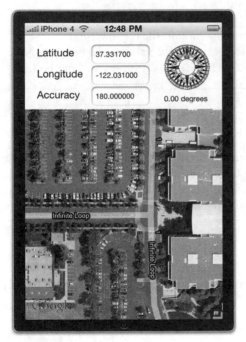

FIGURE 20-14

How It Works

Getting directional information is similar to getting location data; you use the Core Location framework. Instead of calling the startUpdatingLocation method of the CLLocationManager object, you call the startUpdatingHeading method:

```
//---get the compass readings---
[lm startUpdatingHeading];
```

When directional information is available, the `locationManager:didUpdateHeading:` method will continually fire:

```
- (void)locationManager:(CLLocationManager *)manager
        didUpdateHeading:(CLHeading *)newHeading {

    heading.text = [NSString stringWithFormat:@"%.2f degrees",
                    newHeading.magneticHeading];

    // -- -- headings is in degrees -- --
    double d = newHeading.magneticHeading;

    // -- -- convert degrees to radians -- --
    double radians = d / 57.2957795;

    compass.transform = CGAffineTransformMakeRotation(-radians);
}
```

The `magneticHeading` property of the `CLHeading` parameter will contain the readings in degrees, with 0 representing magnetic North. The `ImageView` is then rotated based on the value of the heading. Note that you need to convert the degrees into radians for the `CGAffineTransformMakeRotation()` method.

Rotating the Map

The previous section showed how you can programmatically rotate the image of a compass based on the directional heading information obtained from the Core Location framework. Using this concept, you could also rotate the map whenever the direction of your device changes. This is very useful when you are using the map for navigational purposes. By itself, the Map View does not support map rotation, but the following Try It Out shows how you can improvise.

TRY IT OUT   Rotating the Map

1. Using the LBS project, double-click the `LBSViewController.xib` file to edit it in Interface Builder.

2. Drag and drop a View view from the Library and set its size and location via its Size Inspector window as follows (see also Figure 20-15):

   ➤ X: 0

   ➤ Y: 120

   ➤ W: 320

   ➤ H: 340

3. In the Attributes Inspector window for the View, check the Clip Subviews option (see Figure 20-16).

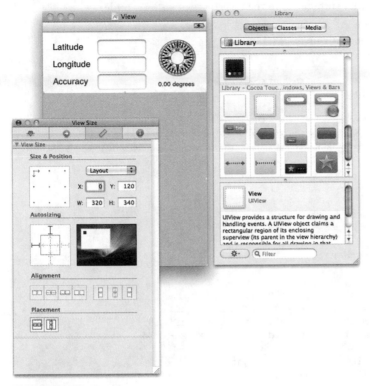

FIGURE 20-15

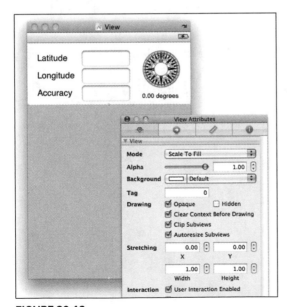

FIGURE 20-16

4. In Xcode, add the following bold statements to the LBSViewController.h file:

```
#import <UIKit/UIKit.h>
#import <CoreLocation/CoreLocation.h>
#import <MapKit/MapKit.h>

@interface LBSViewController : UIViewController
    <CLLocationManagerDelegate,
    MKMapViewDelegate> {
    IBOutlet UITextField *accuracyTextField;
    IBOutlet UITextField *latitudeTextField;
    IBOutlet UITextField *longitudeTextField;
    CLLocationManager *lm;

    MKMapView *mapView;

    IBOutlet UIImageView *compass;
    IBOutlet UILabel *heading;

    IBOutlet UIView *viewForMap;
}

@property (retain, nonatomic) CLLocationManager *lm;
@property (retain, nonatomic) UITextField *accuracyTextField;
@property (retain, nonatomic) UITextField *latitudeTextField;
@property (retain, nonatomic) UITextField *longitudeTextField;

@property (nonatomic, retain) UIImageView *compass;
@property (nonatomic, retain) UILabel *heading;

@property (nonatomic, retain) UIView *viewForMap;

@end
```

5. In Interface Builder, Control-click and drag the File's Owner item and drop it over the newly added View view. Select viewForMap.

6. Add the following bold statements to the LBSViewController.m file:

```
#import "LBSViewController.h"

@implementation LBSViewController

@synthesize lm;
@synthesize latitudeTextField;
@synthesize longitudeTextField;
@synthesize accuracyTextField;

@synthesize compass;
@synthesize heading;

@synthesize viewForMap;

- (void)viewDidLoad {
```

```objc
    self.lm = [[CLLocationManager alloc] init];
    lm.delegate = self;
    lm.desiredAccuracy = kCLLocationAccuracyBest;
    lm.distanceFilter = kCLDistanceFilterNone;
    [lm startUpdatingLocation];

    //---get the compass readings---
    [lm startUpdatingHeading];

    //---display the map in a region---
    mapView = [[MKMapView alloc]
                initWithFrame:CGRectMake(-90, -80, 500,500)];
                // initWithFrame:CGRectMake(0, 120, 320, 340)];

    mapView.delegate = self;
    mapView.mapType = MKMapTypeHybrid;

    // [self.view addSubview:mapView];
    [self.viewForMap addSubview:mapView];

    [super viewDidLoad];
}

- (void)locationManager:(CLLocationManager *)manager
        didUpdateHeading:(CLHeading *)newHeading {

    heading.text = [NSString stringWithFormat:@"%.2f degrees",
                    newHeading.magneticHeading];

    //---headings is in degress---
    double d = newHeading.magneticHeading;

    //---convert degrees to radians---
    double radians = d/57.2957795;

    compass.transform = CGAffineTransformMakeRotation(-radians);

    //---rotate the map---
    mapView.transform = CGAffineTransformMakeRotation(-radians);
}

- (void)dealloc {
    [viewForMap release];
    [compass release];
    [heading release];
    [mapView release];
    [lm release];
    [latitudeTextField release];
    [longitudeTextField release];
    [accuracyTextField release];
    [super dealloc];
}
```

7. Deploy the application to a real iPhone device. Observe that as you rotate the iPhone, the map will rotate as well (see Figure 20-17).

FIGURE 20-17

How It Works

How the map rotates is actually very simple. While you might first assume that the easiest way would be to apply the transformation to the `mapView`, doing so not only rotates the map, it also rotates the entire rectangle (see Figure 20-18).

FIGURE 20-18

The trick is to embed the `mapView` within another View view and rotate it within the View. Hence, you added another View view (`viewForMap`) in the View window and set it to Clip Subviews. Essentially, all the views added to this View will not display beyond its boundary.

Instead of displaying the map in the original size, you now need to set it to a minimum of 466.90 x 466.90 pixels. This is the length of the diagonal of the viewable rectangle of the map. For simplicity, round it up to 500 x 500 pixels.

The `mapView` is now added to `viewForMap`, instead of `self.view`:

```
// [self.view addSubview:mapView];
[self.viewForMap addSubview:mapView];
```

Recall that the initial position of the `mapView` was (0, 120):

```
//---display the map in a region---
mapView = [[MKMapView alloc]
          initWithFrame:CGRectMake(0, 120, 320, 340)];
```

But it must now be changed to (-90, -80):

```
//---display the map in a region---
mapView = [[MKMapView alloc]
               initWithFrame:CGRectMake(-90, -80, 500,500)];
          // initWithFrame:CGRectMake(0, 120, 320, 340)];
```

Figure 20-19 shows how the new coordinate of (-90, -80) was derived. Remember that when you try to add a view to another, the coordinate specified is always with respect to the view you are adding to. In this case, the reference point (0,0) is at `viewForMap`.

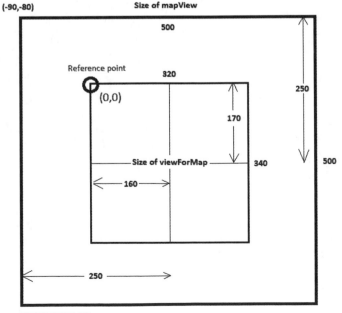

FIGURE 20-19

Finally, to rotate the map, apply the `CGAffineTransformMakeRotation()` method to the `mapView`:

```
//---rotate the map---
mapView.transform = CGAffineTransformMakeRotation(-radians);
```

Displaying Annotations

So far, you have used Core Location to report your current location and heading, and then used Map Kit to display a map representing your location. A visual improvement you can make to the project is to add a pushpin to the map, representing your current location.

In the following Try It Out, you learn how to add annotations to the map in Map Kit. Annotations enable you to display pushpins on the map, denoting specific locations.

TRY IT OUT **Displaying a Pushpin**

1. Continuing with the `LBS` project, add a new Objective-C class file to the `Classes` folder of the project (see Figure 20-20).

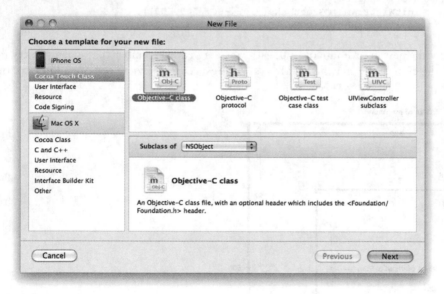

FIGURE 20-20

2. Name it `MyAnnotation.m`. Once it is added, you should see the `MyAnnotation.h` and `MyAnnotation.m` files under the `Classes` folder (see Figure 20-21).

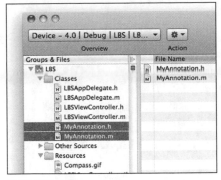

FIGURE 20-21

3. Populate the MyAnnotation.h file as follows:

```objc
#import <Foundation/Foundation.h>
#import <MapKit/MapKit.h>

@interface MyAnnotation : NSObject <MKAnnotation> {
    CLLocationCoordinate2D coordinate;
    NSString *title;
    NSString *subtitle;
}

@property (nonatomic, readonly) CLLocationCoordinate2D coordinate;
@property (nonatomic, retain) NSString *title;
@property (nonatomic, retain) NSString *subtitle;

-(id)initWithCoordinate:(CLLocationCoordinate2D) c
                  title:(NSString *) t
               subtitle:(NSString *) st;
-(void) moveAnnotation: (CLLocationCoordinate2D) newCoordinate;

-(NSString *)subtitle;
-(NSString *)title;

@end
```

4. Populate the MyAnnotation.m file as follows:

```objc
#import "MyAnnotation.h"

@implementation MyAnnotation

@synthesize coordinate;
@synthesize title;
@synthesize subtitle;

-(NSString *)subtitle {
    return subtitle;
```

```
}

-(NSString *)title {
    return title;
}

-(id)initWithCoordinate:(CLLocationCoordinate2D) c
                  title:(NSString *) t
               subtitle:(NSString *) st {
    coordinate = c;
    self.title = t;
    self.subtitle = st;
    return self;
}

-(void) moveAnnotation: (CLLocationCoordinate2D) newCoordinate {
    coordinate = newCoordinate;
}

- (void) dealloc{
    [title release];
    [subtitle release];
    [super dealloc];
}

@end
```

5. In the LBSViewController.h file, add the following bold statements:

```
#import <UIKit/UIKit.h>
#import <CoreLocation/CoreLocation.h>
#import <MapKit/MapKit.h>

#import "MyAnnotation.h"

@interface LBSViewController : UIViewController
    <CLLocationManagerDelegate,
    MKMapViewDelegate> {
    IBOutlet UITextField *accuracyTextField;
    IBOutlet UITextField *latitudeTextField;
    IBOutlet UITextField *longitudeTextField;
    CLLocationManager *lm;

    MKMapView *mapView;

    IBOutlet UIImageView *compass;
    IBOutlet UILabel *heading;

    IBOutlet UIView *viewForMap;

    MyAnnotation *annotation;
}

@property (retain, nonatomic) CLLocationManager *lm;
@property (retain, nonatomic) UITextField *accuracyTextField;
```

```
@property (retain, nonatomic) UITextField *latitudeTextField;
@property (retain, nonatomic) UITextField *longitudeTextField;

@property (nonatomic, retain) UIImageView *compass;
@property (nonatomic, retain) UILabel *heading;

@property (nonatomic, retain) UIView *viewForMap;

@end
```

6. In the `LBSViewController.m` file, add the following bold statements:

```
- (void) locationManager:(CLLocationManager *) manager
       didUpdateToLocation:(CLLocation *) newLocation
              fromLocation:(CLLocation *) oldLocation {

    //---display latitude---
    NSString *lat = [[NSString alloc] initWithFormat:@"%f",
                         newLocation.coordinate.latitude];
    latitudeTextField.text = lat;

    //---display longitude---
    NSString *lng = [[NSString alloc] initWithFormat:@"%f",
                         newLocation.coordinate.longitude];
    longitudeTextField.text = lng;

    //---display accuracy---
    NSString *acc = [[NSString alloc] initWithFormat:@"%f",
                         newLocation.horizontalAccuracy];
    accuracyTextField.text = acc;

    [acc release];
    [lat release];
    [lng release];

    //---update the map---
    MKCoordinateSpan span;
    span.latitudeDelta=.002;
    span.longitudeDelta=.002;
    MKCoordinateRegion region;
    region.center = newLocation.coordinate;
    region.span = span;
    [mapView setRegion:region animated:TRUE];

    //---display an annotation here---
    if (annotation) {
        [annotation moveAnnotation:newLocation.coordinate];
    }
    else {
        annotation = [[MyAnnotation alloc]
            initWithCoordinate:newLocation.coordinate
                         title:@"You are here"
                      subtitle:[NSString
                          stringWithFormat:@"Lat: %@. Lng: %@",
                          latitudeTextField.text,
```

```
                                longitudeTextField.text]];
            [mapView addAnnotation:annotation];
        }
    }

    - (void)dealloc {
        [annotation release];
        [viewForMap release];
        [compass release];
        [heading release];
        [mapView release];
        [lm release];
        [latitudeTextField release];
        [longitudeTextField release];
        [accuracyTextField release];
        [super dealloc];
    }
```

7. Press Command-R to test the application on the iPhone 4 Simulator. You'll see the pushpin inserted into the current position. When you tap on it, it displays the information in the annotation view as shown in Figure 20-22. Also observe that as you test it on a real device, the pushpin is relocated on the map to represent your current location as you move.

FIGURE 20-22

How It Works

You first created the `MyAnnotation` class, which inherits from the `MKAnnotation` base class. Within the `MyAnnotation` class, you implemented several properties (including `coordinate`, which specifies the center point of the annotation) and methods, in particular:

> ➤   `title` — Returns the title to be displayed on the annotation.

> ➤   `subtitle` — Returns the subtitle to be displayed on the annotation.

> ➤   `moveAnnotation:` — Changes the location of the annotation.

As the location of the device changes, you display an annotation to represent the current location:

```
//---display an annotation here---
if (annotation) {
    [annotation moveAnnotation:newLocation.coordinate];
}
else {
    annotation = [[MyAnnotation alloc]
        initWithCoordinate:newLocation.coordinate
                     title:@"You are here"
                  subtitle:[NSString
                     stringWithFormat:@"Lat: %@. Lng: %@",
                     latitudeTextField.text,
                     longitudeTextField.text]];
    [mapView addAnnotation:annotation];
}
```

Note that if an annotation is already present, you simply move its position by calling the `moveAnnotation:` method.

Reverse Geocoding

While knowing your location coordinates is useful, and displaying your location on the Google Maps is cool, the capability to know your current address is even cooler! The process of finding your address from a pair of latitude and longitude coordinates is known as *reverse geocoding*. The following Try It Out shows how to obtain the address of a location given its latitude and longitude. You will do so via the API exposed by the Map Kit.

TRY IT OUT   Obtaining an Address from Latitude and Longitude

1.   Continuing with the LBS project, add the following bold statements to the `LBSViewController.h` file:

```
#import <UIKit/UIKit.h>
#import <CoreLocation/CoreLocation.h>
#import <MapKit/MapKit.h>
#import "MyAnnotation.h"

#import <MapKit/MKReverseGeocoder.h>

@interface LBSViewController : UIViewController
```

```
        <CLLocationManagerDelegate,
        MKMapViewDelegate,
        MKReverseGeocoderDelegate> {
        IBOutlet UITextField *accuracyTextField;
        IBOutlet UITextField *latitudeTextField;
        IBOutlet UITextField *longitudeTextField;
        CLLocationManager *lm;

        MKMapView *mapView;

        IBOutlet UIImageView *compass;
        IBOutlet UILabel *heading;

        IBOutlet UIView *viewForMap;

        MyAnnotation *annotation;

        NSString *location;
        MKReverseGeocoder *geocoder;
}

@property (retain, nonatomic) CLLocationManager *lm;
@property (retain, nonatomic) UITextField *accuracyTextField;
@property (retain, nonatomic) UITextField *latitudeTextField;
@property (retain, nonatomic) UITextField *longitudeTextField;

@property (nonatomic, retain) UIImageView *compass;
@property (nonatomic, retain) UILabel *heading;

@property (nonatomic, retain) UIView *viewForMap;

@end
```

2. In the LBSViewController.m file, add the following bold statements:

```
- (void) locationManager:(CLLocationManager *) manager
      didUpdateToLocation:(CLLocation *) newLocation
            fromLocation:(CLLocation *) oldLocation {

    //---perform reverse geocoding---
    if (!geocoder) {
        geocoder=[[MKReverseGeocoder alloc]
                initWithCoordinate:newLocation.coordinate];
        geocoder.delegate = self;
        [geocoder start];
    }

    //---display latitude---
    NSString *lat = [[NSString alloc] initWithFormat:@"%f",
                        newLocation.coordinate.latitude];
    latitudeTextField.text = lat;

    //---display longitude---
    NSString *lng = [[NSString alloc] initWithFormat:@"%f",
                        newLocation.coordinate.longitude];
```

```
    longitudeTextField.text = lng;

    //---display accuracy---
    NSString *acc = [[NSString alloc] initWithFormat:@"%f",
                        newLocation.horizontalAccuracy];
    accuracyTextField.text = acc;

    [acc release];
    [lat release];
    [lng release];

    //---update the map---
    MKCoordinateSpan span;
    span.latitudeDelta=.002;
    span.longitudeDelta=.002;
    MKCoordinateRegion region;
    region.center = newLocation.coordinate;
    region.span = span;
    [mapView setRegion:region animated:TRUE];

    //---display an annotation here---
    if (annotation) {
        [annotation moveAnnotation:newLocation.coordinate];
    }
    else {
        annotation = [[MyAnnotation alloc]
            initWithCoordinate:newLocation.coordinate
                    title:@"You are here"
                subtitle:[NSString
                    stringWithFormat:@"Lat: %@. Lng: %@",
                    latitudeTextField.text,
                    longitudeTextField.text]];
        [mapView addAnnotation:annotation];
    }
}

- (void)reverseGeocoder:(MKReverseGeocoder *)geo
        didFailWithError:(NSError *)error{
    [geocoder release];
    geocoder = nil;
}

- (void)reverseGeocoder:(MKReverseGeocoder *)geo
        didFindPlacemark:(MKPlacemark *)placemark {
    location = [NSString stringWithFormat:@"%@, %@",
                    placemark.locality, placemark.country];
    annotation.subtitle = location;
    [geocoder release];
    geocoder = nil;
}
```

3. Press Command-R to test the application on the iPhone 4 Simulator. Notice that the Annotation view now displays the address of the location (see Figure 20-23).

FIGURE 20-23

How It Works

To perform reverse geocoding, use the MKReverseGeocoder class available in the Map Kit framework:

```
MKReverseGeocoder *geocoder;
```

When a location is obtained (via the locationManager:didUpdateToLocation:fromLocation: event), you instantiate the MKReverseGeocoder class by setting it to a location coordinate:

```
//---perform reverse geocoding---
if (!geocoder) {
    geocoder=[[MKReverseGeocoder alloc]
                initWithCoordinate:newLocation.coordinate];
    geocoder.delegate = self;
    [geocoder start];
}
```

The MKReverseGeocoder class works asynchronously, and will fire the reverseGeocoder:didFindPlacemark: event when an address has been found. Hence, you need to implement the MKReverseGeocoderDelegate protocol in the View Controller:

```
@interface LBSViewController : UIViewController
    <CLLocationManagerDelegate,
    MKMapViewDelegate,
    MKReverseGeocoderDelegate> {
```

When the address is found, you display the address as the subtitle of the annotation:

```
- (void)reverseGeocoder:(MKReverseGeocoder *)geo
        didFindPlacemark:(MKPlacemark *)placemark {
    location = [NSString stringWithFormat:@"%@, %@",
                placemark.locality, placemark.country];
    annotation.subtitle = location;
    [geocoder release];
    geocoder = nil;
}
```

If the address cannot be found, the reverseGeocoder:didFailWithError: event will be fired:

```
- (void)reverseGeocoder:(MKReverseGeocoder *)geo
        didFailWithError:(NSError *)error{
```

```
    [geocoder release];
    geocoder = nil;
}
```

Displaying a Disclosure Button

When displaying an annotation on the map, it is customary to provide users with the option to select the annotation so that more details about the location can be shown. For example, the user may want to know the detailed address of the location, or you can provide routing information for the selected location. In Map Kit, you can add this option through a disclosure button. The following Try It Out shows how to display the disclosure button in an annotation.

TRY IT OUT Displaying a Disclosure Button

1. Continuing with the LBS project, add the following methods to the LBSViewController.m file:

```
- (MKAnnotationView *)mapView:(MKMapView *)aMapView
            viewForAnnotation:(id)ann {

    NSString *identifier = @"myPin";
    MKPinAnnotationView *pin = (MKPinAnnotationView *)
        [aMapView dequeueReusableAnnotationViewWithIdentifier:identifier];
    if (pin == nil) {
        pin = [[[MKPinAnnotationView alloc] initWithAnnotation:ann
                                            reuseIdentifier:identifier]
                                            autorelease];
    } else {
        pin.annotation = ann;
    }

    //---display a disclosure button on the right---
    UIButton *myDetailButton =
        [UIButton buttonWithType:UIButtonTypeDetailDisclosure];
    myDetailButton.frame = CGRectMake(0, 0, 23, 23);
    myDetailButton.contentVerticalAlignment =
        UIControlContentVerticalAlignmentCenter;
    myDetailButton.contentHorizontalAlignment =
        UIControlContentHorizontalAlignmentCenter;

    [myDetailButton addTarget:self
                        action:@selector(checkButtonTapped:)
            forControlEvents:UIControlEventTouchUpInside];

    pin.rightCalloutAccessoryView = myDetailButton;
    pin.enabled = YES;
    pin.animatesDrop=TRUE;
    pin.canShowCallout=YES;

    return pin;
```

```
    }

    -(void) checkButtonTapped:(id) sender {
        //---know which button was clicked;
        // useful for multiple pins on the map---
        // UIControl *btnClicked = sender;
        UIAlertView *alert =
            [[UIAlertView alloc] initWithTitle:@"Your Current Location"
                                        message:location
                                        delegate:self
                               cancelButtonTitle:@"OK"
                               otherButtonTitles:nil];
        [alert show];
        [alert release];
    }
```

2. Press Command-R to test the application on the iPhone 4 Simulator. The Annotation view now displays a disclosure button to the right of it (see Figure 20-24). Clicking the button displays an Alert view.

FIGURE 20-24

How It Works

What you did was override the `mapView:viewForAnnotation:` method (defined in the `MKMapViewDelegate` protocol), which is fired every time you add an annotation to the map.

Notice the following block of code:

```
NSString *identifier = @"myPin";
MKPinAnnotationView *pin = (MKPinAnnotationView *)
    [aMapView dequeueReusableAnnotationViewWithIdentifier:identifier];
if (pin == nil) {
    pin = [[[MKPinAnnotationView alloc] initWithAnnotation:ann
                                          reuseIdentifier:identifier]
                                          autorelease];
} else {
    pin.annotation = ann;
}
```

It tries to reuse any annotation objects that are currently not visible on the screen. Imagine you have 10,000 annotations on the map; maintaining MKPinAnnotationView objects in memory is not a feasible option (too much memory is used). Hence, this code tries to reuse MKPinAnnotationView objects that are currently not visible on the screen.

The following code block displays a disclosure button next to the annotation:

```
//---display a disclosure button on the right---
UIButton *myDetailButton =
    [UIButton buttonWithType:UIButtonTypeDetailDisclosure];
myDetailButton.frame = CGRectMake(0, 0, 23, 23);
myDetailButton.contentVerticalAlignment =
    UIControlContentVerticalAlignmentCenter;
myDetailButton.contentHorizontalAlignment =
    UIControlContentHorizontalAlignmentCenter;

[myDetailButton addTarget:self
                        action:@selector(checkButtonTapped:)
            forControlEvents:UIControlEventTouchUpInside];

pin.rightCalloutAccessoryView = myDetailButton;
pin.enabled = YES;
pin.animatesDrop=TRUE;
pin.canShowCallout=YES;
```

When the disclosure button is clicked, it fires the checkButtonTapped: method:

```
-(void) checkButtonTapped:(id) sender {
    //---know which button was clicked;
    // useful for multiple pins on the map---
    // UIControl *btnClicked = sender;
    UIAlertView *alert =
        [[UIAlertView alloc] initWithTitle:@"Your Current Location"
                                      message:location
                                      delegate:self
                            cancelButtonTitle:@"OK"
                            otherButtonTitles:nil];
    [alert show];
    [alert release];
}
```

In this case, you simply display an Alert view. You can also display another View window to show more detailed information.

SUMMARY

This chapter explained how to use the Map Kit framework to display the Google Maps in your iPhone application. You also saw how to use the Core Location framework to help you obtain your location information. Combining the Map Kit and the Core Location frameworks enables you to create very compelling location-based services.

EXERCISES

1. Name the property of the `MKMapView` class that enables you to show your current location on the map.

2. Name the protocol that you need to implement in order to monitor changes in your map.

3. Name the method that you need to call to start updating your location.

4. Name the method that you need to call to start updating your heading.

5. Name the class responsible for reverse geocoding.

Answers to the Exercises can be found in Appendix E, on Wrox.com.

▶ **WHAT YOU LEARNED IN THIS CHAPTER**

TOPIC	KEY CONCEPTS
Framework for displaying Google Maps	Map Kit
Framework for obtaining geographical location	Core Location
Class for displaying Google Maps	`MKMapView`
Showing current location on the map	`showsUserLocation`
Monitoring changes in the map	Implement the `MKMapViewDelegate` protocol.
Changing the zoom level of the map	Set the `latitudeDelta` and `longitudeDelta` properties of the map.
Monitoring changes in location	Implement the `CLLocationManagerDelegate` protocol.
Getting location updates	Call the `startUpdatingLocation` method.
Getting directional updates	Call the `startUpdatingHeading` method.
Rotating the map	Embed the `MapView` in another View and rotate the `MapView`.
Displaying annotations	Create a class that inherits from the `MKAnnotation` base class.

21

Background Applications

WHAT YOU WILL LEARN IN THIS CHAPTER

➤ How background code execution works in your iPhone applications

➤ Monitoring application states

➤ How to detect and opt out of background execution

➤ How to track location information in the background

➤ Creating local notifications

One of the main features of iOS 4 is its support for background applications. Unlike the previous versions of the iPhone OS, iOS 4 does not automatically terminate your application when you press the Home button on your device. Instead, your application is put into a suspended state and all processing is paused. When you tap on the application icon again, the application resumes from its suspended state and continues execution. If your application should continue executing in the background, you need to modify it to inform the OS.

In this chapter, you will examine how background execution works and some of the limitations placed on your applications. In particular, you will learn how to modify the location application covered in Chapter 20 so that it will continue working even after the user has switched it to the background. Last but not least, you will learn about the local notification feature that is new in iOS 4.

UNDERSTANDING BACKGROUND EXECUTION ON THE IPHONE

While iOS 4 supports background code execution, there are several things that you need to understand before you write your application:

➤ In order to support background code execution, all applications must be compiled against the iPhone 4 SDK. In other words, if you have downloaded an application from the App Store that is compiled using an older SDK (prior to 4.0), the application will still terminate when you press the Home button on your iPhone 4 device.

➤ Background code execution is supported only on certain devices. Specifically, only iPod third-generation, iPhone 3GS, and iPhone 4 devices support background code execution. Running iOS 4 on any other devices does not enable background code execution.

➤ Background code execution is limited to three specific types of applications:

  ➤ **Audio** — Playing music in the background

  ➤ **Location** — Getting location data in the background

  ➤ **VOIP** — Making phone calls through an Internet connection

➤ If an application does not meet any of the preceding three criteria, it will be suspended when the Home button is pressed.

➤ When an application switches to the background (regardless of whether it is allowed to execute in the background or not), you should always disconnect all network connections (with the exception of VOIP applications). Applications that have active network connections are automatically terminated by the OS when they enter background mode. For example, if your location-based application is transmitting location data to a remote server, you should disable the transmission when the application is switched to the background. While you can continue receiving location data, transmitting it over a network is prohibited when the application is in the background. In this scenario, you might want to log the location data to a database and resend it to the remote server when the application is in the foreground again.

Programming multi-tasking iPhone applications can be a very complex task. The following sections touch on some of the basics to get you started quickly.

Examining the Different Application States

The iOS 4 includes additional events that you can handle in your application delegate so that you can monitor your application's current state. The following Try It Out shows the various states that an application goes through.

TRY IT OUT Handling States Events

codefile States.zip available for download at Wrox.com

1. Using Xcode, create a View-based Application (iPhone) project and name it States.

2. Add the following bold code to the StatesAppDelegate.m file:

```
#import "StatesAppDelegate.h"
#import "StatesViewController.h"

@implementation StatesAppDelegate

@synthesize window;
```

```objc
@synthesize viewController;

- (BOOL)application:(UIApplication *)application
didFinishLaunchingWithOptions:(NSDictionary *)launchOptions {

    NSLog(@"application:didFinishLaunchingWithOptions:");
    // Override point for customization after application launch.

    // Add the view controller's view to the window and display.
    [window addSubview:viewController.view];
    [window makeKeyAndVisible];

    return YES;
}

- (void)applicationWillResignActive:(UIApplication *)application {

    NSLog(@"applicationWillResignActive:");
    /*
     Sent when the application is about to move from active to inactive
    state. This can occur for certain types of temporary interruptions (such
    as an incoming phone call or SMS message) or when the user quits the
    application and it begins the transition to the background state.

     Use this method to pause ongoing tasks, disable timers, and throttle
    down OpenGL ES frame rates. Games should use this method to pause the
    game.
     */
}

- (void)applicationDidEnterBackground:(UIApplication *)application {

    NSLog(@"applicationDidEnterBackground:");
    /*
     Use this method to release shared resources, save user data,
    invalidate timers, and store enough application state information to
    restore your application to its current state in case it is terminated later.
     If your application supports background execution, called instead of
    applicationWillTerminate: when the user quits.
     */
}

- (void)applicationWillEnterForeground:(UIApplication *)application {

    NSLog(@"applicationWillEnterForeground:");
    /*
     Called as part of transition from the background to the inactive
    state: here you can undo many of the changes made on entering the background.
     */
}

- (void)applicationDidBecomeActive:(UIApplication *)application {

    NSLog(@"applicationDidBecomeActive:");
    /*
```

```
       Restart any tasks that were paused (or not yet started) while the
    application was inactive. If the application was previously in the
    background, optionally refresh the user interface.
      */
}

- (void)applicationWillTerminate:(UIApplication *)application {

    NSLog(@"applicationWillTerminate:");
    /*
    Called when the application is about to terminate.
    See also applicationDidEnterBackground:.
    */
}
```

3. In Xcode, press Command-Shift-R to display the Debugger Console window.

4. Press Command-R to test the application on the iPhone 4 Simulator.

5. Observe the output in the Debugger Console window (see Figure 21-1).

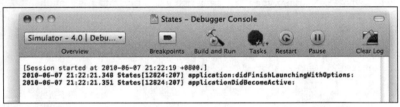

FIGURE 21-1

6. On the iPhone 4 Simulator, press the Home button to send the application to the background. Observe the output in the Debugger Console window again:

```
2010-06-07 21:23:03.928 States[12824:207] applicationWillResignActive:
2010-06-07 21:23:03.963 States[12824:207] applicationDidEnterBackground:
```

7. In the Home screen of the iPhone 4 Simulator, click the application icon to start it again. Observe the output of the Debugger Console window:

```
2010-06-07 21:23:32.090 States[12824:207] applicationWillEnterForeground:
2010-06-07 21:23:32.091 States[12824:207] applicationDidBecomeActive:
```

How It Works

This exercise demonstrates the various states that an application goes through when it is loaded and when it goes into background mode.

In general, you should save your application state in the `applicationDidEnterBackground:` event when the application goes into the background. When an application goes into the background, execution of the application is suspended.

When the application returns to the foreground, you should restore its state in the `applicationDidBecomeActive:` event.

Opting Out of Background Mode

Although the default behavior of all applications compiled using the iPhone 4 SDK is to support background mode, you can override this behavior by adding an entry to your application's `Info.plist` file. The following Try It Out demonstrates how.

TRY IT OUT Disabling Background Mode

1. Using the same project created in the previous section, add a new key to the `States-info.plist` file and label the key `UIApplicationExitsOnSuspend` (see Figure 21-2).

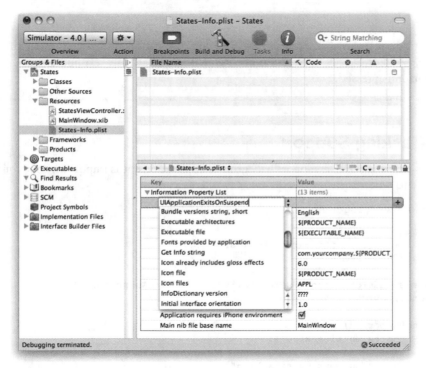

FIGURE 21-2

2. Enable the check box displayed next to the key (note that the key has now changed to the friendly name "Application does not run in background" (see Figure 21-3).

3. Press Command-R to test the application on the iPhone 4 Simulator again. When the application has been loaded onto the Simulator, press the Home button. Observe the output shown on the Debugger Console window (see Figure 21-4).

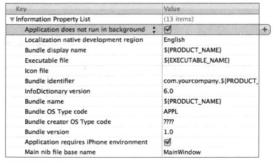

FIGURE 21-3

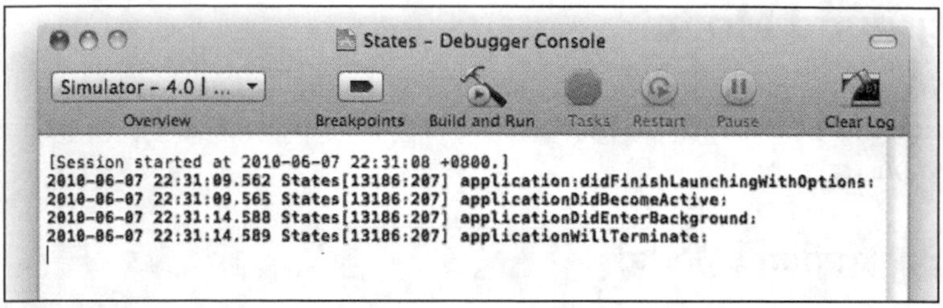

FIGURE 21-4

How It Works

This example shows how to disable the background mode for your application. When you enable the `UIApplicationExitsOnSuspend` key in your application, the iOS will automatically terminate your application when the Home button is pressed.

Detecting Multi-Tasking Support

Because not all devices running the iOS support background applications, it is important that your applications have a way to detect this.

You can do so via the following code snippet:

```
- (void)viewDidLoad {
    UIDevice *device = [UIDevice currentDevice];
    bool backgroundSupported = NO;

    if ([device respondsToSelector:@selector(isMultitaskingSupported)])
        backgroundSupported = device.multitaskingSupported;

    if (backgroundSupported)
        NSLog(@"Supports multitasking");
    else {
        NSLog(@"Does not support multitasking");
    }
    [super viewDidLoad];
}
```

Tracking Locations in the Background

Now that you have seen the basics of how an application behaves when it is suspended and how to disable multi-tasking for an application, this section looks at an example showing how an application can continue to run even when it is in the background.

One of the three types of applications permitted to run in the background is the location-based services application. In Chapter 20, you learned how to use the Core Location framework to obtain geographical data. The limitation with the example shown in that chapter is that as soon as the application goes into the background, your application will no longer be able to receive location updates.

The following Try It Out demonstrates how to enable the application to continue receiving location updates even as it goes into the background.

TRY IT OUT Tracking Locations in the Background

1. Using the LBS project created in Chapter 20, select the LBS-Info.plist file and add a new key to it.

2. Right-click the newly created key and select Show Raw Keys/Values (see Figure 21-5).

FIGURE 21-5

3. Add the key named UIBackgroundModes (see Figure 21-6).

4. Expand the key and set its first value to location (see Figure 21-7).

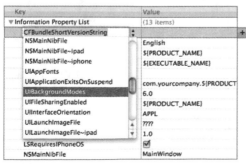

FIGURE 21-6

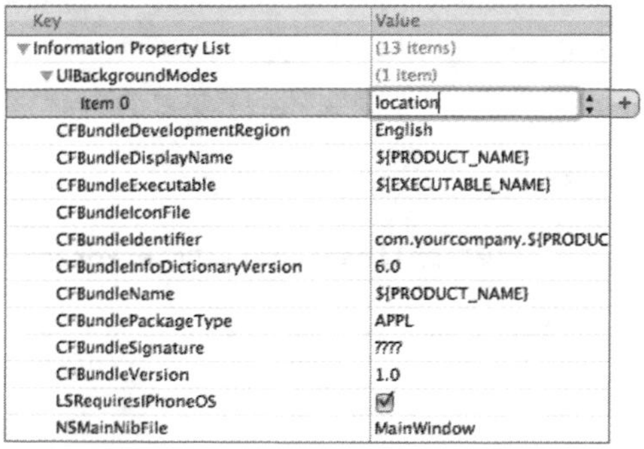

FIGURE 21-7

5. In the `LBSAppDelegate.m` file, add the following bold statements:

```objc
#import "LBSAppDelegate.h"
#import "LBSViewController.h"

@implementation LBSAppDelegate

@synthesize window;
@synthesize viewController;

- (BOOL)application:(UIApplication *)application
didFinishLaunchingWithOptions:(NSDictionary *)launchOptions {

    // Override point for customization after application launch.

    // Add the view controller's view to the window and display.
    [window addSubview:viewController.view];
    [window makeKeyAndVisible];

    return YES;
}

- (void)applicationWillResignActive:(UIApplication *)application {

    NSLog(@"applicationWillResignActive:");
    /*
     Sent when the application is about to move from active to inactive
    state. This can occur for certain types of temporary interruptions (such
    as an incoming phone call or SMS message) or when the user quits the
    application and it begins the transition to the background state.
     Use this method to pause ongoing tasks, disable timers, and throttle
    down OpenGL ES frame rates. Games should use this method to pause the game.
     */
}

- (void)applicationDidEnterBackground:(UIApplication *)application {

    NSLog(@"applicationDidEnterBackground:");
    /*
     Use this method to release shared resources, save user data,
    invalidate timers, and store enough application state information to
    restore your application to its current state in case it is terminated later.
     If your application supports background execution, called instead of
    applicationWillTerminate: when the user quits.
     */
}

- (void)applicationWillEnterForeground:(UIApplication *)application {

    NSLog(@"applicationWillEnterForeground:");
    /*
     Called as part of transition from the background to the inactive
    state: here you can undo many of the changes made on entering the background.
     */
```

```
}

- (void)applicationDidBecomeActive:(UIApplication *)application {

    NSLog(@"applicationDidBecomeActive:");
    /*
     Restart any tasks that were paused (or not yet started) while the
     application was inactive. If the application was previously in the
     background, optionally refresh the user interface.
     */
}

- (void)applicationWillTerminate:(UIApplication *)application {

    NSLog(@"applicationWillTerminate:");
    /*
     Called when the application is about to terminate.
     See also applicationDidEnterBackground:.
     */
}
```

6. In the `LBSViewController.m` file, add the following bold statements:

```
- (void) locationManager:(CLLocationManager *) manager
       didUpdateToLocation:(CLLocation *) newLocation
            fromLocation:(CLLocation *) oldLocation {

    //...
    //...
    //---display accuracy---
    NSString *acc = [[NSString alloc] initWithFormat:@"%f",
                           newLocation.horizontalAccuracy];
    accuracyTextField.text = acc;

    //---print out the lat and long---
    NSLog(@"%@|%@",latitudeTextField.text, longitudeTextField.text);

    [acc release];
    [lat release];
    [lng release];

    //---update the map---
    MKCoordinateSpan span;
    //...
    //...
}
```

7. Press Command-R to test the application on a real device. When the application has finished loading on the device, press the Home button to send the application to the background. Observe the output shown in the Debugger Console window (press Command-Shift-R in Xcode). You may need to move your device so that it can get new location updates:

```
2010-07-07 23:03:54.176 LBS[2408:307] applicationDidBecomeActive:
2010-07-07 23:03:54.865 LBS[2408:307] 1.125160|100.850620
```

```
2010-07-07 23:03:56.719 LBS[2408:307] applicationWillResignActive:
2010-07-07 23:03:56.849 LBS[2408:307] applicationDidEnterBackground:
2010-07-07 23:04:13.544 LBS[2408:307] 1.125195|100.850548
2010-07-07 23:05:30.114 LBS[2408:307] 1.125136|100.850717
2010-07-07 23:08:57.057 LBS[2408:307] 1.125250|100.850394
2010-07-07 23:09:11.354 LBS[2408:307] 1.125181|100.850464
2010-07-07 23:10:13.610 LBS[2408:307] 1.125181|100.850464
```

How It Works

In order to enable your application to continue receiving location data even when it goes into the background, you need to set the `UIBackgroundModes` key in the `Info.plist` file to `location`. The `UIBackgroundModes` key is an array, and it can contain one or more of the following values:

➤   `location`

➤   `audio`

➤   `voip`

Note that no change to your code is required in order to enable your application to run in the background — you need only set the `UIBackgroundModes` key. The output shown in the Debugger Console window proves that even though the application has gone into the background, it continues to receive location data:

```
2010-07-07 23:03:56.719 LBS[2408:307] applicationWillResignActive:
2010-07-07 23:03:56.849 LBS[2408:307] applicationDidEnterBackground:
2010-07-07 23:04:13.544 LBS[2408:307] 1.125195|100.850548
2010-07-07 23:05:30.114 LBS[2408:307] 1.125136|100.850717
```

Making Your Location Apps More Energy Efficient

The project that you modified in the previous section enables you to continuously track your location even though the application may be running in the background. While some scenarios require you to track all location changes, many do not. For example, your application may just need to track a point every few hundred meters. In this case, it is important to prevent the application from continuously tracking every single point, as this takes a heavy toll on the battery.

Instead of using the `startUpdatingLocation` method of the `CLLocationManager` class to receive location updates, you can use the new `startMonitoringSignificantLocationChanges` method, like this:

```
- (void)viewDidLoad {
    self.lm = [[CLLocationManager alloc] init];
    lm.delegate = self;
    lm.desiredAccuracy = kCLLocationAccuracyBest;

    // lm.distanceFilter = kCLDistanceFilterNone;
    // [lm startUpdatingLocation];
    [lm startMonitoringSignificantLocationChanges];

    //...
```

```
//...
//...
[super viewDidLoad];
}
```

The startMonitoringSignificantLocationChanges method reports location data only when the device has moved a significant distance. Specifically, it reports location data only when it detects that the device has switched to another cell tower. As such, this method works only with iPhones (and only iPhone 3GS and iPhone 4; the older iPhone 3G does not support this feature). If you use this method to track location, the distanceFilter property is not needed. When a location update is received, it calls the same locationManager:didUpdateToLocation:fromLocation: method to report location data.

Using the startMonitoringSignificantLocationChanges method greatly reduces the power consumption of your device, as it does not use the power-intensive GPS radio. Note also that if you use this feature, there is no need to have the UIBackgroundModes key in the Info.plist file — the OS will automatically wake your application up from suspended mode to receive the location data.

If your application is terminated when a new location update event is received, it will automatically relaunch your application. To determine whether the application is restarted due to a change in location, you can check for the UIApplicationLaunchOptionsLocationKey key in the application's delegate's application:didFinishLaunchingWithOptions: event, like this:

```objc
#import "LBSAppDelegate.h"
#import "LBSViewController.h"

@implementation LBSAppDelegate

@synthesize window;
@synthesize viewController;

- (BOOL)application:(UIApplication *)application
didFinishLaunchingWithOptions:(NSDictionary *)launchOptions {

    //---if application is restarted due to changes in location---
    if ([launchOptions
        objectForKey:UIApplicationLaunchOptionsLocationKey]) {

        UIAlertView *alert = [[UIAlertView alloc]
            initWithTitle:@"LBS app restarted"
                message:@"App restarted due to changes in location."
            delegate:self
        cancelButtonTitle:@"OK"
        otherButtonTitles:nil];

        [alert show];
        [alert release];
    }
    // Override point for customization after application launch.

    // Add the view controller's view to the window and display.
    [window addSubview:viewController.view];
```

```
        [window makeKeyAndVisible];

        return YES;
    }
```

Once the application is restarted, you should create another instance of the CLLocationManager class and start the monitoring again.

To stop monitoring for location changes, use the stopMonitoringSignificantLocationChanges method:

```
    [lm stopMonitoringSignificantLocationChanges];
```

LOCAL NOTIFICATION

In Chapter 19, you learned about the Apple Push Notification service (APNs), which enables an application to receive notifications, even if it is no longer running on the device. Using the APNs, the provider of an application can continuously keep the user updated, by pushing messages directly to the user through Apple's Push server.

In addition to the APNs, the iPhone also supports another notification framework, *local notifications*. While the notifications for APNs are sent by the application provider, the notifications sent by a local notification are scheduled by the application and delivered by the iOS on the same device. For example, suppose you are writing a to-do list application. At a specific time, your application will display notifications to the user, reminding them of some future tasks. This scenario is a perfect example of the use of local notifications. Another good use of a local notification is that of a location application. The user may be running your application in the background, and when it detects that the user is in the vicinity of a certain location, it can display a notification.

The following example illustrates the building blocks that you need to have in place in order to create an application that uses local notifications.

TRY IT OUT Creating Local Notifications

codefile LocalNotification.zip available for download at Wrox.com

1. Using Xcode, create a new View-based Application (iPhone) project and name it LocalNotification.
2. Double-click on the LocalNotificationViewController.xib file to edit it in Interface Builder.
3. Populate the View window with the following views (see Figure 21-8):
   ➤ Label (name it **Enter notification message**)
   ➤ Text Field
   ➤ Two Buttons (name them **Set** and **Cancel all notifications**)
4. In the LocalNotificationViewController.h file, add the following bold statements:

```
#import <UIKit/UIKit.h>

@interface LocalNotificationViewController : UIViewController {
```

```
    IBOutlet UITextField *message;
}

@property (nonatomic, retain) UITextField *message;

-(IBAction) btnSet:(id) sender;
-(IBAction) btnCancelAll:(id) sender;

@end
```

FIGURE 21-8

5. Back in Interface Builder, perform the following actions:

➤ Control-click the File's Owner item and drag and drop it over the Text Field. Select message.

➤ Control-click the Set button and drag and drop it over the File's Owner item. Select btnSet:.

➤ Control-click the Set button and drag and drop it over the File's Owner item. Select btnCancelAll:.

6. In the LocalNotificationViewController.m file, add the following bold statements:

```
#import "LocalNotificationViewController.h"

@implementation LocalNotificationViewController

@synthesize message;

-(IBAction) btnSet:(id) sender {
    UILocalNotification *localNotification =
```

```
        [[UILocalNotification alloc] init];

    //---set the notification to go off in 5 seconds time---
    localNotification.fireDate =
        [[NSDate alloc] initWithTimeIntervalSinceNow:5];

    //---the message to display for the alert---
    localNotification.alertBody = message.text;

    localNotification.applicationIconBadgeNumber = 1;

    //---uses the default sound---
    localNotification.soundName = UILocalNotificationDefaultSoundName;

    //---title for the button to display---
    localNotification.alertAction = @"View Details";

    //---schedule the notification---
    [[UIApplication sharedApplication]
        scheduleLocalNotification:localNotification];

    [localNotification release];
}

-(IBAction) btnCancelAll:(id) sender {
    //---cancel all notifications---
    [[UIApplication sharedApplication] cancelAllLocalNotifications];
}

- (void)dealloc {
    [message release];
    [super dealloc];
}
```

7. In the `LocalNotificationAppDelegate.m` file, add the following bold statements:

```
#import "LocalNotificationAppDelegate.h"
#import "LocalNotificationViewController.h"

@implementation LocalNotificationAppDelegate

@synthesize window;
@synthesize viewController;

- (void)application:(UIApplication *)application
didReceiveLocalNotification:(UILocalNotification *)notification {
    UIAlertView *alert = [[UIAlertView alloc]
        initWithTitle:@"Inside application:didReceiveLocalNotification:"
                message:notification.alertBody
                delegate:self
    cancelButtonTitle:@"OK"
    otherButtonTitles:nil];

    [alert show];
    [alert release];
}

- (BOOL)application:(UIApplication *)application
```

```
didFinishLaunchingWithOptions:(NSDictionary *)launchOptions {
    UILocalNotification *localNotification =
        [launchOptions objectForKey:
            UIApplicationLaunchOptionsLocalNotificationKey];

    if (localNotification) {
        UIAlertView *alert = [[UIAlertView alloc]
          initWithTitle:@"Inside application:didFinishLaunchingWithOptions:"
                message:localNotification.alertBody
               delegate:self
      cancelButtonTitle:@"OK"
      otherButtonTitles:nil];
        [alert show];
        [alert release];
    }

    // Override point for customization after application launch.

    // Add the view controller's view to the window and display.
    [window addSubview:viewController.view];
    [window makeKeyAndVisible];

    return YES;
}
```

8. Press Command-R to test the application on the
    iPhone 4 Simulator.

9. Enter a message **Time's up!** and click the Set button
    to set the local notification to fire in five seconds (see
    Figure 21-9). Exit the application immediately by press-
    ing the Home button. The application will go into the
    background.

10. About five seconds later, the notification will
    appear (see Figure 21-10). If you click the View Details
    button, the application will return to the foreground.
    The Alert view (see Figure 21-11) shows that the
    `application:didReceiveLocalNotification:` event
    in the application delegate was fired.

11. Enter a notification message again and click the Set
    button again. This time, press the Home button to exit
    the application and then double-click the Home button
    and terminate the application so that it does not run in
    the background anymore.

12. About five seconds later, the notification will appear
    again. If you click the View Details button, the appli-
    cation will return to the foreground. This time, the
    Alert view shows that the `application:didFinishLaunchingWithOptions:`
    event in the application delegate was fired instead (see Figure 21-12).

FIGURE 21-9

FIGURE 21-10

FIGURE 21-11

FIGURE 21-12

How It Works

Creating a local notification is very straightforward:

```
UILocalNotification *localNotification =
    [[UILocalNotification alloc] init];
```

Once you have obtained an instance of the `UILocalNotification` class, you need to configure the object with various information, such as the time in which the notification will fire, the message to display, the badge number to display for your application icon, the sound to play, as well as the caption of the button to display:

```
//---set the notification to go off in 5 seconds time---
localNotification.fireDate =
    [[NSDate alloc] initWithTimeIntervalSinceNow:5];

//---the message to display for the alert---
localNotification.alertBody = message.text;

localNotification.applicationIconBadgeNumber = 1;

//---uses the default sound---
localNotification.soundName = UILocalNotificationDefaultSoundName;

//---title for the button to display---
localNotification.alertAction = @"View Details";
```

In the preceding code, you use the `fireDate` property to set the local notification to fire in five seconds. The `alertBody` property sets the message to display. The `applicationIconBadgeNumber` property displays a badge number next to the application's icon (this badge number will be displayed when the local notification fires). The `soundName` property enables you to specify the filename of a sound resource that is bundled with your application. If you want to play the system's default sound, use the `UILocalNotificationDefaultSoundName` constant. Finally, the `alertAction` property enables you to customize the button caption of the notification (see Figure 21-13).

FIGURE 21-13

To schedule a future local notification, use the `scheduleLocalNotification:` method of the `UIApplication` class:

```
//---schedule the notification---
[[UIApplication sharedApplication]
    scheduleLocalNotification:localNotification];
```

If you want to display the notification instantly, use the `presentLocalNotificationNow:` method instead:

```
//---display the notification now---
[[UIApplication sharedApplication]
    presentLocalNotificationNow:localNotification];
```

This is very useful for cases in which your application is executing in the background and you want to display a notification to draw the user's attention.

When the notification is displayed (it will be displayed only if the application is not in the foreground), the user has two options: close the notification or view the application that generated the notification. When the user views the notification, the `application:didReceiveLocalNotification:` method in the application's delegate will be called:

```
- (void)application:(UIApplication *)application
didReceiveLocalNotification:(UILocalNotification *)notification {
    UIAlertView *alert = [[UIAlertView alloc]
        initWithTitle:@"Inside application:didReceiveLocalNotification:"
            message:notification.alertBody
            delegate:self
    cancelButtonTitle:@"OK"
    otherButtonTitles:nil];

    [alert show];
    [alert release];
}
```

Here, you can simply print out the details of the notification through the `notification` parameter.

Note that the `application:didReceiveLocalNotification:` method is also called when the application is running and the local notification is fired. In this case, the local notification will not appear.

If the application is not running when the local notification occurs, viewing the application will invoke the `application:didFinishLaunchingWithOptions:` method instead:

```
- (BOOL)application:(UIApplication *)application
didFinishLaunchingWithOptions:(NSDictionary *)launchOptions {
    UILocalNotification *localNotification =
        [launchOptions objectForKey:
            UIApplicationLaunchOptionsLocalNotificationKey];

    if (localNotification) {
        UIAlertView *alert = [[UIAlertView alloc]
          initWithTitle:@"Inside application:didFinishLaunchingWithOptions:"
              message:localNotification.alertBody
              delegate:self
    cancelButtonTitle:@"OK"
    otherButtonTitles:nil];
        [alert show];
        [alert release];
    }

    // Override point for customization after application launch.

    // Add the view controller's view to the window and display.
    [window addSubview:viewController.view];
    [window makeKeyAndVisible];

    return YES;
}
```

To obtain details about the notification, you have to use the `launchOptions` parameter, by querying the details using the `UIApplicationLaunchOptionsLocalNotificationKey` constant.

To cancel all scheduled notifications, you can call the `cancelAllLocalNotifications` method of the `UIApplication` class:

```
//---cancel all notifications---
[[UIApplication sharedApplication] cancelAllLocalNotifications];
```

SUMMARY

In this chapter, you have seen how background execution works and how you can utilize it to make your applications more useful. Combining all the different concepts discussed in this chapter will enable you to write compelling iPhone applications. Note that at the time of writing, the multi-tasking feature of iOS applies only to the newer iPhone 3GS and iPhone 4. Support for multi-tasking on the iPad will be available by the end of 2010.

EXERCISES

1. Name the three types of applications that are allowed to execute in the background.

2. Which devices support multi-tasking?

3. For the `CLLocationManager` class, when should you use the `startUpdatingLocation` and `startMonitoringSignificantLocationChanges` methods? Why?

4. What is the difference between Apple Push Notification service and local notifications?

Answers to the Exercises can be found in Appendix E, on Wrox.com.

▶ **WHAT YOU LEARNED IN THIS CHAPTER**

TOPIC	KEY CONCEPTS
Opting out of background execution	Use the `UIApplicationExitsOnSuspend` key.
Tracking locations in the background	Use the `UIBackgroundModes` key.
Monitoring significant location changes	Use the `startMonitoringSignificantLocationChanges` method.
Creating local notifications	Use the `UILocalNotification` class.
Scheduling a local notification	`[[UIApplication sharedApplication]` `    scheduleLocalNotification:localNotification];`
Presenting a local notification	`[[UIApplication sharedApplication]` `    presentLocalNotificationNow:localNotification];`

PART V
Appendices

- ▶ **APPENDIX A:** Testing on an Actual Device
- ▶ **APPENDIX B:** Getting Around in Xcode
- ▶ **APPENDIX C:** Getting Around in Interface Builder
- ▶ **APPENDIX D:** Crash Course in Objective-C
- ▶ **APPENDIX E:** Answers to Exercises (found online at Wrox.com)

Testing on an Actual Device

Although the iPhone Simulator is a very handy tool that enables you to test your iPhone/iPad applications without needing an actual device, nothing beats testing on a real device. This is especially true when you are ready to roll out your application to the world — you must ensure that it works correctly on real devices. In addition, if your application requires access to hardware features on an iPhone, iPod touch, or iPad, such as the accelerometer, gyroscope, and GPS, you need to test it on a real device — the iPhone Simulator is simply not adequate.

This appendix walks through the steps you need to take to test your applications on a real device, be it the iPhone, iPod touch, or iPad. In addition, you will also learn how to prepare your application for submission to the App Store.

SIGNING UP FOR THE IPHONE DEVELOPER PROGRAM

The first step toward testing your application on a real device is to sign up for the iPhone Developer Program at `http://developer.apple.com/iphone/program/`. Two programs are available: Standard and Enterprise. For most developers who want to release applications on the App Store, the Standard program, which costs $99, is sufficient. Check out `http://developer .apple.com/iphone/program/apply.html` to learn more about the differences between the Standard and Enterprise programs.

If you just want to test your application on your actual iPhone/iPod touch, sign up for the Standard program.

OBTAINING THE UDID OF YOUR DEVICE

To test your application on your device, you need to perform a series of steps to prepare your Mac and your device. The following sections walk you through the necessary steps, from obtaining your certificate to deploying your application onto the device.

First, you need to obtain the 40-character identifier that uniquely identifies your device. This identifier is known as the UDID — Unique Device Identifier. Every device sold by Apple has a unique UDID. To do so, connect your device to your Mac and start Xcode. Choose Window ⇨ Organizer to launch the Organizer application. Figure A-1 shows the Organizer application displaying the identifier of my iPhone. Copy the identifier and save it somewhere; you will need it later.

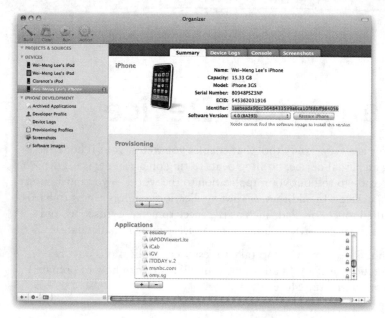

FIGURE A-1

LOGGING IN TO THE IPHONE PROVISIONING PORTAL

Once you have signed up for the iPhone Developer Program, you can log in to the iPhone Dev Center website located at `http://developer.apple.com/iphone/index.action`. Figure A-2 shows the page displayed after you have logged in to the iPhone Dev Center.

On the right side of the page, you will see a section named iPhone Developer Program. The first item listed under this section is iPhone Provisioning Portal. This portal contains all the details about preparing your Mac and devices for testing and deployment. Click the iPhone Provisioning Portal item to display the window shown in Figure A-3.

The pane on the left contains several links to pages where you can submit various information required to prepare your Mac and devices for testing. The center pane contains the welcome message and a Launch Assistant button. If you are using this page for the first time, the Launch Assistant provides an easy-to-follow series of guided instructions to help you test your applications on your devices. However, to help you better understand the details of the process, the following sections describe each step by walking through the various links displayed on the left side of the page.

FIGURE A-2

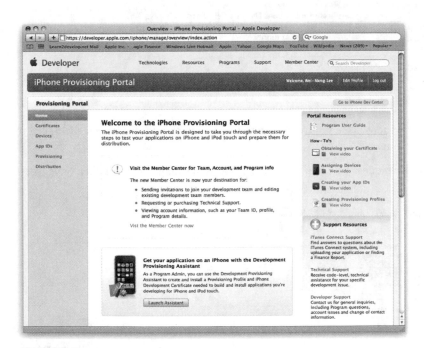

FIGURE A-3

GENERATING A CERTIFICATE

The first step toward testing your application on a real device is to obtain a digital certificate from Apple so that Xcode can use it to code-sign your application. Any applications that are run on your devices must be code-signed. For testing purposes, you will need a *development certificate*. Once you are ready to distribute your application (such as through the App Store), you will then need a *distribution certificate* (discussed later in this Appendix).

To request a development certificate from Apple, you need to generate a certificate signing request (CSR). You can do this using the Keychain Access application located in the `Applications/Utilities/` folder.

In the Keychain Access application, choose Keychain Access ➪ Certificate Assistant and select Request a Certificate From a Certificate Authority (see Figure A-4).

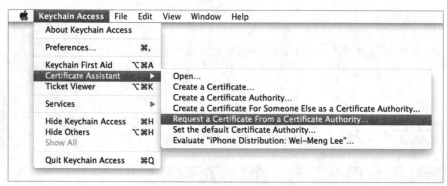

FIGURE A-4

In the Certificate Assistant window (see Figure A-5), enter your e-mail address, check the Saved to disk option, and click Continue.

You will be asked to save the request to a file. Use the default name suggested and click Save (see Figure A-6).

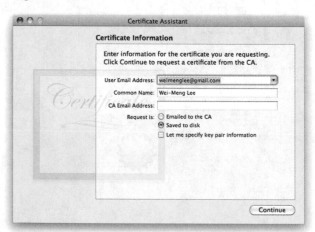

FIGURE A-5
FIGURE A-6

On the iPhone Provisioning Portal page, click the Certificates item displayed on the left (see Figure A-7). Four tabs will be displayed on the right side of the page — Development, Distribution, History, and How To.

In the Development tab, click the Request Certificate button to request a development certificate from Apple. You will see a detailed list of instructions telling you to generate a certificate request using the Keychain Access application (see Figure A-8). As you have already performed this step earlier in this Appendix, click the Choose file button to upload the certificate request file to Apple. After the file is selected, click Submit to send it to Apple.

FIGURE A-7

FIGURE A-8

As shown in Figure A-9, the development certificate will now have a status of Pending Issuance.

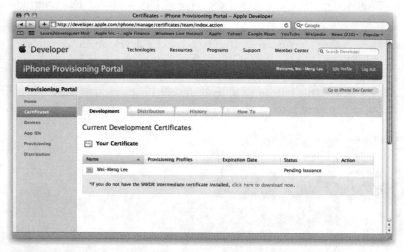

FIGURE A-9

Simply refresh the page or click the Development tab once more and your development certificate will now be ready (see Figure A-10).

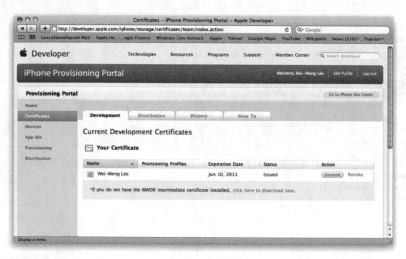

FIGURE A-10

Click the Download button to download the development certificate. When it is downloaded to your Mac, double-click the `developer_identity.cer` file. When prompted, click OK. The certificate will now be installed in the Keychain Access application, which you can verify (see Figure A-11).

FIGURE A-11

REGISTERING YOUR DEVICES

The next step is to register your devices with the iPhone Provisioning Portal so that you can later associate them with the provisioning profiles (more on this shortly).

Back on the iPhone Provisioning Portal page, click the Devices item displayed on the left side of the page (see Figure A-12). On the right of the page, you will see that you can both add devices and upload a list of devices to register.

FIGURE A-12

Click the Add Devices button to register one or more devices. Give your device a name and enter its Device ID (see Figure A-13). You obtained the Device ID (UDID) of your device earlier, in the "Obtaining the UDID of Your Device" section. To register additional devices, click the plus (+) button. Then click Submit.

NOTE *For the Standard Program, you can register up to 100 devices for testing. All added devices count toward your 100-device limit, whether you use them or not. In other words, if you register five devices and then lose them in the bar, you can register only 95 more devices — the slots taken up by the other five devices cannot be recovered. You can reset the list only when you renew your membership annually.*

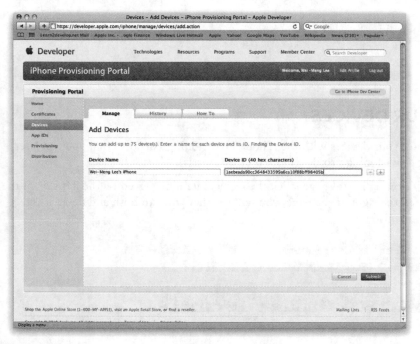

FIGURE A-13

CREATING AN APPLICATION ID

The next step of the process is to create an *Application ID* (*App ID*) that you will use to identify your application. An App ID is a series of characters used to uniquely identify an application (or applications) on your iPhone. An App ID is represented in the following format: *<Bundle Seed ID>.<CF Bundle Identifier>*.

On the iPhone Provisioning Portal page, click the App IDs item on the left (see Figure A-14).

Click the New App ID button to create a new App ID. On the right of the page, you enter the details for the App ID (see Figure A-15).

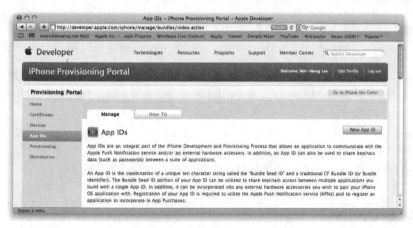

FIGURE A-14

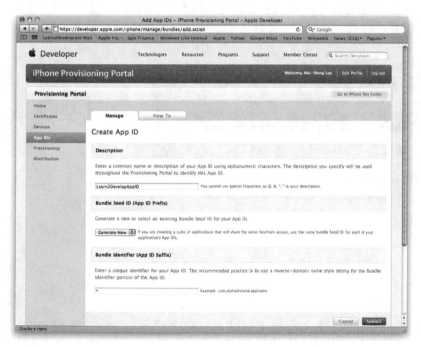

FIGURE A-15

Enter a description for the App ID you are creating. For this example, it is `Learn2DevelopAppID`. This name will be used to identify your App ID. You will leave the Bundle Seed ID to be automatically generated for you. For the Bundle Identifier, you have two options:

➤ Give it a unique identifier, e.g., *com.yourcompany.appname*

➤ Use a wildcard character (*) as the trailing character, e.g., *com.yourcompany.**, or simply use *

Using the wildcard character allows you to use a single App ID for all your applications, while if you use a unique identifier for the Bundle Identifier, you will need to have a unique App ID for each application.

In general, it is easier to use the wildcard character, as you can use one App ID for all your applications. Here, I used the * for the Bundle Identifier. When you compile your application, this wildcard will be substituted with the Bundle Identifier specified in the `info.plist` file in your Xcode.

CREATING A PROVISIONING PROFILE

In order for your application to be able to execute on a device, the device must be provisioned with a file known as a *provisioning profile*.

On the iPhone Provisioning Portal page, click the Provisioning item displayed on the left (see Figure A-16).

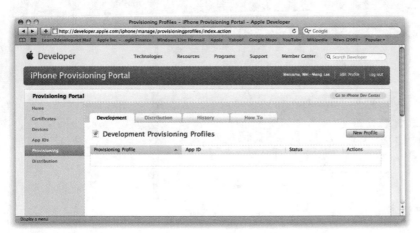

FIGURE A-16

Under the Development tab, shown in Figure A-17, provide a name for your provisioning profile, check the certificate name, select the App ID created in the previous section, and then check all the device names that you want to test on. Click Submit.

The provisioning profile that you have created will now be pending issuance (see Figure A-18).

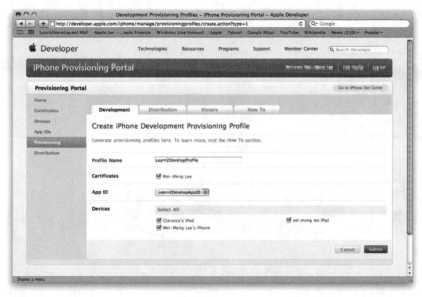

FIGURE A-17

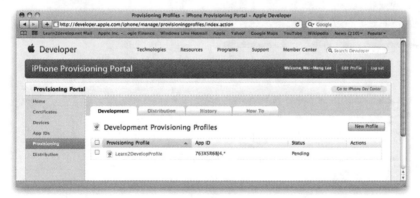

FIGURE A-18

Refresh the page or click the Development tab again and the provisioning profile should now be ready for download (see Figure A-19). Download the generated provisioning profile onto your Mac by clicking the Download button.

FIGURE A-19

Drag and drop the downloaded provisioning profile onto the Xcode icon that is on the Dock (see Figure A-20).

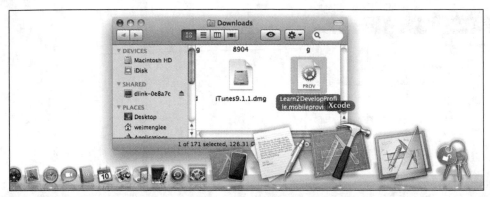

FIGURE A-20

Doing so installs the provisioning profile onto the Organizer application (part of Xcode; see Figure A-21). It also installs the provisioning profile onto your connected iPhone, iPod touch, or iPad device.

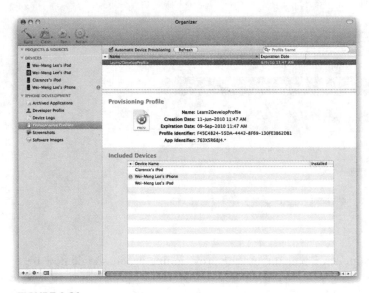

FIGURE A-21

To verify that the provisioning profile is indeed installed on your device, select the device that is currently connected to your Mac and view the Provisioning section of the Summary tab (see Figure A-22).

 NOTE *If you don't see the provisioning profile, simply disconnect your device and connect again. If, after reconnecting the device, the provisioning profile is not there, click the "+" button to manually add the provisioning profile to your device.*

You are now almost ready to deploy your iPhone application onto your iPhone, iPod touch, or iPad. In Xcode, select Device – 4.0 ➪ Debug and press Command-R. When you are prompted to sign your application using the certificate, click Always Allow (see Figure A-23).

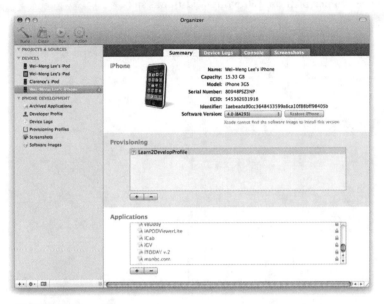

FIGURE A-22

FIGURE A-23

UNDERSTANDING APPLICATION ID AND THE WILDCARD

Earlier, I mentioned that you can use the wildcard character for your App ID. If you do not wish to use the wildcard character, you need to perform the following additional step.

Figure A-24 assumes that you have an App ID called `HelloWorldAppID`.

In Figure A-25, the provisioning profile `HelloWorldProfile` is associated with this App ID.

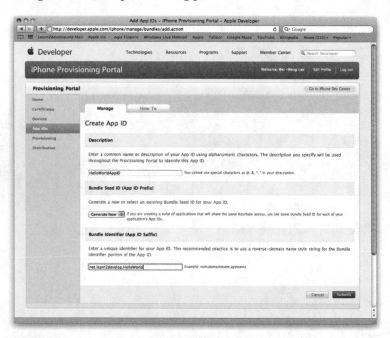

FIGURE A-24

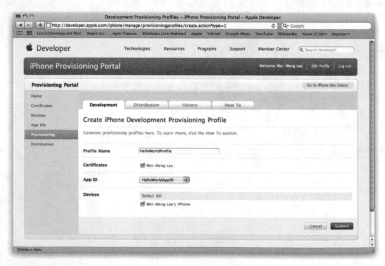

FIGURE A-25

If you were to install the `HelloWorldProfile` provisioning profile onto your device, you would have to modify the Bundle Identifier in your Xcode project to match the Bundle Identifier (`net.learn2develop .HelloWorld`) specified in the `HelloWorldAppID` App ID. To do so, expand the Targets item in your Xcode project and click the Info button located in the toolbar (see Figure A-26).

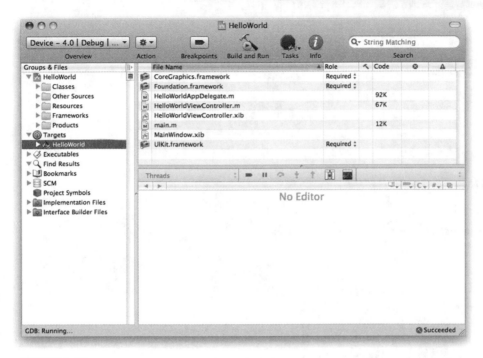

FIGURE A-26

In the Build tab, under the Code Signing Identity setting, observe that only the `Learn2DevelopProfile` (which uses the * character) matches the application identifier (see Figure A-27). The `HelloWorldProfile` does not match the application, as the application identifier is not the same. Your application identifier at the moment is `com.yourcompany .HelloWorld`.

Click the Properties tab and set the Identifier to `net.learn2develop.HelloWorld` (see Figure A-28).

Once this is done, the `HelloWorldProfile` will now match your Bundle Identifier (see Figure A-29).

You will then be able to sign your application based on this provisioning profile.

FIGURE A-27

FIGURE A-28

FIGURE A-29

PREPARING FOR APP STORE SUBMISSION

Preparing for submission to the App Store is very similar to preparing your application for testing on your device. Instead of using a development certificate, you use a *distribution certificate*. Also, instead of using a development provisioning profile, you use a *distribution provisioning profile*.

To create a distribution certificate, repeat the same process outlined earlier for creating the development certificate. The distribution certificate is created in the Distribution tab (see Figure A-30).

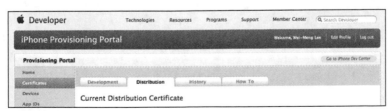

FIGURE A-30

For the distribution provisioning profile, select Provisioning from the panel on the left, and then click the Distribution tab (see Figure A-31). Click the New Profile button to create a new distribution provisioning profile.

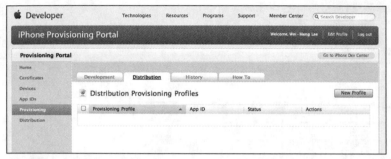

FIGURE A-31

You need to select the distribution method (App Store; see Figure A-32), name the distribution provisioning profile, and select the App ID. Note that there is no need to select the devices because the application will be hosted on the App Store and available to all users.

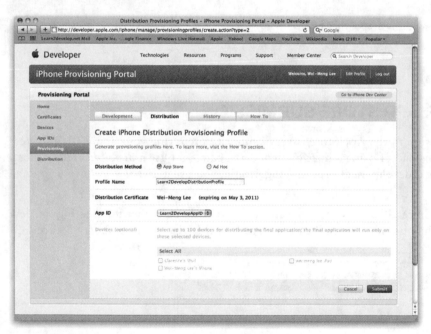

FIGURE A-32

Once the distribution provisioning profile is created, download it and install it in Xcode.

To prepare your application for submission, select your project name in Xcode and click the Info button. Select the Configurations tab (see Figure A-33) and then select Release. Click the Duplicate button to make a copy of it.

Name the duplicate **Distribution** (see Figure A-34).

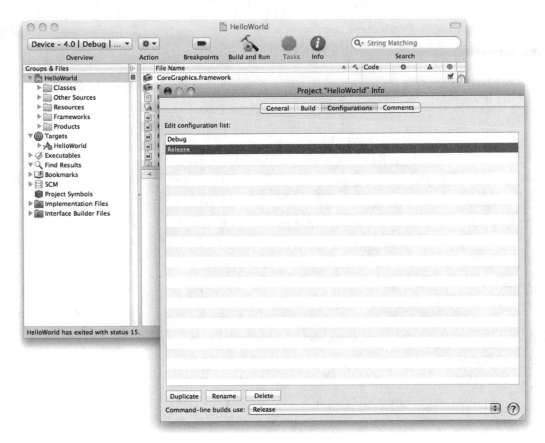

FIGURE A-33

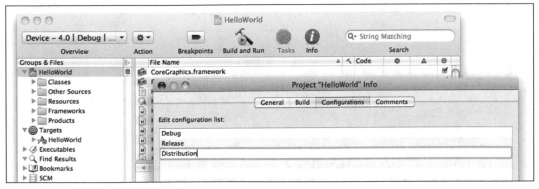

FIGURE A-34

Back in Xcode, select the HelloWorld item listed under Targets and click the Info button. Select the Build tab and set the following items:

➤ **Configuration** — Distribution (see Figure A-35)

➤ **Any iPhone OS Device** — iPhone Distribution:<*Your Name*>

Under the Overview item in the toolbar of Xcode, select Distribution (see Figure A-36). Then, compile the application by selecting Build ➪ Build.

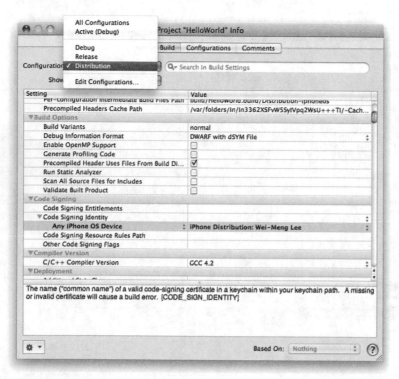

FIGURE A-35

 NOTE *You need to ensure that your application has an icon that is 57 x 57 pixels in size. Otherwise, your application will not be compiled correctly and will be rejected by Apple when it is submitted for approval.*

You can verify that the application is built and signed correctly by selecting Build ➪ Build Results. Ensure that the code signing process is performed correctly (see Figure A-37).

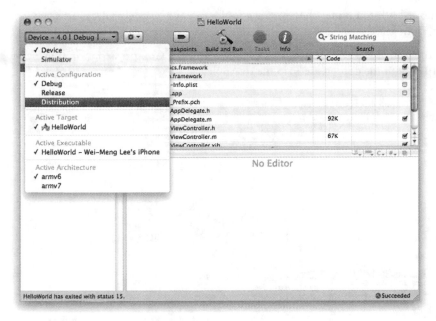

FIGURE A-36

FIGURE A-37

The binary that is compiled is listed under the `Products` folder in your Xcode project. To see its location on your Mac, right-click the .app file and select Reveal in Finder (see Figure A-38).

There are two files in the folder. Right-click the .app file and select the Compress option (see Figure A-39). You will need to submit the compressed zip file to Apple.

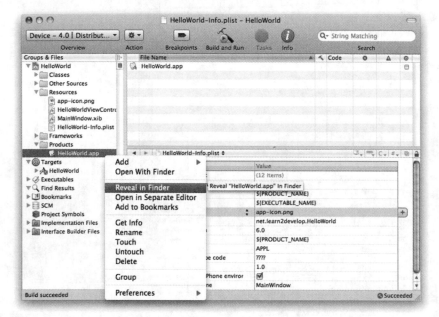

FIGURE A-38

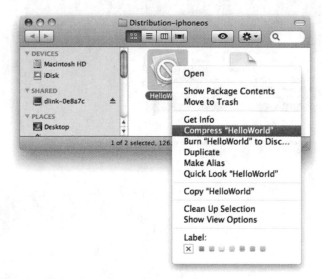

FIGURE A-39

For submission to the App Store, you use the iTunes Connect page shown earlier on the right side of the iPhone Dev Center (refer to Figure A-2).

Inside iTunes Connect, you can find detailed instructions for submitting your application to the App Store (see Figure A-40). Details about submitting the application are beyond the scope of this book.

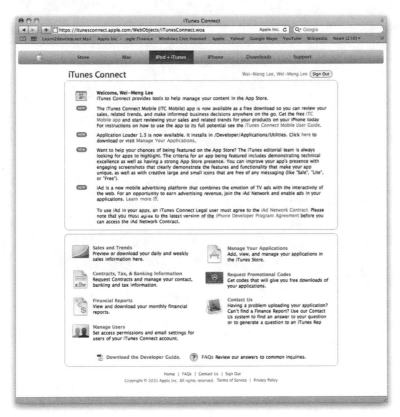

FIGURE A-40

SUMMARY

In this appendix, you have seen the various steps required to deploy your application to your iPhone, iPod touch, or iPad. Although the number of steps may seem intimidating, it is actually quite a straightforward process. The iPhone Developer Program allows you to provision up to 100 devices for testing purposes. After a device is provisioned, you can use the development certificate to deploy your applications onto it. For submission to the App Store, you need a distribution certificate and a provisioning profile.

Getting Around in Xcode

Xcode is the integrated development environment (IDE) that Apple uses for developing Mac OS X, iPhone, and iPad applications. It is a suite of applications that includes a set of compilers, documentation, and Interface Builder (discussed in Appendix C).

Using Xcode, you can build your iPhone and iPad applications from the comfort of an intelligent text editor, coupled with many different tools to help debug your applications. If you are new to Xcode, this appendix can serve as a useful guide to get you started quickly. Appendix C covers the Interface Builder in more detail.

LAUNCHING XCODE

The easiest way to launch Xcode is to type **Xcode** in the textbox of Spotlight. Alternatively, you can launch Xcode by navigating to the `/Developer/Applications/` folder and double-clicking the Xcode icon.

> **NOTE** *For convenience, you can also drag the Xcode icon to the Dock so that in the future you can launch it directly from there.*

At the time of writing, the version of Xcode available is version 3.2.3.

Project Types Supported

Xcode supports the building of iPhone, iPad, and Mac OS X applications. When you create a new project in Xcode (which you do by choosing File ➪ New Project), the New Project dialog appears, as shown in Figure B-1.

As shown on the left, you can create two main project types: iPhone OS and Mac OS X. Under the iPhone OS category are the Application and Library items.

FIGURE B-1

If you select the Application item, you will see all the different project types you can create:

➤ Navigation-based Application (iPhone only)

➤ OpenGL ES Application (iPhone and iPad)

➤ Split View-based Application (iPad only)

➤ Tab Bar Application (iPhone and iPad)

➤ Utility Application (iPhone only)

➤ View-based Application (iPhone and iPad)

➤ Window-based Application (iPhone and iPad)

For the Navigation-based Application, Split View-based Application, Utility Application, and Window-based Application project types, you have the option to use Core Data for storage.

NOTE *Core Data is part of the Cocoa API that was first introduced with the iPhone SDK 3.0. It is basically a framework for manipulating data without worrying about the details of storage and retrieval. A discussion of Core Data is beyond the scope of this book.*

Select the project type you want to create and click the Choose button. Then name the project.

When the project is created, Xcode displays all the files that make up your project (see Figure B-2).

FIGURE B-2

The Xcode window is divided into five sections:

➤ **Toolbar** — Displays the buttons for commonly performed actions.

➤ **Groups and Files List** — Displays the files in a project. Files are grouped into folders and categories for easier management.

➤ **Status Bar** — Displays the status information about the current action.

➤ **Detail View** — Displays the files contained in the folders and groups selected in the Groups and Files List section.

➤ **Editor** — Displays the appropriate editor showing the file currently selected.

To edit a code file, click the filename of a file to open the appropriate editor. For example, if you click an .h or .m file, the code editor in which you can edit your source code is displayed (see Figure B-3).

Click a .plist file, and the XML Property List editor launches (see Figure B-4).

FIGURE B-3

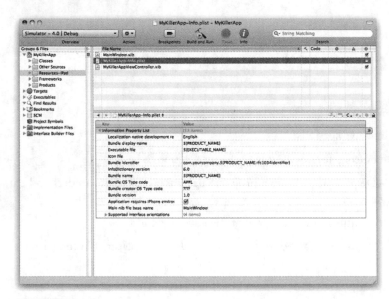

FIGURE B-4

Customizing the Toolbar

The Xcode window contains the toolbar section, in which you can place your favorite items for quick access. By default, the following items are placed in the toolbar:

➤   **Overview** — Enables you to select target settings such as the active SDK (iOS version and device versus Simulator) as well as active configurations (Debug or Release).

➤ **Action** — Specifies the action you can perform with a selected item.

➤ **Breakpoints** — Toggles the Build and Run item (see the next item) to Build and Debug so that you can attach a debugger to the application.

➤ **Build and Run** — Enables you to build and deploy the application.

➤ **Tasks** — Stops any operation in progress.

➤ **Info** — Displays detailed information about a selected item.

➤ **Search** — Filters the items currently displayed in the Detail View section.

You can add items to the toolbar by right-clicking the toolbar and selecting Customize Toolbar. A drop-down pane then shows all the items that you can add to the toolbar (see Figure B-5). To add an item, just drag it directly onto the toolbar.

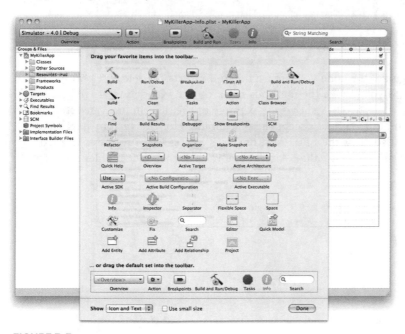

FIGURE B-5

Code Sense

One of the most common features of a modern IDE is *code completion*, whereby the IDE automatically tries to complete the statement you are typing based on the current context. In Xcode, the code-completion feature is known as *Code Sense*. For example, if you type the letters **uial** in a method, such as the `viewDidLoad()` method, Code Sense automatically suggests the `UIAlertView` class, as shown in Figure B-6 (note that the suggested characters are displayed in gray). To accept the suggested word, simply press the Tab or Enter key, or Ctrl-/.

```
// Implement viewDidLoad to
- (void)viewDidLoad {
    UIAlertView
    [super viewDidLoad];
}
```

FIGURE B-6

You can also invoke the Code Sense feature by pressing the Esc key or F5. Code Sense displays a list of words starting with the letters you have typed (see Figure B-7).

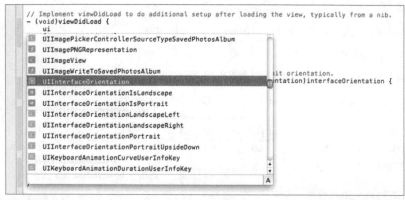

FIGURE B-7

Xcode automatically recognizes the code you are typing and inserts the relevant parameters' placeholders. For example, if you invoke the methods of an object, Xcode inserts the placeholders of the various parameters. Figure B-8 shows an example of the placeholders inserted for the `UIAlertView` object after you type "**i.**" To accept the placeholders for the various parameters, press the Tab key (you can also press the Enter key, or Ctrl-/). Press Ctrl-/ to move to each parameter placeholder and then enter a value. Alternatively, click each placeholder and type over it.

```
// Implement viewDidLoad to do additional setup after loading the view, typically from a nib.
- (void)viewDidLoad {
    UIAlertView *alert = [[UIAlertView alloc] initWithTitle:(NSString *)title message:(NSString *)message delegate
    [super viewDidLoad];
}
```

FIGURE B-8

Running the Application

To execute an application, you first select the active SDK to use. You also choose whether you want to test it on a real device or use the included iPhone Simulator (the iPhone Simulator 4 simulates the iPhone, whereas the iPhone Simulator 3.2 simulates the iPad). You do so by selecting from the Overview list (see Figure B-9).

To run the application, press Command-R, and Xcode builds and deploys the application onto the selected device or Simulator.

FIGURE B-9

DEBUGGING YOUR APPLICATIONS

Debugging your iPhone applications is an essential part of your development journey. Xcode includes debugger utilities that help you trace and examine your code as you execute your application. The following sections describe some of the tips and tricks that you can employ when developing your iPhone applications.

Errors

When you try to run your application, Xcode first tries to build the project before it can deploy the application onto the real device or Simulator. Any syntax errors that Xcode detects are immediately highlighted with the exclamation icons. Figure B-10 shows an Xcode-highlighted syntax error. The error with the code block is the missing brace symbol ([) for the [[UIAlertView alloc] statement.

```
    // Implement viewDidLoad to do additional setup after loading the view, typically from a nib.
    - (void)viewDidLoad {
        UIAlertView *alert = [UIAlertView alloc] initWithTitle:@"Hello World!"    ⓘ Expected ',' or ';' before 'initWi...
                                                  message:@"Hello, my World"
                                                  delegate:self
                                          cancelButtonTitle:@"OK"
                                          otherButtonTitles:nil];
        [alert show];
        [alert release];
        [super viewDidLoad];
    }
```

FIGURE B-10

You can also click the error icon located at the lower-right corner of the window to view the list of errors (see Figure B-11).

FIGURE B-11

Warnings

Objective-C is a case-sensitive language; therefore, a common mistake made by beginners is mixing up the capitalization for some of the method names. Consider the block of code shown in Figure B-12.

Can you spot the error? Syntactically, the statements are correct. However, one of the parameters appears with the wrong capitalization: `initwithTitle:` was misspelled — it should be `initWithTitle:` (note the capital "W"). When you compile the program, Xcode will not flag this code as an error; instead, it issues a warning message (as shown in the figure).

```
// Implement viewDidLoad to do additional setup after loading the view, typically from a nib.
- (void)viewDidLoad {
    UIAlertView *alert = [[UIAlertView alloc] initwithTitle:@"Hello World!"
                                             message:@"Hello, my World"
                                             delegate:self
                                             cancelButtonTitle:@"OK"
                                             otherButtonTitles:nil];
        ⚠ No '-initwithTitle:message:delegate:cancelButtonTitle:otherButtonTitles:' method found
    [alert show];
    [alert release];
    [super viewDidLoad];
}
```

FIGURE B-12

Pay special attention to a warning message in Xcode, and verify that the method name is spelled correctly, including case. Failing to do so may result in a runtime exception.

When a runtime exception occurs, the best way to troubleshoot the error is to open the Debugger Console window by pressing Shift-Command-R. The Debugger Console window displays all the debugging information that is printed when Xcode debugs your application. This window usually contains the clue that helps you determine exactly what went wrong behind the scenes. Figure B-13 shows the content of the Debugger Console window when an exception occurs. To determine the cause of the crash, scroll to the bottom of the window and look for the section displayed in bold. In this case, note the reason stated — the problem is with the `UIAlertView` object.

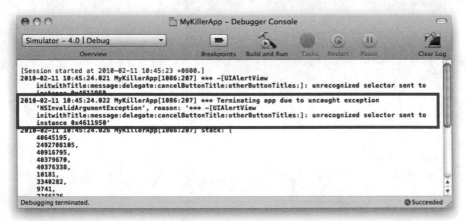

FIGURE B-13

Setting Breakpoints

Setting breakpoints in your code is helpful when debugging your application. Breakpoints enable you to execute your code line-by-line and examine the values of variables so you can check that they perform as expected.

In Xcode, you set a breakpoint by clicking the left column of the code editor — a breakpoint arrow will appear (see Figure B-14).

```
- (void)willRotateToInterfaceOrientation:(UIInterfaceOrientation)toInterfaceOrientation
                          duration:(NSTimeInterval)duration {

    if (toInterfaceOrientation == UIInterfaceOrientationPortrait) {
        btn.frame = CGRectMake(20,20,280,37);
    } else {
        btn.frame = CGRectMake(180,243,280,37);
    }
}
```

FIGURE B-14

> **NOTE** You can toggle the state of a breakpoint by clicking it to enable or disable it. Breakpoints displayed in dark blue are enabled; those displayed in light blue are disabled. To remove a breakpoint, click on it and drag it out of its resting place. It will vanish.

After you have set breakpoints in your application, press Command-Y to debug your application. The code will stop at your breakpoints.

> **NOTE** If you press Command-R to run the application, your code will not stop at the breakpoints.

When the application reaches the breakpoint you have set, Xcode indicates the current line of execution with a red arrow (see Figure B-15).

```
- (void)willRotateToInterfaceOrientation:(UIInterfaceOrientation)toInterfaceOrientation
                          duration:(NSTimeInterval)duration {

    if (toInterfaceOrientation == UIInterfaceOrientationPortrait) {
        btn.frame = CGRectMake(20,20,280,37);
    } else {
        btn.frame = CGRectMake(180,243,280,37);
    }
}
```

FIGURE B-15

At this juncture, you can do several things:

➤ **Step Into (Shift-Command-I)** — Step into the statements in a function/method.

➤ **Step Over (Shift-Command-O)** — Execute all the statements in a function or method and continue to the next statement.

➤ **Step Out (Shift-Command-T)** — Finish executing all the statements in a function or method and continue to the next statement after the function call.

➤ **If you want to resume the execution of your application, press Option-Command-P.** You can also examine the values of variables and objects by clicking the Show Debugger button (shown enclosed by the box in Figure B-16). You can also move your mouse over the objects and variables you are interested in to view their values.

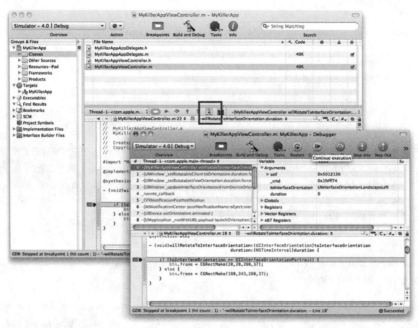

FIGURE B-16

Using NSLog

In addition to setting breakpoints to trace the flow of your application, you can use the NSLog() function to print debugging messages to the Debugger Console window. The following statement in bold prints a message to the Debugger Console window when the application changes orientation:

```
- (void)willRotateToInterfaceOrientation:(UIInterfaceOrientation)
toInterfaceOrientation duration:(NSTimeInterval) duration {
    NSLog(
        @"In the willRotateToInterfaceOrientation:duration: event handler");

    UIInterfaceOrientation destOrientation = toInterfaceOrientation;
    if (destOrientation == UIInterfaceOrientationPortrait) {
        btn.frame = CGRectMake(20,20,280,37);
    }
    else {
        btn.frame = CGRectMake(180,243,280,37);
    }
}
```

Figure B-17 shows the output in the Debugger Console window (press Shift-Command-R to display it).

FIGURE B-17

Documentation

During the course of your development, you often need to check the various methods, classes, and objects used in the iPhone SDK. The best way to check them out is to refer to the documentation. Xcode enables you to quickly and easily browse the definitions of classes, properties, and methods through the use of the Option key. To view the help documentation for an item, simply press the Option key. The cursor changes to cross-hairs. Double-click the item you want to check out, and a small window showing the summary of the selected item appears (see Figure B-18). Clicking the book icon (see the callout on the figure) on the top-right corner of the window displays the full Developer Documentation window.

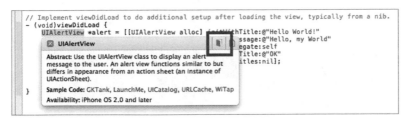

FIGURE B-18

C
Getting Around in Interface Builder

Interface Builder is one of the tools included with the iPhone SDK. It is a visual design tool that you can use to build the user interface of your iPhone applications. Although it is not strictly required for the development of your iPhone applications, Interface Builder plays an integral role in your journey of learning about iPhone application development. This appendix covers some of the important features of Interface Builder.

.XIB WINDOW

The most direct way to launch Interface Builder is to double-click any of the .xib files in your Xcode project. For example, if you have created a View-based Application project, there are two .xib files in the Resources folder of Xcode. Double-clicking either of them launches Interface Builder.

When Interface Builder is launched, the first window that you see has the same name as your .xib file (see Figure C-1).

Within this window are several items; and depending on what you have double-clicked, you should see some of the following:

- ➤ File's Owner
- ➤ First Responder
- ➤ View, Table View, Window, and so on
- ➤ Some View Controllers and delegates

FIGURE C-1

By default, the `.xib` window is displayed in icon mode. But you can also switch to list mode, where you can view some of the items in more detail. For example, Figure C-2 shows that when viewed in list mode, the View item displays a hierarchy of views contained within a typical View Controller.

DESIGNING THE VIEW

To design the user interface of your application, you typically double-click the View (or Table view or other) item

FIGURE C-2

on the `.xib` window to visually display the window. To populate your View window with views, you drag and drop objects listed in the Library window (see the "Library" section for more information on the Library window). Figure C-3 shows a Label view being dropped and positioned onto the View window.

As you position the view on the window, gridlines appear to guide you.

The View window also allows you to rotate the orientation of your view so that you can see how your view looks when it is rotated to the landscape orientation (see Figure C-4; clicking the arrow in the upper-right corner rotates the window).

FIGURE C-3

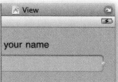

FIGURE C-4

INTERFACE BUILDER KEYBOARD SHORTCUTS

As you add more views to the View window, you begin to realize that you are spending a lot of time figuring out their actual sizes and locations with respect to other views. Here are two tips to make your life easier:

To make a copy of a view on the View window, simply Option-click and drag a view.

If a view is currently selected, pressing the Option key and then moving the mouse over the view displays that view's size information (see the left of Figure C-5). If you move the mouse over another view, it displays the distance between that view and the selected view (see the right of Figure C-5).

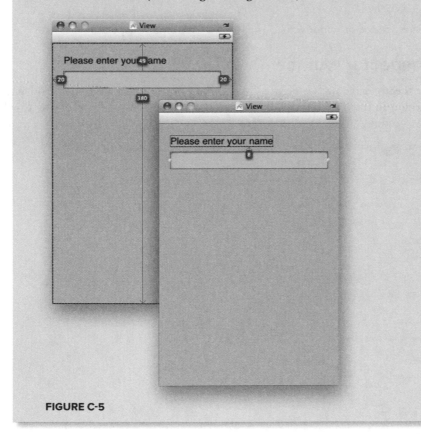

FIGURE C-5

INSPECTOR WINDOW

To customize the various attributes and properties of views, Interface Builder provides an Inspector window that is divided into four windows:

➤ Attributes Inspector

➤ Connections Inspector

➤ Size Inspector

➤ Identity Inspector

You can invoke the Inspector window by choosing Tools ➪ Inspector.

The following sections discuss each of the Inspector windows in more detail.

Attributes Inspector Window

The Attributes Inspector window (see Figure C-6) is where you configure the attributes of views in Interface Builder. The window content is dynamic and varies according to what is selected in the View window.

To open the Attributes Inspector window, choose Tools ➪ Attributes Inspector.

Connections Inspector Window

The Connections Inspector window (see Figure C-7) is where you connect the outlets and actions to your View Controller in Interface Builder. Its content is dynamic and varies according to what is selected in the View window.

To open the Connections Inspector window, choose Tools ➪ Connections Inspector.

FIGURE C-6

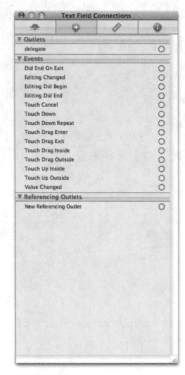

FIGURE C-7

Size Inspector Window

The Size Inspector window (see Figure C-8) is where you configure the size and positioning of views in Interface Builder.

Open it by selecting Tools ➪ Size Inspector.

Identity Inspector Window

The Identity Inspector window (see Figure C-9) is where you configure the various properties of your selected view.

Open the Identity Inspector window by choosing Tools ➪ Identity Inspector.

LIBRARY

The Library (Tools ➪ Library) contains a set of views that you can use to build the user interface of your iPhone application. Figure C-10 shows part of the Library's set of views.

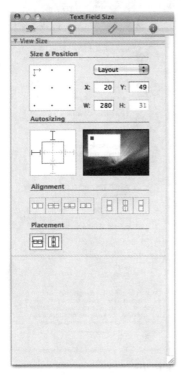

FIGURE C-8

FIGURE C-9

FIGURE C-10

You can configure the Library to display its views in different modes (see Figure C-11):

➤ Icons

➤ Icons and Labels (which is the mode shown in Figure C-10)

➤ Icons and Descriptions

➤ Small Icons and Labels

Figure C-12 shows the Library displayed in the Icons and Descriptions mode.

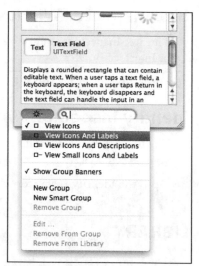

FIGURE C-11

OUTLETS AND ACTIONS

Outlets and actions are fundamental mechanisms in iPhone programming through which your code can connect to the views in your user interface (UI). When you use outlets, your code can programmatically reference the views on your UI, with actions serving as event handlers that handle the different events fired by the various views.

Although you can write code to connect actions and outlets, Interface Builder simplifies the process by enabling you to use the drag-and-drop technique.

Creating Outlets and Actions

To create an action in Interface Builder, open the Library window and click the Classes tab. Select the View Controller that you are working on and then select Actions in the drop-down list at the lower part of the window (see Figure C-13; in this example the selected View Controller is `HelloWorldViewController`).

Click the plus sign (+) button and name your action. Remember to include the colon (:) character at the end of the action name if you want to pass additional arguments in to the action (useful when you have multiple views connected to an action). The colon character enables the action to have an input parameter of type `id` (which you can change to other types), like this:

```
-(IBAction) myAction1:(id) sender;
```

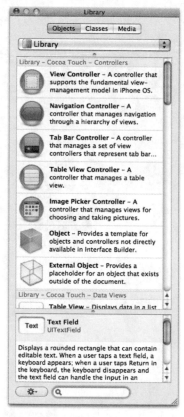

FIGURE C-12

Be sure to note that in Figure C-13 the action is listed under the `HelloWorldViewController.xib` header. This is because the action is defined within Interface Builder.

Likewise, select Outlets in the drop-down list to add an outlet to your View Controller. Click the plus sign (+) button in the Outlets section to create an outlet (see Figure C-14). It is always good to denote the specific type for the outlet that you are defining.

FIGURE C-13   **FIGURE C-14**

 NOTE *You can delete outlets and actions that you have created in Interface Builder by clicking the minus (–) button.*

Using the preceding example, if you want the outlet to connect to a `UITextField` view, you should specify the type of `myOutlet1` as `UITextField` rather than `id`.

After the outlet and action are created using Interface Builder, you still need to define them in the `.h` file, like this:

```
#import <UIKit/UIKit.h>

@interface HelloWorldViewController : UIViewController {
    IBOutlet UITextField *myTextField;
}

-(IBAction) myAction1:(id) sender;

@end
```

NOTE *Whether you are in Xcode or Interface Builder, be sure to save the file after you have modified it. When a* `.xib` *file in Interface Builder has been modified but not yet saved, the close window icon at the top, left corner of the window will contain a black dot (see the top of Figure C-15). When the file is saved, the black dot disappears (see the bottom of Figure C-15).*

In the Library window in Interface Builder, you can see that both the outlet and action are now listed under the `HelloWorldViewController.h` header (see Figure C-16). If you click the plus sign (+) button again, another outlet or action will be listed under the `HelloWorldViewController.xib` header until you define the outlet or action in the `.h` file.

 NOTE *It is not strictly necessary to create your actions and outlets in Interface Builder. However, doing so enables you to connect the views before writing any code. This is useful if you have designers and developers working on different aspects of the project.*

 NOTE *Outlets and actions defined in the* `.h` *file cannot be deleted in the Library window by clicking the minus sign (–) button. They must be deleted in the* `.h` *file.*

Actually, it is much simpler to define the outlets and actions directly in the `.h` files of your View Controllers first. That saves you the trouble of defining them in the Library window of Interface Builder.

Alternatively, if you do not want to manually type in the declaration of the outlets and actions in your View Controller class, you can create the outlets and actions in Interface Builder (as just described), select the File's Owner item, and then choose File ⇨ Write Class Files. This causes Interface Builder to generate the code for the outlets and actions that you have added in the Library window. When you use this option, Interface Builder first asks whether you want to replace or merge with the View Controller files (if they are already present). Replacing the files causes the existing files to be replaced, and all the changes you have made to the file will be gone. Therefore, this is not the recommended option. Merging the files enables you to select the segments of code that you want to merge into your existing files. This is the safer option.

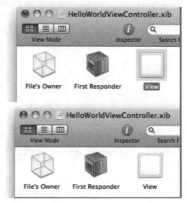

FIGURE C-15

FIGURE C-16

Take note that for code generated by Interface Builder, the outlets will not be exposed as properties. You must manually add the code to expose the properties using the @property keyword and the @synthesize keyword to generate the getters and setters for the properties.

 NOTE *In general, it is always easier to define the outlets and actions manually, rather than have Interface Builder do it for you.*

Connecting Outlets and Actions

You have two options for connecting the outlets and actions to the views; they are discussed in the following sections.

Method 1

To connect outlets, Control-click and drag the File's Owner item to the view to which you want to connect (see Figure C-17).

When you release the mouse button, a list appears from which you can select the correct outlet. When defining your outlets (in the Library window or in code), remember that you can specify the type of view your outlet is referring to. When you release the mouse button, Interface Builder lists only the outlets that match the type of view you have selected. For example, if you defined `myOutlet1` as `UIButton` and you Control-click and drag the File's Owner item to a Text Field view on the View window, `myOutlet1` does not appear in the list of outlets.

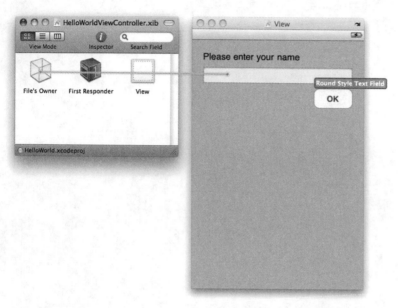

FIGURE C-17

To connect actions, Control-click and drag the view to the File's Owner item in the `.xib` window (see Figure C-18).

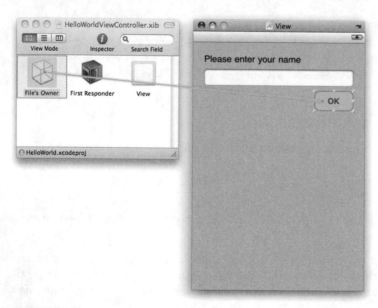

FIGURE C-18

When you release the mouse button, a list appears from which you can select the correct action.

When you have connected the outlets and actions, a good practice is to view all the connections in the File's Owner item by right-clicking it. Figure C-19 shows that the File's Owner item is connected to the Text Field view through the myOutlet1 outlet, and the Button's Touch Up Inside event is connected to the myAction1: action.

How does the Button know that it is the Touch Up Inside event (and not other events) that should be connected to the myAction1: action when you Control-click and drag the Button to the File's Owner item? The Touch Up Inside event is such a commonly used event that it is the default event selected when you perform a Control-click and drag action. What if you want to connect an event other than the default event? The second method shows you how.

FIGURE C-19

Method 2

An alternative method for connecting outlets is to right-click the File's Owner item and connect the outlet to the view directly (see Figure C-20).

To connect actions, you can connect the relevant action with the views to which you want to connect (see Figure C-21). When you release the mouse button, the list of available events appears, and you can select the event you want.

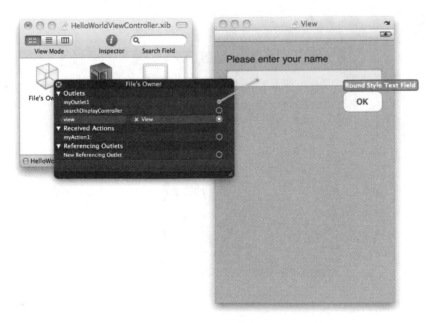

FIGURE C-20

Alternatively, you can right-click the view in question and connect the relevant events to the File's Owner item (see Figure C-22). When you release the mouse button, a list of actions appears. Select the action to which you want to connect.

FIGURE C-21

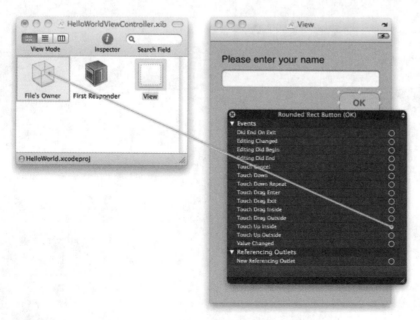

FIGURE C-22

As mentioned earlier, it is always good to right-click the File's Owner item after all the connections are made. One very common mistake that developers tend to make is changing the name of the actions or outlets after the connections are made. For example, suppose you now change the original outlet name from myOutlet1 to myTextField:

```
IBOutlet UITextField *myTextField;
```

Now, if you right-click the File's Owner item in Interface Builder, you will see that the original connection is displayed in yellow (see Figure C-23), together with a triangle icon on the right. All broken connections in Interface Builder are displayed in yellow. To remedy this, click the "x" button to remove the connection and connect the appropriate outlet again.

FIGURE C-23

Crash Course in Objective-C

Objective-C is an object-oriented programming language used by Apple primarily for programming Mac OS X and iPhone/iPad applications. It is an extension to the standard ANSI C language and hence it should be an easy language to pick up if you are already familiar with the C programming language. This appendix assumes that you already have some background in C programming and focuses on the object-oriented aspects of the language. If you are coming from a Java or .NET background, many of the concepts should be familiar to you; you just have to understand the syntax of Objective-C and, in particular, pay attention to the section on memory management.

Objective-C source code files are contained in two types of files:

- ➤ .h — header files
- ➤ .m — implementation files

For the discussions that follow, assume that you have created a View-based Application project using Xcode and added an empty class named SomeClass to your project.

DIRECTIVES

If you observe the content of the SomeClass.h file, you will notice that at the top of the file is an #import statement:

```
#import <Foundation/Foundation.h>

@interface SomeClass : NSObject {

}

@end
```

The #import statement is known as a *preprocessor directive*. In C and C++, you use the #include preprocessor directive to include a file's content with the current source. In

Objective-C, you use the `#import` statement to do the same, except that the compiler ensures that the file is included at most only once. To import a header file from one of the frameworks, you specify the header filename using angle brackets (<>) in the `#import` statement. To import a header file from within your project, you use the " and " characters, as in the case of the `SomeClass.m` file:

```
#import "SomeClass.h"

@implementation SomeClass

@end
```

CLASSES

In Objective-C, you will spend a lot of time dealing with classes and objects. Hence it is important that you understand how classes are declared and defined in Objective-C.

@interface

To declare a class, you use the `@interface` compiler directive, like this:

```
@interface SomeClass : NSObject {

}
```

This is done in the header file (`.h`) and the class declaration contains no implementation. The preceding code declares a class named `SomeClass`, and this class inherits from the base class named `NSObject`.

 NOTE *While you typically put your code declaration in an* `.h` *file, you can also put it inside an* `.m` *if need be. This is usually done for small projects.*

 NOTE `NSObject` *is the root class of most Objective-C classes. It defines the basic interface of a class and contains methods common to all classes that inherit from it.* `NSObject` *also provides the standard memory management and initialization framework used by most objects in Objective-C as well as reflection and type operations.*

In a typical View Controller class, the class inherits from the `UIViewController` class, such as in the following:

```
@interface HelloWorldViewController : UIViewController {

}
```

@implementation

To implement a class declared in the header file, you use the `@implementation` compiler directive, like this:

```
#import "SomeClass.h"

@implementation SomeClass

@end
```

This is done in a separate file from the header file. In Objective-C, you define your class in an .m file. Note that the class definition ends with the `@end` compiler directive.

 NOTE *As mentioned earlier, you can also put your declaration inside an* .m *file. Hence, in your* .m *file you would then have both the* `@interface` *and* `@implementation` *directives.*

@class

If your class references another class defined in another file, you need to import the header file of that file before you can use it. Consider the following example where you have defined two classes — `SomeClass` and `AnotherClass`. If you are using an instance of `AnotherClass` from within `SomeClass`, you need to import the `AnotherClass.h` file, as in the following code snippet:

```
//--SomeClass.h--
#import <Foundation/Foundation.h>
#import "AnotherClass.h"

@interface SomeClass : NSObject {
    //---an object from AnotherClass---
    AnotherClass *anotherClass;
}

@end

//---AnotherClass.h---
#import <Foundation/Foundation.h>

@interface AnotherClass : NSObject {

}

@end
```

However, if within `AnotherClass` you want to create an instance of `SomeClass`, you will not be able to simply import `SomeClass.h` in `AnotherClass`, like this:

```
//--SomeClass.h--
#import <Foundation/Foundation.h>
```

```
#import "AnotherClass.h"

@interface SomeClass : NSObject {
    //---an object from AnotherClass---
    AnotherClass *anotherClass;
}

@end


//---AnotherClass.h---
#import <Foundation/Foundation.h>
#import "SomeClass.h"        //---cannot simply import here---

@interface AnotherClass : NSObject {
    SomeClass *someClass;  //---using an instance of SomeClass---
}

@end
```

Doing so results in circular inclusion. To prevent that, Objective-C uses the `@class` compiler directive as a forward declaration to inform the compiler that the class you specified is a valid class. You usually use the `@class` compiler directive in the header file, and in the implementation file you can use the `@import` compiler directive to tell the compiler more about the content of the class that you are using.

Using the `@class` compiler directive, the program now looks like this:

```
//--SomeClass.h--
#import <Foundation/Foundation.h>

@class AnotherClass;    //---forward declaration---

@interface SomeClass : NSObject {
    //---an object from AnotherClass---
    AnotherClass *anotherClass;
}

@end


//---AnotherClass.h---
#import <Foundation/Foundation.h>

@class SomeClass;        //---forward declaration---

@interface AnotherClass : NSObject {
    SomeClass *someClass;  //---using an instance of SomeClass---
}

@end
```

> **NOTE** *Another notable reason to use forward declaration where possible is that it will reduce your compile times because the compiler does not need to traverse as many included header files and their includes, etc.*

Class Instantiation

To create an instance of a class, you typically use the `alloc` keyword (more on this in the Memory Management section) to allocate memory for the object and then return it to a variable of the class type:

```
SomeClass *someClass = [SomeClass alloc];
```

In Objective-C, you need to prefix an object name with the `*` character when you declare an object. If you are declaring a variable of primitive type (such as `float`, `int`, `CGRect`, `NSInteger`, and so on), the `*` character is not required. Here are some examples:

```
CGRect frame;     //---CGRect is a structure---
int number;       //---int is a primitive type---
NSString *str;    //---NSString is a class
```

Besides specifying the returning class type, you can also use the `id` type, like this:

```
id someClass = [SomeClass alloc];
id str;
```

The `id` type means that the variable can refer to any type of object and hence the `*` is implicitly implied.

Fields

Fields are the data members of objects. For example, the following code shows that `SomeClass` has three fields — `anotherClass`, `rate`, and `name`:

```
//--SomeClass.h--
#import <Foundation/Foundation.h>

@class AnotherClass;   //---forward declaration---

@interface SomeClass : NSObject {
    //---an object from AnotherClass---
    AnotherClass *anotherClass;
    float rate;
    NSString *name;
}

@end

@end
```

Access Privileges

By default, the access privilege of all fields is `@protected`. However, the access privilege can also be `@public` or `@private`. The following list shows the various access privileges:

➤   `@private` — visible only to the class that declares it

➤   `@public` — visible to all classes

➤   `@protected` — visible to the class that declares it as well as to inheriting classes

Using the example shown in the previous section, if you now try to access the fields in `SomeClass` from another class, such as a View Controller, you will not be able to see them:

```
SomeClass *someClass = [SomeClass alloc];
someClass->rate = 5;                    //---rate is declared protected---
someClass->name = @"Wei-Meng Lee";  //---name is declared protected---
```

 NOTE *Observe that to access the fields in a class directly, you use the -> operator.*

To make the `rate` and `name` visible outside the class, modify the `SomeClass.h` file by adding the `@public` compiler directive:

```
//--SomeClass.h--
#import <Foundation/Foundation.h>

@class AnotherClass;   //---forward declaration---

@interface SomeClass : NSObject {
    //---an object from AnotherClass---
    AnotherClass *anotherClass;

@public
    float rate;

@public
    NSString *name;
}

@end
```

The following two statements would now be valid:

```
someClass->rate = 5;                    //---rate is now declared public---
someClass->name = @"Wei-Meng Lee";  //---name is now declared public---
```

Although you can access the fields directly, doing so goes against the design principles of object-oriented programming's rule of encapsulation. A better way is to encapsulate the two fields you want to expose in properties. Refer to the "Properties" section later in this appendix.

Methods

Methods are functions that are defined in a class. Objective-C supports two types of methods — instance methods and class methods.

Instance methods can be called only using an instance of the class. Instance methods are prefixed with the minus sign (-) character.

Class methods can be invoked directly using the class name and do not need an instance of the class in order to work. Class methods are prefixed with the plus sign (+) character.

> **NOTE** *In some programming languages, such as C# and Java, class methods are known as static methods.*

The following code sample shows `SomeClass` with three instance methods and one class method declared:

```
//--SomeClass.h--
#import <Foundation/Foundation.h>

@class AnotherClass;   //---forward declaration---

@interface SomeClass : NSObject {
    //---an object from AnotherClass---
    AnotherClass *anotherClass;
    float rate;
    NSString *name;
}

//---instance methods---
-(void) doSomething;
-(void) doSomething:(NSString *) str;
-(void) doSomething:(NSString *) str withAnotherPara:(float) value;

//---class method---
+(void) alsoDoSomething;

@end
```

The following shows the implementation of the methods that were declared in the header file:

```
#import "SomeClass.h"

@implementation SomeClass

-(void) doSomething {
    //---implementation here---
}

-(void) doSomething:(NSString *) str {
    //---implementation here---
```

```
}

-(void) doSomething:(NSString *) str withAnotherPara:(float) value {
    //---implementation here---
}

+(void) alsoDoSomething {
    //---implementation here---
}

@end
```

To invoke the three instance methods, you first need to create an instance of the class and then call them using the instance created:

```
SomeClass *someClass = [SomeClass alloc];
[someClass doSomething];
[someClass doSomething:@"some text"];
[someClass doSomething:@"some text" withAnotherPara:9.0f];
```

Class methods can be called directly using the class name, as the following shows:

```
[SomeClass alsoDoSomething];
```

In general, you create instance methods when you need to perform some actions that are related to the particular instance of the class (that is, the object). For example, suppose you defined a class that represents the information of an employee. You may expose an instance method that allows you to calculate the overtime wage of an employee. In this case, you use an instance method because the calculation involves data specific to a particular employee object.

Class methods, on the other hand, are commonly used for defining helper methods. For example, you might have a class method called GetOvertimeRate: that returns the rates for working overtime. As all employees get the same rate for working overtime (assuming this is the case for your company), then there is no need to create instance methods, and thus a class method will suffice.

The next section shows how to call methods with a varying number of parameters.

Message Sending (Calling Methods)

In Objective-C, you use the following syntax to call a method:

```
[object method];
```

Strictly speaking, in Objective-C you do not call a method; you send a message to an object. The message to be passed to an object is resolved during runtime and is not enforced at compile time. This is why the compiler does not stop you from running your program even though you may have misspelled the name of a method. It does try to warn you that the target object may not respond to your message, though, because the target object will simply ignore the message. Figure D-1 shows the warning by the compiler when one of the parameters for the UIAlertView's initializer is misspelled (the cancelButtonsTitle: should be cancelButtonTitle:).

NOTE For the ease of understanding, I use the more conventional term of "calling a method" to refer to Objective-C's message sending mechanism.

```
-(IBAction) buttonClicked: (id) sender{
    UIAlertView *alert = [[UIAlertView alloc] initWithTitle:@"Action invoked!"
                                                     message:@"Button clicked!"
                                                    delegate:self
                                           cancelButtonsTitle:@"OK"
                                            otherButtonTitles:nil];
        ⚠ warning: no '-initWithTitle:message:delegate:cancelButtonsTitle:otherButtonTitles:' method found
        (Messages without a matching method signature will be assumed to return 'id' and accept '...' as arguments.)
```

FIGURE D-1

Using the example from the previous section, the doSomething method has no parameter:

```
-(void) doSomething {
    //---implementation here---
}
```

Therefore, you can call it like this:

```
[someClass doSomething];
```

If a method has one or more inputs, you call it using the following syntax:

```
[object method:input1];                          //---one input---
[object method:input1 andSecondInput:input2];   //---two inputs---
```

The interesting thing about Objective-C is the way you call a method with multiple inputs. Using the earlier example:

```
-(void) doSomething:(NSString *) str withAnotherPara:(float) value {
    //---implementation here---
}
```

The name of the preceding method is doSomething:withAnotherPara:.

It is important to note the names of methods and to differentiate those that have parameters from those that do not. For example, doSomething refers to a method with no parameter, whereas doSomething: refers to a method with one parameter, and doSomething:withAnotherPara: refers to a method with two parameters. The presence or absence of colons in a method name dictates which method is invoked during runtime. This is important when passing method names as arguments, particularly when using the @selector (discussed in the Selectors section) notation to pass them to a delegate or notification event.

Method calls can also be nested, as the following example shows:

```
NSString *str = [[NSString alloc] initWithString:@"Hello World"];
```

Here, you first call the alloc class method of the NSString class and then call the initWithString: method of the returning result from the alloc method, which is of type id, a generic C type that Objective-C uses for an arbitrary object.

In general, you should not nest more than three levels because anything more than that makes the code difficult to read.

Properties

Properties allow you to expose your fields in your class so that you can control how values are set or returned. In the earlier example (in the Access Privileges section), you saw that you can directly access the fields of a class using the -> operator. However, this is not the ideal way and you should ideally expose your fields as properties.

Prior to Objective-C 2.0, programmers had to declare methods to make the fields accessible to other classes, like this:

```objc
//--SomeClass.h--
#import <Foundation/Foundation.h>

@class AnotherClass;   //---forward declaration---

@interface SomeClass : NSObject {
    //---an object from AnotherClass---
    AnotherClass *anotherClass;
    float rate;
    NSString *name;
}

//---expose the rate field---
-(float) rate;                          //---get the value of rate---
-(void) setRate:(float) value;          //---set the value of rate

//---expose the name field---
-(NSString *) name;                     //---get the value of name---
-(void) setName:(NSString *) value;     //---set the value of name---

//---instance methods---
-(void) doSomething;
-(void) doSomething:(NSString *) str;
-(void) doSomething:(NSString *) str withAnotherPara:(float) value;

//---class method---
+(void) alsoDoSomething;

@end
```

These methods are known as *getters* and *setters* (or sometimes better known as *accessors* and *mutators*). The implementation of these methods may look like this:

```objc
#import "SomeClass.h"

@implementation SomeClass

-(float) rate {
    return rate;
}

-(void) setRate:(float) value {
```

```
    rate = value;
}

-(NSString *) name {
    return name;
}

-(void) setName:(NSString *) value {
    [value retain];
    [name release];
    name = value;
}

-(void) doSomething {
    //---implementation here---
}

-(void) doSomething:(NSString *) str {
    //---implementation here---
    NSLog(str);
}

-(void) doSomething:(NSString *) str withAnotherPara:(float) value {
    //---implementation here---
}

+(void) alsoDoSomething {
    //---implementation here---
}

@end
```

To set the value of these properties, you need to call the methods prefixed with the set keyword:

```
SomeClass *sc = [[SomeClass alloc] init];
[sc setRate:5.0f];
[sc setName:@"Wei-Meng Lee"];
```

Alternatively, you can use the dot notation introduced in Objective-C 2.0:

```
SomeClass *sc = [[SomeClass alloc] init];
sc.rate = 5;
sc.name = @"Wei-Meng Lee";
```

To obtain the values of properties, you can either call the methods directly or use the dot notation in Objective-C 2.0:

```
NSLog([sc name]); //---call the method---
NSLog(sc.name);   //---dot notation
```

To make a property read only, simply remove the method prefixed with the set keyword.

Notice that within the setName: method, you have various statements using the retain and release keywords. These keywords relate to memory management in Objective-C; you learn more about them in the "Memory Management" section, later in this appendix.

In Objective-C 2.0, you don't need to define getters and setters in order to expose fields as properties. You can do so via the @property and @synthesize compiler directives. Using the same example, you can use the @property to expose the rate and name fields as properties, like this:

```
//--SomeClass.h--
#import <Foundation/Foundation.h>

@class AnotherClass;    //---forward declaration---

@interface SomeClass : NSObject {
    //---an object from AnotherClass---
    AnotherClass *anotherClass;
    float rate;
    NSString *name;
}

@property float rate;
@property (retain, nonatomic) NSString *name;

//---instance methods---
-(void) doSomething;
-(void) doSomething:(NSString *) str;
-(void) doSomething:(NSString *) str withAnotherPara:(float) value;

//---class method---
+(void) alsoDoSomething;

@end
```

The first @property statement defines rate to be a property. The second statement defines name as a property as well, but it also specifies the behavior of this property. In this case, it indicates the behavior as retain and nonatomic, which you learn more about in the section on memory management later in this appendix. In particular, nonatomic means that the property is not accessed in a thread-safe manner. This is alright if you are not writing multi-threaded applications. Most of the time, you will use the retain and nonatomic combination when declaring properties.

In the implementation file, rather than define the getter and setter methods, you can simply use the @synthesize keyword to get the compiler to automatically generate the getters and setters for you:

```
#import "SomeClass.h"

@implementation SomeClass

@synthesize rate, name;
```

As shown, you can combine several properties using a single @synthesize keyword. However, you can also separate them into individual statements:

```
@synthesize rate;
@synthesize name;
```

You can now use your properties as usual:

```
//---setting using setRate---
[sc setRate:5.0f];
[sc setName:@"Wei-Meng Lee"];

//---setting using dot notation---
sc.rate = 5;
sc.name = @"Wei-Meng Lee";

//---getting---
NSLog([sc name]); //---using the name method
NSLog(sc.name);   //---dot notation
```

To make a property read only, use the `readonly` keyword. The following statement makes the `name` property read only:

```
@property (readonly) NSString *name;
```

Initializers

When you create an instance of a class, you often initialize it at the same time. For example, in the earlier example (in the Class Instantiation section), you had this statement:

```
SomeClass *sc = [[SomeClass alloc] init];
```

The `alloc` keyword allocates memory for the object, and when an object is returned, the `init` method is called on the object to initialize the object. Recall that in `SomeClass`, you do not define a method named `init`. So where does the `init` method come from? It is actually defined in the `NSObject` class, which is the base class of most classes in Objective-C. The `init` method is known as an initializer.

If you want to create additional initializers, you can define methods that begin with the `init` word. (The use of the `init` word is more of a norm than a hard-and-fast rule.)

```
//--SomeClass.h--
#import <Foundation/Foundation.h>

@class AnotherClass;    //---forward declaration---

@interface SomeClass : NSObject {
    //---an object from AnotherClass---
    AnotherClass *anotherClass;
    float rate;
    NSString *name;
}

@property float rate;
@property (retain, nonatomic) NSString *name;

//---instance methods---
-(void) doSomething;
```

```
-(void) doSomething:(NSString *) str;
-(void) doSomething:(NSString *) str withAnotherPara:(float) value;

//---class method---
+(void) alsoDoSomething;

- (id)initWithName:(NSString *) n;
- (id)initWithName:(NSString *) n andRate:(float) r;

@end
```

The preceding example contains two additional initializers: initWithName: and initWithName:andRate:. You can provide the implementations for the two initializers as follows:

```
#import "SomeClass.h"

@implementation SomeClass

@synthesize rate, name;

- (id)initWithName:(NSString *) n {
    return [self initWithName:n andRate:0.0f];
}

- (id)initWithName:(NSString *) n andRate:(float) r {
    if (self = [super init]) {
        self.name = n;
        self.rate = r;
    }
    return self;
}

//...
//...
```

Note that in the initWithName:andRate: initializer implementation, you first call the init initializer of the super (base) class so that its base class is properly initialized, which is necessary before you can initialize the current class:

```
- (id)initWithName:(NSString *) n andRate:(float) r {
    if (self = [super init]) {
        self.name = n;
        self.rate = r;
    }
    return self;
}
```

The rule for defining an initializer is simple: If a class is initialized properly, it should return a reference to self (hence the id type). If it fails, it should return nil.

For the `initWithName:` initializer implementation, notice that it calls the `initWithName:andRate:` initializer:

```
- (id)initWithName:(NSString *) n {
    return [self initWithName:n andRate:0.0f];
}
```

In general, if you have multiple initializers, each with different parameters, you should chain them by ensuring that they all call a single initializer that performs the call to the super class's `init` initializer. In Objective-C, the initializer that performs the call to the super class's `init` initializer is called the *designated initializer.*

 NOTE *As a general guide, the designated initializer should be the one with the greatest number of parameters.*

To use the initializers, you can now call them during instantiation time:

```
SomeClass *sc1 = [[SomeClass alloc] initWithName:@"Wei-Meng Lee"
                                        andRate:35];
SomeClass *sc2 = [[SomeClass alloc] initWithName:@"Wei-Meng Lee"];
```

MEMORY MANAGEMENT

Memory management in Objective-C programming (especially for iPhone) is a very important topic that every iPhone developer needs to be aware of. As do all other popular languages, Objective-C supports garbage collection, which helps to remove unused objects when they go out of scope and hence releases memory that can be reused. However, because of the severe overhead involved in implementing garbage collection, the iPhone does not support garbage collection. This leaves you, the developer, to manually allocate and de-allocate the memory of objects when they are no longer needed.

This section discusses the various aspects of memory management on the iPhone.

Reference Counting

To help you allocate and de-allocate memory for objects, the iPhone OS uses a scheme known as *reference counting* to keep track of objects to determine whether they are still needed or can be disposed of. Reference counting basically uses a counter for each object, and as each object is created, the count increases by 1. When an object is released, the count decreases by 1. When the count reaches 0, the memory associated with the object is reclaimed by the OS.

In Objective-C, a few important keywords are associated with memory management. The following sections take a look at each of them.

alloc

The `alloc` keyword allocates memory for an object that you are creating. You have seen it in almost all exercises in this book. An example is as follows:

```
NSString *str = [[NSString alloc] initWithString:@"Hello"];
```

In this example, you are creating an `NSString` object and instantiating it with a default string. When the object is created, the reference count of that object is 1. Because you are the one creating it, the object belongs to you, and it is your responsibility to release the memory when you are done with it.

 NOTE *See the "release" section for information on how to release an object.*

So how do you know when an object is owned, and by whom? Consider the following example:

```
NSString *str = [[NSString alloc] initWithString:@"Hello"];
NSString *str2 = str;
```

In this example, you use the `alloc` keyword for `str`, so you own `str`. Therefore, you need to release it when you no longer need it. However, `str2` is simply pointing to `str`, so you do not own `str2`, meaning that you need not release `str2` when you are done using it.

new

Besides using the `alloc` keyword to allocate memory for an object, you can also use the new keyword, like this:

```
NSString *str = [NSString new];
```

The new keyword is functionally equivalent to

```
NSString *str = [[NSString alloc] init];
```

As with the `alloc` keyword, using the new keyword makes you the owner of the object, so you need to release it when you are done with it.

retain

The `retain` keyword increases the reference count of an object by 1. Consider the previous example:

```
NSString *str = [[NSString alloc] initWithString:@"Hello"];
NSString *str2 = str;
```

In that example, you do not own `str2` because you do not use the `alloc` keyword on the object. When `str` is released, the `str2` will no longer be valid.

 NOTE *How do you release* str2, *then? Well, it is autoreleased. See the "Convenience Method and Autorelease" section for more information.*

If you want to make sure that str2 is available even if str is released, you need to use the retain keyword:

```
NSString *str = [[NSString alloc] initWithString:@"Hello"];
NSString *str2 = str;
[str2 retain];
[str release];
```

In the preceding case, the reference count for str is now 2. When you release str, str2 will still be valid. When you are done with str2, you need to release it manually.

 NOTE As a general rule, if you own an object (using alloc or retain), you need to release it.

release

When you are done with an object, you need to manually release it by using the release keyword:

```
NSString *str = [[NSString alloc] initWithString:@"Hello"];

//...do what you want with the object...

[str release];
```

When you use the release keyword on an object, it causes the reference count of that object to decrease by 1. When the reference count reaches 0, the memory used by the object is released.

One important aspect to keep in mind when using the release keyword is that you cannot release an object that is not owned by you. For example, consider the example used in the previous section:

```
NSString *str = [[NSString alloc] initWithString:@"Hello"];
NSString *str2 = str;
[str release];
[str2 release];   //---this is not OK as you do not own str2---
```

Attempting to release str2 will result in a runtime error because you cannot release an object not owned by you. However, if you use the retain keyword to gain ownership of an object, you do need to use the release keyword:

```
NSString *str = [[NSString alloc] initWithString:@"Hello"];
NSString *str2 = str;
[str2 retain];
[str release];
[str2 release];   //---this is now OK as you now own str2---
```

Recall that earlier in the section on properties, you defined the setName: method, where you set the value of the name field:

```
-(void) setName:(NSString *) value {
    [value retain];
```

```
    [name release];
    name = value;
}
```

Notice that you first had to retain the `value` object, followed by releasing the `name` object and then finally assigning the `value` object to `name`. Why do you need to do that as opposed to the following?

```
-(void) setName:(NSString *) value {
    name = value;
}
```

Well, if you were using garbage collection, the preceding statement would be valid. However, because iPhone OS does not support garbage collection, the preceding statement will cause the original object referenced by the `name` object to be lost, thereby causing a memory leak. To prevent that leak, you first retain the `value` object to indicate that you wish to gain ownership of it; then you release the original object referenced by `name`. Finally, assign `value` to `name`:

```
    [value retain];
    [name release];
    name = value;
```

Convenience Method and Autorelease

So far, you learned that all objects created using the `alloc` or `new` keywords are owned by you. Consider the following case:

```
    NSString *str = [NSString stringWithFormat:@"%d", 4];
```

In this statement, do you own the `str` object? The answer is no, you don't. This is because the object is created using one of the *convenience methods* — static methods that are used for allocating and initializing objects directly. In the preceding case, you create an object but you do not own it. Because you do not own it, you cannot release it manually. In fact, objects created using this method are known as *autorelease* objects. All autorelease objects are temporary objects and are added to an *autorelease pool*. When the current method exits, all the objects contained within it are released. Autorelease objects are useful for cases in which you simply want to use some temporary variables and do not want to burden yourself with allocations and de-allocations.

The key difference between an object created using the `alloc` (or `new`) keyword and one created using a convenience method is that of ownership, as the following example shows:

```
        NSString *str1 = [[NSString alloc] initWithFormat:@"%d", 4];
        [str1 release]; //---this is ok because you own str1---

        NSString *str2 = [NSString stringWithFormat:@"%d", 4];
        [str2 release]; //---this is not ok because you don't own str2---
        //---str2 will be removed automatically when the autorelease
        // pool is activated---
```

UNDERSTANDING REFERENCE COUNTING USING AN ANALOGY

When you think of memory management using reference counting, it is always good to use a real-life analogy to put things into perspective.

Imagine a room in the library that you can reserve for studying purposes. Initially, the room is empty and hence the lights are off. When you reserve the room, the librarian increases a counter to indicate the number of persons using the room. This is similar to creating an object using the `alloc` keyword.

When you leave the room, the librarian decreases the counter, and if the counter is now 0, this means that the room is no longer being used and the lights can thus be switched off. This is similar to using the `release` keyword to release an object.

There may be times when you have booked the room and are the only one in the room (hence, the counter is 1) until a friend of yours comes along. He may simply come and visit you and therefore doesn't register with the librarian. Hence, the counter does not increase. Because he is just visiting you and hasn't booked the room, he has no rights to decide whether the lights should be switched off. This is similar to assigning an object to another variable without using the `alloc` keyword. In this case, if you leave the room (release), the lights will be switched off and your friend will have to leave.

Consider another situation in which you are using the room and another person also booked the room and shares it with you. In this case, the counter is now 2. If you leave the room, the counter goes down to 1, but the lights are still on because another person is in the room. This situation is similar when you create an object and assign it to another variable that uses the `retain` keyword. In such a situation, the object is released only when both objects release it.

If you want to take ownership of an object when using a convenience method, you can do so using the `retain` keyword:

```
NSString *str2 = [[NSString stringWithFormat:@"%d", 4] retain];
```

To release the object, you can use either the `autorelease` or `release` keyword. You learned earlier that the `release` keyword immediately decreases the reference count by 1 and that the object is immediately de-allocated from memory when the reference count reaches 0. In contrast, the `autorelease` keyword promises to decrease the reference count by 1, not *immediately*, but sometime later. It is like saying, "Well, I still need the object now, but later on I can let it go." The following code makes it clear:

```
NSString *str = [[NSString stringWithFormat:@"%d", 4] retain];
[str autorelease];  //you don't own it anymore; still available
NSlog(str);         //still accessible for now
```

NOTE *After you have autoreleased an object, do not release it anymore.*

Note that the statement

```
NSString *str2 = [NSString stringWithFormat:@"%d", 4];
```

has the same effect as

```
NSString *str2 = @"4";
```

Although autorelease objects seem to make your life simple by automatically releasing objects that are no longer needed, you have to be careful when using them. Consider the following example:

```
for (int i=0; i<=99999; i++){
    NSString *str = [NSString stringWithFormat:@"%d", i];
    //...
    //...
}
```

You are creating an NSString object for each iteration of the loop. Because the objects are not released until the function exits, you may well run out of memory before the autorelease pool (see next section) can kick in to release the objects.

One way to solve this dilemma is to use an autorelease pool, as discussed in the next section.

REFERENCE COUNTING: THE ANALOGY CONTINUES

Continuing with our analogy of the room in the library, imagine that you are about to sign out with the librarian when you realize that you have left your books in the room. You tell the librarian that you are done with the room and want to sign out now, but because you left your books in the room, you tell the librarian not to switch off the lights yet so that you can go back to get the books. At a later time, the librarian can switch off the lights at his or her own choosing. This is the behavior of autoreleased objects.

Autorelease Pools

All autorelease objects are temporary objects and are added to an *autorelease pool*. When the current method exits, all the objects contained within it are released. However, sometimes you want to control how the autorelease pool is emptied, rather than wait for it to be called by the OS. To do so, you can create an instance of the NSAutoreleasePool class, like this:

```
for (int i=0; i<=99999; i++){
    NSAutoreleasePool *pool = [[NSAutoreleasePool alloc] init];
```

```
NSString *str1 = [NSString stringWithFormat:@"%d", i];
NSString *str2 = [NSString stringWithFormat:@"%d", i];
NSString *str3 = [NSString stringWithFormat:@"%d", i];
//...
//...
[pool release];
}
```

In this example, for each iteration of the loop, an NSAutoreleasePool object is created, and all the autorelease objects created within the loop — str1, str2, and str3 — go into it. At the end of each iteration, the NSAutoreleasePool object is released so that all the objects contained within it are automatically released. This ensures that you have at most three autorelease objects in memory at any one time.

dealloc

You have learned that by using the alloc or the new keyword, you own the object that you have created. You have also seen how to release the objects you own using the release or autorelease keyword. So when is a good time for you to release them?

As a rule of thumb, you should release the objects as soon as you are done with them. So if you created an object in a method, you should release it before you exit the method. For properties, recall that you can use the @property compiler directive together with the retain keyword:

```
@property (retain, nonatomic) NSString *name;
```

Because the values of the property will be retained, it is important that you free it before you exit the application. A good place to do so is in the dealloc method of a class (such as a View Controller):

```
-(void) dealloc {
    [self.name release];    //---release the name property---
    [super dealloc];
}
```

The dealloc method of a class is fired whenever the reference count of its object reaches 0. Consider the following example:

```
SomeClass *sc1 = [[SomeClass alloc] initWithName:@"Wei-Meng Lee"
                                        andRate:35];
//...do something here…
[sc1 release];   //---reference count goes to 0; dealloc will be called---
```

The preceding example shows that when the reference count of sc1 goes to 0 (when the release statement is called), the dealloc method defined within the class will be called. If you do not define this method in the class, its implementation in the base class will be called.

Memory Management Tips

Memory management is a tricky issue in iPhone programming. Although there are tools that you can use to test for memory leaks, this section presents some simple things you can do to detect memory problems that might affect your application.

First, ensure that you implement the `didReceiveMemoryWarning` method in your View Controller:

```
- (void)didReceiveMemoryWarning {
    // Releases the view if it doesn't have a superview.
    [super didReceiveMemoryWarning];
    //---insert code here to free unused objects---
    // Release any cached data, images, etc that aren't in use.
}
```

The `didReceiveMemoryWarning` method will be called whenever your iPhone runs out of memory. You should insert code in this method so that you can free resources/objects that you do not need.

In addition, you should also handle the `applicationDidReceiveMemoryWarning:` method in your application delegate:

```
- (void)applicationDidReceiveMemoryWarning:(UIApplication *)application {
    /*
    Free up as much memory as possible by purging cached
    data objects that can be recreated (or reloaded from
    disk) later.
    */
    //---insert code here to free unused objects---
}
```

In this method, you should stop all memory-intensive activities, such as audio and video playback. You should also remove all images cached in memory.

PROTOCOLS

In Objective-C, a *protocol* declares a programmatic interface that any class can choose to implement. A protocol declares a set of methods, and an adopting class may choose to implement one or more of its declared methods. The class that defines the protocol is expected to call the methods in the protocols that are implemented by the adopting class.

The easiest way to understand protocols is to examine the `UIAlertView` class. As you have experienced in the various chapters in this book, you can simply use the `UIAlertView` class by creating an instance of it and then calling its `show` method:

```
UIAlertView *alert = [[UIAlertView alloc]
                    initWithTitle:@"Hello"
                          message:@"This is an alert view"
                         delegate:self
                cancelButtonTitle:@"OK"
                otherButtonTitles:nil];
[alert show];
```

The preceding code displays an Alert view with one button — OK. Tapping the OK button automatically dismisses the Alert view. If you want to display additional buttons, you can set the `otherButtonTitles:` parameter like this:

```
UIAlertView *alert = [[UIAlertView alloc]
                        initWithTitle:@"Hello"
                             message:@"This is an alert view"
                            delegate:self
                     cancelButtonTitle:@"OK"
                     otherButtonTitles:@"Option 1", @"Option 2", nil];
[alert show];
```

The Alert view now displays three buttons — OK, Option 1, and Option 2. But how do you know which button was tapped by the user? You can determine this by handling the relevant method(s) that will be fired by the Alert view when the buttons are clicked. This set of methods is defined by the `UIAlertViewDelegate` protocol. This protocol defines the following methods:

➤ `alertView:clickedButtonAtIndex:`

➤ `willPresentAlertView:`

➤ `didPresentAlertView:`

➤ `alertView:willDismissWithButtonIndex:`

➤ `alertView:didDismissWithButtonIndex:`

➤ `alertViewCancel:`

If you want to implement any of the methods in the `UIAlertViewDelegate` protocol, you need to ensure that your class, in this case the View Controller, conforms to this protocol. A class conforms to a protocol using angle brackets (<>), like this:

```
@interface ObjCTestViewController : UIViewController
    <UIAlertViewDelegate> {  //---this class conforms to the
                             // UIAlertViewDelegate protocol---

}

@end
```

NOTE *To conform to more than one delegate, separate the protocols with commas, such as* `<UIAlertViewDelegate, UITableViewDataSource>`.

After the class conforms to a protocol, you can implement the method in your class:

```
- (void)alertView:(UIAlertView *)alertView
clickedButtonAtIndex:(NSInteger)buttonIndex {

    NSLog([NSString stringWithFormat:@"%d", buttonIndex]);

}
```

Delegate

In Objective-C, a delegate is just an object that has been assigned by another object as the object responsible for handling events. Consider the case of the UIAlertView example that you have seen previously:

```
UIAlertView *alert = [[UIAlertView alloc]
                        initWithTitle:@"Hello"
                            message:@"This is an alert view"
                        delegate:self
                    cancelButtonTitle:@"OK"
                    otherButtonTitles:@"Option 1", @"Option 2", nil];
[alert show];
```

The initializer of the UIAlertView class includes a parameter called the delegate. Setting this parameter to self means that the current object is responsible for handling all the events fired by this instance of the UIAlertView class. If you don't need to handle events fired by this instance, you can simply set it to nil:

```
UIAlertView *alert = [[UIAlertView alloc]
                        initWithTitle:@"Hello"
                            message:@"This is an alert view"
                        delegate:nil
                    cancelButtonTitle:@"OK"
                    otherButtonTitles:@"Option 1", @"Option 2", nil];
[alert show];
```

If you have multiple buttons on the Alert view and want to know which button was tapped, you need to handle the methods defined in the UIAlertViewDelegate protocol. You can either implement it in the same class in which the UIAlertView class was instantiated (as shown in the previous section), or create a new class to implement the method, like this:

```
//--SomeClass.m--
@implementation SomeClass

- (void)alertView:(UIAlertView *)alertView
clickedButtonAtIndex:(NSInteger)buttonIndex {

    NSLog([NSString stringWithFormat:@"%d", buttonIndex]);

}
@end
```

To ensure that the Alert view knows where to look for the method, create an instance of SomeClass and then set it as the delegate:

```
SomeClass *myDelegate = [[SomeClass alloc] init];
UIAlertView *alert = [[UIAlertView alloc]
                        initWithTitle:@"Hello"
                            message:@"This is an alert view"
                        delegate:myDelegate;
                    cancelButtonTitle:@"OK"
                    otherButtonTitles:@"Option 1", @"Option 2", nil];
[alert show];
```

SELECTORS

In Objective-C, a selector is the name used to select a method to execute for an object. It is used to identify a method. You have seen the use of a selector in some of the chapters in this book. Here is one of them:

```
//---create a Button view---
CGRect frame = CGRectMake(10, 50, 300, 50);
UIButton *button = [UIButton buttonWithType:UIButtonTypeRoundedRect];
button.frame = frame;
[button setTitle:@"Click Me, Please!"
        forState:UIControlStateNormal];
button.backgroundColor = [UIColor clearColor];
[button addTarget:self
              action:@selector(buttonClicked:)
    forControlEvents:UIControlEventTouchUpInside];
```

The preceding code shows that you are dynamically creating a UIButton object. In order to handle the event (for example, the Touch Up Inside event) raised by the button, you need to call the addTarget:action:forControlEvents: method of the UIButton class:

```
[button addTarget:self
              action:@selector(buttonClicked:)
    forControlEvents:UIControlEventTouchUpInside];
```

The action: parameter takes in an argument of type SEL (selector). In the preceding code, you pass in the name of the method that you have defined — buttonClicked: — which is defined within the class:

```
-(IBAction) buttonClicked: (id) sender {
    //...
}
```

Alternatively, you can create an object of type SEL and then instantiate it by using the NSSelectorFromString function (which takes in a string containing the method name):

```
NSString *nameOfMethod = @"buttonClicked:";
SEL methodName = NSSelectorFromString(nameOfMethod);
```

The call to the addTarget:action:forControlEvents: method now looks like this:

```
[button addTarget:self
              action:methodName
    forControlEvents:UIControlEventTouchUpInside];
```

 NOTE When naming a selector, be sure to specify the full name of the method. For example, if a method name has one or more parameters, you need to add a ":" in the sector, such as:

```
NSString *nameOfMethod = @"someMethod:withPara1:andPara2:";
```

NOTE *Because Objective-C is an extension of C, it is common to see C functions interspersed throughout your Objective-C application. C functions use the parentheses () to pass in arguments for parameters.*

CATEGORIES

A category in Objective-C allows you to add methods to an existing class without the need to subclass it. You can also use a category to override the implementation of an existing class.

 NOTE *In some languages (such as C#), a category is known as an extension method.*

As an example, imagine that you want to test whether a string contains a valid e-mail address. You can add an isEmail method to the NSString class so that you can call the isEmail method on any NSString instance, like this:

```
NSString *email = @"weimenglee@gmail.com";
if ([email isEmail]) {
    //...
}
```

To do so, you can simply create a new class file and code it as follows:

```
//--Utils.h--
#import <Foundation/Foundation.h>

//---NSString is the class you are extending---
@interface NSString (stringUtils)

//---the method you are adding to the NSString class---
-(BOOL) isEmail;

@end
```

Basically, it looks the same as declaring a new class except that it does not inherit from any other class. The stringUtils is a name that identifies the category you are adding, and you can use any name you want.

Next, you need to implement the method(s) you are adding:

```
//--Utils.m--
#import "Utils.h"

@implementation NSString (Utilities)

- (BOOL) isEmail {
```

```
NSString *emailRegEx =
@"(?:[a-z0-9!#$%\\&'*+/=?\\^_`{|}~-]+(?:\\.[a-z0-9!#$%\\&'*+/=?\\^_`{|}"
@"~-]+)*|\"(?:[\\x01-\\x08\\x0b\\x0c\\x0e-\\x1f\\x21\\x23-\\x5b\\x5d-\\"
@"x7f]|\\\\[\\x01-\\x09\\x0b\\x0c\\x0e-\\x7f])*\")@(?:(?:[a-z0-9](?:[a-"
@"z0-9]*[a-z0-9])?\\.)+[a-z0-9](?:[a-z0-9]*[a-z0-9])?|\\[(?:(?:25[0-5"
@"]|2[0-4][0-9]|[01]?[0-9][0-9]?)\\.){3}(?:25[0-5]|2[0-4][0-9]|[01]?[0-"
@"9][0-9]?|[a-z0-9-]*[a-z0-9]:(?:[\\x01-\\x08\\x0b\\x0c\\x0e-\\x1f\\x21"
@"-\\x5a\\x53-\\x7f]|\\\\[\\x01-\\x09\\x0b\\x0c\\x0e-\\x7f])+)\\])";

NSPredicate *regExPredicate = [NSPredicate
                              predicateWithFormat:@"SELF MATCHES %@",
                              emailRegEx];

return [regExPredicate evaluateWithObject:self];
}

@end
```

NOTE *The code for validating an e-mail address using regular expression is adapted from* http://cocoawithlove.com/2009/06/ verifying-that-string-is-email-address.html.

You can then test for the validity of an e-mail address using the newly added method:

```
NSString *email = @"weimenglee@gmail.com";
if ([email isEmail])
    NSLog(@"Valid email");
else
    NSLog(@"Invalid email");
```

INDEX

R